Linux Kernel Programming Part 2 - Char Device Drivers and Kernel Synchronization

Create user-kernel interfaces, work with peripheral I/O, and handle hardware interrupts

Kaiwan N Billimoria

BIRMINGHAM - MUMBAI

Linux Kernel Programming Part 2 - Char Device Drivers and Kernel Synchronization

Copyright © 2021 Packt Publishing

Group Product Manager: Wilson D'souza
Publishing Product Manager: Vijin Boricha
Content Development Editor: Romy Dias
Senior Editor: Rahul D'souza
Technical Editor: Shruthi Shetty
Copy Editor: Safis Editing
Project Coordinator: Neil Dmello
Proofreader: Safis Editing
Indexer: Pratik Shirodkar
Production Designer: Shankar Kalbhor

First published: March 2021

Production reference: 1190321

Published by Packt Publishing Ltd.
Livery Place
35 Livery Street
Birmingham
B3 2PB, UK.

ISBN 978-1-80107-951-8

www.packt.com

First, to my dear parents, Diana and Nadir "Nads", for showing me how to live a happy and productive life. To my dear wife, Dilshad (an accomplished financial advisor herself), and our amazing kids, Sheroy and Danesh – thanks for all your love and patience.

– Kaiwan N Billimoria

Packt.com

Subscribe to our online digital library for full access to over 7,000 books and videos, as well as industry leading tools to help you plan your personal development and advance your career. For more information, please visit our website.

Why subscribe?

- Spend less time learning and more time coding with practical eBooks and Videos from over 4,000 industry professionals

- Improve your learning with Skill Plans built especially for you

- Get a free eBook or video every month

- Fully searchable for easy access to vital information

- Copy and paste, print, and bookmark content

Did you know that Packt offers eBook versions of every book published, with PDF and ePub files available? You can upgrade to the eBook version at www.packt.com and as a print book customer, you are entitled to a discount on the eBook copy. Get in touch with us at customercare@packtpub.com for more details.

At www.packt.com, you can also read a collection of free technical articles, sign up for a range of free newsletters, and receive exclusive discounts and offers on Packt books and eBooks.

Contributors

About the author

Kaiwan N Billimoria taught himself BASIC programming on his dad's IBM PC back in 1983. He was programming in C and Assembly on DOS until he discovered the joys of Unix, and by around 1997, Linux!

Kaiwan has worked on many aspects of the Linux system programming stack, including Bash scripting, system programming in C, kernel internals, device drivers, and embedded Linux work. He has actively worked on several commercial/FOSS projects. His contributions include drivers to the mainline Linux OS and many smaller projects hosted on GitHub. His Linux passion feeds well into his passion for teaching these topics to engineers, which he has done for well over two decades now. He's also the author of *Hands-On System Programming with Linux*. It doesn't hurt that he is a recreational ultrarunner too.

Writing this book took a long while; I'd like to thank the team from Packt for their patience and skill! Carlton Borges, Romy Dias, Vijin Boricha, Rohit Rajkumar, Vivek Anantharaman, Nithin Varghese, Hemangi Lotlikar, and all the others. It was indeed a pleasure working with you.

I owe a debt of gratitude to the very able technical reviewers – Donald "Donnie" Tevault and Anil Kumar. They caught a lot of my mistakes and omissions and greatly helped make this book better.

About the reviewers

Donald A. Tevault, but you can call him Donnie, got involved with Linux way back in 2006 and has been working with it ever since. He holds the Linux Professional Institute Level 3 Security certification, and the GIAC Incident Handler certification. Donnie is a professional Linux trainer, and thanks to the magic of the internet, teaches Linux classes literally the world over from the comfort of his living room. He's also a Linux security researcher for an IoT security company.

Anil Kumar is a Linux BSP and firmware developer at Intel. He has over 12 years of software development experience across many verticals, including IoT, mobile chipsets, laptops/Chromebooks, media encoders, and transcoders. He has a master's degree in electronics design from the Indian Institute of Science and a bachelor's degree in electronics and communication from BMS College of Engineering, India. He is an electronics enthusiast and blogger and loves tinkering to create fun DIY projects.

Table of Contents

Preface

This book has been written with a view to helping you learn the fundamentals of Linux character device driver development in a practical, hands-on fashion, along with the necessary theoretical background to give you a well-rounded view of this vast and interesting topic area. To do the topics justice, that book's scope is deliberately kept limited to (mostly) learning how to write `misc` class character device drivers on the Linux OS. This way, you will be able to deeply imbibe the fundamental and necessary driver author skills to then be able to tackle different kinds of Linux driver projects with relative ease.

The focus is on hands-on driver development via the powerful **Loadable Kernel Module (LKM)** framework; the majority of kernel driver development is done in this manner. The focus is kept on working hands-on with driver code, understanding at a sufficiently deep level the internals wherever required, and keeping security in mind.

A recommendation we can't make strongly enough: to really learn and understand the details well, **it's really best that you first read and understand this book's companion,** *Linux Kernel Programming*. It covers various key areas – building the kernel from source, writing kernel modules via the LKM framework, kernel internals including kernel architecture, the memory system, memory alloc/dealloc APIs, CPU scheduling, and more. The combination of the two books will give you a sure and deep edge.

This book wastes no time – the first chapter has you learning the details of the Linux driver framework and how to write a simple yet complete misc class character device driver. Next, you learn how to do something very necessary: efficiently interfacing your driver with user space processes using various technologies (some of which help as debug/diagnostic aids as well!). Understanding, and working with, hardware (peripheral chip) I/O memory is then covered. Detailed coverage of handling hardware interrupts follows. This includes learning and using several modern driver techniques – using threaded IRQs, leveraging resource-managed APIs for drivers, I/O resource allocation, and so on. It covers what top/bottom halves are, working with tasklets and softirqs, and measuring interrupt latencies. Kernel mechanisms you will typically work with – using kernel timers, setting up delays, creating and managing kernel threads and workqueues – are covered next.

The remaining two chapters of this book delve into a relatively complex yet critical-to-understand topic for the modern pro-level driver or kernel developer: understanding and working with kernel synchronization.

The book uses the latest, at the time of writing, 5.4 **Long Term Support** (**LTS**) Linux kernel. It's a kernel that will be maintained (both bug and security fixes) from November 2019 right through December 2025! This is a key point, ensuring that this book's content remains current and valid for years to come!

We very much believe in a hands-on empirical approach: over 20 kernel modules (besides a few user apps and shell scripts) on this book's GitHub repository make the learning come alive, making it fun, interesting, and useful.

We really hope you learn from and enjoy this book. Happy reading!

Who this book is for

This book is primarily for Linux programmers beginning to find their way with device driver development. Linux device driver developers looking to overcome frequent and common kernel/driver development issues, as well as understanding and learning to perform common driver tasks – the modern **Linux Device Model** (**LDM**) framework, user-kernel interfaces, performing peripheral I/O, handling hardware interrupts, dealing with concurrency, and more – will benefit from this book. A basic understanding of Linux kernel internals (and common APIs), kernel module development, and C programming is required.

What this book covers

Chapter 1, *Writing a Simple misc Character Device Driver*, first goes through the very basics – what a driver is supposed to do, the device namespace, the sysfs, and basic tenets of the LDM. We then delve into the details of writing a simple character device driver; along the way, you will learn about the framework – in effect, the internal implementation of the "if it's not a process, it's a file" philosophy/architecture! You'll learn how to implement a misc class character device driver with various methods; several code examples help harden the concepts. Basic copying of data between the user-kernel space and vice versa is covered. Also covered are key security concerns and how to address them (in this context); a "bad" driver giving rise to a privilege escalation issue is actually demonstrated!

Chapter 2, *User-Kernel Communication Pathways*, covers how to communicate between the kernel and the user space, which is critical to you, as a kernel module/driver author. Here, you'll learn about various communication interfaces, or pathways. This is an important aspect of writing kernel/driver code. Several techniques are employed: communication via traditional procfs, the better way for drivers via sysfs, and several others, via debugfs, netlink sockets, and the ioctl(2) system call.

Chapter 3, *Working with Hardware I/O Memory*, covers a key aspect of driver writing – the issue with (and the solution to) accessing hardware memory (mapped memory I/O) from a peripheral device or chip. We cover using the common **memory-mapped I/O (MMIO)** technique as well as the (typically on x86) **port I/O (PIO)** techniques for hardware I/O memory access and manipulation. Several examples from existing kernel drivers are shown as well.

Chapter 4, *Handling Hardware Interrupts*, shows how to handle and work with hardware interrupts in great detail. We start with a brief on how the kernel works with hardware interrupts, then move on to how you're expected to "allocate" an IRQ line (covering modern resource-managed APIs), and how to correctly implement the interrupt handler routine. The modern approach of using threaded handlers (and the why of it), the **Non-Maskable Interrupt (NMI)**, and more, are then covered. The reasons for and using both "top half" and "bottom half" interrupt mechanisms (hardirq, tasklet, and softirqs) in code, as well as key information regarding the dos and don'ts of hardware interrupt handling are covered. Measuring interrupt latencies with the modern [e]BPF toolset, as well as with Ftrace, concludes this key chapter.

Chapter 5, *Working with Kernel Timers, Threads, and Workqueues*, covers how to use some useful (and often employed by drivers) kernel mechanisms – delays, timers, kernel threads, and workqueues. They come in handy in many real-world situations. How to perform both blocking and non-blocking delays (as the situation warrants), setting up and using kernel timers, creating and working with kernel threads, and understanding and using kernel workqueues are all covered here. Several example modules, including three versions of a **simple encrypt decrypt (sed)** example driver, serve to illustrate the concepts learned in code.

Chapter 6, *Kernel Synchronization – Part 1*, first covers the key concepts regarding critical sections, atomicity, what a lock conceptually achieves, and, very importantly, the why of all this. We then cover concurrency concerns when working within the Linux kernel; this moves us naturally on to important locking guidelines, what deadlock means, and key approaches to preventing deadlock. Two of the most popular kernel locking technologies – the mutex lock and the spinlock – are then discussed in depth, along with several (driver) code examples.

Chapter 7, *Kernel Synchronization – Part 2*, continues the journey on kernel synchronization. Here, you'll learn about key locking optimizations – using lightweight atomic and (the more recent) refcount operators to safely operate on integers, using RMW bit operators to safely perform bit ops, and using the reader-writer spinlock over the regular one. Inherent risks, such as cache "false sharing," are discussed as well. An overview of lock-free programming techniques (with an emphasis on per-CPU variables and their usage, along with examples) is then covered. A critical topic, lock debugging techniques, including the usage of the kernel's powerful lockdep lock validator, is then covered. The chapter is rounded off with a brief look at memory barriers (along with an existing kernel network driver's usage of memory barriers).

We again stress that this book is for kernel programmers who are new to writing device drivers; several Linux driver topics are beyond this book's scope and are *not* covered. This includes other types of device drivers (besides character), working with the device tree, and so on. Packt offers other valuable guides to help you gain traction on these topic areas. This book would be an excellent start.

To get the most out of this book

To get the most out of this book, we expect you to have knowledge and experience of the following:

- Know your way around a Linux system, on the command line (the shell).
- The C programming language.
- Know how to write simple kernel modules via the **Loadable Kernel Module (LKM)** framework
- Understand (at least the basics) of key Linux kernel internals concepts: kernel architecture, memory management (plus common dynamic memory alloc/de-alloc APIs), and CPU scheduling.
- It's not mandatory, but experience with Linux kernel programming concepts and technologies will help greatly.

Ideally, we highly recommend reading this book's companion, *Linux Kernel Programming*, first.

The details on hardware and software requirements for this book, as well as their installation, are shown here:

Chapter number	Software required (with version)	Free / proprietary	Download links to the software	Hardware specifications	OS required
All chapters	A recent Linux distribution; we use Ubuntu 18.04 LTS (as well as Fedora 31 / Ubuntu 20.04 LTS); any of these will be suitable. Recommend you install the Linux OS as a **virtual machine** (VM), using Oracle VirtualBox 6.x (or later) as the hypervisor	Free (open source)	Ubuntu (desktop): `https://ubuntu.com/download/desktop` Oracle VirtualBox: `https://www.virtualbox.org/wiki/Downloads`	*Required:* a modern relatively powerful PC or laptop equipped with 4 GB RAM (minimally; the more the better), 25 GB free disk space, and a good internet connection. *Optional:* we also use the Raspberry Pi 3B+ as a test bed.	Linux VM on a Windows host -OR- Linux as a stand-alone OS

Detailed installation steps (software-wise):

1. Install Linux as a VM on a host Windows system; follow one of these tutorials:
   - *Install Linux Inside Windows Using VirtualBox, Abhishek Prakash (It's FOSS!, August 2019):* `https://itsfoss.com/install-linux-in-virtualbox/`
   - Alternately, here's another tutorial to help you do the same: *Install Ubuntu on Oracle VirtualBox* : `https://brb.nci.nih.gov/seqtools/installUbuntu.html`

2. Install the required software packages on the Linux VM:

    1. Log in to your Linux guest VM and first run the following commands within a Terminal window (on a shell):

```
sudo apt update
sudo apt install gcc make perl
```

    2. Install the Oracle VirtualBox Guest Additions now. Reference: *How to Install VirtualBox Guest Additions in Ubuntu*: https://www.tecmint.com/install-virtualbox-guest-additions-in-ubuntu/ (This step only applies if you are running Ubuntu as a VM using Oracle VirtualBox as the hypervisor app.)

    3. To install the packages, take the following steps:

        1. Within the Ubuntu VM, first run the `sudo apt update` command

        2. Now, run the `sudo apt install git fakeroot build-essential tar ncurses-dev tar xz-utils libssl-dev bc stress python3-distutils libelf-dev linux-headers-$(uname -r) bison flex libncurses5-dev util-linux net-tools linux-tools-$(uname -r) exuberant-ctags cscope sysfsutils curl perf-tools-unstable gnuplot rt-tests indent tree pstree smem hwloc bpfcc-tools sparse flawfinder cppcheck tuna hexdump trace-cmd virt-what` command in a single line.

3. Useful resources:

- The Linux kernel official online documentation: https://www.kernel.org/doc/html/latest/.
- The Linux Driver Verification (LDV) project, particularly the *Online Linux Driver Verification Service* page: http://linuxtesting.org/ldv/online?action=rules.
- SEALS - Simple Embedded ARM Linux System: https://github.com/kaiwan/seals/.
- Every chapter of this book has a very useful *Further reading* section as well, detailing more resources.

4. Detailed instructions, as well as additional useful projects, installing a cross-toolchain for ARM, and more, are described in *Chapter 1, Kernel Workspace Setup*, of this book's companion guide, *Linux Kernel Programming, Kaiwan N Billimoria, Packt Publishing.*

We have tested all the code in this book (it has its own GitHub repository as well) on these platforms:

- x86_64 Ubuntu 18.04 LTS guest OS (running on Oracle VirtualBox 6.1)
- x86_64 Ubuntu 20.04.1 LTS guest OS (running on Oracle VirtualBox 6.1)
- x86_64 Ubuntu 20.04.1 LTS native OS
- ARM Raspberry Pi 3B+ (running both its distro kernel as well as our custom 5.4 kernel); lightly tested.

If you are using the digital version of this book, we advise you to type the code yourself or, better, access the code via the GitHub repository (link available in the next section). Doing so will help you avoid any potential errors related to the copying and pasting of code.

For this book, we'll log in as the user named `llkd`. I strongly recommend that you follow the *empirical approach: not taking anyone's word on anything at all, but trying it out and experiencing it for yourself.* Hence, this book gives you many hands-on experiments and kernel driver code examples that you can and must try out yourself; this will greatly aid you in making real progress and deeply learning and understanding various aspects of Linux driver/kernel development.

Download the example code files

You can download the example code files for this book from GitHub at `https://github.com/PacktPublishing/Linux-Kernel-Programming-Part-2`. In case there's an update to the code, it will be updated on the existing GitHub repository.

We also have other code bundles from our rich catalog of books and videos available at `https://github.com/PacktPublishing/`. Check them out!

Download the color images

We also provide a PDF file that has color images of the screenshots/diagrams used in this book. You can download it here: `http://www.packtpub.com/sites/default/files/downloads/9781801079518_ColorImages.pdf`.

Conventions used

There are a number of text conventions used throughout this book.

`CodeInText`: Indicates code words in text, database table names, folder names, filenames, file extensions, pathnames, dummy URLs, user input, and Twitter handles. Here is an example: "The `ioremap()` API returns a KVA of the `void *` type (since it's an address location)."

A block of code is set as follows:

```
static int __init miscdrv_init(void)
{
    int ret;
    struct device *dev;
```

When we wish to draw your attention to a particular part of a code block, the relevant lines or items are set in bold:

```
#define pr_fmt(fmt) "%s:%s(): " fmt, KBUILD_MODNAME, __func__
[...]
#include <linux/miscdevice.h>
#include <linux/fs.h>
[...]
```

Any command-line input or output is written as follows:

```
pi@raspberrypi:~ $ sudo cat /proc/iomem
```

Bold: Indicates a new term, an important word, or words that you see onscreen. For example, words in menus or dialog boxes appear in the text like this. Here is an example: "Select **System info** from the **Administration** panel."

 Warnings or important notes appear like this.

 Tips and tricks appear like this.

Get in touch

Feedback from our readers is always welcome.

General feedback: If you have questions about any aspect of this book, mention the book title in the subject of your message and email us at customercare@packtpub.com.

Errata: Although we have taken every care to ensure the accuracy of our content, mistakes do happen. If you have found a mistake in this book, we would be grateful if you would report this to us. Please visit www.packtpub.com/support/errata, selecting your book, clicking on the Errata Submission Form link, and entering the details.

Piracy: If you come across any illegal copies of our works in any form on the Internet, we would be grateful if you would provide us with the location address or website name. Please contact us at copyright@packt.com with a link to the material.

If you are interested in becoming an author: If there is a topic that you have expertise in and you are interested in either writing or contributing to a book, please visit authors.packtpub.com.

Reviews

Please leave a review. Once you have read and used this book, why not leave a review on the site that you purchased it from? Potential readers can then see and use your unbiased opinion to make purchase decisions, we at Packt can understand what you think about our products, and our authors can see your feedback on their book. Thank you!

For more information about Packt, please visit packt.com.

Section 1: Character Device Driver Basics

Here, we'll cover what a device driver is, namespaces, **Linux Device Model (LDM)** basics, and the character device driver framework. We'll implement simple `misc` drivers (leveraging the kernel's `misc` framework). We'll set up communication between the user and kernel spaces (via various interfaces, such as `debugfs`, `sysfs`, `netlink` sockets, and `ioctl`). You will learn how to work with hardware I/O memory on a peripheral chip, as well as understanding and working with hardware interrupts. You'll also learn how to use kernel features such as kernel-level timers, create kernel threads, and use workqueues.

This section comprises the following chapters:

- Chapter 1, *Writing a Simple misc Character Device Driver*
- Chapter 2, *User-Kernel Communication Pathways*
- Chapter 3, *Working with Hardware I/O Memory*
- Chapter 4, *Handling Hardware Interrupts*
- Chapter 5, *Working with Kernel Timers, Threads, and Workqueues*

1
Writing a Simple misc Character Device Driver

No doubt, device drivers are a vast and interesting topic. Not only that, they are perhaps the most common use of the **Loadable Kernel Module** (**LKM**) framework that we have been using. Here, we shall introduce you to writing a few simple yet complete Linux character device drivers, within a class called `misc`; yes, that's short for miscellaneous. We wish to emphasize that this chapter is limited in its scope and coverage - here, we do not attempt to delve into the deep details regarding the Linux driver model and its many frameworks; instead, we refer you to several excellent books and tutorials on this topic via the *Further reading* section for this chapter. Our aim here is to quickly get you familiar with the overall concepts behind writing a simple character device driver.

Having said that, this book indeed has several chapters that are dedicated to what a driver author needs to know. Besides this introductory chapter, we cover (in detail) how a driver author works with hardware I/O memory, hardware interrupt handling (and its many sub-topics), and kernel mechanisms such as delays, timers, kernel threads, and work queues. Use of various user-kernel communication pathways or interfaces is covered in detail as well. The final two chapters of this book then focus on something very important for any kernel development, including drivers – kernel synchronization.

The other reasons we'd prefer to write a simple Linux *character device driver* and not just our "usual" kernel module are as follows:

- Until now, our kernel modules have been quite simplistic, having only `init` and `cleanup` functions, nothing more. A device driver provides *several* entry points into the kernel; these are the file-related system calls, known as the *driver's methods*. So, we can have an `open()` method, a `read()` method, a `write()` method, an `llseek()` method, an `[unlocked|compat]_ioctl()` method, a `release()` method, and so on.

> FYI, all possible "methods" (functions) the driver author can hook into are in this key kernel data structure: `include/linux/fs.h:file_operations` (more on this in the *Understanding the connection between the process, the driver, and the kernel* section).

- This situation is simply more realistic, and more interesting.

In this chapter, we will cover the following topics:

- Getting started with writing a simple misc character device driver
- Copying data from kernel to user space and vice versa
- A misc driver with a secret
- Issues and security concerns

Technical requirements

I assume that you have gone through the *Preface* section *To get the most out of this book,* and have appropriately prepared a guest VM running Ubuntu 18.04 LTS (or a later stable release) and installed all the required packages. If not, I highly recommend you do this first. To get the most out of this book, I strongly recommend you first set up the workspace environment, including cloning this book's GitHub repository for the code, and work on it in a hands-on fashion. The repository can be found here: `https://github.com/PacktPublishing/Linux-Kernel-Programming-Part-2`.

Getting started with writing a simple misc character device driver

In this section, you will first learn the required background material – understanding the basics of the device file (or node) and its hierarchy. After that, you will learn – by actually writing the code of a very simple `misc` character driver – the kernel framework behind the raw character device driver. Along the way, we shall cover how to create the device node(s) and test the driver via a user space app. Let's get started!

Understanding the device basics

Some quick background is in order.

A **device driver** is the interface between the OS and a peripheral hardware device. It can be written inline – that is, compiled within the kernel image file – or, more commonly, written outside of the kernel source tree as a kernel module (we covered the LKM framework in detail in the companion guide *Linux Kernel Programming, Chapter 4, Writing Your First Kernel Module – LKMs Part 1*, and *Chapter 5, Writing Your First Kernel Module – LKMs Part 2*). Either way, the driver code certainly runs at OS privilege, in kernel space (user space device drivers do exist, but can suffer performance issues; while useful in many circumstances, we don't cover them here. Take a look at the *Further reading* section).

In order for a user space application to gain access to the underlying device driver within the kernel, some I/O mechanism is required. The Unix (and thus Linux) design is to have the process open a special type of file – a **device file**, or **device node**. These files typically live in the /dev directory, and on modern systems are dynamic and auto-populated. The device node serves as an entry point into the device driver.

In order for the kernel to distinguish between device files, it uses two attributes within their inode data structure:

- The type of file – either character (char) or block
- The major and minor number

You will see that the **namespace** – the device type and the {major#, minor#} pair – form a **hierarchy**. Devices (and thus their drivers) are organized within a tree-like hierarchy within the kernel (the driver core code within the kernel takes care of this). The hierarchy is first divided based on device type – block or char. Within that, we have some *n* major numbers for each type, and each major number is further classified via some *m* minor numbers; *Figure 1.1* shows this hierarchy.

Now, the key difference between block and character devices is that block devices have the (kernel-level) capability to be mounted and thus become part of the user-accessible filesystem. Character devices cannot be mounted; thus, storage devices tend to be block-based. Think of it this way (a bit simplistic but useful): if the (hardware) device is not storage, nor a network device, then it's a character device. A huge number of devices fall into the 'character' class, including your typical I2C/SPI (Inter Integrated Circuit / Serial Peripheral Interface) sensor chips (temperature, pressure, humidity, and so on), touchscreens, **Real-Time Clock (RTC)**, media (video, camera, audio), keyboards, mice, and so on. USB forms a class within the kernel for infrastructure support. USB devices can be block devices (pen drives, USB disks), character devices (mice, keyboard, camera) or network (USB dongles) devices.

From 2.6 Linux onward, the {major:minor} pair is a single unsigned 32-bit quantity within the inode, a bitmask (it's the dev_t i_rdev member). Of these 32 bits, the MSB 12 bits represent the major number and the remaining LSB 20 bits represent the minor number. A quick calculation shows that there can therefore be up to $2^{12} = 4,096$ major numbers and 2^{20}, which is one million, minor numbers per major number. So, glance at *Figure 1.1*; within the block hierarchy, there are a possible 4,096 majors, each of which can have up to 1 million minors. Similarly, within the character hierarchy, there are a possible 4,096 majors, each of which can have up to 1 million minors:

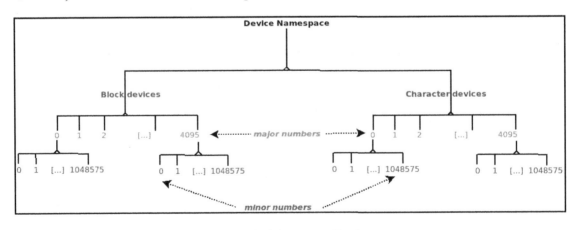

Figure 1.1 – The device namespace or hierarchy

You may be wondering: what exactly does this *major:minor* number pair really mean? Think of the major number as representing the **class** of the device (is it a SCSI disk, a keyboard, a **teletype terminal** (**tty**) or **pseudo-terminal** (**pty**) device, a loopback device (yes, these are pseudo-hardware devices), a joystick, a tape device, a framebuffer, a sensor chip, a touchscreen, and so on?). There's indeed an enormous range of devices; to get a sense of just how many, we urge you to check out the kernel documentation here: `https://www.kernel.org/doc/Documentation/admin-guide/devices.txt` (it's literally the official registry of all available devices for the Linux OS. It's formally called the **LANANA** – the **Linux Assigned Names And Numbers Authority**! Only these folks can officially assign the device node – the type and *major:minor* numbers – to devices).

The minor number's meaning (interpretation) is left completely to the driver author; the kernel does not interfere. Typically, the driver interprets the device's minor number to represent either a physical or logical instance of the device, or to represent a certain functionality. (For example, the **Small Computer System Interface** (**SCSI**) driver – of type block, major `#8` – uses minor numbers to represent logical disk partitions for up to 16 disks. On the other hand, character major `#119` is used by VMware's virtual network control driver. Here, the minors are interpreted as the first virtual network, second virtual network, and so on.) Similarly, all drivers themselves assign meaning to their minor numbers. But every good rule has an exception. Here, the exception to the rule - that the kernel doesn't interpret the minor number – is the `misc` class (type character, major `#10`). It uses the minor numbers as second-level majors. This will be covered in the following section.

A common problem is that of the namespace getting exhausted. A decision taken years back "collects" various miscellaneous character devices - a lot of mice (no, not of the animal kingdom variety), sensors, touchscreens, and so on - into one class called the `misc` or '**miscellaneous**' class, which is assigned character major number `10`. Within the `misc` class live a lot of devices and their corresponding drivers. In effect, they share the same major number and rely on a unique minor number to identify themselves. We shall write a few drivers using precisely this class and leveraging the kernel's 'misc' framework.

Many devices have already been assigned via the **LANANA (Linux Assigned Names And Numbers Authority)** into the `misc` character device class. *Figure 1.2* shows a partial screenshot from `https://www.kernel.org/doc/Documentation/admin-guide/devices.txt` showing the first few `misc` devices, their assigned minor numbers, and a brief description. Do see the reference link for the full list:

```
10 char         Non-serial mice, misc features
                  0 = /dev/logibm           Logitech bus mouse
                  1 = /dev/psaux            PS/2-style mouse port
                  2 = /dev/inportbm         Microsoft Inport bus mouse
                  3 = /dev/atibm            ATI XL bus mouse
                  4 = /dev/jbm              J-mouse
                  4 = /dev/amigamouse       Amiga mouse (68k/Amiga)
                  5 = /dev/atarimouse       Atari mouse
                  6 = /dev/sunmouse         Sun mouse
                  7 = /dev/amigamouse1      Second Amiga mouse
                  8 = /dev/smouse           Simple serial mouse driver
                  9 = /dev/pc110pad         IBM PC-110 digitizer pad
                 10 = /dev/adbmouse         Apple Desktop Bus mouse
                 11 = /dev/vrtpanel         Vr41xx embedded touch panel
                 13 = /dev/vpcmouse         Connectix Virtual PC Mouse
                 14 = /dev/touchscreen/ucb1x00  UCB 1x00 touchscreen
                 15 = /dev/touchscreen/mk712    MK712 touchscreen
                128 = /dev/beep             Fancy beep device
                129 =
                130 = /dev/watchdog         Watchdog timer port
                131 = /dev/temperature      Machine internal temperature
                132 = /dev/hwtrap           Hardware fault trap
                133 = /dev/exttrp           External device trap
                134 = /dev/apm_bios         Advanced Power Management BIOS
                135 = /dev/rtc              Real Time Clock
                137 = /dev/vhci             Bluetooth virtual HCI driver
                139 = /dev/openprom         SPARC OpenBoot PROM
                140 = /dev/relay8           Berkshire Products Octal relay card
                141 = /dev/relay16          Berkshire Products ISO-16 relay card
                142 =
                143 = /dev/pciconf          PCI configuration space
                144 = /dev/nvram            Non-volatile configuration RAM
```

Figure 1.2 – Partial screenshot of misc devices: char type, major # 10

In *Figure 1.2*, the leftmost column has `10 char`, specifying that it's assigned major # 10 under the character type of the device hierarchy (*Figure 1.1*). The columns to the right are in the form `minor# = /dev/<foo>     <description>`; quite obviously, this is the minor number assigned followed by (after the = sign) the device node and a one-line description.

A quick note on the Linux Device Model

Without going into great detail, a quick overview of the modern unified **Linux Device Model (LDM)** is important. Modern Linux, from the 2.6 kernel onward, has a fantastic feature, the LDM, which achieves many goals to do with the system and the devices on it in one broad and bold stroke. Among its many features, it creates a complex hierarchical tree unifying system components, all peripheral devices, and their drivers. This very tree is exposed to user space via the sysfs pseudo-filesystem (analogous to how procfs exposes some kernel and process/thread internal details to user space) and is typically mounted under /sys. Within /sys, you will find several directories – you can consider them to be "viewports" into the LDM. On our x86_64 Ubuntu VM, we show the sysfs filesystem mounted under /sys:

```
$ mount | grep -w sysfs
sysfs on /sys type sysfs (rw,nosuid,nodev,noexec,relatime)
```

Furthermore, take a peek inside:

```
$ ls -F /sys/
block/ bus/ class/ dev/ devices/ firmware/ fs/ hypervisor/ kernel/ module/
power/
```

Think of these directories as viewports into the LDM – different ways of viewing the devices on the system. Of course, as things evolve, more tends to get in than get out (the bloat aspect!). Several non-obvious directories have now made their way in here. Though (as with procfs) sysfs is officially documented as an **Application Binary Interface (ABI)** interface, that's subject to change/deprecation at any time; the reality is that this system is there to stay – and evolve, of course – over time.

The LDM, a bit simplistically, can be thought of as having – and tying together – these major components:

- The **buses** on the system.
- The **devices** on them.
- The **device drivers** that drive the devices (also often referred to as **client** drivers).

A fundamental LDM tenet is that *every single device must reside on a bus*. This might seem obvious: USB devices will be on the USB bus, PCI devices on the PCI bus, I2C devices on the I2C bus, and so on. Thus, under the /sys/bus hierarchy, you will be able to literally "see" all the devices via the buses that they reside on:

```
- $ ls -F /sys/bus/
ac97/          edac/          ishtp/          mmc/           platform/  spi/          xen/
acpi/          eisa/          machinecheck/   nd/            pnp/       thunderbolt/  xen-backend/
cec/           event_source/  mdio_bus/       node/          rapidio/   typec/
clockevents/   gpio/          media/          nvmem/         scsi/      usb/
clocksource/   hdaudio/       mei/            parport/       sdio/      virtio/
container/     hid/           memory/         pci/           serial/    vme/
cpu/           i2c/           memstick/       pci-epf/       serio/     wmi/
dax/           isa/           mipi-dsi/       pci_express/   snd_seq/   workqueue/
- $
```

Figure 1.3 – The different buses or bus driver infrastructure on modern Linux (on an x86_64)

The kernel's driver core provides bus drivers (that are (typically) either part of the kernel image itself or auto-loaded at boot as required), which, of course, makes the buses do their job. What is their job? Critically, they organize and recognize the devices on them. If a new device surfaces (perhaps you plugged in a pen drive), the USB bus driver will recognize the fact and bind it to its (USB mass storage) device driver! Once successfully bound (many terms are used to describe this: bound, enumerated, discovered), the kernel driver framework invokes the registered probe() method (function) of the driver. This probe method now sets up the device, allocating resources, IRQs, memory setup, registering it as required, and so on.

Another key aspect to understand regarding the LDM is that the modern LDM-based driver should typically do the following:

- Register itself to a (specialized) kernel framework.
- Register itself to a bus.

The kernel framework it registers itself to depends on the type of device you are working with; for example, a driver for an RTC chip that resides on the I2C bus will register itself to the kernel's RTC framework (via the rtc_register_device() API) and to the I2C bus (internally via the i2c_register_driver() API). On the other hand, a driver for a network adapter (a NIC) on the PCI bus will typically register itself to the kernel's network infrastructure (via the register_netdev() API) and the PCI bus (via the pci_register_driver() API). Registering with a specialized kernel framework makes your job as a driver author a lot easier – the kernel will often provide helper routines (and even data structures) to take care of I/O details, and so on. For example, take the previously mentioned RTC chip driver.

You needn't know the details of how to communicate with the chip over the I2C bus, bit banging out data on the **Serial Clock (SCL)/Serial Data (SDA)** lines as the I2C protocol demands. The kernel I2C bus framework provides you with convenience routines (such as the typically used `i2c_smbus_*()` APIs) that let you quite effortlessly communicate over the bus to the chip in question!

 If you're wondering how to get more information on these driver APIs, here's the good news: the official kernel documentation has plenty to offer. Do look up *The Linux driver implementer's API guide* here: `https://www.kernel.org/doc/html/latest/driver-api/index.html`.

(We do show some examples of the `probe()` method of a driver in the following two chapters; until then, patience, please.) Conversely, when the device is detached from the bus or the kernel module is unloaded (or the system is shutting down), the detach causes the driver's `remove()` (or `disconnect()`) method to be invoked. Between these, the work of the device via its drivers (both bus and client) is carried out!

Please note that we are glossing over a lot of the inner details here, as they are beyond the scope of this book. The point is to give you a conceptual understanding of the LDM. Do refer to the articles and links in the *Further reading* section for more detailed information.

Here, we wish to keep our driver coverage very simple and minimal, focusing more on the underlying basics. Hence we have chosen to write a driver that uses perhaps the simplest kernel framework – the `misc` or *miscellaneous* kernel framework. In this case, the driver doesn't even need to explicitly register with any bus (driver). In fact, it's more like this: our driver works *directly on the hardware* without the need for any particular bus infrastructure support.

In our particular example using the `misc` kernel framework, since we don't explicitly register with any bus (driver), we don't even require the `probe()`/`remove()` methods. This keeps things simple. On the other hand, once you have understood this simplest of drivers, I encourage you to go further and look at writing device drivers with the typical kernel framework registration plus bus driver registration, thus employing the `probe()`/`remove()` methods. A good way to get started is to learn how to write a simple **platform driver**, registering it with the kernel's `misc` framework and the *platform bus*, a pseudo-bus infrastructure that supports devices that do not physically reside on any physical bus (this is more common than you might at first imagine; several peripherals built into a modern **System on Chip (SoC)** are not on any physical bus, and thus their drivers are typically platform drivers). To get started, look under the kernel source tree in `drivers/` for code invoking the `platform_driver_register()` API. The official kernel documentation here covers platform devices and drivers: `https://www.kernel.org/doc/html/latest/driver-api/driver-model/platform.html#platform-devices-and-drivers`.

As additional help, note the following:
- Do refer to `Chapter 2`, *User-Kernel Communication Pathways*, particularly the *Creating a simple platform device* and *Platform devices* sections.
- An exercise (see the *Questions* section) for this chapter is to write such a driver. I have provided a sample (and very simple) implementation here: `solutions_to_assgn/ch12/misc_plat/`.

We do, however, require the kernel's `misc` framework support, and thus we register ourselves with it. Next, it's also key to understand this: our driver is a logical one, in the sense that there's no actual physical device or chip that it's driving. This is quite often the case (of course, you could say that here, the hardware being worked upon is RAM).

So, if we are to write a Linux character device driver belonging to this `misc` class, we will first need to register ourselves to it. Next, we will be in need of a unique (unused) minor number. Again, there is a way to have the kernel dynamically assign a free minor number to us. The following section covers these aspects and more.

Writing the misc driver code – part 1

Without further ado, let's look at the code to write a simple skeleton character `misc` device driver! (Well, snippets of the actual code; as always, I strongly advise you to `git clone` the book's GitHub repository, view it in detail, and try out the code yourself.)

Let's go through it step by step: in the `init` code of our first device driver (using the LKM framework), we must first **register** our driver with the appropriate Linux kernel's framework; in this case, with the `misc` framework. This is done via the `misc_register()` API. It takes one parameter, a pointer to a data structure of type `miscdevice`, which describes the miscellaneous device we are setting up:

```c
// ch1/miscdrv/miscdrv.c
#define pr_fmt(fmt) "%s:%s(): " fmt, KBUILD_MODNAME, __func__
[...]
#include <linux/miscdevice.h>
#include <linux/fs.h>              /* the fops, file data structures */
[...]

static struct miscdevice llkd_miscdev = {
    .minor = MISC_DYNAMIC_MINOR, /* kernel dynamically assigns a free
minor# */
    .name = "llkd_miscdrv",       /* when misc_register() is invoked, the
kernel
             * will auto-create a device file as /dev/llkd_miscdrv ;
             * also populated within /sys/class/misc/ and
/sys/devices/virtual/misc/ */
    .mode = 0666,                /* ... dev node perms set as specified here */
    .fops = &llkd_misc_fops, /* connect to this driver's 'functionality' */
};

static int __init miscdrv_init(void)
{
    int ret;
    struct device *dev;

    ret = misc_register(&llkd_miscdev);
    if (ret != 0) {
        pr_notice("misc device registration failed, aborting\n");
        return ret;
    }
    [ ... ]
```

In the `miscdevice` structure instance, we do the following:

1. We set the `minor` field to `MISC_DYNAMIC_MINOR`. This has the effect of requesting the kernel to dynamically assign us an available minor number (once registration is successful, this `minor` field gets populated with the actual minor number assigned).

2. We initialize the `name` field. On successful registration, this has the kernel framework automatically create a device node (of the form `/dev/<name>`) on our behalf! As expected, the type will be character, the major number will be `10`, and the minor number will be a dynamically assigned value. This is (part of) the advantage of using a kernel framework; else, we might have had to devise a way to create the device node ourselves; by the way, the `mknod(1)` utility can create a device file when invoked with root privilege (or you have the `CAP_MKNOD` capability); it works by invoking the `mknod(2)` system call!

3. The permissions of the device node will be set to whatever you initialize the `mode` field to (here, we've deliberately kept it permissive and readable-writeable by all via the `0666` octal value).

4. We shall postpone the discussion of the file operations (`fops`) structure member to the section following this one.

All `misc` drivers are of the character type and use the same major number (`10`), but of course require unique minor numbers.

Understanding the connection between the process, the driver, and the kernel

Here, we will delve into just a bit of the kernel internals surrounding the successful registration of a character device driver on Linux. In effect, you will come to understand the workings of the underlying raw character driver framework.

The `file_operations` structure, or the **fops** (pronounced *eff-opps*), as it's commonly referred to, is of critical importance to driver authors; the majority of the members of the fops structure are function pointers – think of them as **virtual methods**. They represent all possible file-related system calls that could be issued on a (device) file. So, it has `open`, `read`, `write`, `poll`, `mmap`, `release`, and several more members (most of which are function pointers). A few of the members of this critical data structure are shown here:

```
// include/linux/fs.h
struct file_operations {
    struct module *owner;
```

```
    loff_t (*llseek) (struct file *, loff_t, int);
    ssize_t (*read) (struct file *, char __user *, size_t, loff_t *);
    ssize_t (*write) (struct file *, const char __user *, size_t, loff_t
*);
[...]
    __poll_t (*poll) (struct file *, struct poll_table_struct *);
    long (*unlocked_ioctl) (struct file *, unsigned int, unsigned long);
    long (*compat_ioctl) (struct file *, unsigned int, unsigned long);
    int (*mmap) (struct file *, struct vm_area_struct *);
    unsigned long mmap_supported_flags;
    int (*open) (struct inode *, struct file *);
    int (*flush) (struct file *, fl_owner_t id);
    int (*release) (struct inode *, struct file *);
[...]
    int (*fadvise)(struct file *, loff_t, loff_t, int);
} __randomize_layout;
```

A key job of the driver author (or the underlying kernel framework) is to populate these function pointers, thus linking them to actual code within the driver. You needn't implement every single function, of course; please refer to the *Handling unsupported methods* section for details.

Now, let's assume you have written your driver to set up functions for some of the f_op methods. Once your driver is registered with the kernel, typically via a kernel framework, when any user space process (or thread) opens a device file registered to this driver, the kernel **Virtual Filesystem Switch** (**VFS**) layer will take over. Without going into deep detail, suffice it to say that the VFS allocates and initializes that process's open file data structure (struct file) for the device file. Now, recall the last line in our struct miscdevice initialization; it's this:

```
    .fops = &llkd_misc_fops, /* connect to this driver's 'functionality' */
```

This line of code has a key effect: it ties the process's file operations pointer (which is within the process' open file structure) to the device driver's file operations structure. The *functionality – what the driver will do –* is now set up for this device file!

Let's flesh this out. Now (after your driver has initialized itself), a user-mode process opens your driver's device file, by issuing the `open(2)` system call on it. Assuming all goes well (and it should), the process is now connected to your driver via the `file_operations` structure pointers deep inside the kernel. Here's a critical point: after the `open(2)` system call returns successfully, and the process issues any file-related system call `foo()` on that (device) file, the kernel VFS layer will, be having in an object-oriented fashion (we have pointed this out before in this book!), blindly and trustingly invoke the registered `fops->foo()` method! The file opened by the user space process, typically a device file in `/dev`, is internally represented by the `struct file` metadata structure (a pointer to this, `struct file *filp`, is passed along to the driver). So, in terms of pseudo-code, when user space issues a file-related system call `foo()`, this is what the kernel VFS layer effectively does:

```
/* pseudocode: kernel VFS layer (not the driver) */
if (filp->f_op->foo)
    filp->f_op->foo(); /* invoke the 'registered' driver method
corresponding to 'foo()' */
```

Thus, if the user space process that opened a device file invokes the `read(2)` system call upon it, the kernel VFS will invoke `filp->f_op->read(...)`, in effect, redirecting control to the device driver. Your job as the device driver author is to provide the functionality of `read(2)`! The same goes for all other file-related system calls. This, essentially, is how Unix and Linux implement the well-known *if it's not a process, it's a file* design principle.

Handling unsupported methods

You don't have to populate every member of the `f_ops` structure, only those that your driver supports. If that's the case, and you have populated a few methods but left out, say, the `poll` method, and a user space process invokes `poll(2)` on your device (perhaps you've documented the fact that it's not supposed to, but what if it does?), then what will happen? In cases like this, the kernel VFS, detecting that the `foo` pointer (in this example, `poll`) is `NULL`, returns an appropriate negative integer (in effect, following the same 0/-E protocol). The `glibc` code will multiply this by –1 and set the calling process's `errno` variable to that value, signaling that the system call failed.

Two points to be aware of:

- Quite often, the negative `errno` value returned by the VFS isn't very intuitive. (For example, if you've set the `read()` function pointer of f_op to NULL, the VFS causes the `EINVAL` value to be sent back. This has the user space process think that `read(2)` failed because of an "`Invalid argument`" error, which simply isn't the case at all!)
- The `lseek(2)` system call has the driver seek to a prescribed location in the file – here, of course, we mean in the device. The kernel deliberately names the f_op function pointer as `llseek` (notice the two 'l's). This is simply to remind you that the return value from `lseek` can be a 64-bit (long long) quantity. Now, for the majority of hardware devices, the `lseek` value is not meaningful, thus most drivers do not need to implement it (unlike filesystems). Now, the issue is this: even if you do not support `lseek` (you've set the `llseek` member of f_op to NULL), it still returns a random positive value, thus causing the user-mode app to incorrectly conclude that it succeeded. Hence, if you aren't implementing `lseek`, you are to do the following:
    1. Explicitly set `llseek` to the special `no_llseek` value, which will cause a failure value (`-ESPIPE`; `illegal seek`) to be returned.
    2. In such cases, you are to also invoke the `nonseekable_open()` function in your driver's `open()` method, specifying that the file is non-seekable (this is often called like this in the `open()` method: `return nonseekable_open(struct inode *inode, struct file *filp);`. The details, and more, are covered in the LWN articles here: `https://lwn.net/Articles/97154/`. You can see the changes this wrought to many drivers here: `https://lwn.net/Articles/97180/`).

An appropriate value to return if you aren't supporting a function is `-ENOSYS`, which will have the user-mode process see the error `Function not implemented` (when it invokes the `perror(3)` or `strerror(3)` library APIs). This is clear, unambiguous; the user space developer will now understand that your driver does not support this function. Thus, one way to implement your driver is to set up pointers to all the file operation methods, and write a routine for all file-related system calls (the f_op methods) in your driver. For the ones you do support, write the code; for the ones you do not implement, just return the value `-ENOSYS`. Though a bit painstaking to do, it will result in unambiguous return values to user space.

Writing the misc driver code – part 2

Armed with this knowledge, look again at the `init` code of `ch1/miscdrv/miscdrv.c`. You will see that, just as described in the previous section, we have initialized the `fops` member of the `miscdev` struct to a `file_operations` structure, thus setting up the functionality of the driver. The relevant code snippet (from our driver) is as follows:

```
static const struct file_operations llkd_misc_fops = {
    .open = open_miscdrv,
    .read = read_miscdrv,
    .write = write_miscdrv,
    .release = close_miscdrv,
};

static struct miscdevice llkd_miscdev = {
    [ ... ]
    .fops = &llkd_misc_fops,      /* connect to this driver's
'functionality' */
};
```

So, now you can see it: when a user space process (or thread) that has opened our device file invokes, say, a `read(2)` system call, the kernel VFS layer will follow the pointers (generically, `filp->f_op->foo()`) and invoke the function, `read_miscdrv()`, in effect handing over control to the device driver! How exactly the read method is written is covered in the next section.

Continuing with the `init` code of our simple `misc` driver:

```
    [ ... ]
    /* Retrieve the device pointer for this device */
    dev = llkd_miscdev.this_device;
    pr_info("LLKD misc driver (major # 10) registered, minor# = %d,"
            " dev node is /dev/%s\n", llkd_miscdev.minor,
llkd_miscdev.name);
    dev_info(dev, "sample dev_info(): minor# = %d\n", llkd_miscdev.minor);
    return 0;      /* success */
}
```

Our driver retrieves a pointer to the `device` structure – it's something required by every driver. Within the `misc` kernel framework, it's available within the `this_device` member of our `miscdevice` structure.

Next, `pr_info()` shows the minor number dynamically obtained. The `dev_info()` helper routine is more interesting: as a driver author, you are **expected to use these** `dev_xxx()` **helpers** when emitting `printk`; it will also prefix useful information about the device. The only difference in syntax between the `dev_xxx()` and `pr_xxx()` helpers is that the first parameter to the former is the pointer to the device structure.

Okay, let's get our hands dirty! We build the driver and `insmod` it into kernel space (we use our `lkm` helper script to do so):

```
$ ../../lkm miscdrv
Version info:
Distro:        Ubuntu 20.04.1 LTS
Kernel: 5.4.0-58-generic
------------------------------
sudo rmmod miscdrv 2> /dev/null
------------------------------
[sudo] password for llkd:
 ^--[FAILED]
------------------------------
sudo dmesg -C
------------------------------
------------------------------
make || exit 1
------------------------------

--- Building : KDIR=/lib/modules/5.4.0-58-generic/build ARCH= CROSS_COMPILE= EXTRA_CFLAGS=-DDEBUG ---

make -C /lib/modules/5.4.0-58-generic/build M=/home/llkd/Learn-Linux-Kernel-Development/ch12/miscdrv modules
make[1]: Entering directory '/usr/src/linux-headers-5.4.0-58-generic'
  CC [M]  /home/llkd/Learn-Linux-Kernel-Development/ch12/miscdrv/miscdrv.o
  Building modules, stage 2.
  MODPOST 1 modules
  CC [M]  /home/llkd/Learn-Linux-Kernel-Development/ch12/miscdrv/miscdrv.mod.o
  LD [M]  /home/llkd/Learn-Linux-Kernel-Development/ch12/miscdrv/miscdrv.ko
make[1]: Leaving directory '/usr/src/linux-headers-5.4.0-58-generic'
------------------------------
sudo insmod ./miscdrv.ko && lsmod|grep miscdrv
------------------------------
miscdrv              20480  0
------------------------------
dmesg
------------------------------
[  140.074879] miscdrv:miscdrv_init(): miscdrv: LLKD misc driver (major # 10) registered, minor# = 56, dev node is
/dev/llkd_miscdrv
[  140.075924] misc llkd_miscdrv: sample dev_info(): minor# = 56
$
$ ls -l /dev/llkd_miscdrv
crw-rw-rw- 1 root root 10, 56 Jan  2 17:23 /dev/llkd_miscdrv
$
```

Figure 1.4 – Screenshot of building and loading our miscdrv.ko skeleton misc driver on an x86_64 Ubuntu VM

(By the way, as you can see in *Figure 1.4*, I tried out this misc driver on a more recent distro: Ubuntu 20.04.1 LTS running the 5.4.0-58-generic kernel.) Notice the two prints toward the bottom of *Figure 1.4*; the first is emitted via the pr_info() (prefixed with the pr_fmt() macro content, as explained in the companion guide *Linux Kernel Programming - Chapter 4, Writing Your First Kernel Module - LKMs Part 1* section *Standardizing printk output via the pr_fmt macro*). The second print is emitted via the dev_info() helper routine – it's prefixed with the words misc llkd_miscdrv, indicating that it originated from the kernel's misc framework, and specifically from the llkd_miscdrv device! (The dev_xxx() routines are versatile; depending on the bus they're on, they will display various details. This is useful for debugging and logging purposes. We repeat: you're recommended to use the dev_*() routines when writing drivers.) You can also see that the /dev/llkd_miscdrv device node is indeed created, with the expected type (character) and major and minor pair (10 and 56 here).

Writing the misc driver code – part 3

Now, the init code is done, the driver functionality has been set up via the file operations structure, and the driver is registered to the kernel misc framework. So, what happens next? Well, nothing really, until a process opens the device file (associated with your driver) and performs I/O (Input/Output, i.e., reads/writes) of some sort.

So, let's assume that a user-mode process (or thread) issues the open(2) system call on your driver's device node (recall, the device node has been auto-created when the driver registered itself to the kernel's misc framework). Most important, as you learned in the *Understanding the connection between the process, the driver, and the kernel* section, for any file-related system calls issued upon your device node, the VFS will essentially invoke the driver's (f_op) registered method. So, here, the VFS will do this: filp->f-op->open(), thus invoking our driver's open method within our file_operations structure, which is the open_miscdrv() function!

But how should you, the driver author, implement this code of the open method of your driver? The key point is this: the signature of your open function **should be identical** to that of the file_operation structure open; in fact, this is true of any function. Thus, we implement the open_miscdrv() function like this:

```
/*
 * open_miscdrv()
 * The driver's open 'method'; this 'hook' will get invoked by the kernel
VFS
 * when the device file is opened. Here, we simply print out some relevant
info.
```

```
 * The POSIX standard requires open() to return the file descriptor on
success;
 * note, though, that this is done within the kernel VFS (when we return).
So,
 * all we do here is return 0 indicating success.
 * (The nonseekable_open(), in conjunction with the fop's llseek pointer
set to
 * no_llseek, tells the kernel that our device is not seek-able).
 */
static int open_miscdrv(struct inode *inode, struct file *filp)
{
    char *buf = kzalloc(PATH_MAX, GFP_KERNEL);

    if (unlikely(!buf))
        return -ENOMEM;
    PRINT_CTX(); // displays process (or atomic) context info
    pr_info(" opening \"%s\" now; wrt open file: f_flags = 0x%x\n",
        file_path(filp, buf, PATH_MAX), filp->f_flags);
    kfree(buf);
    return nonseekable_open(inode, filp);
}
```

Notice how the signature of our `open` routine, the `open_miscdrv()` function, precisely matches that of the `f_op` structure's `open` function pointer (you can always lookup the `file_operations` structure for 5.4 Linux here at https://elixir.bootlin.com/linux/v5.4/source/include/linux/fs.h#L1814).

In this simple driver, in our `open` method, we don't really have much to do. We allocate some memory for a buffer (to hold the pathname of our device) via `kzalloc()`, issue our `PRINT_CTX()` macro (it's in the `convenient.h` header) to show the current context – the process that is currently opening the device. We then emit a `printk` (via `pr_info()`) showing a few VFS layer details (the pathname and open flags value); you can get the path name of a file by using the convenience API `file_path()`, as we do here (to do so, we need to allocate and, after usage, free a kernel memory buffer). Then, as we don't support seeking in this driver, we invoke the `nonseekable_open()` API (as discussed in the *Handling unsupported methods* section).

The open(2) system call on the device file should succeed. The user-mode process will now have a valid file descriptor – a handle to the open file (which, here, is actually a device node). Now, let's say the user-mode process wants to read data from the hardware; it therefore issues the read(2) system call. As explained already, the kernel VFS will now auto-invoke our driver's read method, read_miscdrv(). Again, its signature exactly imitates the read function signature from the file_operations data structure. Here's the simple code of our driver's read method:

```
/*
 * read_miscdrv()
 * The driver's read 'method'; it has effectively 'taken over' the read
syscall
 * functionality! Here, we simply print out some info.
 * The POSIX standard requires that the read() and write() system calls
return
 * the number of bytes read or written on success, 0 on EOF (for read) and
-1 (-ve errno)
 * on failure; we simply return 'count', pretending that we 'always
succeed'.
 */
static ssize_t read_miscdrv(struct file *filp, char __user *ubuf, size_t
count, loff_t *off)
{
        pr_info("to read %zd bytes\n", count);
        return count;
}
```

The preceding comment is self-explanatory. Within it, we emit pr_info(), showing the number of bytes the user space process wants to read. Then, we simply return the number of bytes read, implying success! In reality, we have done (essentially) nothing. The remaining driver methods are quite similar.

Testing our simple misc driver

Let's test our really simple skeleton misc character driver (in the ch1/miscdrv directory; we assume you have built and inserted it as shown in *Figure 1.4*). We test it by issuing open(2), read(2), write(2), and close(2) system calls upon it; how exactly can we do so? We can always write a small C program to do precisely this, but an easier way is to use the useful dd(1) "disk duplicator" utility. We use it like this:

```
dd if=/dev/llkd_miscdrv of=readtest bs=4k count=1
```

Internally dd opens the file we pass it as a parameter (/dev/llkd_miscdrv) via if= (here, it's the first parameter to dd; if= specifies the input file), it will read from it (via the read(2) system call, of course). The output is to be written to the file specified by the parameter of= (the second parameter to dd, and is a regular file named readtest); the bs specifies the block size to perform I/O in and count is the number of times to perform I/O). After performing the required I/O, the dd process will close(2) the files. This sequence is reflected in the kernel log (*Figure 1.5*):

```
$ lsmod |grep -w miscdrv
miscdrv                20480  0
$ dd if=/dev/llkd_miscdrv of=readtest bs=4k count=1 ; dmesg
1+0 records in
1+0 records out
4096 bytes (4.1 kB, 4.0 KiB) copied, 0.00120891 s, 3.4 MB/s
[  140.074879] miscdrv:miscdrv_init(): miscdrv: LLKD misc driver (major # 10) registered, minor# = 56, dev
 node is /dev/llkd_miscdrv
[  140.075924] misc llkd_miscdrv: sample dev_info(): minor# = 56
[ 2630.766139] miscdrv:open_miscdrv(): 002)  dd :2404   | ...0   /* open_miscdrv() */
[ 2630.769117] miscdrv:open_miscdrv():  opening "/dev/llkd_miscdrv" now; wrt open file: f_flags = 0x8000
[ 2630.771107] miscdrv:read_miscdrv(): to read 4096 bytes
[ 2630.771628] miscdrv:close_miscdrv(): closing "/dev/llkd_miscdrv"
$ hexdump readtest
0000000 0000 0000 0000 0000 0000 0000 0000 0000
*
0001000
$
```

Figure 1.5 – Screenshot showing us minimally testing our miscdrv driver's read method via dd(1)

After verifying that our driver (LKM) is inserted, we issue the dd(1) command, having it read 4,096 bytes from our device (as the block size (bs) is set to 4k and count to 1). We have it write the output (via the of= option switch) to a file named readtest. Looking up the kernel log, you can see (*Figure 1.5*) that the dd process has indeed opened our device (our PRINT_CTX() macro's output shows that it's the process context currently running the code of our driver!). Next, we can see (via the output from pr_fmt()) that control goes to our driver's read method, within which we emit a simple printk and return the value 4096 signifying success (though we really didn't read anything!). The device is then closed by dd. Furthermore, a quick check with the hexdump(1) utility reveals that we did indeed receive 0x1000 (4,096) nulls (as expected) from the driver (in the file readtest; do realize that this is the case because dd initialized it's read buffer to NULLs).

The PRINT_CTX() macro we have used within the code lives within our convenient.h header. Do take a look; it's quite instructive (we try and emulate the kernel Ftrace infrastructure's latency output format, which reveals a lot of detail in a small space, a single line of output). This is explained in detail in Chapter 4, *Handling Hardware Interrupts*, in the *Fully figuring out the context* section. Don't worry about all the details for now...

Figure 1.6 shows how we (minimally) test writing to our driver, again via dd(1). This time we read 4k of random data (by leveraging the kernel's built-in mem driver's /dev/urandom facility), and write the random data to our device node; in effect, to our 'device':

```
$ sudo dmesg -C; dd if=/dev/urandom of=/dev/llkd_miscdrv bs=4k count=1 ; dmesg
1+0 records in
1+0 records out
4096 bytes (4.1 kB, 4.0 KiB) copied, 0.00229645 s, 1.8 MB/s
[ 7350.977886] miscdrv:open_miscdrv(): 001)  dd :6911   |  ...0   /* open_miscdrv() */
[ 7350.983078] miscdrv:open_miscdrv():  opening "llkd_miscdrv" now; wrt open file: f_flags = 0x8241
[ 7350.988068] miscdrv:write_miscdrv(): to write 4096 bytes
[ 7350.989450] miscdrv:close_miscdrv(): closing "llkd_miscdrv"
$
```

Figure 1.6 – Screenshot showing us minimally testing our miscdrv driver's write method via dd(1)

(By the way, I have also included a simple user space test app for the driver; it can be found here: ch1/miscdrv/rdwr_test.c. I will leave it to you to read its code and try out.)

You might be thinking: we did apparently succeed in reading and writing data to and from user space to our driver, but, hang on, we never actually saw any data transfer taking place within the driver code. Yes, this is the topic of the next section: how you will actually copy the data from the user space process buffer into your kernel driver's buffer, and vice versa. Read on!

Copying data from kernel to user space and vice versa

A primary job of the device driver is to enable user space applications to transparently both read and write data to the peripheral hardware device (typically a chip of some sort; it may not be hardware at all though), treating the device as though it were simply a regular file. Thus, to read data from the device, the application opens the device file corresponding to that device, thus obtaining a file descriptor, and then simply issues a `read(2)` system call using that `fd` (*step 1* in *Figure 1.7*)! The kernel VFS intercepts the read, and, as we have seen, has control flow to the underlying device driver's read method (which is a C function, of course). The driver code now "talks" to the hardware device, actually performing the I/O, the read operation. (The specifics of how exactly the hardware read (or write) is performed depends very much on the type of hardware – is it a memory-mapped device, a port, a network chip, and so on? We will not delve further into this here; the next chapter does.) The driver, having read data from the device, now places this data into a kernel buffer, `kbuf` (*step 2* in the following diagram. Of course, we assume the driver author allocated memory for it via `[k|v]malloc()` or another suitable kernel API).

We now have the hardware device data in a kernel space buffer. How should we transfer it to the user space process's memory buffer? We shall exploit kernel APIs that make it easy to do so; this is covered next.

Leveraging kernel APIs to perform the data transfer

Now, as mentioned previously, let's assume your driver has read in the hardware data, and that it's now present in a kernel memory buffer. How do we transfer it to user space? A naive approach would be to simply try and perform this via `memcpy()`, but *no*, that does not work (why? one, it's insecure and two, it's very arch-dependent; it works on some architectures and not on others). So, a key point: the kernel provides a couple of inline functions to transfer data from kernel to user space and vice versa. They are `copy_to_user()` and `copy_from_user()`, respectively, and are indeed very commonly used.

Using them is simple. Both take three parameters: the `to` pointer (destination buffer), the `from` pointer (source buffer), and n, the number of bytes to copy (think of it as you would for a `memcpy` operation):

```
include <linux/uaccess.h>    /* Note! used to be <asm/uaccess.h> upto 4.11
*/

unsigned long copy_to_user(void __user *to, const void *from, unsigned long
n);
unsigned long copy_from_user(void *to, const void __user *from, unsigned
long n);
```

The return value is the number of *uncopied* bytes; in other words, a return value of 0 indicates success and a non-zero return value indicates that the given number of bytes were not copied. If a non-zero return occurs, you should (following the usual 0/-E return convention) return an error indicating an I/O fault by returning -EIO or -EFAULT (which thus sets `errno` in user space to the positive counterpart). The following (pseudo) code illustrates how a device driver can use the `copy_to_user()` function to copy some data from kernel to user space:

```
static ssize_t read_method(struct file *filp, char __user *ubuf, size_t
count, loff_t *off)
{
    char *kbuf = kzalloc(...);
    [ ... ]
    /* ... do what's required to get data from the hardware device into
kbuf ... */
    if (copy_to_user(buf, kbuf, count)) {
        dev_warn(dev, "copy_to_user() failed\n");
        goto out_rd_fail;
    }
    [ ... ]
    return count;    /* success */
out_rd_fail:
    kfree(kbuf);
 return -EIO; /* or -EFAULT */
}
```

Here, of course, we assume you have a valid allocated kernel memory buffer, `kbuf`, and a valid device pointer (`struct device *dev`). *Figure 1.7* illustrates what the preceding (pseudo) code is trying to achieve:

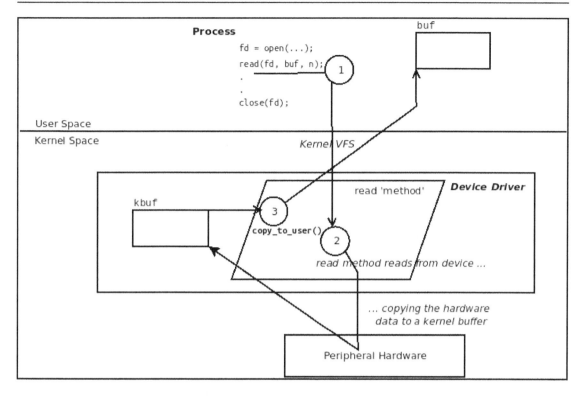

Figure 1.7 – Read: copy_to_user(): copying data from the hardware to a kernel buffer and from there to a user space buffer

The same semantics apply to using the `copy_from_user()` inline function. It is typically used in the context of the driver's write method, pulling in the data written by the user space process context to a kernel space buffer. We will leave it to you to visualize this.

It is also important to realize that both routines (`copy_[from|to]_user()`) might, during their run, cause the process context to (page) fault and thus sleep; in other words, to invoke the scheduler. Hence, **they can only be used in a process context where it's safe to sleep and never in any kind of atomic or interrupt context** (we explain more on the `might_sleep()` helper – a debug aid – in `Chapter 4`, *Handling Hardware Interrupts*, in the *Don't block – spotting possibly blocking code paths* section).

For the curious reader (I hope you are one!), here are some links with a bit more of a detailed explanation on why you cannot just use a simple `memcpy()` but must use the `copy_[from|to]_user()` inline functions to copy data from and to the kernel and user spaces:

- https://stackoverflow.com/questions/14970698/copy-to-user-vs-memcpy
- https://www.quora.com/Why-we-need-copy_from_user-as-the-kernel-can-acc ess-all-the-memory-If-we-see-the-copy_from_user-implementation-again- we-are-copying-data-to-the-kernel-memory-using-memcpy-Doesnt-it-an extra-overhead.

In the following section, we shall write a more complete `misc` framework character device driver, which will actually perform some I/O, reading and writing data.

A misc driver with a secret

Now that you understand how to copy data between user and kernel space (and the reverse), let's write another device driver (`ch1/miscdrv_rdwr`) based on our previous skeleton (`ch1/miscdrv/`) miscellaneous driver. The key difference is that we use a few global data items (within a structure) throughout, and actually perform some I/O in the form of reads and writes. Here, let's introduce the notion of a **driver context or private driver data structure**; the idea is to have a conveniently accessible data structure that contains all relevant information in one place. Here, we name this structure `struct drv_ctx` (see it in the code listing that follows). On driver initialization, we allocate memory to and initialize it.

Okay, there's no real secret here, it just makes it sound interesting. One of the members within this driver context data structure of ours is a so-called secret message (it's the `drv_ctx.oursecret` member, along with some (fake) statistics and config words). This is the simple "driver context" or private data structure we propose using:

```
// ch1/miscdrv_rdwr/miscdrv_rdwr.c
[ ... ]
/* The driver 'context' (or private) data structure;
 * all relevant 'state info' reg the driver is here. */
struct drv_ctx {
    struct device *dev;
    int tx, rx, err, myword;
    u32 config1, config2;
    u64 config3;
#define MAXBYTES 128 /* Must match the userspace app; we should actually
                      * use a common header file for things like this */
```

```
        char oursecret[MAXBYTES];
};
static struct drv_ctx *ctx;
```

Great; now let's move on to seeing and understanding the code.

Writing the 'secret' misc device driver's code

We've divided this discussion on the implementation details of our secret misc character device driver into five parts: driver initialization, the read method, the write method functionality implementation, the driver cleanup, and finally, the userspace application that will use our device driver.

Our secret driver – the init code

In the `init` code of our secret device driver (a kernel module, of course, thus invoked upon `insmod(8)`), we first register the driver as a `misc` character driver with the kernel (via the `misc_register()` API, as seen in the *Writing the misc driver code – part 1* section earlier; we won't repeat this code here).

Next, we allocate kernel memory for our driver's "context" structure – via the useful managed allocation `devm_kzalloc()` API (as you learned in the companion guide *Linux Kernel Programming*, `Chapter 8`, *Kernel Memory Allocation for Module Authors – Part 1*, in the *Using the kernel's resource-managed memory allocation APIs* section) – and initialize it. Notice that you must ensure you first get the device pointer `dev` before you can use this API; we retrieve it from our `miscdevice` structure's `this_device` member (as seen):

```
// ch1/miscdrv_rdwr/miscdrv_rdwr.c
[ ... ]
static int __init miscdrv_rdwr_init(void)
{
    int ret;
    struct device *dev;

    ret = misc_register(&llkd_miscdev);
    [ ... ]
    dev = llkd_miscdev.this_device;
    [ ... ]
    ctx = devm_kzalloc(dev, sizeof(struct drv_ctx), GFP_KERNEL);
    if (unlikely(!ctx))
        return -ENOMEM;

    ctx->dev = dev;
```

```
        strscpy(ctx->oursecret, "initmsg", 8);
        [ ... ]
        return 0;            /* success */
}
```

Okay, clearly, we have initialized the `dev` member of our `ctx` private structure instance as well as the 'secret' string to the `'initmsg'` string (not a very convincing secret, but let's leave it at that). The idea here is that when a user space process (or thread) opens our device file and issues `read(2)` upon it, we pass back (copy) the secret to it; we do so by invoking the `copy_to_user()` helper function! Similarly, when the user-mode app writes data to us (yes, via the `write(2)` system call), we consider that data written to be the new secret. So, we fetch it from its user space buffer – via the `copy_from_user()` helper function – and update it in driver memory.

> Why not simply use the `strcpy()` (or `strncpy()`) API to initialize the `ctx->oursecret` member? This is very important: they aren't safe enough security-wise. Also, the `strlcpy()` API has been marked as **deprecated** by the kernel community (https://www.kernel.org/doc/html/latest/process/deprecated.html#strlcpy). In general, always avoid using deprecated stuff, as documented in the kernel documentation here: https://www.kernel.org/doc/html/latest/process/deprecated.html#deprecated-interfaces-language-features-attributes-and-conventions.

Quite clearly, the interesting parts of this new driver are the I/O functionality – the *read* and *write* methods; on with it!

Our secret driver – the read method

We will first show the relevant code for the read method – this is how a user space process (or thread) can read in the secret information housed within our driver (in its context structure):

```
static ssize_t
read_miscdrv_rdwr(struct file *filp, char __user *ubuf, size_t count,
loff_t *off)
{
    int ret = count, secret_len = strlen(ctx->oursecret);
    struct device *dev = ctx->dev;
    char tasknm[TASK_COMM_LEN];

    PRINT_CTX();
    dev_info(dev, "%s wants to read (upto) %zd bytes\n",
```

```
        get_task_comm(tasknm, current), count);

            ret = -EINVAL;
            if (count < MAXBYTES) {
            [...] << we don't display some validity checks here >>

            /* In a 'real' driver, we would now actually read the content of
        the
             * [...]
             * Returns 0 on success, i.e., non-zero return implies an I/O
        fault).
             * Here, we simply copy the content of our context structure's
             * 'secret' member to userspace. */
            ret = -EFAULT;
            if (copy_to_user(ubuf, ctx->oursecret, secret_len)) {
                dev_warn(dev, "copy_to_user() failed\n");
                goto out_notok;
            }
            ret = secret_len;

            // Update stats
            ctx->tx += secret_len; // our 'transmit' is wrt this driver
            dev_info(dev, " %d bytes read, returning... (stats: tx=%d,
        rx=%d)\n",
                    secret_len, ctx->tx, ctx->rx);
        out_notok:
            return ret;
        }
```

The `copy_to_user()` routine does its job – it copies the `ctx->oursecret` source buffer to the destination pointer, the `ubuf` user space buffer, for `secret_len` bytes, thus transferring the secret to the user space app. Now, let's check out the driver's write method.

Our secret driver – the write method

The end user can change the secret by writing a new secret into the driver, via a `write(2)` system call to the driver's device node. The kernel redirects the write (via the VFS layer) to our driver's write method (as you learned in the *Understanding the connection between the process, the driver, and the kernel* section):

```
static ssize_t
write_miscdrv_rdwr(struct file *filp, const char __user *ubuf, size_t
count, loff_t *off)
{
    int ret = count;
    void *kbuf = NULL;
```

```
        struct device *dev = ctx->dev;
        char tasknm[TASK_COMM_LEN];

        PRINT_CTX();
        if (unlikely(count > MAXBYTES)) { /* paranoia */
            dev_warn(dev, "count %zu exceeds max # of bytes allowed, "
                    "aborting write\n", count);
            goto out_nomem;
        }
        dev_info(dev, "%s wants to write %zd bytes\n", get_task_comm(tasknm,
current), count);

        ret = -ENOMEM;
        kbuf = kvmalloc(count, GFP_KERNEL);
        if (unlikely(!kbuf))
            goto out_nomem;
        memset(kbuf, 0, count);

        /* Copy in the user supplied buffer 'ubuf' - the data content
         * to write ... */
        ret = -EFAULT;
        if (copy_from_user(kbuf, ubuf, count)) {
            dev_warn(dev, "copy_from_user() failed\n");
            goto out_cfu;
        }

        /* In a 'real' driver, we would now actually write (for 'count' bytes)
         * the content of the 'ubuf' buffer to the device hardware (or
         * whatever), and then return.
         * Here, we do nothing, we just pretend we've done everything :-)
         */
        strscpy(ctx->oursecret, kbuf, (count > MAXBYTES ? MAXBYTES : count));
        [...]
        // Update stats
        ctx->rx += count; // our 'receive' is wrt this driver

        ret = count;
        dev_info(dev, " %zd bytes written, returning... (stats: tx=%d,
rx=%d)\n",
                count, ctx->tx, ctx->rx);
out_cfu:
        kvfree(kbuf);
out_nomem:
        return ret;
    }
```

We employ the `kvmalloc()` API to allocate memory for a buffer to hold the user data that we will copy in. The actual copying is done via the `copy_from_user()` routine, of course. Here, we use it to copy the data passed by the user space app to our kernel buffer, `kbuf`. We then (via the `strscpy()` routine) update our driver's context structure's `oursecret` member to this value, thus updating the secret! (A subsequent read on the driver will now reveal the new secret.) Also, do notice the following:

- How we now consistently use the `dev_xxx()` helpers in place of the usual `printk` routines. This is recommended for device drivers.
- The (now typical) usage of `goto` to perform optimal error handling.

This covers the meat of the driver.

Our secret driver – cleanup

It's important to realize that we must free any buffers we have allocated. Here, however, as we performed a managed allocation in the `init` code (`devm_kzalloc()`), we have the benefit of not needing to worry about cleanup; the kernel handles it. Of course, in the driver's cleanup code path (invoked upon `rmmod(8)`), we deregister the `misc` driver with the kernel:

```
static void __exit miscdrv_rdwr_exit(void)
{
    misc_deregister(&llkd_miscdev);
    pr_info("LLKD misc (rdwr) driver deregistered, bye\n");
}
```

You will notice that we also, seemingly uselessly, use two global integers, `ga` and `gb`, in places in this version of the driver. Indeed, they have no real meaning here; the reason we have them at all becomes clear only in the last two chapters of this book, on kernel synchronization. Please ignore them for now.

 On this note, you'll perhaps realize that the way we have arbitrarily accessed global data in this driver **can cause concurrency issue** (*data races!*); yes indeed; we shall set aside the deep and crucial coverage of kernel concurrency and synchronization to the book's last two chapters.

Our secret driver – the user space test app

Writing just the kernel component, the device driver, isn't quite enough; you also have to write a user space application that will actually make use of the driver. We will do so here. (Again, you could simply use dd(1) as well.)

In order to use the device driver, the user space app must first, of course, open the device file corresponding to it. (Here, to save space, we don't show the app code in its entirety, just the most relevant portions of it. We expect you to have cloned the book's Git repository and to work on the code.) The code to open the device file is as follows:

```
// ch1/miscdrv_rdwr/rdwr_test_secret.c
int main(int argc, char **argv)
{
    char opt = 'r';
    int fd, flags = O_RDONLY;
    ssize_t n;
    char *buf = NULL;
    size_t num = 0;
[...]
    if ('w' == opt)
        flags = O_WRONLY;
    fd = open(argv[2], flags, 0);
    if (fd == -1) {
    [...]
```

The second argument to this app is the device file to open. In order to read or write, the process will require memory:

```
    if ('w' == opt)
        num = strlen(argv[3])+1;     // IMP! +1 to include the NULL byte!
    else
        num = MAXBYTES;
    buf = malloc(num);
    if (!buf) {
        [...]
```

Moving along, let's see the block of code to have the app invoke a read or write (depending on the first parameter being r or w) on the (pseudo)device (for conciseness, we don't show the error handling code):

```
    if ('r' == opt) {
        n = read(fd, buf, num);
        if( n < 0 ) [...]
        printf("%s: read %zd bytes from %s\n", argv[0], n, argv[2]);
        printf("The 'secret' is:\n \"%.*s\"\n", (int)n, buf);
    } else {
```

```
        strncpy(buf, argv[3], num);
        n = write(fd, buf, num);
        if( n < 0 ) [ ... ]
        printf("%s: wrote %zd bytes to %s\n", argv[0], n, argv[2]);
    }
    [...]
    free(buf);
    close(fd);
    exit(EXIT_SUCCESS);
}
```

(Before you try out this driver, do ensure the previous `miscdrv` driver's kernel module is unloaded.) Now, ensure that this driver is built and inserted, of course, else it will result in the `open(2)` system call failing. We have shown a couple of trial runs. First, let's build the user-mode app, insert the driver (not shown in *Figure 1.8*), and read from our just-created device node:

```
$ make rdwr_test_secret
gcc rdwr_test_secret.c -o rdwr_test_secret -Os -Wall
$ ./rdwr_test_secret
Usage: ./rdwr_test_secret opt=read/write device_file ["secret-msg"]
 opt = 'r' => we shall issue the read(2), retrieving the 'secret' form the driver
 opt = 'w' => we shall issue the write(2), writing the secret message <secret-msg>
  (max 128 bytes)
$
$ ./rdwr_test_secret r /dev/llkd_miscdrv_rdwr
Device file /dev/llkd_miscdrv_rdwr opened (in read-only mode): fd=3
./rdwr_test_secret: read 7 bytes from /dev/llkd_miscdrv_rdwr
The 'secret' is:
 "initmsg"
$ dmesg
[22226.098941] miscdrv_rdwr:miscdrv_rdwr_init(): LLKD misc driver (major # 10) registered, minor# = 56, dev node is /d
ev/llkd_miscdrv_rdwr
[22226.101663] misc llkd_miscdrv_rdwr: A sample print via the dev_dbg(): driver initialized
[22306.073767] miscdrv_rdwr:open_miscdrv_rdwr(): 001)  rdwr_test_secre :21178  | ...0   /* open_miscdrv_rdwr() */
[22306.083516] misc llkd_miscdrv_rdwr:  opening "llkd_miscdrv_rdwr" now; wrt open file: f_flags = 0x8000
[22306.085804] miscdrv_rdwr:read_miscdrv_rdwr(): 001)  rdwr_test_secre :21178  | ...0   /* read_miscdrv_rdwr() */
[22306.087772] misc llkd_miscdrv_rdwr: rdwr_test_secre wants to read (upto) 128 bytes
[22306.088851] misc llkd_miscdrv_rdwr:  7 bytes read, returning... (stats: tx=7, rx=0)
[22306.089910] miscdrv_rdwr:close_miscdrv_rdwr(): 001)  rdwr_test_secre :21178  | ...0   /* close_miscdrv_rdwr() */
[22306.091768] misc llkd_miscdrv_rdwr:  filename: "llkd_miscdrv_rdwr"
$
```

Figure 1.8 – miscdrv_rdwr: (minimally) testing the read; the original secret is revealed

The user-mode app successfully receives 7 bytes from the driver; it's the (initial) secret value, which it displays. The kernel log reflects the driver initialization, and a few seconds later, you can see (via the `dev_xxx()` instances of `printk` we emitted) that the `rdwr_test_secret` app runs the drivers' code in process context. The opening of the device, the running of the subsequent read, and the close methods are clearly seen. (Notice how the process name is truncated to `rdwr_test_secre`; this is as the task structure's `comm` member is the process name truncated to 16 characters.)

In *Figure 1.9*, we show the complementary act of writing to our device node, changing the secret value; a subsequent read indeed reveals that it has worked:

```
$ ./rdwr_test_secret w /dev/llkd_miscdrv_rdwr "buy llkd ;-)"
Device file /dev/llkd_miscdrv_rdwr opened (in write-only mode): fd=3
./rdwr_test_secret: wrote 13 bytes to /dev/llkd_miscdrv_rdwr
$
$ dmesg |tail -n7
[22947.258677] miscdrv_rdwr:open_miscdrv_rdwr(): 002) rdwr_test_secre :21692  |  ...0   /* open_miscdrv_rdwr() */
[22947.275457] misc llkd_miscdrv_rdwr:  opening "llkd_miscdrv_rdwr" now; wrt open file: f_flags = 0x8001
[22947.281975] miscdrv_rdwr:write_miscdrv_rdwr(): 002)  rdwr_test_secre :21692   |  ...0   /* write_miscdrv_rdwr() */
[22947.287363] misc llkd_miscdrv_rdwr: rdwr_test_secre wants to write 13 bytes
[22947.289870] misc llkd_miscdrv_rdwr:  13 bytes written, returning... (stats: tx=7, rx=13)
[22947.292109] miscdrv_rdwr:close_miscdrv_rdwr(): 002)  rdwr_test_secre :21692   |  ...0   /* close_miscdrv_rdwr() */
[22947.295415] misc llkd_miscdrv_rdwr:  filename: "llkd_miscdrv_rdwr"
$
$ ./rdwr_test_secret r /dev/llkd_miscdrv_rdwr
Device file /dev/llkd_miscdrv_rdwr opened (in read-only mode): fd=3
./rdwr_test_secret: read 12 bytes from /dev/llkd_miscdrv_rdwr
The 'secret' is:
 "buy llkd ;-)"
$
```

Figure 1.9 – miscdrv_rdwr: (minimally) testing the write; a new, excellent secret is written

The portion of the kernel log where the write takes place is highlighted in *Figure 1.9*. It works; I definitely encourage you to try this out yourself, looking up the kernel log as you go along.

Now, it's time to dig a little deeper. The reality is that as a driver author, you have to learn to be really careful regarding *security*, else all kinds of nasty surprises lie in wait. The next section gives you an understanding of this key area.

Issues and security concerns

An important consideration, for the budding driver author, is security. The trouble is, naive usage of even the very common `copy_[from|to]_user()` functions within your driver can let a malicious user quite easily – and illegally – overwrite memory to their advantage in both user and kernel spaces. How? The following section explains this in some detail; then, we will even show you a (bit contrived, but nevertheless, working) hack.

Hacking the secret driver

Think about this: we have the `copy_to_user()` helper routine; the first parameter is the destination `to` address, which should be a user space virtual address (a UVA), of course. Regular usage will comply with this and provide a legal and valid user space virtual address as the destination address, and all will be well.

But what if we don't? What if we pass another user space address, or, check this out – a *kernel* virtual address (a KVA) – in its place? The `copy_to_user()` code will now, running with kernel privileges, overwrite the destination with whatever data is in the source address (the second parameter) for the number of bytes in the third parameter! Indeed, hackers often attempt techniques such as this, to insert code posing as data into a user space buffer and execute it with kernel privilege, leading to a quite deadly **privilege escalation** (privesc) scenario.

To clearly demonstrate the adverse effects of not carefully designing and implementing a driver, we deliberately introduce errors (bugs, really!) into both the read and write methods of a 'bad' version of our previous driver (although here, we only consider the scenario with respect to the very common `copy_[from|to]_user()` routines and nothing else).

To get a more hands-on feel for this, we will write a "bad" version of our `ch1/miscdrv_rdwr` driver. We'll call it (ever so cleverly) `ch1/bad_miscdrv`. In this version, we deliberately have two buggy code paths built into it:

- One within the driver's read method
- The other, the more exciting one, as you shall soon see, within the write method.

Let's check both out. We'll begin with the buggy read.

Bad driver – buggy read()

To help you see what's changed in the code, we first perform a `diff(1)` of this (deliberately) bad driver code with our previous (good) version, yielding the differences, of course (in the following snippet, we curtail the output to only what's most relevant):

```
// in ch1/bad_miscdrv
$ diff -u ../miscdrv_rdwr/miscdrv_rdwr.c bad_miscdrv.c
[ ... ]
+#include <linux/cred.h>            // access to struct cred
#include "../../convenient.h"
[ ... ]
static ssize_t read_miscdrv_rdwr(struct file *filp, char __user *ubuf,
[ ... ]
+ void *kbuf = NULL;
+ void *new_dest = NULL;
[ ... ]
+#define READ_BUG
+//#undef READ_BUG
+#ifdef READ_BUG
[ ... ]
+ new_dest = ubuf+(512*1024);
```

```
+#else
+ new_dest = ubuf;
+#endif
[ ... ]
+ if (copy_to_user(new_dest, ctx->oursecret, secret_len)) {
[ ... ]
```

So, it should be quite clear: in our 'bad' driver's read method, if the READ_BUG macro is defined, we alter the user space destination pointer to point to an illegal location (512 KB beyond the location we should actually copy the data to!). This demonstrates the point here: we can do arbitrary stuff like this because we are running with kernel privileges. That it will cause issues and bugs is a separate matter.

Let's try it: first, do ensure that you've built and loaded the bad_miscdrv kernel module (you can use our lkm convenience script to do so). Our trial run, issuing a read(2) system call via our ch1/bad_miscdrv/rdwr_test_hackit user-mode app, results in failure (see the following screenshot):

```
$ ./rdwr_test_hackit r /dev/bad_miscdrv ; dmesg
Device file /dev/bad_miscdrv opened (in read-only mode): fd=3
./rdwr_test_hackit: dest buf addr = 0x5597245d46b0
read failed: Bad address
Tip: see kernel log
[ 1717.226989] bad_miscdrv:bad_miscdrv_init(): LLKD 'bad' misc driver (major # 10) registered, minor# = 56
[ 1717.227811] misc bad_miscdrv: A sample print via the dev_dbg(): (bad) driver initialized
[ 1733.006497] bad_miscdrv:open_miscdrv_rdwr(): 001)  rdwr_test_hacki :7714   | ...0   /* open_miscdrv_rdwr() */
[ 1733.007379] misc bad_miscdrv:  opening "bad_miscdrv" now; wrt open file: f_flags = 0x8000
[ 1733.008053] bad_miscdrv:read_miscdrv_rdwr(): 001)  rdwr_test_hacki :7714   | ...0   /* read_miscdrv_rdwr() */
[ 1733.008975] misc bad_miscdrv: rdwr_test_hacki wants to read (upto) 128 bytes
[ 1733.009476] misc bad_miscdrv: dest addr = 0x5597246546b0
[ 1733.009912] misc bad_miscdrv: copy_to_user() failed
[ 1733.010316] bad_miscdrv:close_miscdrv_rdwr(): 001)  rdwr_test_hacki :7714   | ...0   /* close_miscdrv_rdwr() */
[ 1733.011187] misc bad_miscdrv:  filename: "bad_miscdrv"
$
```

Figure 1.10 – Screenshot showing our bad_miscdrv misc driver performing a "bad" read

Ah, this is interesting; our test application's (rdwr_test_hackit) read(2) system call does indeed fail, with the perror(3) routine indicating the cause of failure as Bad address. But why? Why didn't the driver, running with kernel privileges, actually write to the destination address (here, 0x5597245d46b0, the wrong one; as we know, it's attempting to write 512 KB *ahead* of the correct destination address. We deliberately wrote the driver's read method code to do so).

This is because kernel ensures that the `copy_[from|to]_user()` routines will (ideally) fail when attempting to read or write illegal addresses! Internally, several checks are done: `access_ok()` is a simple one merely ensuring that I/O is performed within the expected segment (user or kernel). Modern Linux kernels have superior checking; besides the simple `access_ok()` check, the kernel then wades through – if enabled – the **KASAN (Kernel Address Sanitizer**, a compiler instrumentation feature; KASAN is indeed very useful, a *must-do* during development and test!), checks on object sizes (including overflow checks), and only then does it invoke the worker routine that performs the actual copy, `raw_copy_[from|to]_user()`.

Okay, that's good; now, let's move on to the more interesting case, the buggy write, which we shall arrange (in a contrived manner though) to make into an attack! Read on...

Bad driver – buggy write() – a privesc!

What does the malicious hacker really want, their holy grail? A root shell on the system, of course (*got root?*). With a good deal of contrived code within our driver's write method (thus making this hack not a really good one; it's quite academic), let's go get it! To do so, we modify both the user-mode app as well as the device driver. Let's look at the user-mode app's changes first.

User space test app modifications

We slightly modify the user space application – our process context, in effect. This particular version of the user-mode test app differs from the earlier one in one regard: we now have a macro called `HACKIT`. If it's defined (it is by default), this process will deliberately write only zeroes into the user space buffer and send that to our bad driver's write method. If the driver has the `DANGER_GETROOT_BUG` macro defined (it is by default), then it will write the zeroes into the process's UID member, thus making the user-mode process obtain root privileges!

 In the traditional Unix/Linux paradigm, if the **Real User ID (RUID)** and/or **Effective User ID (EUID)** (they're within the task structure, in `struct cred`) are set to the special value zero (0), it implies that the process has superuser (root) powers. Nowadays, the POSIX Capabilities model is considered a superior way to work with privileges, as it allows assigning fine-grained permissions – *capabilities* – on a thread, as opposed to giving a process or thread complete control over the system as root.

Here's a quick `diff` of the user space test app from the previous version, allowing you to see the changes made to the code (again, we curtail the output to only what's most relevant):

```
// in ch1/bad_miscdrv
$ diff -u ../miscdrv/rdwr_test.c rdwr_test_hackit.c
[ ... ]
+#define HACKIT
[ ... ]
+#ifndef HACKIT
+       strncpy(buf, argv[3], num);
+#else
+       printf("%s: attempting to get root ...\n", argv[0]);
+       /*
+        * Write only 0's ... our 'bad' driver will write this into
+        * this process's current->cred->uid member, thus making us
+        * root !
+        */
+       memset(buf, 0, num);
 #endif
- } else { // test writing ..
            n = write(fd, buf, num);
[ ... ]
+       printf("%s: wrote %zd bytes to %s\n", argv[0], n, argv[2]);
+#ifdef HACKIT
+       if (getuid() == 0) {
+           printf(" !Pwned! uid==%d\n", getuid());
+           /* the hacker's holy grail: spawn a root shell */
+           execl("/bin/sh", "sh", (char *)NULL);
+       }
+#endif
[ ... ]
```

This does imply that the (so-called) secret never gets written; that's okay. Now, let's look at the modifications made to the driver.

Device driver modifications

To see how our bad `misc` driver's write method changes, we will continue looking at the same `diff` (of our bad versus good drivers) that we did in the *Bad driver – buggy read()* section. The comments in the code from the following `diff` operation are quite self-explanatory. Check it out:

```
// in ch1/bad_miscdrv
$ diff -u ../miscdrv_rdwr/miscdrv_rdwr.c bad_miscdrv.c
[...]
```

```
        // << this is within the driver's write method >>
 static ssize_t write_miscdrv_rdwr(struct file *filp, const char __user
*ubuf,
 size_t count, loff_t *off)
 {
        int ret = count;
        struct device *dev = ctx->dev;
+       void *new_dest = NULL;
[ ... ]
+#define DANGER_GETROOT_BUG
+//#undef DANGER_GETROOT_BUG
+#ifdef DANGER_GETROOT_BUG
+       /* Make the destination of the copy_from_user() point to the current
+        * process context's (real) UID; this way, we redirect the driver to
+        * write zero's here. Why? Simple: traditionally, a UID == 0 is what
+        * defines root capability!
+        */
+       new_dest = &current->cred->uid;
+       count = 4; /* change count as we're only updating a 32-bit quantity
*/
+       pr_info(" [current->cred=%px]\n", (TYPECST)current->cred);
+#else
+       new_dest = kbuf;
+#endif
```

The key point from the preceding code is that when the DANGER_GETROOT_BUG macro is defined (it is by default), we set the new_dest pointer to the address of the (real) UID member within the credential structure, which is itself within the task structure (referenced by current) for this process context! (If all of this sounds foreign, please read the companion guide *Linux Kernel Programming*, Chapter 6, *Kernel Internals Essentials – Processes and Threads*). This way, when we invoke the copy_to_user() routine to perform the write to user space, it's going to actually write zeroes to the process UID member within current->cred. A UID of zero is what (traditionally) defines root. Also, notice how we restrict the write to 4 bytes (as we're just writing a 32-bit quantity).

(By the way, the build on our "bad" driver does issue a warning; here, with it being intentional, we merely ignore it):

```
Linux-Kernel-Programming-Part-2/ch1/bad_miscdrv/bad_miscdrv.c:229:11:
warning: assignment discards 'const' qualifier from pointer target type [-
Wdiscarded-qualifiers]
  229 | new_dest = &current->cred->uid;
      |                 ^
```

Here's the `copy_from_user()` code invocation:

```
[...]
+           dev_info(dev, "dest addr = " ADDRFMT "\n", (TYPECST)new_dest);
            ret = -EFAULT;
-           if (copy_from_user(kbuf, ubuf, count)) {
+           if (copy_from_user(new_dest, ubuf, count)) {
                dev_warn(dev, "copy_from_user() failed\n");
                goto out_cfu;
            }
[...]
```

Clearly, the preceding `copy_to_user()` routine will write the user-supplied buffer, `ubuf`, into the `new_dest` destination buffer – which, crucially, we have made point to `current->cred->uid` – for `count` bytes.

Let's get root now

Of course, the proof of the pudding is in the eating, yes? So, let's give our hack a spin; here, we assume that you've first unloaded any previous version of our 'misc' drivers, and built and loaded the `bad_miscdrv` kernel module into memory:

```
$ make rdwr_test_hackit
gcc rdwr_test_hackit.c -o rdwr_test_hackit -Os -Wall
$ ./rdwr_test_hackit
Usage: ./rdwr_test_hackit opt=read/write device_file ["secret-msg"]
 opt = 'r' => we shall issue the read(2), retreiving the 'secret' form the driver
 opt = 'w' => we shall issue the write(2), writing the secret message <secret-msg>
  (max 128 bytes)
$
$ ./rdwr_test_hackit w /dev/bad_miscdrv "no secret"
Device file /dev/bad_miscdrv opened (in write-only mode): fd=3
./rdwr_test_hackit: attempting to get root ...
./rdwr_test_hackit: wrote 4 bytes to /dev/bad_miscdrv
 !Pwned! uid==0
#
# id
uid=0(root) gid=1001(llkd) groups=1001(llkd),27(sudo)
#
```

Figure 1.11 – Screenshot showing our bad_miscdrv misc driver performing a "bad" write, resulting in root – a privesc!

Check it out; **we indeed got root!** Our `rdwr_test_hackit` app, detecting that we do have root (via a simple `getuid(2)` system call), then does the logical thing: it execs a root shell (via an `execl(3)` API), and voilà, we land up in a root shell. We show the kernel log:

```
$ dmesg
[ 63.847549] bad_miscdrv:bad_miscdrv_init(): LLKD 'bad' misc driver (major
# 10) registered, minor# = 56
[ 63.848452] misc bad_miscdrv: A sample print via the dev_dbg(): (bad)
driver initialized
[ 84.186882] bad_miscdrv:open_miscdrv_rdwr(): 000) rdwr_test_hacki :2765 |
...0 /* open_miscdrv_rdwr() */
[ 84.190521] misc bad_miscdrv: opening "bad_miscdrv" now; wrt open file:
f_flags = 0x8001
[ 84.191557] bad_miscdrv:write_miscdrv_rdwr(): 000) rdwr_test_hacki :2765 |
...0 /* write_miscdrv_rdwr() */
[ 84.192358] misc bad_miscdrv: rdwr_test_hacki wants to write 4 bytes to
(original) ubuf = 0x55648b8f36b0
[ 84.192971] misc bad_miscdrv: [current->cred=ffff9f67765c3b40]
[ 84.193392] misc bad_miscdrv: dest addr = ffff9f67765c3b44 count=4
[ 84.193803] misc bad_miscdrv: 4 bytes written, returning... (stats: tx=0,
rx=4)
[ 89.002675] bad_miscdrv:close_miscdrv_rdwr(): 000) [sh]:2765 | ...0 /*
close_miscdrv_rdwr() */
[ 89.005992] misc bad_miscdrv: filename: "bad_miscdrv"
$
```

You can see how it's worked: the original user-mode buffer `ubuf` kernel virtual address is `0x55648b8f36b0`. In the hack, we modify it to the new destination address (kernel virtual address), `0xffff9f67765c3b44`, which is (in this case) the kernel virtual address of the UID member of `struct cred` (within the process's task structure). Not only that, but our driver also modifies the number of bytes to write (`count`) to 4 (bytes), as we're updating a 32-bit quantity.

Do note: these hacks are just that – hacks. They could certainly cause your system to become unstable (when run on our "debug" kernel, KASAN, in fact, detected a null pointer dereference!).

These demos prove nothing but the fact that you as a kernel and/or driver author must be alert to programming issues, security, and more at all times. With this, we complete this section and indeed the chapter.

Summary

This concludes this chapter on writing a simple `misc` class character device driver on the Linux OS; so, awesome, you now know the basics of writing a device driver on Linux!

The chapter began with an introduction to device basics, and importantly, the very brief essentials of the modern LDM. You then learned how to write a simple first character device driver, registering with the kernel's `misc` framework. Along the way, you also understood the connection between the process, the driver, and the kernel VFS. Copying data between user and kernel address spaces is essential; we saw how to do so. A more comprehensive demo `misc` driver (our 'secret' driver) showed you how to perform I/O – reads and writes – ferrying data between user and kernel space. A key part of this chapter is the last section, where you learned (well, made a start at least) about security and the driver; a "hack" even demonstrated a *privesc* attack!

As mentioned before, there's much more to this vast topic of writing drivers on Linux; indeed, whole books are devoted to it! Do check out the *Further reading* section for this chapter to find relevant books and online references.

In the following chapter you will learn a key task for a driver author - how exactly can you efficiently interface your device driver with user space processes; several useful approaches are covered in detail and contrasted. Do ensure you're clear on this chapter's material, work on the exercises given, review the *Further reading* resources and then dive into the next one.

Questions

1. Load up the first `miscdrv` skeleton `misc` driver kernel module and issue `lseek(2)` on it; what happens? (Does it succeed? What's the return value from `lseek`?) If not, okay, how will you fix this?

2. Write a `misc` class character driver that behaves as a simple converter program (assume its path name is `/dev/convert`). For example, writing the temperature in Fahrenheit units, it should return (write to the kernel log) the temperature in Celsius. Thus, doing `echo 98.6 > /dev/convert` should result in the value `37 C` being written to the kernel log. Additionally, do the following:
    1. Validate that the data passed to your driver is a numeric value.
    2. How will you handle floating-point values? (Tip: refer to the section *Floating point not allowed in the kernel* in *Linux Kernel Programming, Chapter 5, Writing Your First Kernel Module LKMs – Part 2*.)

3. Write a "task display" driver; here, we'd like a user space process to write a thread (or process) PID to it. When you now read from the driver's device node (assume its path name is `/dev/task_display`), you should receive details regarding the task (which is pulled from its task structure, of course). For example, doing `echo 1 > /dev/task_display` followed by `cat /dev/task_display` should have the driver emit task details of PID 1 to the kernel log. Don't forget to add validity checks (check the PID is valid, and so on).

4. (A bit more advanced:) Write a "proper" LDM-based driver; the `misc` drivers covered here did register with the kernel's `misc` framework, but simply, implicitly, used the raw character interface as the bus. The LDM prefers that a driver must register with a kernel framework and a bus driver. Hence, write a "demo" driver that registers itself with the kernel's `misc` framework and the platform bus. This will involve creating a fake platform device as well. (*Note the following tips*:
   a) Do refer to `Chapter 2`, *User-Kernel Communication Pathways*, particularly the *Creating a simple platform device* and *Platform devices* sections.
   b) A possible solution to this driver can be found here: `solutions_to_assgn/ch12/misc_plat/`.)

 You will find some of the questions answered in the book's GitHub repo: `https://github.com/PacktPublishing/Linux-Kernel-Programming-Part-2/tree/main/solutions_to_assgn`.

Further reading

- Linux device drivers books:

    - *Linux Device Drivers Development*, John Madieu, Packt, Oct 2017: `https://www.amazon.in/Linux-Device-Drivers-Development-Madieu/dp/1785280007/ref=sr_1_2?keywords=linux+device+driverqid=1555486515s=bookssr=1-2` ; excellent coverage, as well as very recent (as of this writing; it covers the 4.13 kernel)

- *Linux Driver Development for Embedded Processors - Second Edition: Learn to develop embedded Linux drivers with kernel 4.9 LTS*, Alberto Liberal de los Rios: `https://www.amazon.in/Linux-Driver-Development-Embedded-Processors-ebook/dp/B07L512BHG/ref=sr_1_6?crid=3RLFFZQXGAMF4keywords=linux+driver+development+embeddedqid=1555486342s=books sprefix=linux+driver+%2Cstripbooks%2C270sr=1-6-catcorr`; very good, as well as recent (4.9 kernel)
- *Essential Linux Device Drivers*, Sreekrishnan Venkateswaran, Pearson: `https://www.amazon.in/Essential-Drivers-Prentice-Software-Development/dp/0132396556/ref=tmm_hrd_swatch_0?_encoding=UTF8qid=sr=`; simply excellent, wide coverage
- *Linux Device Drivers*, Rubini, Hartmann, Corbet, 3rd Edition: `https://www.amazon.in/Linux-Device-Drivers-Kernel-Hardware/dp/8173668493/ref=sr_1_1?keywords=linux+device+driverqid=1555486515s=bookssr=1-1`; venerable (but) old – the famous LDD3 book

- Official kernel documentation:
    - The Linux Kernel Device Model: `https://www.kernel.org/doc/html/latest/driver-api/driver-model/overview.html#the-linux-kernel-device-model`.
    - The kernel driver API manual; this is one of the PDF documents generated by doing `make pdfdocs` within a recent Linux kernel source tree.

    - Deprecated Interfaces, Language Features, Attributes, and Conventions: `https://www.kernel.org/doc/html/latest/process/deprecated.html#deprecated-interfaces-language-features-attributes-and-conventions`.

- Practical tutorials:
    - *Device Drivers, Part 8: Accessing x86-Specific I/O-Mapped Hardware*, Anil K Pugalia, OpenSourceForU, July 2011: `https://opensourceforu.com/2011/07/accessing-x86-specific-io-mapped-hardware-in-linux/`
    - User space device drivers; check out this interesting video presentation by Chris Simmonds: *How to Avoid Writing Device Drivers for Embedded Linux*: `https://www.youtube.com/watch?v=QIO2pJqMxjEt=909s`

2
User-Kernel Communication Pathways

Consider this scenario: you've successfully developed a device driver for, say, a pressure sensor device (perhaps by using the kernel's I2C APIs to fetch the pressure from the chip via the I2C protocol). So, you have the current pressure value in a variable within the driver, which of course implies that it's within kernel memory space. The issue at hand is, how exactly do you now have a *user space application retrieve this value?* Well, as we learned in the previous chapter, you can always include a `.read` method in the driver's *fops* structure. When the user space app issues a `read(2)` system call, control will be diverted (via the **virtual file system (VFS)**) to your driver's *read method.* In there, you perform `copy_to_user()` (or equivalent), resulting in the user mode app receiving the value. However, but there are other, sometimes superior, ways to do this.

In this chapter, you'll understand the various communication interfaces or pathways that are available – as a means to communicate or interface between user and kernel address spaces. This is an important aspect of writing driver code, for without this knowledge, how will you be able to achieve a key thing – efficiently transfer information between a kernel-space component (often, this is a device driver, but it could be anything, really) and a user space process or thread? Not only that, some of the techniques that we shall learn about are often used for debugging (and/or diagnostics) purposes as well. In this chapter, we will cover several techniques to effect communication between the kernel and user (virtual) address spaces: communication via the traditional proc filesystem, *procfs*, the better way for drivers via the sys filesystem, *sysfs*, via a debug filesystem, *debugfs*, via *netlink sockets*, and via the `ioctl(2)` system call.

The following topics will be covered in this chapter:

- Approaches to communicating/interfacing a kernel driver with a user space C app
- Interfacing via the proc filesystem (procfs)
- Interfacing via the sys filesystem (sysfs)
- Interfacing via the debug filesystem (debugfs)
- Interfacing via netlink sockets
- Interfacing via the ioctl system call
- Comparing the interfacing methods – a table

Let's get started!

Technical requirements

I assume you have gone through the *Preface*, the relevant section being *To get the most out of this book,* and have appropriately prepared a guest **virtual machine** (**VM**) running Ubuntu 18.04 LTS (or a later stable release) and installed all the required packages. If not, I recommend you do this first.

To get the maximum out of this book, I strongly recommend you first set up the workspace environment, including cloning this book's GitHub repository (`https://github.com/PacktPublishing/Linux-Kernel-Programming-Part-2`) for the relevant code, and work on it in a hands-on fashion.

Approaches to communicating/interfacing a kernel driver with a user space C app

As we mentioned in the introduction, in this chapter, we wish to learn how to efficiently transfer information between a kernel-space component (often, this is a device driver, but it could be anything, really), and a user space process or thread. To begin, let's simply enumerate various techniques available to the kernel or driver author to communicate or interface with a user space C application. Well, the user space component could be a C app, a shell script (both of which we typically show in this book), or even other apps such as C++/Java apps, Python/Perl scripts, and more.

As we saw in the companion guide, *Linux Kernel Programming*, in *Chapter 4, Writing Your First Kernel Module – LKMs Part 1*, in the *Library and System Call APIs* subsection, the essential interface between user space applications and the kernel that includes the device drivers are the system call APIs. Now, in the previous chapter, you learned the basics of writing a character device driver for Linux. Within that, you also learned how to transfer data between user and kernel address spaces by having a user mode application open the device file and issue read(2) and write(2) system calls. This resulted in the driver's read/write method being invoked by the VFS and your driver performing the data transfer via the copy_{from|to}_user() APIs. So, the question here is: if we have already covered that, then what else is there to learn about in this regard?

Ah, quite a bit! The reality is that there are several other techniques of interfacing between a user mode app and the kernel. Certainly, they all very much depend upon using system calls; after all, there is no other (synchronous, programmatic) way to enter the kernel from the user space! Nevertheless, the techniques differ. The aim of this chapter is to show you various communication interfaces that are available, as of course, depending on the project, one might be more suitable than others to use. Let's look at the various techniques that will be used in this chapter to interface between the user and kernel address spaces:

- Via the traditional procfs interface
- Via sysfs
- Via debugfs
- Via netlink sockets
- Via the ioctl(2) system call

Throughout this chapter, we will discuss these interfacing techniques in detail by providing driver code examples. In addition, we will also briefly explore how conducive they are to the purpose of *debugging*. So, let's begin with using the procfs interface.

Interfacing via the proc filesystem (procfs)

In this section, we shall cover what the proc filesystem is and how you can leverage it as an interface between user and kernel address spaces. The proc filesystem is a powerful and easy-to-program interface, often used for status reporting and debugging core kernel systems.

 Note that from version 2.6 Linux onward and for upstream contribution, this interface is *not* to be used by driver authors (it's strictly meant for kernel-internal usage only). Nevertheless, for completeness, we will cover it here.

Understanding the proc filesystem

Linux has a virtual filesystem named *proc*; the default mount point for it is /proc. The first thing to realize regarding the proc filesystem is that its content is *not* on a non-volatile disk. Its content is in RAM, and is thus volatile. The files and directories you can see under /proc are pseudo files that have been set up by the kernel code for proc; the kernel hints at this fact by (almost) always showing the file's *size* as zero:

```
$ mount | grep -w proc
proc on /proc type proc (rw,nosuid,nodev,noexec,relatime)
$ ls -l /proc/
total 0
dr-xr-xr-x  8 root  root           0 Jan 27 11:13 1/
dr-xr-xr-x  8 root  root           0 Jan 29 08:22 10/
dr-xr-xr-x  8 root  root           0 Jan 29 08:22 11/
dr-xr-xr-x  8 root  root           0 Jan 29 08:22 11550/
[...]
-r--r--r--  1 root  root           0 Jan 29 08:22 consoles
-r--r--r--  1 root  root           0 Jan 29 08:19 cpuinfo
-r--r--r--  1 root  root           0 Jan 29 08:22 crypto
-r--r--r--  1 root  root           0 Jan 29 08:20 devices
-r--r--r--  1 root  root           0 Jan 29 08:22 diskstats
[...]
-r--r--r--  1 root  root           0 Jan 29 08:22 vmstat
-r--r--r--  1 root  root           0 Jan 29 08:22 zoneinfo
$
```

Let's summarize a few critical points regarding Linux's powerful proc filesystem.

The objects under /proc (files, directories, soft links, and so on) are all pseudo objects; they live in RAM!

Directories under /proc

The directories under /proc whose names are integer values represent processes currently alive on the system. The name of the directory is the PID of the process (technically, it's the TGID of the process. We covered TGID/PID in the companion guide *Linux Kernel Programming* in *Chapter 6, Kernel and Memory Management Internals Essentials*).

This folder – /proc/PID/ – contains information regarding this process. So, for example, for the *init* or *systemd* process (always PID 1), you can examine detailed information about this process (its attributes, open files, memory layout, children, and so on) under the /proc/1/ folder.

As an example, here, we will gain a root shell and do ls /proc/1:

```
$ sudo -i
root@llkd-vbox:~# ls /proc/1
arch_status      cpuset    limits      net            personality    smaps_rollup    timerslack_ns
autogroup        cwd       loginuid    ns             projid_map     stack           uid_map
auxv             environ   map_files   numa_maps      root           stat            wchan
cgroup           exe       maps        oom_adj        sched          statm
clear_refs       fd        mem         oom_score      schedstat      status
cmdline          fdinfo    mountinfo   oom_score_adj  sessionid      syscall
comm             gid_map   mounts      pagemap        setgroups      task
coredump_filter  io        mountstats  patch_state    smaps          timers
root@llkd-vbox:~# ▉
```

Figure 2.1 – Screenshot of performing ls /proc/1 on an x86_64 guest system

The complete details regarding the pseudo files and folders under /proc/<PID>/... can be found on the man page of proc(5) (by doing man 5 proc); do try it out and refer to it!

 Note that the precise content under /proc varies from both the kernel version and the (CPU) architecture; x86_64 tends to have the richest content.

The purpose behind the proc filesystem

The *purpose* behind the proc filesystem is two-fold:

- One, it is a simple interface for developers, system administrators, and anyone really to look deep inside the kernel so that they can gain information regarding the internals of processes, the kernel, and even hardware. Using this interface only requires you to know basic shell commands such as cd, cat, echo, ls, and so on.
- Two, as the *root* user and, at times, the owner, you can write into certain pseudo files under /proc/sys, thus tuning various kernel parameters. This feature is called **sysctl**. As an example, you can tune various IPv4 networking parameters in /proc/sys/net/ipv4/. They are all documented here: https://www.kernel.org/doc/Documentation/networking/ip-sysctl.txt.

Changing the value of a proc-based tunable is easy; for example, let's change the maximum number of threads allowed at any given point in time on the box. Run the following commands as *root*:

```
# cat /proc/sys/kernel/threads-max
15741
# echo 10000 > /proc/sys/kernel/threads-max
# cat /proc/sys/kernel/threads-max
10000
#
```

With that, we're done. However, it should be clear that the preceding operation is *volatile* – the change only applies to this session; a power cycle or reboot will result in it reverting back to the default value of course. How, then, do we make the change permanent? The short answer: use the sysctl(8) utility; refer to its man page for more details.

Are you ready to write some procfs-interfacing code now? Not so fast – the next section informs you as to why this may *not* be a great idea after all.

procfs is off-bounds to driver authors

Even though we could use the proc filesystem to interface with a user mode app, there is an important point to note here! You must realize that procfs is, like many similar facilities within the kernel, an **Application Binary Interface (ABI)**. The kernel community makes no promises that it remains stable and exactly the way it is today, just as is the case with the kernel *APIs* and their internal data structures as well. In fact, ever since the 2.6 kernel, the kernel folks have made this very clear – *device driver authors (and the like) are not supposed to use procfs* for their own purposes or their interfaces, debug or otherwise. Earlier, with 2.6 Linux, it was quite common to use proc for said purposes (abused, as per the kernel community, as proc is meant for kernel internal use only!).

So, if procfs is considered off-bounds, or deprecated, to us as driver authors, then what facility do we use to communicate with user space processes? Driver authors are to use the sysfs facility to *export* their interfaces. In reality, it's not just sysfs; there are several choices available to you such as sysfs, debugfs, netlink sockets, and the ioctl system call. We will cover these in detail later in this chapter.

Hang on, though; again, the reality is that this "rule" regarding the non-usage of procfs for driver authors are for the community. What this means is that if you intend to *upstream* your driver or kernel module to the mainline kernel, thus contributing your code under the GPLv2 license, *then* all the community rules definitely apply. If not, it's really up to you to decide. Of course, following the kernel community's guidelines and rules can only be a good thing; we definitely recommend that you do so. In terms of discouraging the use of proc by non-core stuff such as drivers, unfortunately, there is no recent kernel documentation available for the proc API/ABI.

 On the 5.4.0 kernel, there are around 70-odd callers of the `proc_create()` kernel API, several of which being (typically older) drivers and filesystems.

Nevertheless (you have been warned!), let's learn how to interact a user space process with kernel code via procfs.

Using procfs to interface with the user space

As a kernel module or device driver developer, we can actually create our own entries under `/proc`, leveraging this as a simple interface to the user space. How can we do this? The kernel provides APIs that create directories and files under procfs. We will learn how to use them in this section.

Basic procfs APIs

Here, we do not intend to delve into the gory details of the procfs API set; rather, we shall cover just enough to have you be able to understand and use them. For deeper detail, do refer to the ultimate resource: the kernel code base. The routines we will cover here have been exported, thus making them available to driver authors like you. Also, as we mentioned earlier, all the procfs file objects are really pseudo objects, in the sense that they exist only in RAM.

 Here, we are assuming you understand how to design and implement a simple LKM; you'll find more details in the companion guide to this book, *Linux Kernel Programming*, in the fourth and fifth chapters.

Let's begin by exploring a few simple procfs APIs that allow you to perform a few key tasks – creating a directory under the proc filesystem, creating (pseudo) files under there, and deleting them, respectively. For all of these tasks, ensure you include the relevant header file; that is, `#include <linux/proc_fs.h>`:

1. Create a directory named `name` under `/proc`:

```
struct proc_dir_entry *proc_mkdir(const char *name,
                        struct proc_dir_entry *parent);
```

The first parameter is the name of the directory, while the second parameter is the pointer to the parent directory to create it under. Passing `NULL` here creates the directory under the root; that is, under `/proc`. Save the return value, as you will typically use it as a parameter in subsequent APIs.

The `proc_mkdir_data()` routine allows you to pass along a data item (a `void *`) as well; note that it's exported via `EXPORT_SYMBOL_GPL`.

2. Create a procfs (pseudo) file called `/proc/parent/name`:

```
struct proc_dir_entry *proc_create(const char *name, umode_t mode,
                        struct proc_dir_entry *parent,
                        const struct file_operations *proc_fops);
```

The key parameter here is `struct file_operations`, which we introduced in the previous chapter. You are expected to populate it with the "methods" to be implemented (more on this follows). Think about it: this is really powerful stuff; using the `fops` structure, you can set up "callback" functions within your driver (or kernel module) that the kernel's proc filesystem layer will honor: when a user space process reads from your proc file, it (the VFS) will invoke the driver's `.read` method or callback function. If a user space app writes, it will invoke the driver's `.write` callback!

3. Remove a procfs entry:

```
void remove_proc_entry(const char *name, struct proc_dir_entry
*parent)
```

This API removes the specified `/proc/name` entry and frees it (if not in use); similarly (and often much more convenient), use the `remove_proc_subtree()` API to remove an entire sub-tree within `/proc` (typically on cleanup or if an error occurs).

Now that we know the basics, the empirical approach demands that we put these APIs to practice! To do so, let's figure out what directories/files to create under /proc.

The four procfs files we will create

To help clearly illustrate the usage of procfs as an interfacing technology, we will have our kernel module create a directory under /proc. Within that directory, it will create four procfs (pseudo) files. Note that, by default, all procfs files have their *owner:group* attributes as *root:root*. Now, create a directory called /proc/proc_simple_intf and, under it, create four (pseudo) files. The names and attributes of the four procfs (pseudo) files under the /proc/proc_simple_intf directory, are shown in the following table:

Name of procfs 'file'	R: action on read callback, invoked via user space read	W: action on write callback, invoked via user space write	Procfs 'file' permissions
llkdproc_dbg_level	Retrieves (to the user space) the current value of the global variable; that is, debug_level	Updates the debug_level global variable to the value written by the user space	0644
llkdproc_show_pgoff	Retrieves (to the user space) the kernel's PAGE_OFFSET value	– no write callback –	0444
llkdproc_show_drvctx	Retrieves (to the user space) the current values within the driver's "context" structure; that is, drv_ctx	– no write callback –	0440
llkdproc_config1 (also treated as dbg_level)	Retrieves (to user space) the current value of the context variable; that is, drvctx->config1	Updates the driver context member, drvctx->config1, to the value written by the user space	0644

We'll look at the APIs and actual code to create the proc_simple_intf directory under /proc and the four files mentioned previously under it shortly. (Due to a lack of space, we won't actually show all the code; just the code with respect to the "debug level" get-and-set; this is not an issue, the remainder of the code is conceptually very similar).

Trying out the dynamic debug_level procfs control

First, let's check out the "driver context" data structure that we shall use throughout this chapter (in fact, we first used it in the previous chapter):

```
// ch2/procfs_simple_intf/procfs_simple_intf.c
[ ... ]
/* Borrowed from ch1; the 'driver context' data structure;
 * all relevant 'state info' reg the driver and (fictional) 'device'
 * is maintained here.
 */
struct drv_ctx {
    int tx, rx, err, myword, power;
    u32 config1; /* treated as equivalent to 'debug level' of our driver */
    u32 config2;
    u64 config3;
#define MAXBYTES    128
    char oursecret[MAXBYTES];
};
static struct drv_ctx *gdrvctx;
static int debug_level;    /* 'off' (0) by default ... */
```

Here, we can also see that we have a global integer named debug_level; this will provide dynamic control over the debug verbosity of the "project". The debug level is assigned a range of [0-2], where we have the following:

- 0 implies *no debug messages* (the default).
- 1 is *medium debug* verbosity.
- 2 implies *high debug* verbosity.

The beauty of the whole schema – and indeed the whole point here – is that we shall be able to query and set this debug_level variable from the user space via a procfs interface that we've created! This will allow the end user (who, for security reasons, requires *root* access) to dynamically vary the debug level at runtime (a fairly common feature found in many products).

Before diving into the code-level details, let's try it out so that we know what to expect:

1. Here, using our lkm convenience wrapper script, we must build and insmod(8) the kernel module (ch2/proc_simple_intf in this book's source tree):

```
$ cd <booksrc>/ch2/proc_simple_intf
$ ../../lkm procfs_simple_intf         <-- builds the kernel
module
Version info:
```

```
[...]
[24826.234323] procfs_simple_intf:procfs_simple_intf_init():321:
proc dir (/proc/procfs_simple_intf) created
[24826.240592] procfs_simple_intf:procfs_simple_intf_init():333:
proc file 1 (/proc/procfs_simple_intf/llkdproc_debug_level) created
[24826.245072] procfs_simple_intf:procfs_simple_intf_init():348:
proc file 2 (/proc/procfs_simple_intf/llkdproc_show_pgoff) created
[24826.248628] procfs_simple_intf:alloc_init_drvctx():218:
allocated and init the driver context structure
[24826.251784] procfs_simple_intf:procfs_simple_intf_init():368:
proc file 3 (/proc/procfs_simple_intf/llkdproc_show_drvctx) created
[24826.255145] procfs_simple_intf:procfs_simple_intf_init():378:
proc file 4 (/proc/procfs_simple_intf/llkdproc_config1) created
[24826.259203] procfs_simple_intf initialized
$
```

Here, we built and inserted the kernel module; dmesg(1) displays the kernel *printks* showing that one of the procfs files we created is the one pertaining to the dynamic debug facility (highlighted in bold here; since these are pseudo files, the file size will appear as 0 bytes).

2. Now, let's test it by querying the current value of debug_level:

```
$ cat /proc/procfs_simple_intf/llkdproc_debug_level
debug_level:0
$
```

3. Great, it's zero – the default – as expected. Now, let's change the debug level to 2:

```
$ sudo sh -c "echo 2 >
/proc/procfs_simple_intf/llkdproc_debug_level"
$ cat /proc/procfs_simple_intf/llkdproc_debug_level
debug_level:2
$
```

Notice how we had to issue echo as *root*. As we can see, the debug level has indeed changed (to a value of 2)! Attempting to set the value out of range is caught as well (and the debug_level variable's value is reset to its last valid value), as shown here:

```
$ sudo sh -c "echo 5 >
/proc/procfs_simple_intf/llkdproc_debug_level"
sh: echo: I/O error
$ dmesg
[...]
[ 6756.415727] procfs_simple_intf: trying to set invalid value for
debug_level [allowed range: 0-2]; resetting to previous (2)
```

Right; it worked as expected. However, the question is, how did all this work at the code level? Read on to find out!

Dynamically controlling debug_level via procfs

Let's answer the aforementioned question – *how is it done in code?* It's quite straightforward, really:

1. First off, within the `init` code of the kernel module, we must create our procfs directory, naming it after the name of our kernel module:

   ```
   static struct proc_dir_entry *gprocdir;
   [...]
   gprocdir = proc_mkdir(OURMODNAME, NULL);
   ```

2. Again, within the `init` code of the kernel module, we must create the `procfs` file that controls the project's "debug level":

   ```
   // ch2/procfs_simple_intf/procfs_simple_intf.c
   [...]
   #define PROC_FILE1          "llkdproc_debug_level"
   #define PROC_FILE1_PERMS    0644
   [...]
   static int __init procfs_simple_intf_init(void)
   {
       int stat = 0;
       [...]
       /* 1. Create the PROC_FILE1 proc entry under the parent dir
   OURMODNAME;
        * this will serve as the 'dynamically view/modify debug_level'
        * (pseudo) file */
       if (!proc_create(PROC_FILE1, PROC_FILE1_PERMS, gprocdir,
                        &fops_rdwr_dbg_level)) {
       [...]
       pr_debug("proc file 1 (/proc/%s/%s) created\n", OURMODNAME,
   PROC_FILE1);
       [...]
   ```

   Here, we used the `proc_create()` API to create the *procfs* file and "linked" it to the supplied `file_operations` structure.

3. The fops structure (technically, `struct file_operations`) is the key data structure here. As we learned in `Chapter 1`, *Writing a Simple misc Character Device Driver*, it's where we assign *functionality* to the various file operations on the device, or, as in this case, the procfs file. Here's the code initializing our fops:

```
static const struct file_operations fops_rdwr_dbg_level = {
    .owner = THIS_MODULE,
    .open = myproc_open_dbg_level,
    .read = seq_read,
    .write = myproc_write_debug_level,
    .llseek = seq_lseek,
    .release = single_release,
};
```

4. The `open` method of fops points to a function we must define:

```
static int myproc_open_dbg_level(struct inode *inode, struct file *file)
{
    return single_open(file, proc_show_debug_level, NULL);
}
```

Using the kernel's `single_open()` API, we register the fact that, whenever this file is read – which is ultimately done via the `read(2)` system call from the user space – the proc filesystem will "call back" our `proc_show_debug_level()` routine (the second parameter to `single_open()`).

 We won't bother with the internal implementation of the `single_open()` API here; if you're curious, you can always look it up here: `fs/seq_file.c:single_open()`.

So, to summarize, to register a "read" method with procfs, we do the following:

- Initialize the `fops.open` pointer to a `foo()` function.
- In the `foo()` function, call `single_open()`, providing the read callback function as the second parameter.

There's some history here; without getting too deep into it, suffice it to say that the older working of procfs had issues. Notably, you couldn't transfer more than a single page of data (with read or write) without manually iterating over the content. The *sequence iterator* functionality that was introduced with 2.6.12 fixed these issues. Nowadays, using `single_open()` and its ilk (the `seq_read`, `seq_lseek`, and `seq_release` built-in kernel functions) is the simpler and correct approach to using procfs.

5. So, what about when user space *writes* (via the `write(2)` system call) into a proc file? Simple: in the preceding code, you can see that we have registered the `fops_rdwr_dbg_level.write` method as the `myproc_write_debug_level()` function, implying that this function will be *called back* whenever this (pseudo) file is written to (it's explained in *Step 6*, following the *read* callback).

The code of the *read* callback function that we registered via `single_open` is as follows:

```
/* Our proc file 1: displays the current value of debug_level */
static int proc_show_debug_level(struct seq_file *seq, void *v)
{
    if (mutex_lock_interruptible(&mtx))
        return -ERESTARTSYS;
    seq_printf(seq, "debug_level:%d\n", debug_level);
    mutex_unlock(&mtx);
    return 0;
}
```

`seq_printf()` is conceptually similar to the familiar `sprintf()` API. It correctly prints – to the `seq_file` object – the data supplied to it. When we say "prints" here, what we really mean is that it effectively passes the data buffer to the user space process or thread that issued the read system call that got us here in the first place, in effect *transferring the data to the user space*.

Oh yes, what's with the `mutex_{un}lock*()` APIs? They are for something critical – *locking*. We will provide a detailed discussion on locking in `Chapter 6`, *Kernel Synchronization – Part 1*, and `Chapter 7`, *Kernel Synchronization – Part 2*; for now, just understand that these are required synchronization primitives.

6. The `write` callback function we registered via `fops_rdwr_dbg_level.write` is as follows:

```
#define DEBUG_LEVEL_MIN     0
#define DEBUG_LEVEL_MAX     2
[...]
/* proc file 1 : modify the driver's debug_level global variable as
per what user space writes */
static ssize_t myproc_write_debug_level(struct file *filp,
                const char __user *ubuf, size_t count, loff_t *off)
{
    char buf[12];
    int ret = count, prev_dbglevel;
    [...]
    prev_dbglevel = debug_level;
    // < ... validity checks (not shown here) ... >
    /* Get the user mode buffer content into the kernel (into 'buf')
*/
    if (copy_from_user(buf, ubuf, count)) {
        ret = -EFAULT;
        goto out;
    }
    [...]
    ret = kstrtoint(buf, 0, &debug_level); /* update it! */
    if (ret)
        goto out;
  if (debug_level < DEBUG_LEVEL_MIN || debug_level >
DEBUG_LEVEL_MAX) {
            [...]
            debug_level = prev_dbglevel;
            ret = -EFAULT; goto out;
    }
    /* just for fun, let's say that our drv ctx 'config1'
        represents the debug level */
    gdrvctx->config1 = debug_level;
    ret = count;
out:
    mutex_unlock(&mtx);
    return ret;
}
```

In our write method's implementation (notice how similar it is in structure to a character device driver's write method), we performed some validity checking and then copied in the data the user space process wrote to us (recall how we used the `echo` command to write to the procfs file) via the usual `copy_from_user()` function. We then used the kernel's built-in `kstrtoint()` API (there are several in a similar vein) to convert the string buffer into an integer, storing the result in our global variable; that is, `debug_level`! Again, we validate it, and if all's well, we also set (just as an example) our driver context's `config1` member to the same value and then return a success message.

7. The remainder of the kernel module's code is very similar – we set up the functionality for the remaining three procfs files. I leave it to you to browse through the code in detail and try it out.

8. One more quick demo: let's set `debug_level` to 1 and then dump the driver context structure (via the third procfs file we created):

```
$ cat /proc/procfs_simple_intf/llkdproc_debug_level
debug_level:0
$ sudo sh -c "echo 1 >
/proc/procfs_simple_intf/llkdproc_debug_level"
```

9. Okay, the `debug_level` variable will now have a value of 1; now, let's dump the driver context structure:

```
$ cat /proc/procfs_simple_intf/llkdproc_show_drvctx
cat: /proc/procfs_simple_intf/llkdproc_show_drvctx: Permission
denied
$ sudo cat /proc/procfs_simple_intf/llkdproc_show_drvctx
prodname:procfs_simple_intf
tx:0,rx:0,err:0,myword:0,power:1
config1:0x1,config2:0x48524a5f,config3:0x424c0a52
oursecret:AhA xxx
$
```

We need *root* access to do this. Once done, we can clearly see all the members of our `drv_ctx` data structure. Not only that, but we verified that the `config1` member, highlighted in bold, now has a value of 1, thus reflecting the "debug level" as designed.

Also, notice how the output is deliberately generated to the user space in a highly parseable format, almost JSON-like. Of course, as a small exercise, you could arrange to do precisely that!

A large number of recent **Internet of Things** (**IoT**) products use RESTful APIs to communicate; the format that's parsed is typically JSON. Getting in the habit of designing and implementing your kernel-to-user (and vice versa) communication in easily parsable formats (such as JSON) is only going to help.

With that, you have learned how exactly to create a procfs directory, a file within it, and, most importantly, how to create and use the read and write callback functions so that when a user mode process reads or writes your proc file, you can respond appropriately from deep within the kernel. As we mentioned earlier, due to a lack of space, we will not describe the code driving the remaining three procfs files we have created and used. This is very similar conceptually to what we have just covered. We expect you to read through and try it out!

A few misc procfs APIs

Let's conclude this section by looking at a few remaining miscellaneous procfs APIs. You can create a symbolic or soft link within /proc by using the proc_symlink() function.

Next, the proc_create_single_data() API can be very useful; it's used as a "shortcut", where you require just a "read" method to be attached to a procfs file:

```
struct proc_dir_entry *proc_create_single_data(const char *name, umode_t
mode, struct
        proc_dir_entry *parent, int (*show)(struct seq_file *, void *),
void *data);
```

Using this API thus eliminates the need for a separate fops data structure. We can use this function to create and work with our second procfs file – the llkdproc_show_pgoff file:

```
... proc_create_single_data(PROC_FILE2, PROC_FILE2_PERMS, gprocdir,
proc_show_pgoff, 0) ...
```

When read from the user space, the kernel's VFS and proc layer code paths will invoke the registered method – the proc_show_pgoff() function of our module – within which we trivially invoke seq_printf() to send the value of PAGE_OFFSET to the user space:

```
seq_printf(seq, "%s:PAGE_OFFSET:0x%px\n", OURMODNAME, PAGE_OFFSET);
```

Furthermore, note the following regarding the `proc_create_single_data` API:

- You can make use of the fifth parameter to `proc_create_single_data()` to pass any data item to the read callback (retrieved there as a `seq_file` member called `private`, very similar to how we used `filp->private_data` in the previous chapter).
- Several typically older drivers within the kernel mainline do make use of this function to create their procfs interfaces. Among them is the RTC driver (which sets up an entry at `/proc/driver/rtc`). The SCSI `megaraid` driver (`drivers/scsi/megaraid`) uses this routine no fewer than 10 times to set up its proc interfaces (when a config option is enabled; it is by default).

> Be careful! I find that on an Ubuntu 18.04 LTS system running the distro (default) kernel, this API – `proc_create_single_data()` – isn't even available, so the build fails. On our custom "vanilla" 5.4 LTS kernel, it works just fine.
>
> In addition, there is some documentation on the procfs API we've set here, though this tends to be for internal usage and not for modules: `https://www.kernel.org/doc/html/latest/filesystems/api-summary.html#the-proc-filesystem`.
>
> So, as we mentioned previously, with the procfs APIs it's a case of **Your Mileage May Vary (YMMV)**! Carefully test your code before release. It's probably best to follow the kernel community guidelines and simply say **No** to procfs as a driver interfacing technique. Worry not – we'll look at better ones throughout this chapter!

This completes our coverage on using procfs as a useful communication interface. Now, let's learn how to use a more appropriate one for drivers – the sysfs interface.

Interfacing via the sys filesystem (sysfs)

A critical feature of the 2.6 Linux kernel release was the advent of what is called the modern *device model*. Essentially, a series of complex tree-like hierarchical data structures model all devices present on the system. Actually, it goes well beyond this; the **sysfs** tree encompasses the following (among other things):

- Every bus present on the system (it can be a virtual or pseudo bus as well)

- Every device present on every bus
- Every device driver bound to a device on a bus

Thus, it's not just peripheral devices but also the underlying system buses, the devices on each bus and the device driver bound or that will bind to a device, that are created at runtime and maintained by the device model. The inner workings of this model are invisible to you, as a typical driver author; you don't really have to worry about it. On system boot, and whenever a new device becomes visible, the *driver core* (part of the built-in kernel machinery) generates the required virtual files under the sysfs tree. (Conversely, when a device is removed or detached, its entry disappears from the tree.)

Recall, though, from the *Interfacing with the proc filesystem* section, that using procfs for a device driver's interfacing purposes is not really the right approach, at least for code that wants to move upstream. So, what *is* the right approach? Ah, *creating sysfs (pseudo) files is considered the "correct way" for device drivers to interface with the user space.*

So, now we see it! sysfs is a virtual filesystem typically mounted on the /sys directory. In effect, sysfs, very similarly to procfs, is a kernel-exported tree of information (device and other) that's sent to the user space. You can think of sysfs as having different *viewports* into the modern device model. Via sysfs, you can view the system in several different ways or via different "viewports"; for example, you can view the system via the various buses it supports (the *bus* view – PCI, USB, platform, I2C, SPI, among several others), via various "classes" of devices (the *class* view), via the *devices* themselves, via the *block* devices viewport, and so on. The following screenshot showing the content of /sys on my Ubuntu 18.04 LTS VM shows this to be the case:

```
$ ls /sys/
block/   class/   devices/   fs/             kernel/   power/
bus/     dev/     firmware/  hypervisor/     module/
$
```

Figure 2.2 – Screenshot showing the content of sysfs (/sys) on an x86_64 Ubuntu VM

As we can see, with sysfs, there are several other viewports via that you can use to look into the system as well. Of course, in this section, we wish to understand how to interface a device driver to the user space via sysfs, how to write the code to create our driver (pseudo) files under sysfs, and how to register the read/write callbacks from them. Let's begin by looking at the basic sysfs APIs.

Creating a sysfs (pseudo) file in code

One way to create a pseudo (or virtual) file under sysfs is via the `device_create_file()` API. Its signature is as follows:

```
drivers/base/core.c:int device_create_file(struct device *dev,
                           const struct device_attribute *attr);
```

Let's consider its two parameters one by one; first, there is a pointer to `struct device`. The second parameter is a pointer to a device attribute structure; we shall explain and work on it a bit later (in the *Setting up the device attributes and creating the sysfs file* section). For now, let's focus on the first parameter only – the device structure. It seems quite intuitive – a device is represented by a metadata structure called `device` (it is part of the driver core; you can look up its full definition in the `include/linux/device.h` header).

Note that when you write (or work on) a "real" device driver, chances are high that a generic *device structure* will exist or come into being. This often happens upon *registering* the device; an underlying device structure is usually made available as a member of a specialized structure for that device. For example, all structures, such as `platform_device`, `pci_device`, `net_device`, `usb_device`, `i2c_client`, `serial_port` and so on, have a `struct device` member embedded within them. Thus, you can use that device structure pointer as a parameter to the API for the purpose of creating files under sysfs. Rest assured, you shall soon see this being done in code! So, let's get going by getting ourselves a device structure by creating a simple "platform device". You'll learn how to do this in the next section!

Creating a simple platform device

Clearly, in order to create a (pseudo) file under sysfs, we somehow require, as the first parameter to `device_create_file()`, a pointer to a `struct device`. However, for our demo sysfs driver here and now, we don't actually have any real device, and therefore no `struct device`, to work on!

So, can't we create an *artificial* or *pseudo device* and simply use it? Yes, but how, and more crucially, why exactly should we have to do this? It's critical to understand that the modern **Linux Device Model (LDM)** is built on three key components: **an underlying bus must exist that devices live on, and devices are "bound to" and driven by device drivers.** (We already mentioned this in Chapter 1, *Writing a Simple misc Character Device Driver*, in the *A quick note on the Linux Device Model* section).

All of these must be registered to the driver core. Now, don't worry about the buses and the bus drivers that drive them; they will be registered and handled internally by the kernel's driver core subsystem. When there is no real *device*, however, we will have to create a pseudo one in order to work with the model. Again, there are several ways to do such things, but we shall create **a** *platform device.* This device will "live" on a pseudo bus (that is, it exists only in software) known as the *platform bus*.

Platform devices

A quick but important aside: *platform devices* are often used to represent the variety of devices on a **System on Chip** (**SoC**) within an embedded board. The SoC is typically a very sophisticated chip that integrates various components into its silicon. Besides processing units (CPUs/GPUs), it might house several peripherals too, including Ethernet MAC, USB, multimedia, serial UART, clock, I2C, SPI, flash chip controllers, and so on. A reason we need these components to be enumerated as a platform device is that there is no physical bus within the SoC; thus, the platform bus is used.

Traditionally, the code that was used to instantiate these SoC platform devices was kept in a "board" file (or files) within the kernel source (arch/<arch>/...). Due to it becoming overloaded, it's been moved outside the pure kernel source into a useful hardware description format called the **Device Tree** (within **Device Tree Source** (**DTS**) files that are themselves with the kernel source tree).

On our Ubuntu 18.04 LTS guest VM, let's look at the platform devices under sysfs:

```
$ ls /sys/devices/platform/
alarmtimer  'Fixed MDIO bus.0'   intel_pmc_core.0   platform-framebuffer.0
reg-dummy
serial8250 eisa.0  i8042  pcspkr power rtc_cmos uevent
$
```

The *Bootlin* website (previously called *Free Electrons*) offers superb materials on embedded Linux, drivers, and so on. This link on their site leads to excellent material on the LDM: https://bootlin.com/pub/conferences/2019/elce/opdenacker-kernel-programming-device-model/.

Back to the driver: we bring our (artificial) platform device into existence by registering it to the (already existing) platform bus driver via the `platform_device_register_simple()` API. The moment we do so, the driver core will *generate* the required sysfs directories and a few boilerplate sysfs entries (or files). Here, in the init code of our sysfs demo driver, we will set up a (simplest possible) *platform device* by registering it to the driver core:

```
// ch2/sysfs_simple_intf/sysfs_simple_intf.c
include <linux/platform_device.h>
static struct platform_device *sysfs_demo_platdev;
[...]
#define PLAT_NAME    "llkd_sysfs_simple_intf_device"
sysfs_demo_platdev =
    platform_device_register_simple(PLAT_NAME, -1, NULL, 0);
[...]
```

The `platform_device_register_simple()` API returns a pointer to `struct platform_device`. One of this structure's members is `struct device dev`. We now have what we've been after: a *device structure*. Also, it's key to note that when this registration API runs, the effect is visible within sysfs. You can easily see the new platform device, plus a few boilerplate sysfs objects, being created by the driver core here (made visible to us via sysfs); let's build and *insmod* our kernel module to see this:

```
$ cd <...>/ch2/sysfs_simple_intf
$ make && sudo insmod ./sysfs_simple_intf.ko
[...]
$ ls -l /sys/devices/platform/llkd_sysfs_simple_intf_device/
total 0
-rw-r--r-- 1 root root 4.0K Feb 15 20:22 driver_override
-rw-r--r-- 1 root root 4.0K Feb 15 20:22 llkdsysfs_debug_level
-r--r--r-- 1 root root 4.0K Feb 15 20:22 llkdsysfs_pgoff
-r--r--r-- 1 root root 4.0K Feb 15 20:22 llkdsysfs_pressure
-r--r--r-- 1 root root 4.0K Feb 15 20:22 modalias
drwxr-xr-x 2 root root 0 Feb 15 20:22 power/
lrwxrwxrwx 1 root root 0 Feb 15 20:22 subsystem -> ../../../bus/platform/
-rw-r--r-- 1 root root 4.0K Feb 15 20:21 uevent
$
```

We can create a `struct device` in different ways; the generic way is to set up and issue the `device_create()` API. An alternate means to creating a sysfs file, while bypassing the need for a device structure, is to create a "object" and invoke the `sysfs_create_file()` API. (Links to tutorials that use both these approaches can be found in the *Further reading* section). Here, we prefer to use a "platform device" as it's the closer approach to writing a (platform) driver.

There's yet another valid approach. As we saw in `Chapter 1`, *Writing a simple misc Character Device Driver*, we built a simple character driver conforming to the kernel's `misc` framework. There, we instantiated a `struct miscdevice`; once registered (via the `misc_register()` API), this structure will contain a member called `struct device *this_device;`, thus allowing us to use it as a valid device pointer! Thus, we could have simply extended our earlier `misc` device driver and used it here. However, in order to learn a bit about platform drivers, we've chosen that approach. (We leave the approach of extending our earlier `misc` device driver so that it can use sysfs APIs and create/use sysfs files as an exercise to you).

Back to our driver, compared to the init code, in the *cleanup* code, we must un-register our platform device:

```
platform_device_unregister(sysfs_demo_platdev);
```

Now, let's tie all this knowledge together and actually see the code that generates the sysfs files, along with their read and write callback functions!

Tying it all together – setting up the device attributes and creating the sysfs file

As we mentioned at the beginning of this section, the `device_create_file()` API is the one we'll use to create our sysfs file:

```
int device_create_file(struct device *dev, const struct device_attribute
*attr);
```

In the previous section, you learned how we obtain a device structure (the first parameter for our API). Now, let's figure out how to initialize and use the second parameter; that is, the `device_attribute` structure. The structure itself is defined as follows:

```
// include/linux/device.h
struct device_attribute {
    struct attribute attr;
    ssize_t (*show)(struct device *dev, struct device_attribute *attr,
                    char *buf);
    ssize_t (*store)(struct device *dev, struct device_attribute *attr,
                    const char *buf, size_t count);
};
```

The first member, attr, essentially consists of the *name* of the sysfs file and its *mode* (permission bitmask). The other two members are function pointers ("virtual functions", analogous to those in the **file operations** or **fops** structure):

- show: Represents the *read callback* function
- store: Represents the *write callback* function

Our job is to initialize this device_attribute structure, thus setting up the sysfs file. While you can always manually initialize it, there's an easier approach: the kernel provides (several) macros for initializing struct device_attribute; among them is the DEVICE_ATTR() macro:

```
// include/linux/device.h
define DEVICE_ATTR(_name, _mode, _show, _store) \
    struct device_attribute dev_attr_##_name = __ATTR(_name, _mode, _show,
_store)
```

Notice the "stringification" that's performed by dev_attr_##_name, ensuring that the structure's name is suffixed with the name that's passed as the first parameter to DEVICE_ATTR. Furthermore, the actual "worker" macro, named __ATTR(), actually instantiates a device_attribute structure in code at preprocessing time, with (via stringification) the name of the structure becoming dev_attr_<name>:

```
// include/linux/sysfs.h
#define __ATTR(_name, _mode, _show, _store) { \
    .attr = {.name = __stringify(_name), \
    .mode = VERIFY_OCTAL_PERMISSIONS(_mode) }, \
    .show = _show, \
    .store = _store, \
}
```

Furthermore, the kernel defines additional simple wrapper macros over these macros in order to specify the *mode* (permissions for the sysfs file), thus making it even simpler for you, the driver author. Among them is DEVICE_ATTR_RW(_name), DEVICE_ATTR_RO(_name), and DEVICE_ATTR_WO(_name):

```
#define DEVICE_ATTR_RW(_name) \
    struct device_attribute dev_attr_##_name = __ATTR_RW(_name)
#define __ATTR_RW(_name) __ATTR(_name, 0644, _name##_show, _name##_store)
```

With this code, we can create a **read-write (RW)**, **read-only (RO)**, or **write-only (WO)** sysfs file. Now, we wish to set up a sysfs file that can be read and written to. Internally, this is a "hook" or callback for us to query or set a debug_level global variable just as we did in the sample kernel module on procfs earlier!

Now that we have sufficient background, let's delve into the code!

The code for implementing our sysfs file and its callbacks

Let's look at the relevant parts of the code for our simple *sysfs interfacing driver* and try things out, step by step:

1. Set up the device attribute structure (via the `DEVICE_ATTR_RW` macro; see the preceding section for more information) and create our first sysfs (pseudo) file:

```
// ch2/sysfs_simple_intf/sysfs_simple_intf.c

#define SYSFS_FILE1 llkdsysfs_debug_level
// [... <we show the actual read/write callback functions just a
bit further down> ...]
static DEVICE_ATTR_RW(SYSFS_FILE1);

int __init sysfs_simple_intf_init(void)
{
  [...]
/* << 0. The platform device is created via the
platform_device_register_simple() API; code already shown above ...
>> */

  // 1. Create our first sysfile file : llkdsysfs_debug_level
  /* The device_create_file() API creates a sysfs attribute file for
   * given device (1st parameter); the second parameter is the
pointer
   * to it's struct device_attribute structure dev_attr_<name> which
was
   * instantiated by our DEV_ATTR{_RW|RO} macros above ... */
  stat = device_create_file(&sysfs_demo_platdev->dev,
&dev_attr_SYSFS_FILE1);
  [...]
```

From the definition of the macros shown here, we can infer that `static DEVICE_ATTR_RW(SYSFS_FILE1);` instantiates an initialized `device_attribute` structure with the name `llkdsysfs_debug_level` (as that's what the `SYSFS_FILE1` macro evaluates to) and a mode of `0644`; the read callback name will be `llkdsysfs_debug_level_show()` and the write callback name will be `llkdsysfs_debug_level_store()`!

2. Here's the relevant code for the read and write callbacks (again, we won't show the entire code here). First, let's look at the read callback:

```
/* debug_level: sysfs entry point for the 'show' (read) callback */
static ssize_t llkdsysfs_debug_level_show(struct device *dev,
                                            struct device_attribute
*attr,
                                            char *buf)
{
        int n;
        if (mutex_lock_interruptible(&mtx))
                return -ERESTARTSYS;
        pr_debug("In the 'show' method: name: %s,
debug_level=%d\n",
                dev->kobj.name, debug_level);
        n = snprintf(buf, 25, "%d\n", debug_level);
        mutex_unlock(&mtx);
        return n;
}
```

How does this work? On reading our sysfs file, the preceding callback function is invoked. Within it, simply writing into the user-supplied buffer pointer, `buf` (its third parameter; we used the kernel `snprintf()` API to do so), has the effect of transferring the value provided (here, `debug_level`) to the user space!

3. Let's build and `insmod(8)` the kernel module (for convenience, we will use our `lkm` wrapper script to do so):

```
$ ../../lkm sysfs_simple_intf           // <-- build and insmod it
[...]
[83907.192247] sysfs_simple_intf:sysfs_simple_intf_init():237:
sysfs file [1]
(/sys/devices/platform/llkd_sysfs_simple_intf_device/llkdsysfs_debu
g_level) created
[83907.197279] sysfs_simple_intf:sysfs_simple_intf_init():250:
sysfs file [2]
(/sys/devices/platform/llkd_sysfs_simple_intf_device/llkdsysfs_pgof
f) created
[83907.201959] sysfs_simple_intf:sysfs_simple_intf_init():264:
sysfs file [3]
(/sys/devices/platform/llkd_sysfs_simple_intf_device/llkdsysfs_pres
sure) created
[83907.205888] sysfs_simple_intf initialized
$
```

4. Now, let's list and read the sysfs file pertaining to the debug-level:

```
$ ls -l
/sys/devices/platform/llkd_sysfs_simple_intf_device/llkdsysfs_debug
_level
-rw-r--r-- 1 root root 4096 Feb   4 17:41
/sys/devices/platform/llkd_sysfs_simple_intf_device/llkdsysfs_debug
_level
$ cat
/sys/devices/platform/llkd_sysfs_simple_intf_device/llkdsysfs_debug
_level
0
```

This reflects the fact that debug-level is currently 0.

5. Now, let's peek at the code of our *write callback* for the debug-level sysfs file:

```
#define DEBUG_LEVEL_MIN 0
#define DEBUG_LEVEL_MAX 2

static ssize_t llkdsysfs_debug_level_store(struct device *dev,
                                           struct device_attribute
*attr,
                                           const char *buf, size_t
count)
{
        int ret = (int)count, prev_dbglevel;
        if (mutex_lock_interruptible(&mtx))
                return -ERESTARTSYS;

        prev_dbglevel = debug_level;
        pr_debug("In the 'store' method:\ncount=%zu, buf=0x%px
count=%zu\n"
        "Buffer contents: \"%.*s\"\n", count, buf, count,
(int)count, buf);
        if (count == 0 || count > 12) {
                ret = -EINVAL;
                goto out;
        }

        ret = kstrtoint(buf, 0, &debug_level); /* update it! */
        // < ... validity checks ... >
        ret = count;
 out:
        mutex_unlock(&mtx);
        return ret;
}
```

Again, it should be clear that the `kstrtoint()` kernel API is used to convert the user space `buf` string into an integer value, which we then validate. Also, the third parameter to `kstrtoint` is the integer to write to, thus updating it!

6. Now, let's try updating the value of `debug_level` from its sysfs file:

```
$ sudo sh -c "echo 2 >
/sys/devices/platform/llkd_sysfs_simple_intf_device/llkdsysfs_debug
_level"
$ cat
/sys/devices/platform/llkd_sysfs_simple_intf_device/llkdsysfs_debug
_level
2
$
```

Voila – it works!

7. As we did when we interfaced with procfs, we have provided more code in the sysfs code example. Here, we have another (read-only) sysfs interface to display the value of PAGE_OFFSET, plus a new one. Imagine that this driver's job is to retrieve a "pressure" value (perhaps via an I2C-driven pressure sensor chip). Let's imagine we have done so, and stored this pressure value in an integer global variable named `gpressure`. To "show" the user space the current pressure value, we must use a sysfs file. Here it is:

 Internally, for the purpose of this demo, we have randomly set the `gpressure` global variable to a value of 25.

```
$ cat
/sys/devices/platform/llkd_sysfs_simple_intf_device/llkdsysfs_press
ure
25$
```

Look carefully at the output; why does the prompt appear immediately after 25? Because we just printed the value as-is – no newline, nothing; that's what is expected. The code that displays the "pressure" value is simple indeed:

```
/* show 'pressure' value: sysfs entry point for the 'show' (read) callback
*/
static ssize_t llkdsysfs_pressure_show(struct device *dev,
                    struct device_attribute *attr, char *buf)
{
        int n;
```

```
        if (mutex_lock_interruptible(&mtx))
                return -ERESTARTSYS;
        pr_debug("In the 'show' method: pressure=%u\n", gpressure);
        n = snprintf(buf, 25, "%u", gpressure);
        mutex_unlock(&mtx);
        return n;
}
/* The DEVICE_ATTR{_RW|RO|WO}() macro instantiates a struct
device_attribute dev_attr_<name> here...    */
static DEVICE_ATTR_RO(llkdsysfs_pressure);
```

With that, you've learned how to interface with the user space via sysfs! As usual, I urge you to actually write the code and try out these skills yourself; take a look at the *Questions* section at the end of this chapter and try out the (relevant) assignments yourself. Now, let's continue with sysfs, understanding an important *rule* regarding its ABI.

The "one value per sysfs file" rule

So far, you have understood how to create and make use of sysfs for user space kernel interfacing purposes, but there is a key point that we have been ignoring. There is a "rule" regarding using sysfs files, which states that you must only read or write exactly one value! Think of this as the *one-value-per-file* rule.

So, as in the example where we used the "pressure" value, we merely return the current value of the pressure, nothing more. Thus, sysfs, unlike the other interfacing technologies, is not quite suited to those cases where you might want to return arbitrary long-winded information packets (say, the contents of the driver context structure) to the user space; in other words, it's not suited to pure "debugging" purposes.

The kernel documents and "rules" regarding the usage of sysfs can be found here: https://www.kernel.org/doc/html/latest/admin-guide/sysfs-rules.html#rules-on-how-to-access-information-in-sysfs. In addition, there is documentation on the sysfs API here: https://www.kernel.org/doc/html/latest/filesystems/api-summary.html#the-filesystem-for-exporting-kernel-objects.

The kernel typically provides several different means of creating sysfs objects; for example, with the sysfs_create_files() API, you can create multiple sysfs files in one go: int __must_check sysfs_create_files(struct kobject *kobj, const struct attribute * const *attr);. Here, you are expected to supply a pointer to a kobject and a pointer to a list of attribute structures.

This concludes our discussion of sysfs as an interfacing technology; in summary, sysfs is indeed considered the *right way* for driver authors to display and/or set a particular driver value to and from the user space. Due to the "one value per sysfs file" convention, sysfs is really not ideally suited to debugging information dispensation. This neatly brings us to our next topic – debugfs!

Interfacing via the debug filesystem (debugfs)

Imagine for a moment, the quandary faced by you, a driver developer, on Linux: you want to implement an easy yet elegant way to provide debug "hooks" from your driver to the user space. For example, the user simply performing a cat(1) on a (pseudo) file should result in your driver's "debug callback" function being invoked. It will then proceed to dump some status information (perhaps a "driver context" structure) to the user mode process, which will faithfully dump it to stdout.

Okay, no problem: in the days before the 2.6 release, we could (as you learned in the *Interfacing via the proc filesystem (procfs)* section) happily use the procfs layer to interface our driver with the user space. Then, from 2.6 Linux onward, the kernel community vetoed this approach. We were told to strictly stop using procfs and instead use the sysfs layer as the means to interface our drivers with the user space. However, as we saw in the *Interfacing via the sys filesystem (sysfs)* section, it has a strict *one-value-per-file* rule. This is actually great for reporting or sending single values from and to the driver (typically, environment sensor values and similar), but quickly rules out all but the most trivial debug interfaces to the user space. We could use the ioctl approach (as we shall see) to set up a debug interface but it's quite a bit harder to do so.

So, what can you do? Luckily, there is an elegant solution in place from around 2.6.12 Linux onward called debugfs. The "debug filesystem" is very easy to use and quite explicit in communicating the fact that driver authors (anyone, in fact) can use it for whatever purpose they choose! There is no one-value-per-file rule – forget that, there are no rules.

Of course, just as with the other filesystem-based approaches we have dealt with – procfs, sysfs, and now debugfs – the kernel community clearly claims that all these interfaces are an ABI, and thus, that their stability and lifespan is something that is *not* guaranteed. While that is the formal stance that's adopted, the reality is that these interfaces have become de facto ones in the real world; stripping them out without preamble one fine day wouldn't really serve anybody.

The following screenshot shows the content of debugfs on our x86-64 Ubuntu 18.04.3 LTS guest (running the "custom" 5.4.0 kernel we built back in our companion book *Linux Kernel Programming, Chapter 3, Building the 5.0 Linux kernel from Source, Part 2!*):

```
root@llkd-vbox:~# uname -r
5.4.0-llkd01
root@llkd-vbox:~# mount |grep -w debugfs
debugfs on /sys/kernel/debug type debugfs (rw,relatime)
root@llkd-vbox:~# ls /sys/kernel/debug
acpi             dynamic_debug        opp              soundwire
bdi              error_injection      pinctrl          split_huge_pages
block            extfrag              pmc_core         suspend_stats
cec              fault_around_bytes   pm_qos           swiotlb
cleancache       frontswap            pwm              sync
clear_warn_once  gpio                 ras              tracing
clk              hid                  regmap           usb
device_component iosf_sb              regulator        virtio-ports
devices_deferred kprobes              sched_debug      wakeup_sources
dma_buf          mce                  sched_features   x86
dri              memcg_slabinfo       sleep_time       zswap
root@llkd-vbox:~# █
```

Figure 2.3 – Screenshot revealing the content of the debugfs filesystem on an x86_64 Linux VM

As with procfs and sysfs, due to debugfs being a kernel feature (it's a virtual filesystem, after all!), the precise content within it is highly dependent on the kernel version and CPU architecture. As we mentioned previously, by looking at this screenshot, it should now be obvious that there are plenty of real-world "users" of debugfs.

Checking for the presence of debugfs

First off, in order to make use of the powerful *debugfs* interface, it must be enabled within the kernel config. The relevant Kconfig macro is CONFIG_DEBUG_FS. Let's check whether it's enabled on our 5.4 custom kernel:

Here, we are assuming you have the CONFIG_IKCONFIG and CONFIG_IKCONFIG_PROC options set to y, thus allowing us to use the /proc/config.gz pseudo file to access the current kernel's configuration.

```
$ zcat /proc/config.gz | grep -w CONFIG_DEBUG_FS
CONFIG_DEBUG_FS=y
```

Indeed it is; it's typically enabled by default in distributions.

Next, the default mount point of debugfs is `/sys/kernel/debug`. Thus, we can see that it is internally dependent on the sysfs kernel feature being present and mounted, which it is by default. Let's check where debugfs is mounted on our Ubuntu 18.04 x86_64 VM:

```
$ mount | grep -w debugfs
debugfs on /sys/kernel/debug type debugfs (rw,relatime)
```

It is available and mounted at the expected location; that is, `/sys/kernel/debug`.

Of course, it's always a best practice to never assume that this will always be the location where it's mounted; in your script or user mode C program, take the trouble to check and verify it. In fact, allow me to rephrase this: *it's always a good practice to never assume anything; making assumptions is a really good source of bugs.*

By the way, an interesting Linux feature is that filesystems can be mounted in different, even multiple, locations; also, some folks prefer to create a symbolic link to `/sys/kernel/debug` as `/debug`; it's up to you, really.

As usual, our intention here is to create our (pseudo) files under the debugfs umbrella, and then register and make use of the read/write callbacks from them, for the purpose of interfacing our driver with the user space. To do so, we need to understand the basic usage of the debugfs API. We will point you to the documentation for this in the next section.

Looking up the debugfs API documentation

The kernel supplies succinct and superb documentation on using the debugfs API (courtesy of Jonathan Corbet, LWN) here: `https://www.kernel.org/doc/Documentation/filesystems/debugfs.txt` (of course, you can also look it up directly within the kernel codebase).

I urge you to refer to this document to learn how to use the debugfs APIs, since it's easy to read and understand; this way, you can avoid unnecessarily repeating the same information here. In addition to the aforementioned document, the modern kernel documentation system (the "Sphinx"-based one) also provides quite detailed debugfs API pages: `https://www.kernel.org/doc/html/latest/filesystems/api-summary.html?highlight=debugfs#the-debugfs-filesystem`.

Note that all debugfs APIs are exported as GPL-only to kernel modules (thus necessitating the module being released under the "GPL" license (this can be dual licensed, but one must be "GPL")).

An interfacing example with debugfs

Debugfs, being deliberately designed with a "no particular rules" mindset, makes it the ideal interface to use *for debug purposes*. Why? It allows you to construct any arbitrary byte stream and send it off to the user space, including a binary "blob" with the `debugfs_create_blob()` API.

Our previous example kernel modules with procfs and sysfs constructed and used three to four (pseudo) files. For a quick demo with debugfs, we shall just stick to two "files":

- `llkd_dbgfs_show_drvctx`: As you'll have no doubt guessed, when read, it will cause the current content of our (by now familiar) "driver context" data structure to be dumped to the console; we shall ensure the pseudo file's mode is read-only (by root).
- `llkd_dbgfs_debug_level`: This file's mode shall be read-write (by root only); when read, it will display the current value of `debug_level`; when an integer is written to it, we shall update the value of `debug_level` within the kernel module to the value passed.

Here, in the init code of our kernel module, we will first create a directory under `debugfs`:

```
// ch2/debugfs_simple_intf/debugfs_simple_intf.c

static struct dentry *gparent;
[...]
static int debugfs_simple_intf_init(void)
{
    int stat = 0;
    struct dentry *file1, *file2;
    [...]
    gparent = debugfs_create_dir(OURMODNAME, NULL);
```

Now that we have a starting point – a directory – let's move on and create the debugfs (pseudo) files under it.

Creating and using the first debugfs file

For readability and to save space, we won't show the error handling code sections here.

Just as in the example with procfs, we must allocate and initialize an instance of our "driver context" data structure (we haven't shown the code here as it's repetitive, so please refer to the GitHub source).

Then, via the generic `debugfs_create_file()` API, we must create a `debugfs` file, associating it with a `file_operations` structure. This, in effects, gets just a read callback registered:

```
static const struct file_operations dbgfs_drvctx_fops = {
    .read = dbgfs_show_drvctx,
};
[...]
// < ... init function ... >
    /* Generic debugfs file + passing a pointer to a data structure as a
     * demo.. the 4th param is a generic void * ptr; it's contents will be
     * stored into the i_private field of the file's inode.
     */
#define DBGFS_FILE1 "llkd_dbgfs_show_drvctx"
    file1 = debugfs_create_file(DBGFS_FILE1, 0440, gparent,
                (void *)gdrvctx, &dbgfs_drvctx_fops);
    [...]
```

From 5.8 Linux onward (recall that we're working with the 5.4 LTS kernel), the return value of several of the debugfs creation APIs have been removed (they will return `void`); Greg Kroah-Hartman's patch mentions that this was done as no one was using them. This is quite typical of Linux – unneeded features are stripped off, and kernel evolution continues...

Clearly, the "read" callback is our `dbgfs_show_drvctx()` function. As a reminder, this function gets auto-invoked by the debugfs layer whenever the `debugfs` file (`llkd_dbgfs_show_drvctx`) is read; here's the code for our debugfs read callback function:

```
static ssize_t dbgfs_show_drvctx(struct file *filp, char __user * ubuf,
                        size_t count, loff_t * fpos)
{
    struct drv_ctx *data = (struct drv_ctx *)filp->f_inode->i_private;
                    // retrieve the "data" from the inode
#define MAXUPASS 256   // careful- the kernel stack is small!
    char locbuf[MAXUPASS];

    if (mutex_lock_interruptible(&mtx))
        return -ERESTARTSYS;

    /* As an experiment, we set our 'config3' member of the drv ctx stucture
     * to the current 'jiffies' value (# of timer interrupts since boot);
```

```
 * so, every time we 'cat' this file, the 'config3' value should change!
 */
data->config3 = jiffies;
snprintf(locbuf, MAXUPASS - 1,
        "prodname:%s\n"
        "tx:%d,rx:%d,err:%d,myword:%d,power:%d\n"
        "config1:0x%x,config2:0x%x,config3:0x%llx (%llu)\n"
        "oursecret:%s\n",
        OURMODNAME,
        data->tx, data->rx, data->err, data->myword, data->power,
        data->config1, data->config2, data->config3, data->config3,
        data->oursecret);

    mutex_unlock(&mtx);
    return simple_read_from_buffer(ubuf, MAXUPASS, fpos, locbuf,
                                   strlen(locbuf));
}
```

Notice how we retrieve the "data" pointer (our driver context structure) by dereferencing the debugfs files' inode member, which is called i_private.

As we mentioned in Chapter 1, *Writing a Simple misc Character Device Driver*, using the data pointer to dereference the driver context structure from the file's inode is one of a number of similar, common techniques employed by driver authors to avoid the use of globals. Here, gdrvctx *is* a global, so it's a moot point; we are simply using it to demonstrate the typical use case.

Using the snprintf() API, we can populate a local buffer with the current content of our driver's "context" structure, and then, via the simple_read_from_buffer() API, pass it up to the user space app that issued the read, which typically causes it to be displayed on the Terminal/console window. This simple_read_from_buffer() API is a wrapper over copy_to_user().

Let's give it a spin:

```
$ ../../lkm debugfs_simple_intf
[...]
[200221.725752] dbgfs_simple_intf: allocated and init the driver context
structure
[200221.728158] dbgfs_simple_intf: debugfs file 1
<debugfs_mountpt>/dbgfs_simple_intf/llkd_dbgfs_show_drvctx created
[200221.732167] dbgfs_simple_intf: debugfs file 2
<debugfs_mountpt>/dbgfs_simple_intf/llkd_dbgfs_debug_level created
[200221.735723] dbgfs_simple_intf initialized
```

As we can see, the two debugfs files are created as expected; let's verify this (be careful here; you can only look into debugfs as *root*):

```
$ ls -l /sys/kernel/debug/dbgfs_simple_intf
ls: cannot access '/sys/kernel/debug/dbgfs_simple_intf': Permission denied
$ sudo ls -l /sys/kernel/debug/dbgfs_simple_intf
total 0
-rw-r--r-- 1 root root 0 Feb  7 15:58 llkd_dbgfs_debug_level
-r--r----- 1 root root 0 Feb  7 15:58 llkd_dbgfs_show_drvctx
$
```

The pseudo files have been created and have the correct permissions. Now, let's read (as root user) from the `llkd_dbgfs_show_drvctx` file:

```
$ sudo cat /sys/kernel/debug/dbgfs_simple_intf/llkd_dbgfs_show_drvctx
prodname:dbgfs_simple_intf
tx:0,rx:0,err:0,myword:0,power:1
config1:0x0,config2:0x48524a5f,config3:0x102fbcbc2 (4345023426)
oursecret:AhA yyy
$
```

It works; performing the read again a few seconds later. Notice how the value of `config3` has changed. Why? Recall that we set it to the `jiffies` value – the number of timer "ticks"/interrupts – that have occurred since system boot:

```
$ sudo cat /sys/kernel/debug/dbgfs_simple_intf/llkd_dbgfs_show_drvctx |
grep config3
config1:0x0,config2:0x48524a5f,config3:0x102fbe828 (4345030696)
$
```

Having created and used our first debugfs file, let's understand the second debugfs file.

Creating and using the second debugfs file

Let's move on to the second debugfs file. We will create it using an interesting shortcut helper debugfs API named `debugfs_create_u32()`. This API *automatically* sets up internal callbacks, allowing you to read/write upon the specified unsigned 32-bit global variable within the driver. The main advantage of this "helper" routine is that you don't need to explicitly provide a `file_operations` structure or even any callback routines. The debugfs layer "understands" and internally sets things up so that reading or writing the numeric (global) variable will always just work! Take a look at the following code in the *init* codepath, which creates and sets up our second debugfs file:

```
static int debug_level;    /* 'off' (0) by default ... */
[...]
```

```
    /* 3. Create the debugfs file for the debug_level global; we use the
     * helper routine to make it simple! There is a downside: we have no
     * chance to perform a validity check on the value being written.. */
#define DBGFS_FILE2    "llkd_dbgfs_debug_level"
    file2 = debugfs_create_u32(DBGFS_FILE2, 0644, gparent, &debug_level);
    [...]
    pr_debug("%s: debugfs file 2 <debugfs_mountpt>/%s/%s created\n",
             OURMODNAME, OURMODNAME, DBGFS_FILE2);
```

It's as simple as that! Now, reading this file will produce the current value of debug_level;
writing to it will set it to the value written. Let's do this:

```
$ sudo cat /sys/kernel/debug/dbgfs_simple_intf/llkd_dbgfs_debug_level
0
$ sudo sh -c "echo 5 >
/sys/kernel/debug/dbgfs_simple_intf/llkd_dbgfs_debug_level"
$ sudo cat /sys/kernel/debug/dbgfs_simple_intf/llkd_dbgfs_debug_level
5
$
```

This works, but there is a downside to this "shortcut" approach: since this is all done
internally, there is no way for us to *validate* the value being written. Thus, here, we wrote
the value 5 to debug_level; it worked, but it's an invalid value (at least let's assume that's
the case)! So, how can this be corrected? Simple: do not use this helper method; instead, do
it the "usual" way via the generic debugfs_create_file() API (as we did for the first
debugfs file). The advantage here is that as we set up explicit callback routines for read and
write, by specifying them within a fops structure, we have control over the value being
written (I leave doing this to you, as an exercise). Like life, it's a trade-off; you win some,
you lose some.

Helper debugfs APIs for working on numeric globals

You have just learned how to use the debugfs_create_u32() helper API to set up a
debugfs file to read/write an unsigned 32-bit integer global. The fact is, the debugfs layer
provides a bunch of similar "helper" APIs to implicitly read/write on numeric (integer)
global variables within your module.

The helper routines for creating debugfs entries that can read/write different bit size unsigned integer (8-, 16-, 32-, and 64-bit) globals follow. The last parameter is the key one – the address of the global integer within the kernel/module:

```
// include/linux/debugfs.h
struct dentry *debugfs_create_u8(const char *name, umode_t mode,
                struct dentry *parent, u8 *value);
struct dentry *debugfs_create_u16(const char *name, umode_t mode,
                struct dentry *parent, u16 *value);
struct dentry *debugfs_create_u32(const char *name, umode_t mode,
                struct dentry *parent, u32 *value);
struct dentry *debugfs_create_u64(const char *name, umode_t mode,
                struct dentry *parent, u64 *value);
```

The preceding APIs work with decimal base; to make using *hexadecimal base* easy, we have the following helpers:

```
struct dentry *debugfs_create_x8(const char *name, umode_t mode,
                struct dentry *parent, u8 *value);
struct dentry *debugfs_create_x16(const char *name, umode_t mode,
                struct dentry *parent, u16 *value);
struct dentry *debugfs_create_x32(const char *name, umode_t mode,
                struct dentry *parent, u32 *value);
struct dentry *debugfs_create_x64(const char *name, umode_t mode,
                struct dentry *parent, u64 *value);
```

 As an aside, the kernel also provides a helper API for those cases where the precise *size* of the variable varies; hence, using the `debugfs_create_size_t()` helper creates a debugfs file appropriate for a variable of size `size_t`.

For drivers that merely need to peek at a numeric global, or update it without any worry about invalid values, these debugfs helper APIs are very useful and are indeed commonly used by several drivers in the mainline kernel (we will look at an example within the MMC driver shortly). To evade the "validity check" issue, often, we can arrange for the *user space* application (or script) to perform validity checking; in fact, this is typically the "right way" to do things.

 The UNIX paradigm has a saying: *provide mechanism, not policy.*

When working with globals that are of the *boolean* type, debugfs provides the following helper API:

```
struct dentry *debugfs_create_bool(const char *name, umode_t mode,
                    struct dentry *parent, bool *value);
```

Reading from the "file" will result in only Y or N (suffixed with a newline) being returned; obviously, Y if the current value of the fourth `value` parameter is non-zero, and N otherwise. When writing, you can write Y or N or 1 or 0; other values will not be accepted.

> Think about it: you can control your "robot" device via your robot device driver by writing 1 to a boolean variable called, say, `power` to turn it on, and use 0 to turn it off! The possibilities are endless.

The kernel documentation on debugfs provides a few more miscellaneous APIs; I leave it to you to have a look. Now that we've covered how to create and use our demo debugfs pseudo files, let's learn how to remove them.

Removing the debugfs pseudo file(s)

When a module is removed (via, say, `rmmod(8)`), we must delete our debugfs files. The older way to do this was via the `debugfs_remove()` API, where each debugfs file had to be individually removed with it (painful, to say the least). The modern approach makes this really simple:

```
void debugfs_remove_recursive(struct dentry *dentry);
```

Pass the pointer to the overall "parent" directory (the one we created first), and the entire branch is recursively removed; perfect.

Not deleting your debugfs files at this point, thus leaving them there on the filesystem in an orphaned state, is asking for trouble! Just think about this: what will happen when someone (attempts to) reads or writes to any of them later? **A kernel bug, or an *Oops*,** that's what.

Seeing a kernel bug – an Oops!

Let's make it happen – a kernel bug! Exciting, yes!?

Okay, to create a kernel bug, we must ensure that when we remove (unload) the kernel module, the API that cleans up (deletes) all the debugfs files, `debugfs_remove_recursive()`, is *not* invoked. Thus, after each module is removed, our debugfs directory and files seem to be present! However, if you try and operate on – read/write – any of them, they'll be in an *orphaned state* and, hence, upon trying to dereference its metadata, the internal debugfs code paths will perform an invalid memory reference, resulting in a (kernel-level) bug.

In the kernel space, a bug is a very serious thing indeed; in theory, it should never, ever happen! This is called an *Oops*; as part of handling this, an internal kernel function is called, which dumps useful diagnostic information via `printk` to the in-memory kernel log buffer, as well as to the console device (on production systems, it might also be directed elsewhere so that it can be retrieved and investigated at a later date; for example, via the kernel's *kdump* mechanism).

Let's introduce a module parameter that controls whether we (quite deliberately) cause an *Oops* to occur or not:

```
// ch2/debugfs_simple_intf/debugfs_simple_intf.c
[...]
/* Module parameters */
static int cause_an_oops;
module_param(cause_an_oops, int, 0644);
MODULE_PARM_DESC(cause_an_oops,
"Setting this to 1 can cause a kernel bug, an Oops; if 1, we do NOT perform
required cleanup! so, after removal, any op on the debugfs files will cause
an Oops! (default is 0, no bug)");
```

In the cleanup code path of our driver, we check if the `cause_an_oops` variable is non-zero and deliberately do *not* (recursively) delete our debugfs file(s), hence setting up the bug:

```
static void debugfs_simple_intf_cleanup(void)
{
        kfree(gdrvctx);
        if (!cause_an_oops)
                debugfs_remove_recursive(gparent);
        pr_info("%s removed\n", OURMODNAME);
}
```

When we "normally" use `insmod(8)`, the scary `cause_an_oops` module parameter is 0 by default, thus ensuring that everything works well. But let's get adventurous! We are building the kernel module and when we insert it, we must pass the parameter while setting it to 1 (notice that here, we're running as *root* on our x86_64 Ubuntu 18.04 LTS guest system on our custom `5.4.0-llkd01` kernel):

```
# id
uid=0(root) gid=0(root) groups=0(root)
# insmod ./debugfs_simple_intf.ko cause_an_oops=1
# cat /sys/kernel/debug/dbgfs_simple_intf/llkd_dbgfs_debug_level
0
# dmesg
[ 2061.048140] dbgfs_simple_intf: allocated and init the driver context
structure
[ 2061.050690] dbgfs_simple_intf: debugfs file 1
<debugfs_mountpt>/dbgfs_simple_intf/llkd_dbgfs_show_drvctx created
[ 2061.053638] dbgfs_simple_intf: debugfs file 2
<debugfs_mountpt>/dbgfs_simple_intf/llkd_dbgfs_debug_level created
[ 2061.057089] dbgfs_simple_intf initialized (fyi, our 'cause an Oops'
setting is currently On)
#
```

Now, let's remove the kernel module – internally, the code that's used to clean up (recursively delete) our debugfs file would not have run. Here, we are actually triggering the kernel bug, the *Oops*, by attempting to read one of our debugfs files:

```
# rmmod debugfs_simple_intf
# cat /sys/kernel/debug/dbgfs_simple_intf/llkd_dbgfs_debug_level
Killed
```

The `Killed` message on the console is ominous! This is a clue that something has gone (dramatically) wrong. Viewing the kernel log confirms that we indeed got an *Oops!* The following (partially cropped) screenshot shows this:

```
[ 2119.775724] dbgfs_simple_intf removed
[ 2124.945311] BUG: unable to handle page fault for address: ffffffffc054d480
[ 2124.948501] #PF: supervisor read access in kernel mode
[ 2124.951069] #PF: error_code(0x0000) - not-present page
[ 2124.953575] PGD 7080e067 P4D 7080e067 PUD 70810067 PMD 7af5e067 PTE 0
[ 2124.956332] Oops: 0000 [#1] SMP PTI
[ 2124.958473] CPU: 1 PID: 4673 Comm: cat Tainted: G           OE    5.4.0-llkd01 #2
[ 2124.961171] Hardware name: innotek GmbH VirtualBox/VirtualBox, BIOS VirtualBox 12/01/2006
[ 2124.963971] RIP: 0010:debugfs_u32_get+0x5/0x20
[ 2124.966355] Code: e5 5d 48 89 06 31 c0 c3 0f 1f 00 66 2e 0f 1f 84 00 00 00 00 00 0f 1f 44 00 00 55 31 c0 89 37 48 89 e5 5d c3 90
0f 1f 44 00 00 <8b> 07 55 48 89 e5 5d 48 89 06 31 c0 c3 0f 1f 40 00 66 2e 0f 1f 84
[ 2124.973702] RSP: 0018:ffffa239808cbe00 EFLAGS: 00010246
[ 2124.976101] RAX: ffffffffbaa0b490 RBX: 0000000000000000 RCX: ffffa239808cbee8
[ 2124.978880] RDX: ffff92db34814440 RSI: ffffa239808cbe10 RDI: ffffffffc054d480
[ 2124.981827] RBP: ffffa239808cbe48 R08: ffffffffbb48a380 R09: 0000000000000000
[ 2124.984674] R10: 0000000000000000 R11: 0000000000000000 R12: ffff92db3cda0250
[ 2124.987504] R13: ffffa239808cbee8 R14: ffff92db3cda0200 R15: 0000000000020000
[ 2124.990426] FS:  00007f0e123d3540(0000) GS:ffff92db3db00000(0000) knlGS:0000000000000000
[ 2124.993462] CS:  0010 DS: 0000 ES: 0000 CR0: 0000000080050033
[ 2124.996008] CR2: ffffffffc054d480 CR3: 000000004ccba001 CR4: 00000000000606e0
[ 2124.998808] Call Trace:
[ 2125.000850]  ? simple_attr_read+0x6b/0xf0
[ 2125.003305]  debugfs_attr_read+0x49/0x70
[ 2125.005576]  __vfs_read+0x1b/0x40
[ 2125.007776]  vfs_read+0x8e/0x130
[ 2125.009799]  ksys_read+0xa7/0xe0
[ 2125.011934]  __x64_sys_read+0x1a/0x20
[ 2125.013896]  do_syscall_64+0x57/0x190
[ 2125.015921]  entry_SYSCALL_64_after_hwframe+0x44/0xa9
[ 2125.018103] RIP: 0033:0x7f0e11ee0081
[ 2125.020150] Code: fe ff ff 48 8d 3d 67 9c 0a 00 48 83 ec 08 e8 a6 4c 02 00 66 0f 1f 44 00 00 48 8d 05 81 08 2e 00 8b 00 85 c0 75
13 31 c0 0f 05 <48> 3d 00 f0 ff ff 77 57 f3 c3 0f 1f 44 00 00 41 54 55 49 89 d4 53
[ 2125.027032] RSP: 002b:00007ffceb55a5a8 EFLAGS: 00000246 ORIG_RAX: 0000000000000000
[ 2125.029474] RAX: ffffffffffffffda RBX: 0000000000020000 RCX: 00007f0e11ee0081
[ 2125.032055] RDX: 0000000000020000 RSI: 00007f0e123b1000 RDI: 0000000000000003
[ 2125.034592] RBP: 0000000000020000 R08: 00000000ffffffff R09: 0000000000000000
[ 2125.037051] R10: 0000000000000022 R11: 0000000000000246 R12: 00007f0e123b1000
[ 2125.039547] R13: 0000000000000003 R14: 00007f0e123b10f0 R15: 0000000000020000
[ 2125.041867] Modules linked in: vboxsf(OE) vboxvideo(OE) vmwgfx drm_kms_helper syscopyarea sysfillrect snd_intel8x0 sysimgblt snd
```

Figure 2.4 – A partial screenshot of a kernel Oops, a kernel-level bug

Since provided kernel debugging details is beyond the scope of this book, we will not delve into the details here. Nevertheless, figuring out a little bit is quite intuitive. Look carefully at the preceding screenshot: in the `BUG:` statement, you can see the **kernel virtual address (kva)** whose lookup caused the bug, known as the Oops (we covered the kva space in the companion guide, *Linux Kernel Programming – Chapter 7, Memory Management Internals Essentials*; this is really key information for driver authors):

```
CPU: 1 PID: 4673 Comm: cat Tainted: G OE 5.4.0-llkd01 #2
```

This shows the CPU (1) that the process context (`cat`) was running on, the tainted flags, and the kernel version. One of the really key pieces of output is as follows:

```
RIP: 0010:debugfs_u32_get+0x5/0x20
```

This tells you that the CPU instruction pointer (the register named RIP on the x86_64) was in the `debugfs_u32_get()` function at an offset of `0x5` bytes from the start of the machine code of the function (furthermore, the kernel figures out that the length of the function is `0x20` bytes)!

 Combining this information with powerful tools such as `objdump(1)` and `addr2line(1)` can help to literally pinpoint the location of the bug in code!

The CPU registers are dumped; even better, the *call trace* or the *call stack* – the *content of the kernel mode stack* of the process context (please refer to *Linux Kernel Programming*, in *Chapter 6*, *Kernel Internals Essentials, Processes and Threads*, for details on the kernel stack) – shows you the code that led up to this point; that is, the crash (read the stack trace bottom-up). Another quick tip: if a kernel function in the call trace's output is preceded by a `?` symbol, just ignore it (it's perhaps a previous "blip" that was left behind).

 Realistically, a kernel bug on a production system *must* cause the entire system to panic (halt). On non-production systems (like what we're running on), a kernel panic may or may not occur; here, it doesn't. Nevertheless, a kernel bug must be treated with the highest level of severity, it's indeed a show-stopper and must be fixed. The procfs file, `/proc/sys/kernel/panic_on_oops`, is set to `0` by most distros, but on production systems, it will typically be set to the value `1`.

The moral here is clear: there is no auto cleanup being performed by debugfs; we have to do it. Right, let's wrap up this discussion on debugfs by looking up some actual real-world usage within the kernel.

Debugfs – actual users

As we mentioned previously, there are several "real-world" users of the debugfs API; can we spot some of them? Well, here's one way: simply search under the kernel source tree's `drivers/` directory for files named `*debugfs*.c`; you might be surprised (I found 114 such files in the 5.4.0 kernel tree!). Let's take a look at a few:

```
$ cd <kernel-source-tree> ; find drivers/ -iname "*debugfs*.c"
drivers/block/drbd/drbd_debugfs.c
drivers/mmc/core/debugfs.c
drivers/platform/x86/intel_telemetry_debugfs.c
[...]
drivers/infiniband/hw/qib/qib_debugfs.c
```

```
drivers/infiniband/hw/hfi1/debugfs.c
[...]
drivers/media/usb/uvc/uvc_debugfs.c
drivers/acpi/debugfs.c
drivers/net/wireless/mediatek/mt76/debugfs.c
[...]
drivers/net/wireless/intel/iwlwifi/mvm/debugfs-vif.c
drivers/net/wimax/i2400m/debugfs.c
drivers/net/ethernet/broadcom/bnxt/bnxt_debugfs.c
drivers/net/ethernet/marvell/mvpp2/mvpp2_debugfs.c
drivers/net/ethernet/mellanox/mlx5/core/debugfs.c
[...]
drivers/misc/genwqe/card_debugfs.c
drivers/misc/mei/debugfs.c
drivers/misc/cxl/debugfs.c
[...]
drivers/usb/mtu3/mtu3_debugfs.c
drivers/sh/intc/virq-debugfs.c
drivers/soundwire/debugfs.c
[...]
drivers/crypto/ccree/cc_debugfs.c
```

Have a look at (some of) them; their code exposes debugfs interfaces. This is not always done for mere debug purposes; many of the debugfs files are for actual production usage! As an example, the MMC driver contains the following line of code, which makes use of the debugfs "helper" API to get an x32 global:

```
drivers/mmc/core/debugfs.c:mmc_add_card_debugfs():
debugfs_create_x32("state", S_IRUSR, root, &card->state);
```

This creates a debugfs file called `state` that, when read, displays the "state" of the card.

Okay, this completes our coverage of how to interface with the user space via the powerful debugfs framework. Our demo debugfs driver created a debugfs directory and two debugfs pseudo files within it; you then learned how to set up and use both read and write callback handlers for them. The "shortcut" APIs (such as `debugfs_create_u32()` and friends) are powerful too. Not only that, but we even managed to generate a kernel bug – an Oops! Now, let's learn how to communicate over a special type of socket, known as a netlink socket.

Interfacing via netlink sockets

Here, you'll learn to interface kernel and user spaces with a familiar and indeed ubiquitous network abstraction – sockets! Programmers familiar with network application programming swear by its advantages.

 Familiarity with network programming in C/C++ with socket APIs helps here. Do see the *Further reading* section for a couple of good tutorials on this topic.

Advantages using sockets

Among others, socket technology provides us with several advantages (over other typical user mode IPC mechanisms such as pipes, SysV IPC/POSIX IPC mechanisms (message queues, shared memory, semaphores, and so on)), as follows:

- Bidirectional simultaneous data transfer (full duplex).
- Lossless on the internet, with at least with some transport layer protocols, such as TCP, and of course, on the localhost, which is the case here.
- High-speed data transfer, especially on localhost!
- Flow control semantics are always in effect.
- Asynchronous communication; messages can be queued, so the sender does not have to wait for the receiver.
- Especially with respect to our topic, in other user<->kernel communication paths (such as procfs, sysfs, debugfs, and ioctl), the user space app must initiate the transfer to the kernel space; with netlink sockets, *the kernel can initiate a transfer.*
- Also, with all the other mechanisms we have seen so far (procfs, sysfs, and debugfs), the various interface files being strewn all over the filesystem(s) can cause kernel namespace pollution; with netlink sockets (and, incidentally, with ioctl), this isn't the case as there are no files.

These advantages can be helpful, depending on the type of product you're working on. Now, let's understand what a netlink socket is.

Understanding what a netlink socket is

So, what is a netlink socket? We shall keep it simple – a *netlink socket* is a "special" socket family that exists only on the Linux OS since version 2.2. Using it, you can set up **Inter-Process Communication (IPC)** between a user mode process (or thread) and a component within the kernel; in our case, a kernel module, which is typically a driver.

It is similar to a UNIX domain datagram socket in many ways; it's meant for communication on the *localhost only* and not across systems. While UNIX domain sockets use a pathname as their namespace (a special "socket" file), netlink sockets use a PID. Pedantically, this is a port ID and not a process ID, although realistically, process IDs are very often used as the namespace. The modern kernel core (besides drivers) uses netlink sockets in many cases – as one example, the iproute2 networking utilities use it to configure wireless drivers. As another interesting example, the udev feature uses netlink sockets to effect communication between the kernel udev implementation and the user space daemon process (udevd or systemd-udevd, for things such as device discovery, device node provisioning, and so on).

Here, we will design and implement a simple user<->kernel messaging demonstration using netlink sockets. To do so, we shall have to write two programs (at a minimum) – one as the user space application that issues socket-based system calls, and another for the kernel-space component (here, a kernel module). We shall have the user space process send a "message" to the kernel module; the kernel module should receive it and print it (into the kernel log buffer). The kernel module will then reply to the user space process, which is blocking on this very event.

So, without further ado, let's dive into writing some code using netlink sockets; we shall begin with the user space application. Read on!

Writing the user space netlink socket application

Follow these steps get the *user space* application running:

1. The first thing we must do is get ourselves a *socket*. Traditionally, a socket is defined as an endpoint of communication; thus, a pair of sockets forms a connection. We will use the `socket(2)` system call to do this. Its signature is `int socket(int domain, int type, int protocol);`.

Without going into too much detail, here's what we do:

- We specify `domain` as part of the special `PF_NETLINK` family, thus requesting a netlink socket.
- Set `type` to `SOCK_RAW` using a raw socket (effectively skipping the transport layer).
- `protocol` is the protocol to use. Since we're using a raw socket, the protocol is left to be implemented either by us or by the kernel; having the kernel netlink code do this is the right approach. Here, we use an unused protocol number; that is, `31`.

2. The next step is to bind the socket via the usual `bind(2)` system call semantics. First, we must initialize a netlink source `socketaddr` structure for this purpose (where we specify the family as a netlink and the PID value as the calling process' PID (for unicast only)). The following code is for the first two steps mentioned here (for clarity, we won't be displaying the error checking code here):

```
// ch2/netlink_simple_intf/userapp_netlink/netlink_userapp.c
#define NETLINK_MY_UNIT_PROTO        31
    // kernel netlink protocol # (registered by our kernel module)
#define NLSPACE 1024

[...]
 /* 1. Get ourselves an endpoint - a netlink socket! */
sd = socket(PF_NETLINK, SOCK_RAW, NETLINK_MY_UNIT_PROTO);
printf("%s:PID %d: netlink socket created\n", argv[0], getpid());

/* 2. Setup the netlink source addr structure and bind it */
memset(&src_nl, 0, sizeof(src_nl));
src_nl.nl_family = AF_NETLINK;
/* Note carefully: nl_pid is NOT necessarily the PID of the sender
process; it's actually 'port id' and can be any unique number */
src_nl.nl_pid = getpid();
src_nl.nl_groups = 0x0; // no multicast
bind(sd, (struct sockaddr *)&src_nl, sizeof(src_nl))
```

3. Next, we must initialize a netlink "destination address" structure. Here, we set the PID member to `0`, a special value indicating that the destination is the kernel:

```
/* 3. Setup the netlink destination addr structure */
memset(&dest_nl, 0, sizeof(dest_nl));
dest_nl.nl_family = AF_NETLINK;
dest_nl.nl_groups = 0x0; // no multicast
dest_nl.nl_pid = 0;        // destined for the kernel
```

4. Next, we must allocate and initialize a netlink "header" data structure. Among other things, it specifies the source PID and, importantly, the data "payload" that we shall deliver to our kernel component. Here, we are making use of helper macros such as NLMSG_DATA() to specify the correct data location within the netlink header structure:

```
/* 4. Allocate and setup the netlink header (including the payload)
*/
nlhdr = (struct nlmsghdr *)malloc(NLMSG_SPACE(NLSPACE));
memset(nlhdr, 0, NLMSG_SPACE(NLSPACE));
nlhdr->nlmsg_len = NLMSG_SPACE(NLSPACE);
nlhdr->nlmsg_pid = getpid();
/* Setup the payload to transmit */
strncpy(NLMSG_DATA(nlhdr), thedata, strlen(thedata)+1);
```

5. Next, an iovec structure must be initialized to reference the netlink header, and a msghdr data structure must be initialized to point to the destination address and iovec:

```
/* 5. Setup the iovec and ... */
memset(&iov, 0, sizeof(struct iovec));
iov.iov_base = (void *)nlhdr;
iov.iov_len = nlhdr->nlmsg_len;
[...]
/* ... now setup the message header structure */
memset(&msg, 0, sizeof(struct msghdr));
msg.msg_name = (void *)&dest_nl;    // dest addr
msg.msg_namelen = sizeof(dest_nl); // size of dest addr
msg.msg_iov = &iov;
msg.msg_iovlen = 1; // # elements in msg_iov
```

6. Finally, the message is sent (transmitted) via the sendmsg(2) system call (which takes the socket descriptor and the aforementioned msghdr structure as a parameter):

```
/* 6. Actually (finally!) send the message via sendmsg(2) */
nsent = sendmsg(sd, &msg, 0);
```

7. The kernel component – a kernel module, which we shall discuss shortly – should now receive the message via its netlink socket and display the message's content; we arrange for it to then politely reply. To grab the reply, our user space app must now perform a blocking read on the socket:

```
/* 7. Block on incoming msg from the kernel-space netlink component
*/
printf("%s: now blocking on kernel netlink msg via recvmsg()
...\n", argv[0]);
nrecv = recvmsg(sd, &msg, 0);
```

We must employ the `recvmsg(2)` system call to do this. When it gets unblocked, it states that the message has been received.

Why so much abstraction and wrapping for data structures? Well, it's how things often evolve – the `msghdr` structure was created so that the `sendmsg(2)` API can use fewer parameters. But that implies the parameters have to go somewhere; they go deep inside `msghdr`, which points to the destination address and `iovec`, whose `base` member points to the netlink header structure, which contains the payload! Whew.

As an experiment, what if we build and run the user mode netlink application prematurely – *without* the kernel-side code in place? It will fail, of course... But how exactly? Well, use the empirical approach. By trying this out via the venerable `strace(1)` utility, we can see that the `socket(2)` system call returns a failure, the cause being `Protocol not supported`:

```
$ strace -e trace=network ./netlink_userapp
socket(AF_NETLINK, SOCK_RAW, 0x1f /* NETLINK_??? */) = -1 EPROTONOSUPPORT
(Protocol not supported)
netlink_u: netlink socket creation failed: Protocol not supported
+++ exited with 1 +++
$
```

This is correct; there is no such `protocol # 31` (31 = `0x1f`, the protocol number we're using) in place *yet* within the kernel! We're yet to do this. So, that's the user space side of things. Now, let's complete the puzzle and have it actually work! We'll do this by seeing how the kernel component (module/driver) is written.

Writing the kernel-space netlink socket code as a kernel module

The kernel provides the base infrastructure for netlink, including APIs and data structures; all the required ones are exported and thus available to you as a module author. We use several of them; the steps to program our kernel netlink component – our kernel module – are outlined here:

1. Just as with the user space app, the first thing we must do is get ourselves a netlink socket. The kernel API is `netlink_kernel_create()`, and its signature is as follows:

   ```
   struct sock * netlink_kernel_create(struct net *, int , struct
   netlink_kernel_cfg *);
   ```

   The first parameter is a generic network structure; we pass the kernel's existing and valid `init_net` structure here. The second parameter is the *protocol number (unit)* to use; we shall specify the same number (31) as we did for the user space app. The third parameter is a pointer to an (optional) netlink configuration structure; here, we only set the input member to a function of ours nullifying the rest. This function is called back when a user space process (or thread) provides any input (that is, transmits something) to the kernel netlink component. So, within our kernel module's `init` routine, we have the following:

   ```
   //
   ch2/netlink_simple_intf/kernelspace_netlink/netlink_simple_intf.c
   #define OURMODNAME              "netlink_simple_intf"
   #define NETLINK_MY_UNIT_PROTO   31
       // kernel netlink protocol # that we're registering
   static struct sock *nlsock;
   [...]
   static struct netlink_kernel_cfg nl_kernel_cfg = {
       .input = netlink_recv_and_reply,
   };
   [...]
   nlsock = netlink_kernel_create(&init_net, NETLINK_MY_UNIT_PROTO,
           &nl_kernel_cfg);
   ```

2. As we mentioned previously, when a user space process (or thread) provides any input (that is, transmits something) to our kernel (netlink) module or driver, the callback function is invoked. It's important to understand that it runs in the process context and not any kind of interrupt context; we use our `convenient.h:PRINT_CTX()` macro to verify this (we will cover this in Chapter 4, *Handling Hardware Interrupts*, in the *Fully figuring out the context* section). Here, we simply display the received message and then reply by sending a sample message to our user space peer process. The data payload that's transmitted from our user space peer process can be retrieved from the socket buffer structure that is passed along to our callback function as a parameter, from a netlink header structure within it. You can see how the data and sender PID are retrieved here:

```
static void netlink_recv_and_reply(struct sk_buff *skb)
{
    struct nlmsghdr *nlh;
    struct sk_buff *skb_tx;
    char *reply = "Reply from kernel netlink";
    int pid, msgsz, stat;

    /* Find that this code runs in process context, the process
     * (or thread) being the one that issued the sendmsg(2) */
    PRINT_CTX();

    nlh = (struct nlmsghdr *)skb->data;
    pid = nlh->nlmsg_pid; /*pid of sending process */
    pr_info("%s: received from PID %d:\n"
        "\"%s\"\n", OURMODNAME, pid, (char *)NLMSG_DATA(nlh));
```

The *socket buffer* data structure – `struct sk_buff` – is considered the critical data structure within the Linux kernel's network protocol stack. It holds all metadata concerning the network packet, including dynamic pointers to it. It has to be quickly allocated and freed (especially when network code runs in interrupt contexts); this is indeed possible because it's on the kernel's slab (SLUB) cache (see details on the kernel slab allocator in the companion guide *Linux Kernel Programming, Chapters 7, Memory Management Internals - Essentials, Chapter 8, Kernel Memory Allocation for Module Authors – Part 1*, and *Chapter 9, Kernel Memory Allocation for Module Authors – Part 2*).

Now, we need to understand that we can retrieve the payload from the network packet by first dereferencing the `data` member of the socket buffer (`skb`) structure that's passed to our callback routine! Next, this `data` member is actually the pointer to the netlink message header structure that's set up by our user space peer. We then dereference it to get the actual payload.

3. We would now like to "reply" to our user space peer process; doing so involves performing a few actions. First, we must allocate a new netlink message with the `nlmsg_new()` API, which is really a thin wrapper over `alloc_skb()`, add a netlink message to the just allocated socket buffer via the `nlmsg_put()` API, and then copy in the data (the payload) into the netlink header using an appropriate macro (`nlmsg_data()`):

```
//--- Let's be polite and reply
msgsz = strlen(reply);
skb_tx = nlmsg_new(msgsz, 0);
[...]
// Setup the payload
nlh = nlmsg_put(skb_tx, 0, 0, NLMSG_DONE, msgsz, 0);
NETLINK_CB(skb_tx).dst_group = 0; /* unicast only (cb is the
     * skb's control buffer), dest group 0 => unicast */
strncpy(nlmsg_data(nlh), reply, msgsz);
```

4. We send the reply to our user space peer process via the `nlmsg_unicast()` API (even multicasting netlink messages are possible):

```
// Send it
stat = nlmsg_unicast(nlsock, skb_tx, pid);
```

5. That only leaves the cleanup (which is invoked when the kernel module is removed); the `netlink_kernel_release()` API is effectively the inverse of `netlink_kernel_create()` as it cleans up the netlink socket, shutting it down:

```
static void __exit netlink_simple_intf_exit(void)
{
    netlink_kernel_release(nlsock);
    pr_info("%s: removed\n", OURMODNAME);
}
```

Now that we have written both the user space app and the kernel module to interface via a netlink socket, let's actually try it out!

Trying out our netlink interfacing project

It's time to verify it all works as advertised. Let's get started:

1. First, build and insert the kernel module into kernel memory:

> Our `lkm` convenience script makes short work of this; this session was carried out on our familiar x86_64 guest VM running Ubuntu 18.04 LTS and a custom 5.4.0 Linux kernel.

```
$ cd <booksrc>/ch2/netlink_simple_intf/kernelspace_netlink
$ ../../../lkm netlink_simple_intf
Version info:
Distro:     Ubuntu 18.04.4 LTS
Kernel: 5.4.0-llkd01
[...]
make || exit 1
[...] Building for: KREL=5.4.0-llkd01 ARCH=x86 CROSS_COMPILE=
EXTRA_CFLAGS= -DDEBUG
  CC [M]
/home/llkd/booksrc/ch13/netlink_simple_intf/kernelspace_netlink/net
link_simple_intf.o
[...]
sudo insmod ./netlink_simple_intf.ko && lsmod|grep
netlink_simple_intf
-------------------------------
netlink_simple_intf    16384  0
[...]
[58155.082713] netlink_simple_intf: creating kernel netlink socket
[58155.084445] netlink_simple_intf: inserted
$
```

2. With that, it's loaded up and ready. Next, we will build and try out our user space application:

```
$ cd ../userapp_netlink/
$ make netlink_userapp
[...]
```

This results in the following output:

```
$ lsmod |grep netlink_simple_intf
netlink_simple_intf    16384  0
$
$ ../userapp_netlink/netlink_userapp
../userapp_netlink/netlink_userapp:PID 7813: netlink socket created
../userapp_netlink/netlink_userapp: bind done
../userapp_netlink/netlink_userapp: destination struct, netlink hdr, payload setup
../userapp_netlink/netlink_userapp: initialized iov structure (nl header folded in)
../userapp_netlink/netlink_userapp: initialized msghdr structure (iov folded in)
../userapp_netlink/netlink_userapp:sendmsg(): *** success, sent 1040 bytes all-inclusive
(see kernel log for dtl)
../userapp_netlink/netlink_userapp: now blocking on kernel netlink msg via recvmsg() ...
../userapp_netlink/netlink_userapp:recvmsg(): *** success, received 44 bytes:
msg from kernel netlink: "Reply from kernel netlink"
$
$ dmesg
[62818.385716] netlink_simple_intf: creating kernel netlink socket
[62818.389860] netlink_simple_intf: inserted
[62838.889120] netlink_recv_and_reply(): [000] netlink_userapp :7813    | ...0
[62838.900928] netlink_simple_intf: received from PID 7813:
               "sample user data to send to kernel via netlink"
[62838.922712] netlink_simple_intf: reply sent
$ █
```

Figure 2.5 – Screenshot showing user<->kernel communication via our sample netlink socket code

It works; the kernel netlink module receives and displays the message that was sent to it from the user space process (PID 7813). The kernel module then replies with its own message to its user space peer, which successfully receives and displays it (via a printf()). Give it a try yourself. When you're done, don't forget to remove the kernel module with sudo rmmod netlink_simple_intf.

 An aside: a connector driver exists within the kernel. Its purpose is to ease the development of netlink-based communication, making it simpler for both kernel and user space developers set up and use a netlink-based communication interface. We will not delve into this here; please refer to the documentation within the kernel (https://elixir.bootlin.com/linux/v5.4/source/Documentation/driver-api/connector.rst). Some sample code is also provided within the kernel source tree (at samples/connector).

With that, you have learned how to interface between a user mode app and a kernel component via the powerful netlink socket mechanism. As we mentioned earlier, it has several actual use cases within the kernel tree. Now, let's move on and cover one more user-kernel interfacing method, via the popular ioctl(2) system call.

Interfacing via the ioctl system call

ioctl is a system call; why the funny name *ioctl*? It's an abbreviation for **input-output control**. While the read and write system calls (among others) are used to effectively transfer *data* from and to a device (or file; remember the UNIX paradigm *if it's not a process, it's a file!*), the *ioctl* system call is used to *issue commands* to the device (via its driver). For example, changing a console device's terminal characteristics, writing a track to a disk when formatting it, sending a control command to a stepper motor, controlling a camera or audio device, and so on, are all instances of commands being sent to a device.

Let's consider a fictitious example. We have a device and are developing a (character) device driver for it. The device has various *registers*, small – typically 8-, 16-, or 32-bit pieces of hardware memory on the device – some of which are control registers. By appropriately performing I/O (reads and writes) on them, we control the device (well, that's really the whole point, isn't it; the actual subject matter regarding the details of working with hardware memory including device registers will be covered in the next chapter). So, how will you, the driver author, communicate or interface with a user space program that wants to perform various control operations on this device? We often architect the user space C (or C++) program to open the device typically by performing an open(2) on its device file, and subsequently issue the read and write system calls.

But, as we just mentioned, the read(2) and write(2) system call APIs are appropriate when *transferring data* while here, instead, we intend to perform **control operations**. So, we need another system call to do so... Do we then need to create and encode a new system call (or calls)? No, it's much simpler than that: we *multiplex via the ioctl system call,* leveraging it to perform any required control operations upon our device! How? Ah, recall from the previous chapter the all-important file_operations (fops) data structure; we will now initialize another member, the .ioctl one, to our ioctl method function, thus allowing our device driver to hook into this system call:

```
static struct file_operations ioct_intf_fops = {
    .llseek = no_llseek,
    .ioctl = ioct_intf_ioctl,
    [...]
};
```

Realistically, we shall have to figure out whether we should use ioctl or the unlocked_ioctl member of the file_operations structure, depending on whether the module is running on Linux kernel version 2.6.36 or later; more on this follows.

In fact, adding new system calls to the kernel is not something you should do lightly! The kernel chaps are *not* open to arbitrarily adding syscalls – it's a security-sensitive interface, after all. More on this is documented here: https://www.kernel.org/doc/html/latest/kernel-hacking/hacking.html#ioctls-not-writing-a-new-system-call.

More on using ioctl for interfacing follows.

Using ioctl in the user and kernel space

The ioctl(2) system call's signature is as follows:

```
#include <sys/ioctl.h>
int ioctl(int fd, unsigned long request, ...);
```

The parameter list is a *varargs – variable arguments –* one. Realistically and typically, we pass either two or three parameters:

- The first parameter is obvious – the file descriptor of the (in our case) device file that was opened.
- The second parameter, called request, is the interesting one: it's the command to be passed to the driver. In reality, it's an *encoding*, encapsulating a so-called ioctl magic number: a number and a type (read/write).
- The (optional) third parameter, often called arg, is also an unsigned long quantity; we use it to either pass some data in the usual fashion to the underlying driver or, often, to return data to the user space by passing its (virtual) address and having the kernel write into it, utilizing C's so-called **value-result** or **in-out** parameter style.

Now, using ioctl correctly is not as trivial as it is with many other APIs. Think about this for a moment: you can easily have a scenario where several user space apps are issuing ioctl(2) system calls (with various commands being issued) to their underlying device drivers. A problem becomes apparent: how will the kernel VFS layer direct the ioctl request to the correct driver? ioctl is typically performed on a char device file that has a unique *(major, minor)* number; hence, how can another driver receive your ioctl command (unless you intentionally, perhaps maliciously, set up the device file(s) in such a manner)?

Nevertheless, a protocol exists to achieve safe and correct usage of ioctl; every application and driver defines a magic number that will be encoded into all its ioctl requests. First, the driver will verify that every ioctl request it receives contains *its* magic number; only then will it proceed to process it; otherwise, it will simply drop it. This, of course, brings up the need for an *ABI* – we need to allocate unique magic numbers (it could be a range) to each "registered" driver. Since this creates an ABI, the kernel document will be the same; you can find details on who is using which magic number (or code) here: `https://www.kernel.org/doc/Documentation/ioctl/ioctl-number.txt`.

Next, an ioctl request to the underlying driver can be one of essentially four things: a command to "write" to the device, a command to "read" from (or query) the device, a command to do both read/write transfers, or neither. This information is (again) *encoded* into a request by defining certain bits to convey the meaning: to make this job easier, we have four helper macros that allows us to construct ioctl commands:

- `_IO(type,nr)`: Encodes an ioctl command with no argument
- `_IOR(type,nr,datatype)`: Encodes an ioctl command for reading data from the kernel/driver
- `_IOW(type,nr,datatype)`: Encodes an ioctl command for writing data to the kernel/driver
- `_IOWR(type,nr,datatype)`: Encodes an ioctl command for read/write transfers

These macros are defined within the user space `<sys/ioctl.h>` header and in the kernel at `include/uapi/asm-generic/ioctl.h`. The typical (and quite obvious) best practice is to create a *common header* file that defines the ioctl commands for an app/driver and includes that file in both the user mode app, as well as the device driver.

Here, as a demonstration, we shall design and implement a user space app and a kernel space device driver to drive a fictional device that communicates via the `ioctl(2)` system call. Thus, we must define some commands to issue via the *ioctl* interface. We will do this in a common header file, as shown here:

```
// ch2/ioctl_intf/ioctl_llkd.h

/* The 'magic' number for our driver; see Documentation/ioctl/ioctl-
number.rst
 * Of course, we don't know for _sure_ if the magic # we choose here this
 * will remain free; it really doesn't matter, this is just for demo
purposes;
 * don't try and upstream this without further investigation :-)
 */
#define IOCTL_LLKD_MAGIC        0xA8
```

```
#define IOCTL_LLKD_MAXIOCTL        3
/* our dummy ioctl (IOC) RESET command */
#define IOCTL_LLKD_IOCRESET     _IO(IOCTL_LLKD_MAGIC, 0)
/* our dummy ioctl (IOC) Query POWER command */
#define IOCTL_LLKD_IOCQPOWER    _IOR(IOCTL_LLKD_MAGIC, 1, int)
/* our dummy ioctl (IOC) Set POWER command */
#define IOCTL_LLKD_IOCSPOWER    _IOW(IOCTL_LLKD_MAGIC, 2, int)
```

We must try and make the names we use in our macros meaningful. Our three commands (highlighted in bold) are all prefixed with IOCTL_LLKD_, indicating that they are all ioctl commands for our fictitious LLKD project; next, they are suffixed with IOC{Q|S}, with IOC implying that it's an ioctl command, Q implying it's a query operation, and S implying it's a set operation.

Now, let's learn how we set things up at the code level from both the user space as well as the kernel space (driver).

User space – using the ioctl system call

The *user space* signature of the ioctl(2) system call is as follows:

```
#include <sys/ioctl.h>
int ioctl(int fd, unsigned long request, ...);
```

Here, we can see that it takes a variable argument list; the arguments to ioctl are as follows:

- **First parameter**: The file descriptor of the file or device (as it will be in our case) to perform the ioctl operation on (we get fd by performing an *open* on the device file).
- **Second parameter**: The request or command being issued to the underlying device driver (or filesystem or whatever fd represents).
- **An optional third (or more) parameter(s)**: Often, the third parameter is an integer (or a pointer to an integer or data structure); we use this method to either pass some additional information to the driver, when issuing a *set* kind of command, or to retrieve some information from the driver via the well-understood *pass-by-reference* C paradigm, where we pass the pointer and have the driver "poke" it, thus treating the parameter as, in effect, a return value.

In effect, ioctl is often used as a *generic* system call. The use of ioctl to perform command operations on both hardware and software is almost embarrassingly large! Please refer to the kernel documentation (`Documentation/ioctl/<...>`) to see many actual real-world examples. For example, you will find details on who is using which magic number (or code) within ioctl here: `https://www.kernel.org/doc/Documentation/ioctl/ioctl-number.txt`.

(Similarly, the `ioctl_list(2)` man page reveals the complete list of ioctl calls in the x86 kernel; these documentation files seem to be pretty old, though. The docs now seem to be here: `https://github.com/torvalds/linux/tree/master/Documentation/userspace-api/ioctl`.)

Let's look at some snippets of the user space C application, particularly when it comes to issuing the `ioctl(2)` system calls (for brevity and readability, we have left out the error checking code; the full code is available in this book's GitHub repository):

```c
// ch2/ioctl_intf/user space_ioctl/ioctl_llkd_userspace.c
#include "../ioctl_llkd.h"
[...]
ioctl(fd, IOCTL_LLKD_IOCRESET, 0);    // 1. reset the device
ioctl(fd, IOCTL_LLKD_IOCQPOWER, &power); // 2. query the 'power status'

// 3. Toggle it's power status
if (0 == power) {
        printf("%s: Device OFF, powering it On now ...\n", argv[0]);
        if (ioctl(fd, IOCTL_LLKD_IOCSPOWER, 1) == -1) { [...]
        printf("%s: power is ON now.\n", argv[0]);
    } else if (1 == power) {
        printf("%s: Device ON, powering it OFF in 3s ...\n", argv[0]);
        sleep(3); /* yes, careful here of sleep & signals! */
        if (ioctl(fd, IOCTL_LLKD_IOCSPOWER, 0) == -1) { [...]
        printf("%s: power OFF ok, exiting..\n", argv[0]);
    }
[...]
```

How does our driver handle these user space-issued ioctls? Let's find out.

Kernel space – using the ioctl system call

In the previous section, we saw that the kernel driver will have to initialize its
`file_operations` structure to include the `ioctl` method. There is more to this, though:
the Linux kernel keeps evolving; in early kernel versions, the developers used a very coarse
granularity lock that, though it worked, quite severely hurt its performance (we will
discuss locking in detail in Chapter 6, *Kernel Synchronization - Part 1*, and Chapter 7, *Kernel
Synchronization - Part 2*). It was so bad that it was nicknamed the **Big Kernel Lock**
(**BKL**)! The good news is that by kernel release 2.6.36, the developers got rid of this
infamous lock. Doing so had some side effects, though: one of them was that the number of
parameters that get sent to the ioctl method within the kernel and thus within our
`file_operations` data structure changed from four to three with the newer method –
christened `unlocked_ioctl`. Thus, for our demo driver, we will initialize the *ioctl* method
with the following when initializing our driver's `file_operations` structure:

```
// ch2/ioctl_intf/kerneldrv_ioctl/ioctl_llkd_kdrv.c
#include "../ioctl_llkd.h"
#include <linux/version.h>
[...]
static struct file_operations ioctl_intf_fops = {
    .llseek = no_llseek,
#if LINUX_VERSION_CODE >= KERNEL_VERSION(2, 6, 36)
    .unlocked_ioctl = ioctl_intf_ioctl, // use the 'unlocked' version
#else
    .ioctl = ioctl_intf_ioctl, // 'old' way
#endif
};
```

Clearly, as it's defined within the fops driver, ioctl is considered a private driver interface
(`driver-private`). Also, this same fact regarding the newer "unlocked" version has to be
taken into account in the function definition within the driver code; our driver does so:

```
#if LINUX_VERSION_CODE >= KERNEL_VERSION(2, 6, 36)
static long ioctl_intf_ioctl(struct file *filp, unsigned int cmd, unsigned
long arg)
#else
static int ioctl_intf_ioctl(struct inode *ino, struct file *filp, unsigned
int cmd, unsigned long arg)
#endif
{
[...]
```

The key code here is the driver's ioctl method. Think about it: once basic validity checks have been done, all the driver really does is perform a *switch-case* on all possible valid ioctl commands issued by the user space app. Let's take a look at the following code (for readability, we will skip the #if LINUX_VERSION_CODE >= ... macro directive and just show the modern ioctl function signature, as well as some validity checks; you can view the full code in this book's GitHub repository):

```
static long ioctl_intf_ioctl(struct file *filp, unsigned int cmd, unsigned
long arg)
{
    int retval = 0;
    pr_debug("In ioctl method, cmd=%d\n", _IOC_NR(cmd));

    /* Verify stuff: is the ioctl's for us? etc.. */
    [...]

    switch (cmd) {
    case IOCTL_LLKD_IOCRESET:
        pr_debug("In ioctl cmd option: IOCTL_LLKD_IOCRESET\n");
        /* ... Insert the code here to write to a control register to reset
           the device ... */
        break;
    case IOCTL_LLKD_IOCQPOWER:  /* Get: arg is pointer to result */
        pr_debug("In ioctl cmd option: IOCTL_LLKD_IOCQPOWER\n"
            "arg=0x%x (drv) power=%d\n", (unsigned int)arg, power);
        if (!capable(CAP_SYS_ADMIN))
            return -EPERM;
        /* ... Insert the code here to read a status register to query the
         * power state of the device ... * here, imagine we've done that
         * and placed it into a variable 'power'
         */
        retval = __put_user(power, (int __user *)arg);
        break;
    case IOCTL_LLKD_IOCSPOWER:  /* Set: arg is the value to set */
        if (!capable(CAP_SYS_ADMIN))
            return -EPERM;
        power = arg;
        /* ... Insert the code here to write a control register to set the
         * power state of the device ... */
        pr_debug("In ioctl cmd option: IOCTL_LLKD_IOCSPOWER\n"
            "power=%d now.\n", power);
        break;
    default:
        return -ENOTTY;
    }
    [...]
```

The `_IOC_NR` macro is used to extract the command number from the `cmd` parameter. Here, we can see that the driver "reacts" to three valid cases of the `ioctl` issued via the user space process:

- On receiving the `IOCTL_LLKD_IOC`**RESET** command, it performs a device reset.
- On receiving the `IOCTL_LLKD_IOC`**Q**`POWER` command, it queries (`Q` for query) and returns the current power status (by poking its value into the third parameter, `arg`, using the *value-result* C programming approach).
- On receiving the `IOCTL_LLKD_IOC`**S**`POWER` command, it sets (`S` for set) the power status (to the value passed in the third parameter, `arg`).

Of course, since we're working with a purely fictional device, our driver does not actually perform any register (or other hardware) work. This driver is simply a template that you can make use of.

What if a hacker attempts to issue a command unknown to our driver in a (rather clumsy) hack? Well, the initial validity checks will catch it; even if they don't, we shall hit the `default` case in our *ioctl* method, resulting in the driver returning `-ENOTTY` to the user space. This will, via glibc "glue" code, set the user space process (or thread's) `errno` value to `ENOTTY`, informing it that the ioctl method cannot be serviced. Our user space `perror(3)` API will display the `Inappropriate ioctl for device` error message. In fact, this is precisely what occurs if a driver has *no* ioctl method (that is, if the ioctl member within the `file_operations` structure is set to `NULL`) and a user space app issues an `ioctl` method against it.

I leave it to you to try out this user space/driver project example; for convenience, once the driver has been loaded (via insmod), you can use the `ch2/userspace_ioctl/cr8devnode.sh` convenience script to generate the device file. Once it's set up, run the user space app; you will find that running it in succession has the "power state" of our fictional device get repeatedly toggled.

ioctl as a debug interface

As we mentioned at the beginning of this chapter, what about using the *ioctl* interface for debug purposes? It can be used for this purpose. You can always insert a "debug" command into the *switch-case* block; it can be used to provide useful information to the user space application on the driver status, the values of key variables (health monitoring too), and more.

Not only that, but unless it's explicitly documented to the end user or customer, the precise commands that are used via the ioctl interface are unknown; thus, you are expected to document the interface while providing sufficient detail for other teams or the customer to make good use of them. This leads to an interesting point: you might choose to deliberately leave a certain ioctl command undocumented; it's now a "hidden" command that can be used by, say, field engineers to examine the device. (I leave doing this as an assignment to you.)

The kernel documentation on ioctl includes this file: `https://www.kernel.org/doc/Documentation/ioctl/botching-up-ioctls.txt`. Though biased toward kernel graphics stack devs, it describes typical design mistakes, trade-offs, and more.

Fantastic – you're almost done! You have learned how to interface a kernel module or driver with a user mode process or thread (within a user space application) via various technologies. We began with procfs, then moved on to using sysfs and debugfs. The netlink socket and the ioctl system call completed our look at these interfacing methods.

But with all this choice, which one should you actually use on a project? The next section will help you make this decision by providing a quick comparison between these various interfacing methods.

Comparing the interfacing methods – a table

In this section, we have created a quick comparison table of the various user-kernel interfacing methods that were described in this chapter, based on a few parameters:

Parameter /Interfacing method	procfs	sysfs	debugfs	netlink socket	ioctl
Ease of development	Easy to learn and use.	(Relatively) easy to learn and use.	(Very) easy to learn and use.	Harder; have to write user space C + driver code + understand socket APIs.	Fair/harder; have to write user space C + driver code.

Appropriate for what use	Core kernel *only* (a few older drivers may still use it); best avoided by drivers.	Device driver interfacing.	Driver (and other) interfacing for production and debug purposes.	Various interfacing: users include device drivers, core networking code, the udev system, and more.	Device driver interfacing mostly (includes many).
Interface visibility	Visible to all; use permissions to control access.	Visible to all; use permissions to control access.	Visible to all; use permissions to control access.	Hidden from the filesystem; doesn't pollute the kernel namespace.	Hidden from the filesystem; doesn't pollute the kernel namespace.
Upstream kernel ABI for driver/module authors*	Usage in drivers is deprecated for mainline.	The "right way"; the formally accepted approach to interface drivers with user space.	Well supported and heavily used in mainline by drivers and other products.	Well supported (since 2.2).	Well supported.
Useful for (driver) debugging purposes	Yes (although not supposed to in mainline).	No/not ideal.	Yes, very useful! "No rules" by design.	No/not ideal.	Yes; (even) via hidden commands.

* As we mentioned earlier, the kernel community documents that procfs, sysfs, and debugfs are all *ABIs;* their stability and lifespan isn't guaranteed. While that is the formal stance adopted by the community, the reality is that plenty of actual interfaces that use these filesystems have become de facto ones used by products in the real world. Nevertheless, we should follow the kernel community's "rules" and guidelines regarding their usage.

Summary

In this chapter, we covered an important aspect of device driver authors – how exactly you can *interface between user and kernel (driver) space.* We walked you through several interfacing methods; we began with an older one, which is interfacing via the venerable proc filesystem (and then mentioned why it's not the preferred method for driver authors). We then moved on to interfacing via the newer 2.6-based *sysfs.* This turns out to be *the* preferred interface for the user space, at least for a device driver. Sysfs has limitations, though (recall the one-value-per-sysfs-file rule). Thus, using the completely free-format *debugfs* interfacing technique makes writing debug (and other) interfaces very simple and powerful indeed. The netlink socket is a powerful interfacing technology and is used by the network subsystem, udev, and a few drivers; it does require some knowledge on socket programming and the kernel socket buffer, though. To perform generic command operations on device drivers, the ioctl system call turns out to be a tremendous multiplexer and is often used by device driver authors (and other components) to interface with the user space.

Armed with this knowledge, you are now in a position to practically integrate your driver-level code with user space applications (or scripts); often, a user mode **graphical user interface (GUI)** will want to display some values that have been received from the kernel or device driver. You now know how to pass these values from the kernel space device driver!

In the next chapter, you will learn about a typical task driver authors must perform: working with hardware chip memory! Do ensure you're clear on this chapter's material, work on the exercises provided, review the *Further reading* resources, and then dive into the next chapter. See you there!

Questions

1. `sysfs_on_misc`: *sysfs assignment #1*: Extend one of the `misc` device drivers we wrote in `Chapter 1`, *Writing a Simple misc Character Device Driver*; set up two sysfs files and their read/write callbacks; test them from user space.

2. `sysfs_addrxlate`: *sysfs assignment #2 (a bit more advanced)*: *Address translation:* Exploiting the knowledge gained from this chapter and from the *Linux Kernel Programming* book, *Chapter 7, Memory Management Internals - Essentials*, the *Direct-mapped RAM and address translation* section, write a simple platform driver that provides two sysfs interface files called `addrxlate_kva2pa` and `addrxlate_pa2kva`. Writing a kva into the sysfs file, `addrxlate_kva2pa`, should have the driver read and translate the *kva* into its corresponding **physical address (pa)**; then, reading from the same file should cause the *pa* to be displayed. Do the same with the `addrxlate_pa2kva` sysfs file.

3. `dbgfs_disp_pgoff`: *debugfs assignment #1*: Write a kernel module that sets up a debugfs file here: `<debugfs_mount_point>/dbgfs_disp_pgoff`. When read, it should display (to user space) the current value of the `PAGE_OFFSET` kernel macro.

4. `dbgfs_showall_threads`: *debugfs assignment #2* : Write a kernel module that sets up a debugfs file here: `<debugfs_mount_point>/dbgfs_showall_threads/dbgfs_showall_threads`. When read, it should display some attributes of every thread that's alive. (This is similar to our code from the *Linux Kernel Programming* book here: `https://github.com/PacktPublishing/Linux-Kernel-Programming/tree/master/ch6/foreach/thrd_showall`. Note that the threads are displayed *only* at insmod time; with a debugfs file, you can display information on all the threads at any time you choose to)!
Suggested output is CSV format: `TGID,PID,current,stack-start,name,#threads`. The `[name]` field in square brackets => kernel thread; `#threads` field should only display a positive integer; no output here implies a single-threaded process; for example: `130,130,0xffff9f8b3cd38000,0xffffc13280420000,[watchdogd])`

5. *ioctl assignment #1*: Using the provided `ch2/ioctl_intf/` code as a template, write a user space C application and a kernel space (char) device driver implementing the `ioctl` method. Add an ioctl command called `IOCTL_LLKD_IOCQPGOFF` to return the value of `PAGE_OFFSET` (within the kernel) to the user space.

6. `ioctl_undoc`: *ioctl assignment #2*: Using the provided `ch2/ioctl_intf/` code as a template, write a user space C application and a kernel space (char) device driver implementing the `ioctl` method. Add a driver context data structure (we used these in several examples), and then allocate and initialize it. Now, in addition to the three previous ioctl commands we used, set up a fourth undocumented command (you can call it `IOCTL_LLKD_IOCQDRVSTAT`). When queried from the user space via `ioctl(2)`, it must return the contents of the driver context data structure to the user space; the user space C app must print out the current content of every member of that structure.

 You will find some of the questions answered in the book's GitHub repo: `https://github.com/PacktPublishing/Linux-Kernel-Programming-Part-2/tree/main/solutions_to_assgn`.

Further reading

You can refer to the following links for more information on the topics covered in this chapter. Some more information on using the very common I2C protocol within a Linux device driver can be found here:

- An article on the I2C protocol basics: *How to use I2C in STM32F103C8T6? STM32 I2C Tutorial*, March 2020: `https://www.electronicshub.org/how-to-use-i2c-in-stm32f103c8t6/`

- Kernel documentation: Implementing I2C device drivers: `https://www.kernel.org/doc/html/latest/i2c/writing-clients.html`

Working with Hardware I/O Memory

In this chapter, we will focus on an important hardware-related aspect of writing a device driver: how exactly to access and perform I/O (input/output, reads and writes) to hardware (or peripheral) I/O memory – the peripheral hardware chip that you are writing the driver for.

The motivation behind the knowledge you will gain in this chapter is straightforward: without this, how will you actually control the device? Most devices are driven by carefully calibrated writes and reads to their hardware registers and/or peripheral memory, also called hardware I/O memory. Linux, being a virtual memory-based OS, requires some abstraction in the way it works with peripheral I/O memory.

In this chapter, we will cover the following topics:

- Accessing hardware I/O memory from the kernel
- Understanding and using memory-mapped I/O
- Understanding and using port-mapped I/O

Let's get started!

Technical requirements

I assume that you have gone through the *Preface* section *To get the most out of this book* and have appropriately prepared a guest VM running Ubuntu 18.04 LTS (or a later stable release) and installed all the required packages. If not, I highly recommend you do this first. To get the most out of this book, I strongly recommend you first set up the workspace environment, including cloning this book's GitHub repository for the code, and work on it in a hands-on fashion. The repository can be found here: `https://github.com/PacktPublishing/Linux-Kernel-Programming-Part-2`.

Accessing hardware I/O memory from the kernel

An interesting issue that you, as a device driver author, will likely face is this: you need to be able to access and work on the I/O memory, the hardware registers, and/or hardware memory of a peripheral chip. This is, in fact, typically the way in which the driver programs the hardware at the level of the "metal": by issuing commands to it via its registers and/or peripheral memory. However, there is an issue to be faced with directly accessing hardware I/O memory on Linux. In this first section, we'll take a look at this issue and provide a solution for it.

Understanding the issue with direct access

Now, of course, this hardware memory on the chip, the so-called I/O memory, is not RAM. The Linux kernel refuses the module or driver author direct access to such hardware I/O memory locations. We already know why: on a modern VM-based OS, all memory access has to be via the **Memory Management Unit (MMU)** and paging tables.

Let's quickly summarize the key aspect of what was seen in the companion guide *Linux Kernel Programming* in *Chapter 7, Memory Management Internals – Essentials*: by default, memory is virtualized, which means that all addresses are virtual and not physical (this includes the addresses within the kernel segment or VAS). Think of it this way: once a virtual address is accessed by a process (or the kernel) for reading or writing or execution, the system has to fetch the memory content at the corresponding physical address. This involves translating the virtual address to the physical address at runtime; hardware optimizations (the CPU caches, **Translation Lookaside Buffers** (TLBs), and so on) can speed this up. The process that is carried out is as follows:

1. First, the CPU caches (L1-D/L1-I, L2, and so on) are checked to see whether the memory referred to by this virtual address is already onboard the CPU cache(s) silicon.
2. If the memory is already onboard, we have a cache hit and the work is done. If not (it's a **Last Level Cache—LLC** miss - expensive!), the virtual address is fed to the microprocessor MMU.
3. The MMU now looks for the corresponding physical address within the processor TLB(s). If it's there, we have a TLB hit and the work is done; if not, we have a TLB miss (this is expensive!).

4. The MMU now walks the paging tables of the user space process that made the access; or, if the kernel made the access, it walks the kernel paging tables, translating the virtual address into the corresponding physical one. At this point, the physical address is placed on the bus and the work is done.

> Please refer to TI's *Technical Reference Manual* for the OMAP35x at `https:/`
> `/www.ti.com/lit/ug/spruf98y/spruf98y.pdf?ts=1594376085647` for
> more information on this; the *MMU Functional Description* topic (page 946)
> is illustrated with excellent diagrams (for our purpose, see *Figures 8.4, 8.6,*
> and *8.7* – the latter is a flowchart depicting the preceding procedures).
>
> Also, we mention the fact that the actual address translation procedure is
> of course very arch-dependent. On some systems, the order is as shown
> here; on others (often on ARM), the MMU (including TLB lookups) is
> performed first, and then the CPU caches are checked.

So, think about this: even normal RAM locations aren't really directly accessed by software running on a modern OS; this is because its memory is virtualized. In such cases, the paging tables (of every process, as well as the kernel itself) enable the OS to be able to runtime translate the virtual address to its physical counterpart. (We have covered these areas in some detail in our companion book, *Linux Kernel Programming*, in *Chapter 7, Memory Management Internals – Essentials*, in the *Virtual addressing and address translation* section; do glance back at it to refresh these key points if you need to.)

Now, if we have a hardware peripheral or chip containing I/O memory, the issue seems even more complicated if we consider the fact that this memory isn't RAM. So, is this memory not being mapped by paging tables? Or is it? In the next section, we'll look at two common solutions to this issue, so read on!

The solution – mapping via I/O memory or I/O port

In order to solve this issue, we must understand that modern processors provide two broad ways by which they can access and work with hardware I/O (peripheral chip) memory:

*   By reserving some region(s) of the processor's address space for these peripheral devices; that is, by using **memory-mapped I/O (MMIO)** as a mapping type for I/O.

- By providing distinct assembly (and the corresponding machine) CPU instructions to directly access the I/O memory. Using such a mapping type for I/O is called **port-mapped I/O** (**PMIO** or simply **PIO**).

We shall consider both of these techniques in the *Understanding and using memory-mapped I/O* and *Understanding and using port-mapped I/O* sections, respectively. Before we do that, though, we need to learn how to politely ask the kernel for permission to use these I/O resources!

Asking the kernel's permission

Think about this for a moment: even if you know which API(s) to use to map or work upon I/O memory in some manner, first, you need to request permission from the OS. After all, the OS is the system's overall resource manager and you must ask it nicely before using its resources. Well, there's more to this, of course – when you ask it, what you're really doing is asking it to set up some internal data structures that allow the kernel to understand which driver or subsystem is using what I/O memory region or port.

Before performing any peripheral I/O, you are expected to ask the kernel for permission to do so, and assuming you get it, you perform the I/O. After this, you are expected to release the I/O region back to the kernel. The following steps are involved in this process:

1. **Before I/O**: Request access to the memory or port region.
2. **Having received the green light from the kernel core, perform the actual I/O**: You use either MMIO or PMIO to do this (details are provided in the following table).
3. **After I/O**: Release the memory or port region back to the OS.

So, how do you perform these request, I/O, and release operations? There are APIs that can do this, and the ones you should use depend on whether you are using MMIO or PMIO. The following table summarizes the APIs you should use before performing I/O and then releasing the region after this work has been done (the actual APIs that perform I/O will be covered later):

Method of access to I/O memory	MMIO	PMIO
Before performing any I/O, request access to the I/O memory/port region.	`request_mem_region()`	`request_region()`
Perform the I/O operation.	(See the *MMIO – performing the actual I/O* section)	(See the *PMIO – performing the actual I/O* section)

| After performing the I/O operation, release the region. | `release_mem_region()` | `release_region()` |

The functions shown in the preceding table are defined as macros in the `linux/ioport.h` header; their signatures are as follows:

```
request_mem_region(start, n, name);  [...] ; release_mem_region(start, n);
request_region(start, n, name);      [...] ; release_region(start, n);
```

All these macros are essentially wrappers over the `__request_region()` and `__release_region()` internal APIs. The parameters for these macros are as follows:

- `start` is the beginning of the I/O memory region or port; for MMIO, it's a physical (or bus) address, while for PMIO, it's a port number.
- `n` is the length of the region that's being requested.
- `name` is any name you'd like to associate the mapped region or port range with. It's usually the name of the driver that performs the I/O operation (you can see it within the proc filesystem; we'll look at this in more detail when we cover how to use MMIO and PMIO).

The return value from the `request_[mem_]region()` APIs/macros is a pointer to a `struct resource` (again, more on this in the *Obtaining the device resources* section). If `NULL` is returned, this implies that the resource failed to be reserved; the driver typically returns –`EBUSY`, signaling that the resource is now busy or unavailable (possibly because another component/driver has already requested and is currently using it).

We will provide some actual examples of using these APIs/macros in the coming sections. Now, let's learn how to actually map and work with I/O memory. We will begin with the common approach that pretty much all modern processors support; that is, MMIO.

Understanding and using memory-mapped I/O

In the MMIO approach, the CPU understands that a certain region (or several) of its address space is reserved for I/O peripheral memory. You can actually look up the region(s) by referring to the physical memory map of a given processor's (or SoC's) datasheet.

To help make this clearer, let's take a look at a real example: the Raspberry Pi. As you'll be aware, this popular board uses a Broadcom BCM2835 (or later) SoC. The *BCM2835 ARM Peripherals* document at `https://github.com/raspberrypi/documentation/blob/master/hardware/raspberrypi/bcm2835/BCM2835-ARM-Peripherals.pdf`, on *page 90*, provides a screenshot of a small portion of its physical memory map. The mapping of the SoC's **General Purpose Input/Output (GPIO)** registers shows a portion of the hardware I/O memory in the processor's address space:

6.1   Register View

The GPIO has 41 registers. All accesses are assumed to be 32-bit.

Address	Field Name	Description	Size	Read/Write
0x 7E20 0000	GPFSEL0	GPIO Function Select 0	32	R/W
0x 7E20 0000	GPFSEL0	GPIO Function Select 0	32	R/W
0x 7E20 0004	GPFSEL1	GPIO Function Select 1	32	R/W
0x 7E20 0008	GPFSEL2	GPIO Function Select 2	32	R/W
0x 7E20 000C	GPFSEL3	GPIO Function Select 3	32	R/W
0x 7E20 0010	GPFSEL4	GPIO Function Select 4	32	R/W
0x 7E20 0014	GPFSEL5	GPIO Function Select 5	32	R/W
0x 7E20 0018	-	Reserved	-	-
0x 7E20 001C	GPSET0	GPIO Pin Output Set 0	32	W
0x 7E20 0020	GPSET1	GPIO Pin Output Set 1	32	W

Figure 3.1 – Physical memory map on the BCM2835 showing the GPIO register bank

Well, the reality is more complex; the BCM2835 SoC has multiple MMUs: one – the VC/ARM MMU (**VC** stands for **VideoCore** here) – translates the ARM bus address into the ARM physical address, after which the regular ARM MMU translates the physical address into a virtual address. Take a look at the diagram on *page 5* of the aforementioned *BCM2835 ARM Peripherals* document to see this.

As we can see, this is a register block (or bank), a collection of 32-bit registers serving a similar purpose (here, GPIO). In the preceding figure, the crucial column for our current purpose is the first one, which is the **Address** column: this is the physical or bus address and is the location in the ARM processor's physical address space where it sees the GPIO registers. It begins at `0x7e20 0000` (as that's the very first address in the preceding screenshot) and has a finite length (here, it's documented as having 41 registers of 32 bits each, so we'll take the length of the region as *41 * 4* bytes).

Using the ioremap*() APIs

Now, as we saw in the *Understanding the issue with direct access* section, attempting to perform I/O directly on these physical or bus addresses simply won't work. The way we should do this is by telling Linux to **map** these bus addresses into the kernel's VAS so that we can access it through **kernel virtual addresses (KVAs)**! How do we do this? The kernel provides APIs for this express purpose; a very common one that driver authors use is the `ioremap()` API. Its signature is as follows:

```
#include <asm/io.h>
void __iomem *ioremap(phys_addr_t offset, size_t size)
```

The `asm/io.h` header becomes an arch-specific header file as required. Notice how the first parameter to `ioremap()` is a physical (or bus) address (it's data type is `phys_addr_t`). This is one of the rare cases in Linux where you, as a driver author, have to supply a physical – not a virtual – address (the other typical case being when performing **Direct Memory Access (DMA)** operations). The second parameter is obvious; this is the size or length of the memory I/O region we must map. When invoked, the `ioremap()` routine will map the I/O chip or peripheral memory starting from `offset` for a length of `size` bytes into the kernel's VAS! This is necessary - running with kernel privilege, your driver can now access this I/O memory region via the return pointer and thus perform I/O on the memory region.

 Think about it! Just like the `mmap()` system call allows you to memory map a region of KVA space to a user space process, the `[devm_]ioremap*()` (and friends) APIs allow you to map a region of peripheral I/O memory to the KVA space.

The `ioremap()` API returns a KVA of the `void *` type (since it's an address location). So, what's the peculiar-looking `__iomem` directive here (`void __iomem *`)? It's simply a compiler attribute that is wiped away at build time; it's merely there to remind us humans (as well as to perform sanity checking or look at static analysis code) that this is an I/O address and not your regular RAM address!

So, for the preceding example, on a Raspberry Pi device, you can map the GPIO register bank to a KVA by doing the following (this isn't the actual code, but an example to show you how `ioremap()` API can be invoked):

```
#define GPIO_REG_BASE      0x7e200000
#define GPIO_REG_LEN       164     // 41 * 4
static void __iomem *iobase;
[...]
if (!request_mem_region(GPIO_REG_BASE, GPIO_REG_LEN, "mydriver")) {
    dev_warn(dev, "couldn't get region for MMIO, aborting\n");
    return -EBUSY;    // or -EINVAL, as appropriate
}
iobase = ioremap(GPIO_REG_BASE, GPIO_REG_LEN);
if (!iobase) // handle any error
    [... perform the required IO ... ]
iounmap(iobase);
release_mem_region(GPIO_REG_BASE, GPIO_REG_LEN);
```

The `iobase` variable now holds the return value from `ioremap()`; it's a KVA, a kernel virtual address. You can now use it, as long as it's non-NULL (you are expected to verify this!). So, in this example, the return value from the `ioremap()` is the place in kernel VAS where the GPIO registers (the peripheral I/O memory) of the Raspberry Pi is now mapped and available.

Once done, you're expected to unmap the mapping (as can be seen in the preceding code fragment) using the `iounmap()` API; the parameter to the `iounmap()` API is obvious - the start of the I/O mapping (the value returned by the `ioremap()`):

```
void iounmap(volatile void __iomem *io_addr);
```

So, when we map the (GPIO registers) I/O memory into kernel VAS, we get a KVA so that we can work with it. Interestingly, the return value from the `ioremap()` API is typically an address within the *vmalloc* region of the kernel VAS (refer back to the companion guide *Linux Kernel Programming* - Chapter 7, *Memory Management Internals – Essentials*, for these details). This is because `ioremap` usually allocates and uses the required virtual memory for mapping from the kernel's vmalloc region (this is not always the case though; variants such as `ioremap_cache()` can use a region outside the vmalloc one). Here, let's say the return value – our `iobase` address – is `0xbbed 8000` (refer to Figure 3.2: with a 2:2 GB VM split here, you can see that the `iobase` return address is indeed a KVA within the kernel's vmalloc region).

The following is a conceptual diagram showing this:

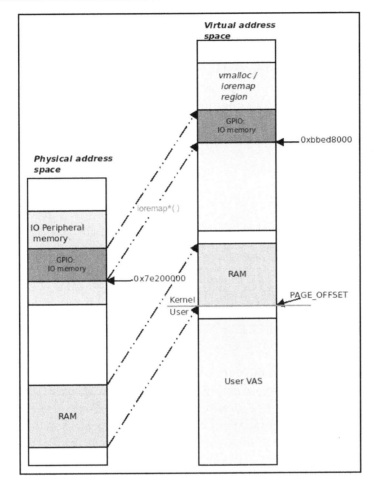

Figure 3.2 – The physical-to-virtual mapping of I/O peripheral memory

Comparing the preceding diagram (*Figure 3.2*) with our detailed diagram of kernel VAS on the Raspberry Pi, which we covered in the companion guide *Linux Kernel Programming* in *Chapter 7, Memory Management Internals - Essentials* (*Figure 7.12*), is something interesting to do.

(It's also educative to see a similar diagram showing the physical/virtual mapping of the memory on the Aarch64 or ARM64 processor; you can look it up in the official ARM documentation; that is, *ARM Cortex-A Series Programmer's Guide for ARMv8-A*, under the *The Memory Management Unit* section – check out *Figure 12.2:* https://developer.arm.com/documentation/den0024/a/The-Memory-Management-Unit.)

The newer breed – the devm_* managed APIs

Now that you understand how to use the `request_mem_region()` and the just-seen `ioremap*()` APIs, guess what? The reality is that both these APIs are now considered deprecated; as a modern driver author, you're expected to use the better resource-managed `devm_*` APIs. (We covered the older ones for a few reasons, including the fact that many older drivers still very much use them, for understanding the basics of using the `ioremap()` resource management APIs, and for completeness.)

First, let's check out the new resource-managed ioremap, known as `devm_ioremap()`, in `lib/devres.c`:

```
/**
 * devm_ioremap - Managed ioremap()
 * @dev: Generic device to remap IO address for
 * @offset: Resource address to map
 * @size: Size of map
 *
 * Managed ioremap(). Map is automatically unmapped on driver detach.
 */
void __iomem *devm_ioremap(struct device *dev, resource_size_t offset,
                resource_size_t size)
```

Just as we learned with regard to the very common `kmalloc/kzalloc` APIs (refer to the companion guide *Linux Kernel Programming, Chapter 8, Kernel Memory Allocation for Module Authors – Part 1*), the `devm_kmalloc()` and the `devm_kzalloc()` APIs simplify life for us as they guarantee that they'll free the memory that's been allocated on device detach or driver removal. In a similar fashion, using `devm_ioremap()` implies that you don't need to explicitly invoke the `iounmap()` API since the kernel's *devres* framework will handle it upon driver detach!

 Again, since this book is not primarily focused on writing device drivers, we shall mention bit not delve into deep details of using the modern **Linux Device Model (LDM)** with the `probe()` and `remove()/disconnect()` hooks. Other literature dedicated to this subject can be found in the *Further reading* section, at the end of this chapter.

Note that the first parameter of any `devm_*()` API is the pointer to `struct device` (we showed you how to obtain this in `Chapter 1`, *Writing a Simple misc Character Device Driver*, when we covered how to write a simple `misc` driver).

Obtaining the device resources

The second parameter of the `devm_ioremap()` API (see its signature in the preceding section) is `resource_size_t offset`. The formal parameter name `offset` is a bit misleading – it's really the physical or bus address of the peripheral I/O memory region that's used to remap to kernel VAS (in fact, the `resource_size_t` data type is nothing but a `typedef` for `phys_addr_t`, a physical address).

> This and the following section's coverage is **important for Linux device driver authors** since it introduces some key ideas (the **Device Tree (DT)**, the platform and `devres` APIs, and so on) and encompasses some very common strategies that are employed.

But how will you obtain this first parameter to the `devm_ioremap()` API - the bus or physical address? An FAQ indeed! Well, of course, this is very device-specific. Having said that, the starting bus or physical address is just one of several I/O resources that the driver author can – and at times, must – specify. The Linux kernel provides a powerful framework – the **I/O resource management** framework – for exactly this purpose in that it allows you to get/set hardware resources.

> There are several kinds of resources available; it includes device MMIO ranges, I/O port ranges, **interrupt request (IRQ)** lines, register offsets, DMAs, and bus values.

Now, in order for all this to work, the I/O resources have to be specified on a per-device basis. There are two broad ways in which this is done:

- **The traditional approach**: By hard-coding them (the I/O resources) into the kernel source tree in what's often called board-specific files. (For example, for the popular ARM CPU, these are typically found at `arch/arm/mach->foo/...`, where `foo` is the machine (`mach`) or platform/board name. As a further example, the number of platform devices defined within these board-specific files was 1,670 with Linux 3.10.6; migrating to the modern DT approach has had this number reduce to 885 for the 5.4.0 kernel source tree.)

- **The modern approach**: By placing them (the I/O resources) in a way that they can be discovered at boot by the OS; this is usually done for embedded systems, such as ARM-32, AArch64, and PPC, by describing the hardware topology of a board or platform (all the hardware stuff on it, such as the SoC, CPUs, peripherals, disks, flash chips, sensor chips, and so on) via a hardware-specific language called the DT (analogous to VHDL). The **Device Tree Source (DTS)** files live under the kernel source tree (for ARM, in `arch/arm/boot/dts/`) and are compiled at kernel build time (via the DT compiler; that is, `dtc`) into a binary format called the **Device Tree Blob (DTB)**. The DTB is typically passed along at boot by the bootloader to the kernel. During early boot, the kernel reads in, flattens, and interprets the DTB, creating platform (and other) devices as required, and then binds them to their appropriate drivers.

 The DT isn't present for x86[_64] systems. The closest equivalent is perhaps the ACPI tables. Also, note that the DT isn't a Linux-specific technology; it was designed to be OS-agnostic, and the generic org is called **Open Firmware (OF)**.

As we mentioned previously, with this modern model, the kernel and/or the device driver must obtain the resource information (which is populated inside a `include/linux/ioport.h:struct resource`) from the DTB. How? One common way in which a platform driver usually does this is via the `platform_get_*()` APIs.

We hope to make this clear with an example from a **Video For Linux (V4L)** media controller driver within the kernel source. This driver is for the SP5 TV mixer on the Samsung Exynos 4 SoC (used in some Galaxy S2 models). There's even some kernel documentation on this, under the *V4L driver-specific documentation* section: `https://www.kernel.org/doc/html/v5.4/media/v4l-drivers/fimc.html#the-samsung-s5p-exynos4-fimc-driver`.

The following code can be found at `drivers/gpu/drm/exynos/exynos_mixer.c`. Here, the driver exploits the `platform_get_resource()` API to obtain the value of the I/O memory resource; that is, the start physical address of the I/O memory for that peripheral chip:

```
struct resource *res;
[...]
res = platform_get_resource(mixer_ctx-pdev, IORESOURCE_MEM, 0);
if (res == NULL) {
    dev_err(dev, "get memory resource failed.\n");
    return -ENXIO;
}
```

```
    mixer_ctx->mixer_regs = devm_ioremap(dev, res-start,
                            resource_size(res));
    if (mixer_ctx->mixer_regs == NULL) {
        dev_err(dev, "register mapping failed.\n");
        return -ENXIO;
    }
    [...]
```

In the preceding code snippet, the driver issues the `platform_get_resource()` API to fetch the pointer to the resource structure for the `IORESOURCE_MEM` type resource (MMIO memory!). It then issues the `devm_ioremap()` API to map this MMIO region into kernel VAS (as explained in some detail in the previous section). Using the `devm` version alleviates the need for manually unmapping the I/O memory when this is done (or due to an error), thus reducing the chance of leaks!

All in one with the devm_ioremap_resource() API

As a driver author, you should become aware of and employ this useful routine: the `devm_ioremap_resource()` managed API performs the job of (validity) checking the requested I/O memory region, requesting it from the kernel (internally via the `devm_request_mem_region()` API), and remapping it (internally via `devm_ioremap()`)! This makes it a useful wrapper for driver authors like you, and its usage is pretty common (in the 5.4.0 kernel code base, it's employed over 1,400 times). Its signature is as follows:

```
void __iomem *devm_ioremap_resource(struct device *dev, const struct
resource *res);
```

Here's a usage example from `drivers/char/hw_random/bcm2835-rng.c`:

```
static int bcm2835_rng_probe(struct platform_device *pdev)
{
    [...]
    struct resource *r;
    [...]
    r = platform_get_resource(pdev, IORESOURCE_MEM, 0);

    /* map peripheral */
    priv->base = devm_ioremap_resource(dev, r);
    if (IS_ERR(priv->base))
        return PTR_ERR(priv->base);
    [...]
```

Again, as is typical with the modern LDM, this code is executed as part of the probe routine of the driver. Also (again, this is very common), the platform_get_resource() API is employed first in order to fetch and place the value of the physical (or bus) address in a resource structure, whose address is passed as the second parameter to devm_ioremap_resource(). The I/O memory, using MMIO, is now checked, requested, and remapped to kernel VAS, ready for the driver to use!

 You may have come across the devm_request_and_ioremap() API which was commonly used for similar purposes; back in 2013, it was replaced with the devm_ioremap_resource() API.

Finally, there are several variants of ioremap(). The [devm_]ioremap_nocache() and ioremap_cache() APIs are such examples and affect the CPU's caching modes.

 Driver authors would do well to carefully read the (arch-specific) comments in the kernel source where these routines are; for example, on the x86 at arch/x86/mm/ioremap.c:ioremap_nocache().

Now, having covered this important section on how to get resource information and use the modern devm_*() managed APIs, let's learn how to interpret the output from /proc with regard to MMIO.

Looking up the new mapping via /proc/iomem

Once you have performed a mapping (via one of the just-covered [devm_]ioremap*() APIs), it can actually be seen via the read-only pseudo-file; that is, /proc/iomem. The reality is that a new entry under /proc/iomem is generated when you successfully call request_mem_region(). Viewing it requires root access (more correctly, you can view it as non-root but will only see all the addresses as 0; this is for security purposes). So, let's take a look at this on our trusty x86_64 Ubuntu guest VM. In the following output, due to lack of space and for clarity, we'll show it partially truncated:

```
$ sudo cat /proc/iomem
[sudo] password for llkd:
00000000-00000fff : Reserved
00001000-0009fbff : System RAM
0009fc00-0009ffff : Reserved
000a0000-000bffff : PCI Bus 0000:00
000c0000-000c7fff : Video ROM
000e2000-000ef3ff : Adapter ROM
```

```
000f0000-000fffff : Reserved
000f0000-000fffff : System ROM
00100000-3ffeffff : System RAM
18800000-194031d0 : Kernel code
194031d1-19e6a1ff : Kernel data
1a0e2000-1a33dfff : Kernel bss
3fff0000-3fffffff : ACPI Tables
40000000-fdffffff : PCI Bus 0000:00
[...]
fee00000-fee00fff : Local APIC
fee00000-fee00fff : Reserved
fffc0000-ffffffff : Reserved
$
```

The really important thing to realize is that the address ranges shown in the left hand-side column are not virtual – **they are physical (or bus) addresses**. You can see where the system (or platform) RAM is mapped. Also, within it, you can see where exactly the kernel code, data, and bss sections are (in terms of physical addresses). In fact, my procmap utility (https://github.com/kaiwan/procmap) uses precisely this information (converting the physical addresses to virtual).

For some contrast, let's run the same command on our Raspberry Pi 3 device (the B+ model sports a Broadcom BCM2837 SoC with a quad-core ARM Cortex A53). Again, due to space restrictions and for clarity, we'll show a partially truncated part of the output:

```
pi@raspberrypi:~ $ sudo cat /proc/iomem
00000000-3b3fffff : System RAM
00008000-00bfffff : Kernel code
00d00000-00e74147 : Kernel data
3f006000-3f006fff : dwc_otg
3f007000-3f007eff : dma@7e007000
[...]
3f200000-3f2000b3 : gpio@7e200000
3f201000-3f2011ff : serial@7e201000
3f201000-3f2011ff : serial@7e201000
3f202000-3f2020ff : mmc@7e202000
[...]
pi@raspberrypi:~ $
```

Notice how the GPIO register bank shows up as `gpio@7e200000`, which, as we saw in *Figure 3.1*, is the physical address. You may be wondering why the format on ARM looks different from that of the x86_64. What does the left column now mean? Here, the kernel allows the BSP/platform team to decide on how exactly they construct and set up (via `/proc/iomem`) the I/O memory regions for display, which makes sense! They know the hardware platform best. We mentioned this previously, but the fact is that the BCM2835 SoC (which the Raspberry Pi uses) has multiple MMUs. One such MMU is the coarse granularity VC/ARM MMU, which translates the ARM bus address into an ARM physical address, after which the regular ARM MMU translates the physical address into a virtual address. Hence, here, the ARM bus address `start-end` values show up in the left column and the ARM physical address shows as suffixed to the @ symbol (`gpio@xxx`). So, for the preceding GPIO registers being mapped, the ARM bus addresses are `3f200000-3f2000b3` and the ARM physical address is `0x7e200000`.

Let's finish this section by mentioning a few more points regarding the `/proc/iomem` pseudo-file:

- `/proc/iomem` displays the physical (and/or bus) addresses currently being mapped by the kernel and/or various device drivers. However, the exact display format is very arch- and device-dependent.
- An entry is generated for `/proc/iomem` whenever the `request_mem_region()` API runs.
- The entry is removed when the corresponding `release_mem_region()` API runs.
- You can find the relevant kernel code at `kernel/resource.c:ioresources_init()`.

So, now that you have the I/O memory region successfully mapped to kernel VAS, how will you actually read/write this I/O memory? What are the APIs for MMIO? The next section delves into this topic.

MMIO – performing the actual I/O

When working with the MMIO approach, the peripheral I/O memory is mapped to the kernel VAS, and thus appears to you – the driver author – as plain old memory, just like RAM. We need to be careful here: there are caveats and cautions to be observed. You are *not* expected to treat the region as plain old RAM and access it directly via the usual C routines!

In the upcoming sections, we'll show you how to perform I/O (reads and writes) for any peripheral I/O region that's been remapped via the MMIO approach. We'll begin with the very common case of performing small (1- to 8-byte) I/O, then move on to repeating I/O, before looking at how to memset and memcpy an MMIO region.

Performing 1- to 8-byte reads and writes on MMIO memory regions

So, how exactly can you access and perform I/O (reads and writes) on peripheral I/O memory via the MMIO approach? The kernel provides APIs allowing you to both read and write chip memory. By using these APIs (or macros/inline functions), you can perform I/O, such as reads and writes, in four possible bit-widths; that is, 8-bit, 16-bit, 32-bit, and, on 64-bit systems, 64-bit:

- MMIO reads: ioread8(), ioread16(), ioread32(), and ioread64()
- MMIO writes: iowrite8(), iowrite16(), iowrite32(), and iowrite64()

The signatures of the **I/O read routines** are as follows:

```
#include <linux/io.h>
u8 ioread8(const volatile void __iomem *addr);
u16 ioread16(const volatile void __iomem *addr);
u32 ioread32(const volatile void __iomem *addr);
#ifdef CONFIG_64BIT
u64 ioread64(const volatile void __iomem *addr);
#endif
```

The single parameter for the ioreadN() APIs is the address of the I/O memory location that must be read from. Typically, it's the return value that's obtained from one of the *ioremap*() APIs we have seen, plus an offset (the offset could be 0). Adding an offset to the base (__iomem) address is a very common thing since hardware designers deliberately lay out registers in such a way that they can be easily sequentially accessed, as an array (or register bank), by software! Driver authors take advantage of this. Of course, there's no shortcut for this as you cannot assume anything – you have to carefully study the datasheet for the particular I/O peripheral you're writing the driver for; the devil lies in the details!

The u8 return type is a typedef specifying an unsigned 8-bit data type (conversely, the s prefix denotes a signed data type). The same goes for the other data types (there's s8, u8, s16, u16, s32, u32, s64, and u64, all very useful and unambiguous).

The signatures of the **I/O write routines** are as follows:

```
#include <linux/io.h>
void iowrite8(u8 value, volatile void __iomem *addr);
void iowrite16(u16 value, volatile void __iomem *addr);
void iowrite32(u32 value, volatile void __iomem *addr);
#ifdef CONFIG_64BIT
void u64 iowrite64(u64 value, const volatile void __iomem *addr);
#endif
```

The first parameter for the `iowriteN()` APIs is the value to write (of the appropriate bit-width), while the second parameter specifies the location to write it to; that is, the MMIO address (again, this is obtained via one of the `*ioremap*()` APIs). Notice that there's no return value. This is because these I/O routines literally work on the hardware, so there's no question of them failing: they always succeed! Now, of course, your driver may still not work, but this could be due to any number of reasons (resource unavailable, wrongly mapped, using the wrong offset, timing or synchronization issues, and so on). However, the I/O routines will still work.

A common test that driver authors use to fundamentally test the driver's/hardware's sanity is that they write a value, n, into a register and read it back; you should get the same value (n). (Of course, this only holds true if the register/hardware won't immediately change or consume it.)

Performing repeating I/O on MMIO memory regions

The `ioread[8|16|32|64]()` and `iowrite[8|16|32|64]()` APIs can work upon small data quantums ranging from 1 to 8 bytes only. But what if we'd like to read or write a few dozen or a few hundred bytes? You can always encode these APIs in a loop. However, the kernel, anticipating exactly this, provides helper routines that are more efficient, that internally use a tight assembly loop. These are the so-called repeating versions of the MMIO APIs:

- For reading, we have the `ioread[8|16|32|64]_rep()` set of APIs.
- For writing, we have the `iowrite[8|16|32|64]_rep()` set of APIs.

Let's look at the signature for one of them; that is, an 8-bit repeating read. The remaining reads are completely analogous:

```
#include <linux/io.h>

void ioread8_rep(const volatile void __iomem *addr, void *buffer, unsigned
int count);
```

This will read `count` bytes from the source address, `addr` (an MMIO location), into the (kernel-space) destination buffer specified by `buffer`. Similarly, the following is the signature for the repeating 8-bit write:

```
void iowrite8_rep(volatile void __iomem *addr, const void *buffer, unsigned
int count);
```

This will write `count` bytes from the source (kernel-space) buffer (`buffer`) into the destination address, `addr` (an MMIO location).

Besides these APIs, the kernel does have a few helpers that are variations of this; for example, for endianness, it provides `ioread32be()`, where `be` is big-endian.

Setting and copying on MMIO memory regions

The kernel also provides helper routines for the `memset()` and `memcpy()` operations when using MMIO. Note that you must use the following helpers:

```
#include linux/io.h

void memset_io(volatile void __iomem *addr, int value, size_t size);
```

This will set the I/O memory from the start address, `addr` (an MMIO location), to the value specified by the `value` parameter for `size` bytes.

For the purpose of copying memory, two helper routines are available, depending on the direction of the memory transfer:

```
void memcpy_fromio(void *buffer, const volatile void __iomem *addr, size_t
size);
void memcpy_toio(volatile void __iomem *addr, const void *buffer, size_t
size);
```

The first copies memory from the MMIO location `addr` to the (kernel-space) destination buffer (`buffer`) for `size` bytes; the second routine copies memory from the (kernel-space) source buffer (`buffer`) to the destination MMIO location `addr` for `size` bytes. Again, for all these helpers, notice that there is no return value; they always succeed. Also, for all the preceding routines, ensure you include the `linux/io.h` header.

Originally, the `asm/io.h` header was typically included. However, now, the `linux/io.h` header is an abstraction layer above it and internally includes the `asm/io.h` file.

Something to be aware of is that the kernel has older helper routines for performing MMIO; these are the `read[b|w|l|q]()` and `write[b|w|l|q]()` API helpers. Here, the letter that's suffixed to the read/write specifies the bit width; it's really very simple:

- b: Byte-wide (8 bits)
- w: Word-wide (16 bits)
- l: Long-wide (32 bits)
- q: Quad-word-wide (64 bits); only available on 64-bit machines

Note that with modern kernels, you are *not* expected to use these routines, but rather the aforementioned `ioread/iowrite[8|16|32|64]()` API helpers. The only reason we're mentioning them here is that there are still several drivers using these older helper routines. The syntax and semantics are completely analogous to the newer helpers, so I'll leave it to you to look them up if required.

Let's end this section by summarizing (without paying too much attention to all the details we've covered so far) the **typical sequence that drivers follow when performing MMIO**:

1. Request the memory region from the kernel
   via `request_mem_region()` (generates an entry in `/proc/iomem`).
2. Remap the peripheral I/O memory to kernel VAS
   via `[devm_]ioremap[_resource|[no]cache]()`; modern drivers typically use
   the managed `devm_ioremap()` (or the `devm_ioremap_resource()` API) to do
   so
3. Perform the actual I/O via one or more of the modern helper routines:
   - `ioread[8|16|32|64]()`
   - `iowrite[8|16|32|64]()`
   - `memset_io()` / `memcpy_fromio()` / `memcpy_toio()`
   - (Older helper routines: `read[b|w|l|q]()` and `write[b|w|l|q]()`)

4. When done, unmap the MMIO region; that is, `iounmap()`. This is only done if
   required (when using the managed `devm_ioremap*()` APIs, this is
   unnecessary).
5. Release the MMIO region back to the kernel via `release_mem_region()` (clears
   the entry in `/proc/iomem`).

With MMIO being a powerful means to communicate with peripheral chips, you might imagine that all drivers (including the so-called bus drivers) are designed and written to use it (and/or port I/O) but this isn't true. This is due to performance issues. After all is said and done, performing MMIO (or PMIO) on a peripheral requires the processor's continuous interaction and attention. This, on many classes of devices (think about streaming high-definition media content on your smartphone or tablet!), is just far too slow. So, what's the high-performance way of communicating with a peripheral device? The answer is DMA, a topic that's unfortunately beyond the scope of this book (do look at the *Further reading* section for suggestions on useful driver books and resources on DMA). So, where is MMIO used? Realistically, it's used for plenty of lower speed peripherals, including for status and control operations.

While MMIO is the most common way of performing I/O on peripherals, port I/O is another. So, let's learn how to work with it.

Understanding and using port-mapped I/O

As we mentioned earlier in the *The solution – mapping via I/O memory or I/O port* section, besides MMIO, there is another way to perform I/O on peripheral device memory called PMIO, or often simply **PIO**. It works quite differently from MMIO. Here, the CPU has distinct assembly (and corresponding machine) instructions to enable it to directly read and write I/O memory locations. Not only that, but this I/O memory range is a separate address space altogether, distinct from RAM. These memory locations are called ports. Don't confuse the term **port** that's being used here with the same term that's used in networking technology; think of this port as an **hardware register** in that it closely approximates the meaning. (While it's usually 8-bit, peripheral chip registers can actually be of three bit widths: 8, 16, or 32 bits.)

The reality is that most modern processors, even if they do support PMIO with a separate I/O port address space, tend to mostly use the MMIO approach for peripheral I/O mapping. The mainstream processor family that does support PMIO and employs it often – in addition to MMIO – is the x86. On these processors, as documented in their **physical memory map**, is a range of address locations reserved for this purpose. This is called the **port address range** and typically - on the x86 - spans from physical address 0x0 to 0xffff; that is, 64 kilobytes in length. What registers does this region contain? Typically, on the x86, there are registers (usually data/status/control) for various I/O peripherals. Some common ones include the i8042 keyboard/mouse controller chip, **DMA controller** (**DMAC**), timers, RTC, and so on. We'll look at these in more detail in the *Looking up the ports via /proc/ioports* section.

PMIO – performing the actual I/O

Port I/O is pretty simple compared to all the hoopla we saw with MMIO. This is because the processor provides machine instructions to directly perform the work. Of course, just like MMIO, you are expected to politely ask the kernel for permission to access a PIO region (we covered this in the *Asking the kernel's permission* section). The APIs for doing this are `request_region()` and `release_region()` (their parameters are identical to their MMIO counterpart APIs).

So, how can you access and perform I/O (reads and writes) upon the *I/O port(s)*? Again, the kernel provides API wrappers over the underlying assembly/machine instructions to do so for both reading and writing. Using them, you can perform I/O reads and writes in three possible bit-widths; that is, 8-bit, 16-bit, and 32-bit:

- PMIO reads: `inb()`, `inw()`, and `inl()`
- PMIO writes: `outb()`, `outw()`, and `outl()`

Quite intuitively, `b` implies byte-wide (8 bits), `w` implies word-wide (16 bits), and `l` implies long-wide (32 bits).

The signatures of the **port I/O read routines** are as follows:

```
#include <linux/io.h>
u8 inb(unsigned long addr);
u16 inw(unsigned long addr);
u32 inl(unsigned long addr);
```

The single parameter for the `in[b|w|l]()` wrappers is the port address of the port I/O memory location that will be read from. We covered this in the *Obtaining the device resources* section (a really key section for driver developers like you!). A **port** is also a resource, which means it can be obtained in the usual manner: on modern embedded systems, this is done by parsing the *device tree* (or ACPI tables); the older way was to hard-code the values within board-specific source files. Actually, for many common peripherals, the port number or port address range is a well-known one, which means it can be hard-coded into the driver (this often occurs in the driver's header files). Again, it's best to not simply assume anything, ensure you refer to the datasheet for the peripheral in question.

Now, let's get back to the APIs. The return value is an unsigned integer (with the bit-width varying, depending on the helper routine being used). It's the current value on that port (register) at the instant the read was issued.

The signatures of the **port I/O write routines** are as follows:

```
#include <linux/io.h>
void outb(u8 value, unsigned long addr);
void outw(u16 value, unsigned long addr);
void outl(u32 value, unsigned long addr);
```

The first parameter is the value to be written to the hardware (port), while the second parameter is the port address of the port I/O memory to write to. Again, as with MMIO, there's no question of failure since these helper I/O routines always succeed. On the x86 at least, a write to an I/O port is guaranteed to be completed before the next instruction is executed.

A PIO example – the i8042

To help make things clearer, let's look at a few code snippets from the device driver for the i8042 keyboard and mouse controller, which, though nowadays considered quite old, is still very common on x86 systems.

You can find a basic schematic of the 8042 controller here: `https://wiki.osdev.org/File:Ps2-kbc.png`.

The interesting bits (for us, at least) are in the driver's header file:

```
// drivers/input/serio/i8042-io.h
/*
 * Register numbers.
 */
#define I8042_COMMAND_REG    0x64
#define I8042_STATUS_REG     0x64
#define I8042_DATA_REG       0x60
```

In the preceding code snippet, we can see the I/O ports or hardware registers that this driver works with. How come the status and data registers resolve to the same I/O port (0x64) address? The *direction* matters: reading it has I/O port 0x64 behave as the status register, while writing to it has it behave as the command register! Furthermore, the datasheet will show you that these are 8-bit registers; so, here, the actual I/O is performed via the inb() and outb() helpers. The driver abstracts these further in small inline routines:

```
[...]
static inline int i8042_read_data(void)
```

```
{
    return inb(I8042_DATA_REG);
}
static inline int i8042_read_status(void)
{
    return inb(I8042_STATUS_REG);
}
static inline void i8042_write_data(int val)
{
    outb(val, I8042_DATA_REG);
}
static inline void i8042_write_command(int val)
{
    outb(val, I8042_COMMAND_REG);
}
```

Of course, the reality is that there's far more that this driver does (than what we've shown here), including handling hardware interrupts, initializing and working with multiple ports, blocking reads and writes, flushing buffers, blinking the keyboard LEDs on kernel panic, and more. We won't look into this any further here.

Looking up the port(s) via /proc/ioports

The kernel provides a viewport into the port address space via the /proc/ioports pseudo-file. Let's check it out on our x86_64 guest VM (again, we're only showing part of the output):

```
$ sudo cat /proc/ioports
[sudo] password for llkd:
0000-0cf7 : PCI Bus 0000:00
  0000-001f : dma1
  0020-0021 : pic1
  0040-0043 : timer0
  0050-0053 : timer1
  0060-0060 : keyboard
  0064-0064 : keyboard
  0070-0071 : rtc_cmos
  0070-0071 : rtc0
[...]
  d270-d27f : 0000:00:0d.0
  d270-d27f : ahci
$
```

We've highlighted the keyboard ports in bold. Notice how the port numbers match what the i8042 driver code we saw previously specifies. Interestingly, running the same command on the Raspberry Pi yields nothing; this is because no driver or subsystem is using any I/O ports. Analogous with MMIO, an entry in `/proc/ioports` is generated when the `request_region()` API runs, and, conversely, is removed when the corresponding `release_region()` API runs.

Now, let's quickly mention a few things with respect to port I/O.

Port I/O – a few remaining points to note

A few more or less miscellaneous points remain on PIO that you as a driver author should take note of:

- Just like MMIO provides the repeating I/O routines (recall the `ioread|iowrite[8|16|32|64]_rep()` helpers), PMIO (or PIO) provides somewhat similar repeating functionality for those cases where you'd like to read or write the same I/O port multiple times. These are the so-called *string versions* of the regular port helper routines; they have an `s` in their name to remind you of this. The kernel source contains a comment that neatly sums this up:

```
// include/asm-generic/io.h
/*
 * {in,out}s{b,w,l}{,_p}() are variants of the above that
repeatedly access a
 * single I/O port multiple times.
 */
we don't show the complete code below, just the 'signature' as such
void insb(unsigned long addr, void *buffer, unsigned int count);
void insw(unsigned long addr, void *buffer, unsigned int count);
void insl(unsigned long addr, void *buffer, unsigned int count);

void outsb(unsigned long addr, const void *buffer, unsigned int
count);
void outsw(unsigned long addr, const void *buffer, unsigned int
count);
void outsl(unsigned long addr, const void *buffer, unsigned int
count);
```

So, for example, the `insw()` helper routine will read a total of count times (that is, *count*2* bytes since it's 2-byte or 16-bit reads each) from the starting `addr`, which is an I/O port address, into the successive locations of the destination buffer at `buffer` (the `readsw()` inline function is the internal implementation).

Similarly, the `outsw()` helper routine writes a total of count times (that is, *count*2* bytes since it's 2-byte or 16-bit reads each), data from the source buffer at `buffer` to the I/O port at `address` (the `writesw()` inline function is the internal implementation).

- Next, the kernel seems to provide helper APIs equivalent to the `in|out[b|w|l]()` ones; that is, `in|out[b|w|l]_p()`. Here, the `_p` suffix implies that a *pause* or delay was introduced into the I/O. Originally, this was meant for slow peripherals; nowadays, though, this seems to have become a backward-compatible moot point: the "delayed I/O" routines are nothing but simple wrappers over the regular routines (in effect there is no delaying).
- There are also user space equivalents of the PIO APIs (you can use one these to, for example, write a user space driver). Of course, successfully issuing the `in|out[b|w|l]()` APIs in user mode requires the issuing process to successfully invoke the `iopl(2)`/`ioperm(2)` system calls, which, in turn, requires root access (or you require to have the `CAP_SYS_RAWIO` capability bit set; this can also be done for security purposes.)

With that, we have concluded our discussion of port I/O, as well as this chapter.

Summary

In this chapter, you learned why we can't just work directly with peripheral I/O memory. Next, we covered how, within the Linux device driver framework, to access and perform I/O (reads and writes) on hardware (or peripheral) I/O memory. You learned that there are two broad ways to do this: via MMIO (the common approach) and P(M)IO.

We learned that systems such as the x86 often employ both approaches as that's how the peripherals are designed. MMIO and/or PMIO access is a key task for any driver – after all, this is how we talk to and control hardware! Not only that, but many of the underlying bus drivers (for various buses on Linux, such as I2C, USB, SPI, PCI, and more) internally use MMIO/PMIO for performing peripheral I/O. So, good job on completing this chapter!

In the next chapter, we'll look at another critical hardware-related area of importance: understanding, dealing with, and working with hardware interrupts.

Questions

Imagine that you have mapped an 8-bit register bank to a peripheral chip (via the `devm_ioremap_resource()` API in your driver's `xxx_probe()` method; assume it succeeds). Now, you want to read the current content in the third 8-bit register. The following is some (pseudo)code that you can use to do this. Study it and spot the bug inside it:

```
char val;
void __iomem *base = devm_ioremap_resource(dev, r);
[...]
val = ioread8(base+3);
```

Can you suggest a fix?

Possible solution to this exercise can be found at `https://github.com/PacktPublishing/Linux-Kernel-Programming-Part-2/tree/main/solutions_to_assgn`.

Further reading

- Modern (and older) *Linux device drivers* books: Working with the LDM:
    - *Linux Device Drivers Development, Madieu*, Packt, October 2017 – This is an excellent resource that provides modern and wide coverage.
    - *Linux Driver Development for Embedded Processors*, Alberto Liberal de los Ríos, second edition, 2018.
    - *Essential Linux Device Drivers*, Sreekrishnan Venkateswaran, Pearson, March 2008 – This is an older book but provides superb coverage on literally all types of Linux drivers!
    - *Linux Device Drivers*, Rubini, Corbet, GK-Hartman, O'Reilly, February 2005 – This is the old Linux drivers bible; how can it possibly be left out?

- Device tree:
    - Device tree specification: https://www.devicetree.org/.
    - *Device Tree Reference*, eLinux: https://elinux.org/Device_Tree_Reference.
    - *Generate and compile the device tree to config the hardware setup of your* Arietta *G25 board*: http://linux.tanzilli.com/ – This provides a very interesting and interactive configuration that can be performed for a device tree!
- DMA:
    - Article: *Introduction to direct memory access*, October 2003: https://www.embedded.com/introduction-to-direct-memory-access/
    - LWN kernel index: articles on DMA: https://lwn.net/Kernel/Index/#Direct_memory_access
    - Linux kernel documentation: *DMAEngine documentation*: https://www.kernel.org/doc/html/latest/driver-api/dmaengine/index.html
    - *Linux kernel has a "DMA test" kernel module; documentation*: https://www.kernel.org/doc/html/latest/driver-api/dmaengine/dmatest.html
    - *Stack Overflow: From the kernel to the user space (DMA)*: https://stackoverflow.com/questions/11137058/from-the-kernel-to-the-user-space-dma
    - Laurent Pinchart – *mastering the dma and iommu apis | ELC 2014*: https://www.youtube.com/watch?v=n07zPcbdX_w
- Hardware/CPU:
    - Intel x86 architecture, Min: https://www.slideshare.net/multics69/intel-x86-architecture

4
Handling Hardware Interrupts

In this chapter, we'll focus on a really key aspect of writing a device driver: what hardware interrupts are and, more importantly, how exactly you, as a driver author, handle them. The fact is, a large percentage of peripherals (that you're interested in writing a device driver for) indicate their need for immediate action via the OS or driver by asserting a hardware interrupt. This is, in effect, an electrical signal that ultimately alerts the processor's control unit (typically, this alert must redirect control to the affected peripheral's interrupt handler routine as it requires immediate attention).

To handle these kinds of interrupts, you need to understand some of the fundamentals of how they work; that is, how the OS handles them and, most importantly, how you as a driver author are expected to work with them. An additional layer of complexity is added by the fact that Linux, being a VM-based rich OS, requires and uses some abstraction in the way it works with interrupts. So, you will begin by learning about the (very) basic workflow regarding how to handle a hardware interrupt. Then, we will look at the topics that a driver author like yourself will be primarily interested in: how exactly to allocate an IRQ and write the code of the handler routine itself – there are some very specific dos and don'ts! We will then cover the motivation behind and the usage of the newer threaded interrupt model, enabling/disabling specific IRQs, viewing information about IRQ lines via proc, and what top and bottom halves are for and how to use them. We'll finish this chapter by answering a few FAQs on interrupt handling.

In this chapter, we will cover the following topics:

- Hardware interrupts and how the kernel handles them
- Allocating the hardware IRQ
- Implementing the interrupt handler routine
- Working with the threaded interrupts model
- Enabling and disabling IRQs

- Viewing all allocated interrupt (IRQ) lines
- Understanding and using top and bottom halves
- A few remaining FAQs answered

Let's get started!

Technical requirements

This chapter assumes that you've gone through the *Preface* section *To get the most out of this book* and have appropriately prepared a guest VM running Ubuntu 18.04 LTS (or a later stable release) and installed all the required packages. If not, I highly recommend you do this first. To get the most out of this book, I strongly recommend you first set up the workspace environment, including cloning this book's GitHub repository for the code, and work on it in a hands-on fashion. The repository can be found here: `https://github.com/PacktPublishing/Linux-Kernel-Programming-Part-2`.

Hardware interrupts and how the kernel handles them

Many, if not most, peripheral controllers use a hardware interrupt to inform the OS or device driver that some (usually urgent) action is required. Typical examples include network adapters (NICs), block devices (disks), USB devices, AV devices, **human interface devices (HIDs)** such as keyboards, mice, touchscreens, and video screens, clocks/timer chips, DMA controllers, and so on. The primary idea behind hardware interrupts is efficiency. Instead of continually polling the chip (on a battery-backed device, this can result in rapidly draining the battery!), the interrupt is a means to have the low-level software run only as and when required.

Here's a quick hardware-level overview (without getting into too much detail): modern system motherboards will have an interrupt controller chip of some sort, which is often called the **[IO][A]PIC**, short for **IO-[Advanced] Programmable Interrupt Controller**, on x86 (the kernel documents for the x86 IO-APIC can be found at `https://www.kernel.org/doc/html/latest/x86/i386/IO-APIC.html#io-apic`) or a **generic interrupt controller (GIC)** on ARM. The PIC (to keep it simple, we'll just use the generic term PIC) has one line to the CPU's interrupt pin. Onboard peripherals capable of asserting interrupts will have an IRQ line to the PIC.

IRQ is the common abbreviated term for **Interrupt ReQuest**; it denotes the interrupt line (or lines) that's allocated to a peripheral device.

Let's say that the peripheral device in question is a network adapter (a NIC) and a network packet is received. The (highly simplified) flow is as follows:

1. The peripheral device (the NIC) now needs to emit (assert) a hardware interrupt; thus, it asserts its line on the PIC (low or high logic as required; all this is internal to the hardware).

2. The PIC, on seeing that a peripheral line has been asserted, saves the asserted line value in a register.

3. The PIC then asserts the CPU's interrupt pin.

4. The control unit on the processor checks for the presence of hardware interrupts on every CPU after every single machine instruction runs. Thus, if a hardware interrupt occurs, it will certainly come to know about it almost immediately. The CPU will then raise a hardware interrupt (of course interrupts can be masked; we'll discuss this in more detail later in the *Enabling and disabling IRQs* section).

5. The low-level (BSP/platform) code on the OS will be hooked into this and will react (this is often code that's at the assembly level); for example, on the ARM-32, the low-level C entry point for a hardware interrupt is `arch/arm/kernel/irq.c:asm_do_IRQ()`.

6. From here, the OS executes code paths that ultimately invoke the registered interrupt handler routine(s) of the driver(s) this interrupt is to be serviced by. (Again, it's not our intention to focus on the hardware layer and even the arch-specific platform-level details of hardware interrupts in this chapter. I'd like to focus on what's of relevance to you as the driver author – how to handle them!).

The hardware interrupt is literally the top priority on the Linux OS: it preempts whatever's currently running – be it user or kernel-space code paths – in order to run. Having said that, later, we will see that on modern Linux kernels, it's possible to employ a threaded interrupt model that changes things; a little patience please – we'll get there!

Now, let's digress. We mentioned an example of a typical peripheral device, a network controller (or NIC), and have essentially said that it services packet transmission and reception (Tx/Rx) via hardware interrupts. This used to be true, but this isn't always the case with modern high-speed NICs (typically 10 Gbps and higher). Why? The answer is interesting: the extreme speed at which interrupts will literally interrupt the processor can cause the system to land in a problematic situation called **livelock**; a situation where it cannot cope with the extremely high interrupt demand! As with deadlocks (covered in `Chapter 6`, *Kernel Synchronization – Part 1*), the system effectively tends to freeze or hang. So, what do we do regarding livelock? Most high-end modern NICs support a polled-mode of operation; modern OSes such as Linux have a network receive path infrastructure called **NAPI** (it's nothing to do with babies, mind you – it's short for **New API**) that allows the driver to switch between interrupt and polled mode based on demand and hence process network packets (on the receive path) more efficiently.

Now that we've introduced hardware interrupts, let's learn how you, as a driver author, can work with them. Most of the remaining sections in this chapter will deal with this. Let's start by learning how to allocate or register an IRQ line.

Allocating the hardware IRQ

Often, a key part of writing a device driver is really the work of trapping into and handling the hardware interrupt that the chip you're writing the driver for emits. How do you do this? The trouble is that the way that hardware interrupts are routed from the interrupt controller chip(s) to the CPU(s) varies widely; it is very platform-specific. The good news is that the Linux kernel provides an abstraction layer to abstract away all the hardware-level differences; it's referred to as the **generic interrupt (or IRQ) handling layer**. Essentially, it performs the required work under the hood and exposes APIs and data structures that are completely generic. Thus, at least theoretically, your code will work on any platform. This **generic IRQ layer** is what we, primarily as driver authors, shall be using, of course; all the APIs and helper routines we use fall into this category.

Recall that it's really the core kernel that, at least initially, handles the interrupt (as we learned in the previous section). It then refers to an array of linked lists (a very common data structure on Linux; here, the index to the array is the IRQ number) to figure out the driver-level function(s) to invoke. (Without going into too much detail, the node on the lists is the IRQ descriptor structure; that is, `include/linux/interrupt.h:struct irqaction`.) But how do you get your driver's interrupt handler function onto this list so that the kernel can invoke it when an interrupt from your device occurs? Ah, that's the key: you register it with the kernel. Modern Linux provides at least four ways (APIs) via which you can register interest in an interrupt line, as follows:

- `request_irq()`
- `devm_request_irq()`
- `request_threaded_irq()`
- `devm_request_threaded_irq()` (recommended!)

Let's tackle them one by one (there are additional routines that are slight variations of them). Along the way, we'll look at some code from a few drivers and learn how to work with threaded interrupts. There's a lot to learn and do; let's get on with it!

Allocating your interrupt handler with request_irq()

Just as we saw with I/O memory and I/O ports, the IRQ line(s) is considered a **resource** that the kernel is in charge of. The `request_irq()` kernel API can be thought of as the traditional means by which driver authors register their interest in an IRQ and allocate this resource to themselves, thus allowing the kernel to invoke their handler when the interrupt asynchronously arrives.

It might strike you that this discussion seems very analogous to user space **signal handling**. There, we call the `sigaction(2)` system call to register interest in a signal. When the signal (asynchronously) arrives, the kernel invokes the registered signal handler (user mode) routine!
There are some key differences here. First, a user space signal handler is not an interrupt; second, the user space signal handler runs purely in non-privileged user mode; in contrast, the kernel space interrupt handler of your driver runs (asynchronously) with kernel privileges and in an interrupted context!

Furthermore, some signals are really the software side effect of a **processor exception** being raised; broadly speaking, the processor will raise a **fault, trap, or abort** when something illegal occurs and it has to "trap" (switch) to kernel space to handle it. A process or thread attempting to access an invalid page (or without sufficient permissions) causes the MMU to raise a fault or an abort; this leads to the OS fault handling code raising the `SIGSEGV` signal upon the process context (i.e. upon `current`)! However, raising an exception of some sort does *not* always imply there's a problem – a system call is nothing but a trap to the OS; that is, a programmed exception (via `syscall` / `SWI` on x86/ARM).

The following comment (which has been partially reproduced in the following snippet) from the kernel source tells us more about what the `request[_threaded]_irq()` API does:

```
// kernel/irq/manage.c:request_threaded_irq()
[...]
 * This call allocates interrupt resources and enables the
 * interrupt line and IRQ handling. From the point this
 * call is made your handler function may be invoked.
```

Actually, `request_irq()` is merely a thin wrapper over the `request_threaded_irq()` API; we will discuss this API later. The signature of the `request_irq()` API is as follows:

```
#include <linux/interrupt.h>

int __must_check
request_irq(unsigned int irq, irq_handler_t (*handler_func)(int, void *),
unsigned long flags, const char *name, void *dev);
```

Always include the `linux/interrupt.h` header file. Let's examine each of the parameters to `request_irq()` one by one:

- `int irq`: This is the IRQ line that you're attempting to register or trap/hook into. This means that when this particular interrupt fires, your interrupt handler function (the second parameter, `handler_func`) is invoked. The question regarding `irq` is: how do I find out what the IRQ number is? We addressed this generic issue in Chapter 3, *Working with Hardware I/O Memory*, in the (really key) *Obtaining the device resources* section. To quickly reiterate, **an IRQ line is a resource**, which means it is obtained in the usual manner – on modern embedded systems, it's obtained by parsing the **Device Tree (DT)**; the older way was to hard code the values within board-specific source files (relax, you will see an example of querying the IRQ line via the DT in the *IRQ allocation – the modern way – the managed interrupt facility* section). On PC-type systems, you might have to resort to interrogating the bus that the device lives on (for cold devices). Here, the PCI bus (and friends) is very common. The kernel even provides PCI helper routines you can use to query resources from it, and thus find out the assigned IRQ line.

- `irq_handler_t (*handler_func)(int, void *)`: This parameter is a pointer to the interrupt handler function (in C, just providing the function's name is sufficient). This, of course, is the code that will be asynchronously invoked when the hardware interrupt fires. Its job is to service the interrupt (more on this later). How does the kernel know where it is? Recall `struct irqaction`, which is the structure that's populated by the `request_irq()` routine. One of its members is `handler`, and is set to this second parameter.

- `unsigned long flags`: This, the third parameter to `request_irq()`, is a flag bitmask. When it's set to zero, it implements its default behavior (we'll discuss some key interrupt flags in the *Setting interrupt flags* section).

- `const char *name`: This is the name of the code/driver that owns the interrupt. Typically, this is set to the name of the device driver (this way, `/proc/interrupts` can show you the name of the driver that is using the interrupt; it's the right-most column; details follow in the *Viewing all allocated interrupt (IRQ) lines* section.)

- `void *dev`: This, the fifth and last parameter to `request_irq()`, allows you to pass any data item you wish to (often called a cookie) to the interrupt handler routine, which is a common software technique. In the second parameter, you can see that the interrupt handler routine is of the `void *` type. This is where this parameter gets passed.

  Most real-world drivers will have some kind of context or private data structure where they store all required information. Furthermore, this context structure is often embedded into the driver's device (often specialized by the subsystem or driver framework) structure. In fact, the kernel typically helps you do so; for example, network drivers use `alloc_etherdev()` to embed their data into `struct net_device`, platform drivers embed their data into the `platform_device.device.platform_data` member of `struct platform_device`, I2C client drivers employ the `i2c_set_clientdata()` helper to "set" their private/context data into the `i2c_client` structure, and so on.

 Note that when you're using a *shared* interrupt (we'll explain this shortly), you *must* initialize this parameter to a non-NULL value (otherwise, how will `free_irq()` know which handler to free?). If you do not have a context structure or anything specific to pass along, passing the `THIS_MODULE` macro here will do the trick (assuming you're writing the driver using the loadable kernel module framework; it's the pointer to your kernel module's metadata structure; that is, `struct module`).

The return value from `request_irq()` is an integer, as per the usual `0/-E` kernel convention (see the companion guide *Linux Kernel Programming - Chapter 4, Writing Your First Kernel Module – LKMs Part 1*, the section *The 0/-E return convention*), it's 0 on success, and a negative `errno` value on failure. As the `__must_check` compiler attribute clearly specifies, you are certainly expected to check for the failure case (this is good programming practice in any case).

Linux Driver Verification (LDV) project: In the companion guide *Linux Kernel Programming, Chapter 1 - Kernel Workspace Setup*, in the section *The LDV - Linux Driver Verification - project*, we mentioned that this project has useful "rules" with respect to various programming aspects of Linux modules (drivers, mostly) as well as the core kernel.

With regard to our current topic, here's one of the rules, a negative one, implying that you *cannot* do this: "*Making no delay when probing for IRQs*" (`http://linuxtesting.org/ldv/online?action=show_rulerule_id=0037`). This discussion really applies to x86[_64] systems. Here, in some circumstances, you might need to physically probe for the correct IRQ line number. For this purpose, the kernel provides an "autoprobe" facility via the `probe_irq_{on|off}()` APIs (`probe_irq_on()` returns a bitmask of potential IRQ lines that can be used). The thing is, a delay is required between the `probe_irq_on()` and `probe_irq_off()` APIs; not invoking this delay can cause issues. The LDV page mentioned previously covers this in some detail, so do take a look. The actual API used to perform the delay is typically `udelay()`. Worry not, we cover it (and several others) in detail in `Chapter 5`, *Working with Kernel Timers, Threads, and Workqueues* in the section *Delaying for a given time in the kernel*.

Where in the driver's code should you call the `request_irq()` API (or its equivalent)? For pretty much all modern drivers that adhere to the modern **Linux Device Model** (**LDM**), the modern kernel framework for devices and drivers, the `probe()` method (this is a function, really) is the right place.

Freeing the IRQ line

Conversely, when the driver is being unloaded or the device is being detached, the `remove()` (or `disconnect()`) method is the right place where you should call the converse routine – `free_irq()` – to free the IRQ line back to the kernel:

```
void *free_irq(unsigned int, void *);
```

The first parameter to `free_irq()` is the IRQ line to free back to the kernel. The second parameter is, again, the same value that's passed to the interrupt handler (via the last parameter to `request_irq()`), so you must typically populate it with either the device structure pointer (which embeds your driver's context or private data structure) or the `THIS_MODULE` macro.

The return value is the *device name* argument that you passed as the fourth parameter of the `request_irq()` routine (yes, it's a string) on success and NULL on failure.

It's important that you, as the driver author, take care to do the following:

- Disable the interrupt on the board before calling `free_irq()` when the IRQ line is being shared
- Call it from process context only

Also, `free_irq()` will only return when any and all the executing interrupts for this IRQ line have completed.

Before we look at some code, we need to briefly cover two additional areas: interrupt flags and the notion of level/edge-triggered interrupts.

Setting interrupt flags

When allocating an interrupt (IRQ line) with the `{devm_}request{_threaded}_irq()` APIs (we'll cover the variants of `request_irq()` shortly), you can specify certain interrupt flags that will affect the interrupt line's configuration and/or behavior. The parameter that's responsible for this is `unsigned long flags` (as we mentioned in the *Allocating your interrupt handler with request_irq()* section). It's important to realize it's a bitmask; you can bitwise-OR several flags to get their combined effect. The flag values fall broadly into a few classes: flags to do with IRQ line sharing, interrupt threading, and suspend/resume behavior. They're all in the `linux/interrupt.h` header in IRQF_foo format. The following are some of the most common ones:

- `IRQF_SHARED`: This allows you to share the IRQ line between several devices (required for devices on the PCI bus).
- `IRQF_ONESHOT`: The IRQ is not enabled after the hardirq handler finishes executing. This flag is typically used by threaded interrupts (covered in the *Working with the threaded interrupts model* section) to ensure that the IRQ remains disabled until the threaded handler completes.

The `__IRQF_TIMER` flag is a special case. It's used to mark the interrupt as a timer interrupt. As seen in the companion guide *Linux Kernel Programming, Chapter 10, The CPU Scheduler - Part 1*, and *Chapter 11, The CPU Scheduler - Part 2*, when we looked at CPU scheduling, that the timer interrupt fires at periodic intervals and is responsible for implementing the kernel's timer/timeout mechanisms, scheduler-related housekeeping, and so on.

The timer interrupt flags are specified by this macro:

```
#define IRQF_TIMER (__IRQF_TIMER | IRQF_NO_SUSPEND | IRQF_NO_THREAD)
```

In addition to specifying that it's marked as the timer interrupt (`__IRQF_TIMER`), the `IRQF_NO_SUSPEND` flag specifies that the interrupt remains enabled even when the system goes into a suspend state. Furthermore, the `IRQF_NO_THREAD` flag specifies that this interrupt cannot use the threaded model (we'll cover this in the *Working with the threaded interrupts model* section).

There are several other interrupt flags we can use, including `IRQF_PROBE_SHARED`, `IRQF_PERCPU`, `IRQF_NOBALANCING`, `IRQF_IRQPOLL`, `IRQF_FORCE_RESUME`, `IRQF_EARLY_RESUME`, and `IRQF_COND_SUSPEND`. We won't cover them explicitly here (take a look at the comment header briefly describing them in the `linux/interrupt.h` header file).

Now, let's gain a brief understanding of what level- and edge-triggered interrupts are.

Understanding level- and edge-triggered interrupts – a brief note

When a peripheral asserts an interrupt, the interrupt controller is triggered to latch this event. The electrical characteristics that it uses to trigger the hardware interrupt in the CPU fall into two broad categories:

- **Level-triggered**: The interrupt is triggered when the level changes (from inactive to active or asserted); until it's deasserted, the line remains in the asserted state. This happens even after your handler returns; if the line is still asserted, you will get the interrupt again.
- **Edge-triggered**: The interrupt triggers only once when the level changes from inactive to active.

Additionally, the interrupt could be high or low triggered, on the rising or falling (clock) edge. The kernel allows this to be configured and specified via additional flags such as `IRQF_TRIGGER_NONE`, `IRQF_TRIGGER_RISING`, `IRQF_TRIGGER_FALLING`, `IRQF_TRIGGER_HIGH`, `IRQF_TRIGGER_LOW`, and so on. These low-level electrical characteristics of the peripheral chip are typically pre-configured within the BSP-level code or specified in the DT.

Level-triggered interrupts force you to understand the interrupt source so that you can correctly deassert (or *ack*) it (in the case of a shared IRQ, after checking that it's for you). Typically, this is the first thing you must do when you're servicing it; otherwise, it will keep firing. For example, if the interrupt is triggered when a certain device register hits the value `0xff`, for example, then the driver must set the register to, say, `0x0` before deasserting it! This is easy to see but can be difficult to handle correctly.

On the other hand, edge-triggered interrupts are easy to work with since no knowledge of the interrupt source is required, but they can also be easy to miss! In general, firmware designers use edge-triggered interrupts (though this isn't a rule). Again, these characteristics are really at the hardware/firmware boundary. You should study the datasheet and any allied documentation (such as Application Notes from the OEM) provided for the peripheral you're writing the driver for.

You might by now realize that writing a device driver (well!) requires two distinct knowledge domains. First, you'll need to have a deep understanding of the hardware/firmware and how it works - it's **theory of operation (TOO)**, its control/data planes, register banks, I/O memory, and so on. Second, you'll need to have a deep (enough) understanding of the OS (Linux) and its kernel/driver framework, how Linux works, memory management, scheduling, interrupt models, and so on. Also, you need to understand the modern LDM and kernel driver frameworks and how to go about debugging and profiling them. The better you get at these things, the better you'll be at writing the driver!

We'll learn how to find out what kind of triggering is being used in the *Viewing all allocated (IRQ) lines* section. Check out the *Further reading* section for more links concerning IRQ edge/level triggering.

Now, let's move on and look at something interesting. To help assimilate what you've learned so far, we'll look at some small snippets of code from a Linux network driver!

Code view 1 – the IXGB network driver

It's time to look at some code. Let's take a look at some small portions of code for the Intel IXGB network adapter driver (which drives several Intel network adapters in the 82597EX series). Among the many available on the market, Intel has a product line called the **IXGB network adapter**. The controller is the Intel 82597EX; these are typically 10-gigabit ethernet adapters meant for servers (Intel's product brief on this controller can be found at `https://www.intel.com/Assets/PDF/prodbrief/pro10GbE_LR_SA-DS.pdf`):

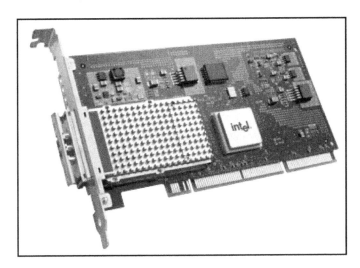

Figure 4.1 – The Intel PRO/10GbE LR server adapter (IXGB, 82597EX) network adapter

First, let's take a look at it invoking `request_irq()` to allocate the IRQ line:

```
// drivers/net/ethernet/intel/ixgb/ixgb_main.c
[...]
int
ixgb_up(struct ixgb_adapter *adapter)
{
    struct net_device *netdev = adapter->netdev;
    int err, irq_flags = IRQF_SHARED;
    [...]
    err = request_irq(adapter->pdev->irq, ixgb_intr, irq_flags,
                    netdev->name, netdev);
    [...]
```

In the preceding code snippet, you can see the driver invoking the `request_irq()` API to allocate this interrupt within the network driver's `ixgb_up()` method. This method is invoked when the network interface is brought up (by networking utilities such as `ip(8)` or (older) `ifconfig(8)`). Let's look at the parameters passed to `request_irq()` here, in turn:

- Here, the IRQ number – the first parameter – is queried from the `irq` member of the `pci_dev` structure (as this device lives on the PCI bus). The `pdev` structure pointer is within this driver's context (or private) metadata structure named `ixgb_adapter`. Its member is called `irq`.
- The second parameter is the pointer to the interrupt handler routine (it's often referred to as the *hardirq handler*; we'll look at all this in a lot more detail later); here, it's the function named `ixgb_intr()`.
- The third parameter is the `flags` bitmask. You can see that here the driver specifies that this interrupt is shared (via the `IRQF_SHARED` flag). It's part of the PCI specification for devices on this bus to share their interrupt lines. This implies that the driver will need to verify that the interrupt is really meant for it. It does this in the interrupt handler (it's usually very hardware-specific code, typically checking a given register for some expected value).
- The fourth parameter is the name of the driver handling this interrupt. It's obtained via the specialized `net_device` structure's `name` member (which has been registered to the kernel's net framework by this driver calling `register_netdev()` in its probe method, `ixgb_probe()`).
- The fifth parameter is the value to pass along to the interrupt handler routine. As we mentioned previously, it's (again) the specialized `net_device` structure (which internally has the driver's context structure (`struct ixgb_adapter`) embedded within it!).

Conversely, when the network interface goes down, the `ixgb_down()` method is invoked by the kernel. When this happens, it disables NAPI and frees up the IRQ line with `free_irq()`:

```
void
ixgb_down(struct ixgb_adapter *adapter, bool kill_watchdog)
{
    struct net_device *netdev = adapter->netdev;
    [...]
    napi_disable(&adapter->napi);
    /* waiting for NAPI to complete can re-enable interrupts */
    ixgb_irq_disable(adapter);
    free_irq(adapter-pdev->irq, netdev);
    [...]
```

Now that you've learned how to trap into a hardware interrupt via `request_irq()`, we need to understand some key points about writing the code of the interrupt handler routine itself, which is where the actual work of handling the interrupt is performed.

Implementing the interrupt handler routine

Often, the interrupt is the hardware peripheral's way of informing the system – the driver, really – that data is available and that it should pick it up. This is what typical drivers do: they grab the incoming data from the device buffers (or port, or whatever). Not just that, it's also possible that there are user mode processes (or threads) that want this data. Thus, they have quite possibly opened the device file and have issued the `read(2)` (or equivalent) system call. This has them currently blocking (sleeping) upon this very event; that is, data arriving from the device.

On detecting that data currently isn't available, the driver's *read* method typically puts the process context to sleep using one of the `wait_event*()` APIs.

So, once your driver's interrupt handler has fetched the data into some kernel buffer, it typically awakens the sleeping readers. They now run through the driver's read method (in process context), pick up the data, and transfer it to the user space buffer as required.

This section has been split into two broad parts. First, we'll learn what we can and cannot do in our interrupt handler. Then, we'll cover the mechanics of writing the code.

Interrupt context guidelines – what to do and what not to do

The interrupt handler routine is your typical C code, with some caveats. A few key points regarding the design and implementation of your hardware interrupt handler are as follows:

- **The handler runs in an interrupt context, so do not block**: First and foremost, this code always runs in an interrupt context; that is, an atomic context. On a preemptible kernel, preemption is disabled, so there are some limitations regarding what it can and cannot do. In particular, it cannot do anything that directly or indirectly invokes the scheduler (`schedule()`)!
  In effect, you **cannot** do the following:
    - Transfer data to and from kernel to user space as it might cause a page fault, which isn't allowed in an atomic context.
    - Use the `GFP_KERNEL` flag in memory allocation. You must use the `GFP_ATOMIC` flag so that the allocation is non-blocking – it either succeeds or fails immediately.
    - Invoke any API that's blocking (that, down the line, calls `schedule()`). In other words, it has to be purely non-blocking code paths. (We covered why in some detail in As seen in the companion guide *Linux Kernel Programming - Chapter 8, Kernel Memory Allocation for Module Authors – Part 1*, in the *Never sleep in interrupt or atomic contexts* section).

- **Interrupt masking**: By default, while your interrupt handler is running, **all** interrupts on the local CPU core where your handler is executing are masked (disabled), and the particular interrupt you're handling is masked **across all cores**. Thus, your code is inherently reentrant-safe.

- **Keep it fast!**: You are writing code that will literally interrupt other processes – other "business" that the system was running before you rudely interrupted it; thus, you must do what's required, as fast as is possible, and return, allowing the interrupted code path to continue. Important system software metrics include the worst-case interrupt length and the worst-case interrupt's disabled time (we'll cover some more on this in the *Measuring metrics and latency* section at the end of this chapter).

These points are important enough to merit more detail, so we'll cover them more thoroughly in the following subsections.

Don't block – spotting possibly blocking code paths

This really boils down to the fact that when you're in an interrupt or atomic context, don't do anything that will call `schedule()`. Now, let's look at what happens if our interrupt handler's pseudocode looks like this:

```
my_interrupt()
{
    struct mys *sp;
    ack_intr();
    x = read_regX();
    sp = kzalloc(SIZE_HWBUF, GFP_KERNEL);
    if (!sp)
        return -ENOMEM;
    sp = fetch_data_from_hw();
    copy_to_user(ubuf, sp, count);
    kfree(sp);
}
```

Did you spot the big fat potential (though perhaps still subtle) bugs here? (Take a moment to spot them before moving on.)

First, the invocation of `kzalloc()` with the `GFP_KERNEL` flag might cause its kernel code to invoke `schedule()`! If it does, this will result in an "Oops," which is a kernel bug. In typical production environments, this causes the kernel to panic (as the *sysctl* named `panic_on_oops` is typically set to `1` in production; doing `sysctl kernel.panic_on_oops` will show you the current setting). Next, the `copy_to_user()` invocation might result in a page fault and therefore necessitate a context switch, which will, of course, invoke `schedule()`; this is just not possible -again, a serious bug - in an atomic or interrupt context!

So, more generically, let's your interrupt handler calls a function, `a()`, with the call chain for `a()` being as follows:

```
a() -- b() -- c() -- [...] -- g() -- schedule() -- [...]
```

Here, you can see that calling `a()` ultimately results in `schedule()` being called, which, as we just pointed out, will result in an "Oops", which is a kernel bug. So, the question here is, how do you, the driver developer, know that when you call `a()`, it results in `schedule()` being called? There are a few points you need to understand and leverage regarding this:

- (As mentioned in the companion guide *Linux Kernel Programming - Chapter 8, Kernel Memory Allocation for Module Authors – Part 1*) One way you can find out in advance if your kernel code will ever enter an atomic or interrupt context is by looking at the kernel directly. When you're configuring the kernel (again, as seen in the companion guide *Linux Kernel Programming*, recall `make menuconfig` from *Linux Kernel Programming - Chapter 2, Building the 5.x Linux Kernel from Source – Part 1*), you can turn on a kernel config option that will help you spot exactly this circumstance. Take a look under the **Kernel Hacking / Lock Debugging** menu. There, you will find a Boolean tunable called **Sleep inside atomic section checking**. Turn it **ON**!

> The config option is named `CONFIG_DEBUG_ATOMIC_SLEEP`; you can always grep your kernel's config file for it. As seen in the companion guide *Linux Kernel Programming - Chapter 5, Writing Your First Kernel Module - LKMs Part 2*, in the *Configuring a debug kernel* section, we specified that this option should be turned ON!

- Next (this is a bit pedantic, but it will help you!), make it a habit to look up the kernel documentation on the function in question (even better, briefly look up its code). The fact that it's a blocking call will usually be documented or specified in the comment header.
- The kernel has a helper macro called `might_sleep()`; it's a useful debugging aid for just these situations! The following screenshot (from the kernel source, `include/linux/kernel.h`) explains it clearly:

```
#ifdef CONFIG_DEBUG_ATOMIC_SLEEP
extern void ___might_sleep(const char *file, int line, int preempt_offset);
extern void __might_sleep(const char *file, int line, int preempt_offset);
extern void __cant_sleep(const char *file, int line, int preempt_offset);

/**
 * might_sleep - annotation for functions that can sleep
 *
 * this macro will print a stack trace if it is executed in an atomic
 * context (spinlock, irq-handler, ...). Additional sections where blocking is
 * not allowed can be annotated with non_block_start() and non_block_end()
 * pairs.
 *
 * This is a useful debugging help to be able to catch problems early and not
 * be bitten later when the calling function happens to sleep when it is not
 * supposed to.
 */
# define might_sleep() \
    do { __might_sleep(__FILE__, __LINE__, 0); might_resched(); } while (0)
```

Figure 4.2 – The comment for might_sleep() is helpful

Along the same lines, the kernel provides helper macros such
as might_resched(), cant_sleep(), non_block_start(), non_block_end(
), and so on.

- Just to remind you, we mentioned pretty much the same thing - regarding not
  blocking within an atomic context - in the companion guide *Linux Kernel
  Programming, Chapter 8, Kernel Memory Allocation for Module Authors Part 1* in the
  Dealing with the GFP flags section (and elsewhere). Furthermore, we also showed
  you how the useful LDV project (mentioned back in companion guide *Linux
  Kernel Programming, Chapter 1, Kernel Workspace Setup*, in the section *The LDV -
  Linux Driver Verification - project*) has caught and fixed several such violations
  within kernel and driver module code.

At the beginning of this section, we mentioned that, often, sleeping user space readers block
upon the arrival of data. Its arrival is typically signaled by the hardware interrupt. Then,
your interrupt handler routine fetches the data into a kernel VAS buffer and wakes up the
sleepers. Hey, isn't that disallowed? No – the wake_up*() APIs are non-blocking in nature.
The thing you need to understand is that they only switch the process' (or thread's) state
from asleep (TASK_{UN}INTERRUPTIBLE) to awake, ready to run (TASK_RUNNING). This
does not invoke the scheduler; the kernel will do that at the next opportunity point (we
discussed CPU scheduling in the companion guide *Linux Kernel Programming, Chapter 10,
The CPU Scheduler – Part 1*, and *Chapter 11, The CPU Scheduler – Part 2*).

Interrupt masking – the defaults and controlling it

Recall that the interrupt controller chip (the PIC/GIC) will have a mask register. The OS can program it **to mask or block hardware interrupts** as required (of course, some interrupts may be unmaskable; the **non-maskable interrupt (NMI)** is a typical case that we discuss later in this chapter).

It's important to realize, though, that keeping interrupts enabled (unmasked) as much as possible is a critical measure of OS quality! Why? If an interrupt(s) is blocked, the peripheral cannot be responded to and the system's performance lags or suffers as a result (merely pressing and releasing a keyboard key results in two hardware interrupts). You must keep interrupts enabled for as long as possible. Locking with the spinlock will cause interrupts and preemption to be disabled! Keep the critical section short (we'll cover locking in depth in the last two chapters of this book).

Next, when it comes to the default behavior on the Linux OS, when a hardware interrupt occurs and that interrupt isn't masked (always the default), let's say it's IRQn (where *n* is the IRQ number), **the kernel ensures that while its interrupt (hardirq) handler executes, all interrupts on the local CPU core where the handler is executing are disabled and IRQn is disabled across all CPUs**. Thus, your handler code is inherently reentrant-safe. This is good as it means you never have to worry about the following:

- Masking interrupts yourself
- When to run atomically, to completion and without interruption, on that CPU core

> As we'll see later, a bottom-half can still be interrupted by a top-half, thus necessitating locking.

While IRQn executes on, say, CPU core 1, other interrupts remain enabled (unmasked) on all CPU cores but core 1. Thus, on multicore system hardware, interrupts can run in parallel on different CPU cores. This is fine as long as they don't step on each other's toes, with respect to global data! If they do, you'll have to employ locking, something we'll cover in detail in this book's last two chapters.

Furthermore, on Linux, **all interrupts are peers**, so there is no priority among them; in other words, they all run at the same priority. Provided it's unmasked, any hardware interrupt can interrupt the system at any point in time; an interrupt can even interrupt interrupts! However, they typically don't do the latter. This is because, as we have just learned, while an interrupt IRQn is running on a CPU core, all the interrupts on that core are disabled (masked) and IRQn is disabled globally (across all cores) until it completes; the exception is an NMI.

Keep it fast

An interrupt is what is suggests: it interrupts normal work on the machine; it's a bit of an annoyance that has to be tolerated. Context has to be saved, the handler has to be executed (along with bottom halves, which we will cover in the *Understanding and using top and bottom halves* section), and then context must be restored to whatever got interrupted. So, you get the idea: it's a critical code path, so don't plod along – **be fast and non-blocking!**

It also brings up the question, how fast is fast? While the answer is, of course, platform-dependent, a heuristic is this: keep your interrupt processing as fast as is possible, **within tens of microseconds**. If it consistently exceeds 100 microseconds, then the need for alternate strategies does come up. We'll cover what you can do when this occurs later in the chapter.

With regard to our simple `my_interrupt()` pseudocode snippet (shown in the *Don't block – spotting possibly blocking code paths* section), first, ask yourself, must I really allocate memory in a critical non-blocking needs-to-execute-fast code path such as an interrupt handler? Can you design the module/driver to allocate the memory earlier (and just use the pointer)?

Again, the reality is that, at times, quite a lot of work has to be done to correctly service the interrupt (network/block drivers are good examples). We shall cover some typical strategies we can use to deal with this shortly.

Writing the interrupt handler routine itself

Now, let's quickly learn the mechanical part of it. The signature of the hardware interrupt handler routine (often referred to as the **hardirq** routine) is as follows:

```
static irqreturn_t interrupt_handler(int irq, void *data);
```

The interrupt handler routine is invoked by the kernel's generic IRQ layer when a hardware IRQ that your driver has registered interest in (via the `request_irq()` or friends APIs) is triggered. It receives two parameters:

- The first parameter is the IRQ line (an integer). Triggering this causes this handler to be invoked.
- The second parameter is the value that was passed via the last parameter to `request_irq()`. As we mentioned previously, it's typically the driver's specialized device structure that embeds the driver context or private data. Because of this, its data type is the generic `void *`, allowing `request_irq()` to pass any type along, typecasting it appropriately in the handler routine and using it.

The handler is regular C code, but with all the caveats we mentioned in the preceding section! Take care to follow those guidelines. Though the details are hardware-specific, typically, your interrupt handler's first responsibility is to clear the interrupt on the board, in effect, acknowledging it and telling the PIC as much. This is usually achieved by writing some specific bits into a specified hardware register on the board or controller; read the datasheet for your particular chip, chipset or hardware device to figure this out. Here, the `in_irq()` macro will return `true`, informing you that your code is currently in a hardirq context.

The rest of the work that's done by the handler is obviously very device-specific. For example, an input driver will want to scan the key code (or touchscreen coordinates or mouse key/movement or whatever) that was just pressed or released from some register or peripheral memory location and perhaps save it in some memory buffer. Alternatively, it might immediately pass it up the stack to a generic input layer above it. We won't try and delve into those details here. Again, the driver framework is what you need to understand for your driver type; this is beyond the scope of this book.

What about the value to return from your hardirq handler? The `irqreturn_t` return value is an `enum` and looks as follows:

```
// include/linux/irqreturn.h

/**
 * enum irqreturn
 * @IRQ_NONE interrupt was not from this device or was not handled
 * @IRQ_HANDLED interrupt was handled by this device
 * @IRQ_WAKE_THREAD handler requests to wake the handler thread
 */
enum irqreturn {
    IRQ_NONE = (0 0),
    IRQ_HANDLED = (1 0),
```

```
    IRQ_WAKE_THREAD = (1 1),
};
```

The preceding comment header clearly points out its meaning. Essentially, the generic IRQ framework insists that you return the `IRQ_HANDLED` value if your driver handled the interrupt. If the interrupt was not yours or you couldn't handle it, you should return the `IRQ_NONE` value. (This helps the kernel detect spurious interrupts as well. If you cannot figure out whether it's your interrupt, simply return `IRQ_HANDLED`.) We'll see how `IRQ_WAKE_THREAD` is used shortly.

Now, let's look at some more code! In the next section, we'll check out the hardware interrupt handler code for two drivers (we came across these earlier in this and the previous chapter).

Code view 2 – the i8042 driver's interrupt handler

In the previous chapter, `Chapter 3`, *Working with Hardware I/O Memory*, in the *A PIO example – the i8042* section, we learned how the i8042 device driver uses some very simple helper routines to perform I/O (read/write) on the I/O ports of the i8042 chip (this is often the keyboard/mouse controller on x86 systems). The following code snippet shows some of the code for its hardware interrupt handler routine; you can clearly see it reading both the status and data registers:

```
// drivers/input/serio/i8042.c
/*
 * i8042_interrupt() is the most important function in this driver –
 * it handles the interrupts from the i8042, and sends incoming bytes
 * to the upper layers.
 */
static irqreturn_t i8042_interrupt(int irq, void *dev_id)
{
    unsigned char str, data;
    [...]
    str = i8042_read_status();
    [...]
    data = i8042_read_data();
    [...]
    if (likely(serio && !filtered))
        serio_interrupt(serio, data, dfl);
 out:
    return IRQ_RETVAL(ret);
}
```

Here, the `serio_interrupt()` call is how this driver passes on the data it read from the hardware to the upper "input" layer, which will process it further and ultimately have it ready for the user space process to consume. (Take a look at the *Questions* section at the end of this chapter; one of the exercises for you to try is writing a simple "key logger" device driver.)

Code view 3 – the IXGB network driver's interrupt handler

Let's take a look at another example. Here, we're looking at the hardware interrupt handler of the Intel IXGB ethernet adapter's device driver, which we mentioned earlier:

```
// drivers/net/ethernet/intel/ixgb/ixgb_main.c
static irqreturn_t
ixgb_intr(int irq, void *data)
{
    struct net_device *netdev = data;
    struct ixgb_adapter *adapter = netdev_priv(netdev);
    struct ixgb_hw *hw = &adapter-hw;
    u32 icr = IXGB_READ_REG(hw, ICR);

    if (unlikely(!icr))
        return IRQ_NONE; /* Not our interrupt */
    [...]
    if (napi_schedule_prep(&adapter-napi)) {
        [...]
        IXGB_WRITE_REG(&adapter-hw, IMC, ~0);
        __napi_schedule(&adapter-napi);
    }
    return IRQ_HANDLED;
}
```

In the preceding code snippet, notice how the driver gains access to its private (or context) metadata structure (`struct ixgb_adapter`) from the `net_device` structure (the specialized structure for network devices) it receives as the second parameter; this is very typical. (Here, the `netdev_priv()` helper used to extract the driver's private structure from the generic `net_device` structure is somewhat analogous to the well-known `container_of()` helper macro. In fact, this helper is also often employed in similar situations.)

Next, it performs a peripheral I/O memory read via the `IXGB_READ_REG()` macro (it's using the MMIO approach – see the previous chapter for details on MMIO; `IXGB_READ_REG()` is a macro that invokes the `readl()` API we covered in the previous chapter – the older style routine for performing a 32-bit MMIO read). Don't miss the key point here: this is how the driver determines whether the interrupt is meant for it, as, recall, it's a shared interrupt! If it is meant for it (the likely case), it proceeds with its job; since this adapter supports NAPI, the driver now schedules polled NAPI reads to suck up network packets as they come in and sends them up the network protocol stack for further processing (well, it's really not that simple; the actual memory transfer work will be performed over DMA).

Now, a diversion but an important one: you need to learn how to allocate the IRQ line the modern way – via the `devm_*` APIs. This is known as the managed approach.

IRQ allocation – the modern way – the managed interrupt facility

Many modern drivers employ the kernel's *devres* or managed APIs framework for various purposes. The managed APIs in modern Linux kernels give you the advantage of not having to worry about freeing up resources that you've allocated (we have covered a few of them already, including `devm_k{m,z}alloc()` and `devm_ioremap{_resource}()`). Of course, you must use them appropriately, typically in the probe method (or `init` code) of the driver.

It is recommended that, when writing drivers, you use this newer API style. Here, we'll show how you to employ the `devm_request_irq()` API in order to allocate (register) your hardware interrupt. Its signature is as follows:

```
#include <linux/interrupt.h>

int __must_check
devm_request_irq(struct device *dev, unsigned int irq, irq_handler_t
handler,
                 unsigned long irqflags, const char *devname, void
*dev_id);
```

The first parameter is the pointer to the `device` structure of the device (which, as we saw in `Chapter 1`, *Writing a Simple misc Character Device Driver*, has to be obtained by registering to the appropriate kernel framework). The five remaining parameters are identical to `request_irq()`; we won't repeat them here. The whole point is that, once registered, you are freed from calling `free_irq()`; the kernel will automatically invoke it as required (on driver removal or device detachment). This greatly helps us developers avoid common and infamous leakage type bugs.

To help clarify its use, let's quickly look at an example. The following is a bit of the code from the V4L TV tuner driver:

```
// drivers/gpu/drm/exynos/exynos_mixer.c
[...]
    res = platform_get_resource(mixer_ctx->pdev, IORESOURCE_IRQ, 0);
    if (res == NULL) {
        dev_err(dev, "get interrupt resource failed.\n");
        return -ENXIO;
    }

    ret = devm_request_irq(dev, res->start, mixer_irq_handler,
                        0, "drm_mixer", mixer_ctx);
    if (ret) {
        dev_err(dev, "request interrupt failed.\n");
        return ret;
    }
    mixer_ctx-irq = res->start;
[...]
```

As we saw in regard to getting the physical address for MMIO in `Chapter 3`, *Working with Hardware I/O Memory*, in the *Obtaining the device resources* section, here, the same driver employs the `platform_get_resource()` API to extract the IRQ number (specifying the type of resource as an IRQ line with `IORESOURCE_IRQ`). Once it has it, it issues the `devm_request_irq()` API to allocate or register the interrupt! As is therefore expected, a search for `free_irq()` in this driver yields no results.

Next, we'll learn what a threaded interrupt is, how to work with one, and, more importantly, the *why* of it.

Working with the threaded interrupts model

As seen in the companion guide *Linux Kernel Programming - Chapter 11, The CPU Scheduler – Part 2*, in the *Converting mainline Linux into an RTOS* section, we covered the real-time patch for Linux (RTL), which allows you to patch, configure, build, and run Linux as an RTOS! If you're hazy on this, please refer back to this. We won't repeat the same information here.

The **Real-Time Linux (RTL)** project's work has been steadily back-ported into the mainline Linux kernel. One of the key changes wrought by RTL was merging the **threaded interrupts** feature into the mainline kernel. This occurred in kernel version 2.6.30 (June 2009). This technology does something that, at first glance, seems very weird: it "converts" the hardware interrupt handler into, essentially, a kernel thread.

As you will learn in the next chapter, a kernel thread is really very similar to a user mode thread – it runs independently, in the process context and has its own task structure (and thus its own PID, TGID, and so on), which means it can be scheduled; that is, when in the runnable state, it fights with other contender threads to run on a CPU core. The key difference is that a user mode thread always has two address spaces – the process VAS that it belongs to (user space) and the kernel VAS, which it switches to when it issues a system call. A kernel thread, on the other hand, runs purely in kernel space and has no view of the user space; it only sees the kernel VAS that it always executes in (technically, its `current-mm` value is always `NULL`!).

So, how do you decide if you should use a threaded interrupt? We need to cover a few more topics before this becomes completely clear (for those of you who are impatient, here's the short answer: use a threaded interrupt handler when (as a quick heuristic) the interrupt work takes over 100 microseconds; skip ahead to the *Hardirqs, tasklets, threaded handlers – what to use when* section and see the table there for a quick look).

Now, let's learn how to employ the threaded interrupt model by checking out the available APIs – both the regular and managed ones. Then, we'll learn how to use the managed version and how to employ it within a driver. After that, we'll look at its internal implementation and delve more into the why of it.

Employing the threaded interrupt model – the API

In order to understand the threaded interrupt model's inner workings, let's take a look at the relevant APIs. We've already covered using the `request_irq()` API. Let's look at its implementation:

```
// include/linux/interrupt.h
static inline int __must_check
request_irq(unsigned int irq, irq_handler_t handler, unsigned long flags,
const char *name, void *dev)
{
    return request_threaded_irq(irq, handler, NULL, flags, name, dev);
}
```

This API is merely a thin wrapper over the `request_threaded_irq()` API! Its signature is as follows:

```
int __must_check
request_threaded_irq(unsigned int irq, irq_handler_t handler,
            irq_handler_t thread_fn,
            unsigned long flags, const char *name, void *dev);
```

The parameters, except for the third one, are identical to `request_irq()`. The following are a few key points to note:

- `irq_handler_t handler`: The second parameter is a pointer to the usual interrupt handler function. We now refer to it as the primary handler. If it's null and `thread_fn` (the third parameter) is non-null, a default primary handler (of the kernel's) is auto-installed (if you're wondering about this default primary handler, we'll cover it in more detail in the *Internally implementing the threaded interrupt* section).
- `irq_handler_t thread_fn`: The third parameter is a pointer to the threaded interrupt function; the API behavior depends on whether you pass this parameter as null or not:
  - If it's non-null, then the actual servicing of the interrupt is performed by this function. It runs within the context (process) of a dedicated kernel thread – it's a threaded interrupt!
  - If it's null, which is the default when you call `request_irq()`, only the primary handler runs, and no kernel thread is created.

The primary handler if specified (second parameter), is run in what's referred to as the **hardirq** or hard interrupt context (as was the case with `request_irq()`). If the primary handler is non-null, then you are expected to write it's code and (minimally) do the following in it:

- Verify the interrupt is for you; if it's not, return `IRQ_NONE`.
- If it is for you, then you can clear and/or disable the interrupt on the board/device.
- Return `IRQ_WAKE_THREAD`; this will cause the kernel to wake up the kernel thread representing your threaded interrupt handler. The name of the kernel thread will be in the format `irq/irq#-name`. This kernel thread will now internally invoke the `thread_fn()` function, where you perform the actual interrupt handling work.

On the other hand, if the primary handler is null, then just your threaded handler – the function specified by the third parameter – will be automatically run **as a kernel thread** by the OS when the interrupt fires.

As with `request_irq()`, the return value from `request_threaded_irq()` is an integer, following the usual `0/-E` kernel convention: 0 on success and a negative `errno` value on failure. You are expected to check it.

Employing the managed threaded interrupt model – the recommended way

Again, using the managed API for allocating a threaded interrupt would be the recommended approach for a modern driver. The kernel provides the `devm_request_threaded_irq()` API for this very purpose:

```
#include linux/interrupt.h

int __must_check
 devm_request_threaded_irq(struct device *dev, unsigned int irq,
             irq_handler_t handler, irq_handler_t thread_fn,
             unsigned long irqflags, const char *devname,
             void *dev_id);
```

All the parameters besides the first one, which is the pointer to the device structure, are the same as those for `request_threaded_irq()`. The key advantage of this is that you don't need to worry about freeing up the IRQ line. The kernel will auto-free it on device detach or driver removal, as we learned with `devm_request_irq()`. As with `request_threaded_irq()`, the return value from `devm_request_threaded_irq()` is an integer, following the usual `0/-E` kernel convention: `0` on success and a negative errno value on failure; you are expected to check it.

 Don't forget! Using the managed `devm_request_threaded_irq()` API is the modern recommended approach for allocating a threaded interrupt. However, note that it won't always be the right approach; see the *Constraints when using a threaded handler* section for more information.

The signature of the threaded interrupt handler function is identical to that for the hardirq interrupt handler:

```
static irqreturn_t threaded_handler(int irq, void *data);
```

The parameters have the same meaning as well.

Threaded interrupts often use the `IRQF_ONESHOT` interrupt flag; the kernel comment in `include/linux/interrupt.h` describes it best:

```
 * IRQF_ONESHOT - Interrupt is not reenabled after the hardirq handler
finished.
 * Used by threaded interrupts which need to keep the
 * irq line disabled until the threaded handler has been run.
```

As a matter of fact, the kernel **insists that you use** the `IRQF_ONESHOT` flag when your driver is incorporating a threaded handler and the primary handler is the kernel default. Not using the `IRQF_ONESHOT` flag would be deadly when level-triggered interrupts are in play. To be safe, the kernel throws an error - when this flag isn't present in the `irqflags` bitmask parameter - even for edge-triggering. If you're curious, the code at `kernel/irq/manage.c:__setup_irq()` checks for just this (link: `https://elixir.bootlin.com/linux/v5.4/source/kernel/irq/manage.c#L1486`).

 A kernel parameter called `threadirqs` exists that you can pass to the kernel command line (via the bootloader). This force threads all the interrupt handlers except those marked explicitly as `IRQF_NO_THREAD`. To find out more about this kernel parameter, go to `https://www.kernel.org/doc/html/latest/admin-guide/kernel-parameters.html`.

In the following subsection, we'll take a look at one of the Linux driver's STM32 microcontrollers. Here, we will focus on how interrupt allocation is done via the "managed" API that we just covered.

Code view 4 – the STM32 F7 microcontroller's threaded interrupt handler

The STM32 F7 is part of a series of microcontrollers that have been manufactured by STMicroelectronics, based on the ARM-Cortex M7F core:

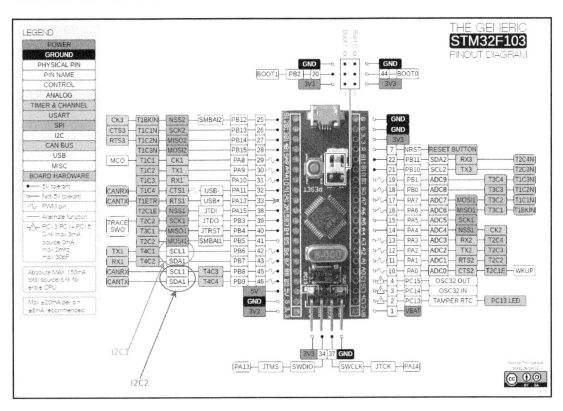

Figure 4.3 – The STM32F103 microcontroller pinout with some I2C pins highlighted (see the lower left)

Image Credit: The preceding image, which has been slightly added to by myself, has been taken from `https://www.electronicshub.org/wp-content/uploads/2020/02/STM32F103C8T6-Blue-Pill-Pin-Layout.gif`. Image by Rasmus Friis Kjekisen. This image falls under Creative Commons CC BY-SA 1.0 (`https://creativecommons.org/licenses/by-sa/1.0/`).

The Linux kernel supports the STM32 F7 via various drivers and DTS files. Here, we'll take a look at a tiny bit of the code for the I2C bus driver (`drivers/i2c/busses/i2c-stm32f7.c`) for this microcontroller. It allocates two hardware interrupts:

- The event IRQ line, via the `devm_request_threaded_irq()` API
- The error IRQ line, via the `request_irq()` API

The code that allocates the IRQ lines is, as expected, within its probe method:

```
// drivers/i2c/busses/i2c-stm32f7.c
static int stm32f7_i2c_probe(struct platform_device *pdev)
{
    struct stm32f7_i2c_dev *i2c_dev;
    const struct stm32f7_i2c_setup *setup;
    struct resource *res;
    int irq_error, irq_event, ret;

    [...]
    irq_event = platform_get_irq(pdev, 0);
    [...]
    irq_error = platform_get_irq(pdev, 1);
    [...]
    ret = devm_request_threaded_irq(&pdev->dev, irq_event,
                stm32f7_i2c_isr_event,
                stm32f7_i2c_isr_event_thread,
                IRQF_ONESHOT,
                pdev->name, i2c_dev);
    [...]
    ret = devm_request_irq(&pdev->dev, irq_error, stm32f7_i2c_isr_error, 0,
                pdev->name, i2c_dev);
```

Let's focus on the call to `devm_request_threaded_irq()`. The first parameter is the pointer to the device structure. Since this is a platform driver (registered via the `module_platform_driver` wrapper macro), its probe method receives the `struct platform_device *pdev` parameter; the `device` structure is extracted from it. The second parameter is the IRQ line to allocate. Again, as we've already seen, it's extracted via a helper routine. Here, this is the `platform_get_irq()` API.

The third parameter specifies the primary handler; that is the hardirq. Since it's non-null, this routine will be invoked when the IRQ is triggered. It performs hardware-specific verification on the device and the I2C transfer, and if all is okay, it returns the `IRQ_WAKE_THREAD` value. This awakens the threaded interrupt routine, the fourth parameter, and the function `stm32f7_i2c_isr_event_thread()` runs as a kernel thread in process context! The `irqflags` parameter, which is set to `IRQF_ONESHOT`, is typical with threaded handlers; it specifies that the IRQ line remains disabled until the threaded handler completes (not just the hardirq). The threaded handler routine does its work and returns `IRQ_HANDLED` when it's finished.

Since the error IRQ line is allocated via the `devm_request_irq()` API, and because we have already covered how to use this API (refer to the *IRQ allocation – the modern way – the managed interrupt facility* section), we won't repeat any information regarding it here.

Now, let's look at how the kernel internally implements the threaded interrupt model.

Internally implementing the threaded interrupt

As we mentioned previously, if the primary handler is null and the thread function is non-null, the kernel uses a default primary handler. The function is called `irq_default_primary_handler()` and all it does is return the `IRQ_WAKE_THREAD` value, thus waking up (and making schedulable) the kernel thread.

Furthermore, the actual kernel thread that runs your `thread_fn` routine is created within the code of the `request_threaded_irq()` API. The call graph (as of version 5.4.0 of the Linux kernel) is as follows:

```
kernel/irq/manage.c:request_threaded_irq() -- __setup_irq() --
      setup_irq_thread() -- kernel/kthread.c:kthread_create()
```

The invocation of the `kthread_create()` API is as follows. Here, you can clearly see how the format of the new kernel thread's name will be in `irq/irq#-name` format:

```
t = kthread_create(irq_thread, new, "irq/%d-%s", irq, new->name);
```

Here (we don't show the code), the new kernel thread is programmed to be set to the `SCHED_FIFO` scheduling policy and the `MAX_USER_RT_PRIO/2` real-time scheduling priority, which typically has a value of `50` (the `SCHED_FIFO` range is from 1 to `99`, and `MAX_USER_RT_PRIO` is `100`). We'll cover why this is important in the *Why use threaded interrupts?* section. If you're unsure about the thread scheduling policy and its priority, please refer to the companion guide *Linux Kernel Programming - Chapter 10, The CPU Scheduler – Part 1*, the *The POSIX scheduling policies* section.

The kernel manages this kernel thread representing the threaded interrupt handler in its entirety. As we've already seen, it creates it on IRQ allocation via the `[devm_]request_threaded_irq()` API; then, the kernel thread simply sleeps. It is awoken on demand by the kernel, whenever the allocated IRQ is triggered; the kernel will destroy it when `free_irq()` is invoked. Don't worry about the details at the moment; we'll cover kernel threads and other interesting topics in the next chapter.

So far, although you have learned how to use the threaded interrupt model, it's not been clearly explained why (and when) you should. The next section will cover this in detail.

Why use threaded interrupts?

A key question that's usually asked is, why should I use threaded interrupts at all when the regular hardirq-type interrupt exists? The complete answer is a bit elaborate; the following are the primary reasons why:

- To really make it real time.
- It eliminates/reduces softirq bottlenecks. Since the threaded handler actually runs its code in process context, it's not considered to be as critical a code path as a hardirq handler; hence, you can take a little longer with interrupt handling.

  - While a hardirq executes IRQn, that IRQ line is disabled on all the cores across the system. If it takes a while to execute to completion (of course, you should design it so that it doesn't), then the system's response can significantly drop; on the other hand, while a threaded handler executes, the hardware IRQ line is enabled by default. This is good for performance and responsiveness. (Note that there will be many cases where the driver will not want this behavior; that is, it will want IRQ to be disabled while it processes it. To do that, specify the `IRQF_ONESHOT` flag.)

In a nutshell, as a quick rule of thumb, **when the interrupt handling consistently takes over 100 microseconds, use the threaded interrupt model** (see the table in *Hardirqs, tasklets, threaded handlers – what to use when* section).

In the following subsections, we will expand on these points.

Threaded interrupts – to really make it real time

This is a key point and requires some explanation.

Prioritization on the standard Linux OS goes from highest to lowest priority as follows (we'll suffix each bullet point with the *context* it runs in; it will be either process or interrupt. If you're unclear on this point, it's very important you understand this; do refer to the companion guide *Linux Kernel Programming - Chapter 6, Kernel Internals Essentials – Processes and Threads*, the *Understanding Process and Interrupt Contexts* section, for more information):

- **Hardware interrupts**: These preempt anything and everything. The hardirq handler runs atomically (to completion, without interruption) on the CPU; context:interrupt.

- **Real-time threads** (the SCHED_FIFO or SCHED_RR scheduling policy), both kernel and user space, with positive real-time priority (rtprio); context:process:
    - A kernel thread at the same realtime priority (current-rtprio) gets a slight priority bump over a user space thread at the same realtime priority.

- **Processor exceptions**: This includes system calls (they're really synchronous exceptions; for example, syscall on the x86, SWI on ARM), page faults, protection faults, and so on; context:process.

- **User mode threads**: They use the SCHED_OTHER scheduling policy by default with an rtprio of 0; context:process.

The following diagram shows relative prioritization on Linux (this diagram is a bit simplistic; a more refined diagram is seen later via *Figure 4.10* and *Figure 4.11*):

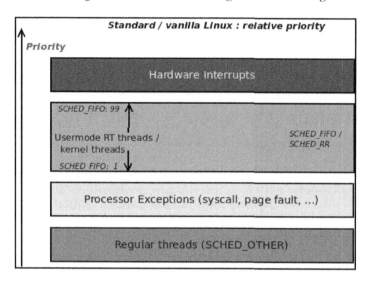

Figure 4.4 – Relative prioritization on the standard Linux OS

Let's say you are working on a real-time multithreaded application. Of the dozens of threads that are alive within the process, three of them (let's call them threads A, B, and C for simplicity) are considered to be critical "real-time" threads. Accordingly, you have the app grant them a scheduling policy of SCHED_FIFO and real-time priorities of 30, 45, and 60 to threads A, B, and C, respectively (if you're unclear on these points, please refer to the companion guide *Linux Kernel Programming - Chapter 10, The CPU Scheduler - Part 1*, and *Chapter 11, The CPU Scheduler - Part 2*, on CPU scheduling). Since it's a real-time app, the maximum time that it can take these threads to complete their work is curtailed. In other words, a *deadline exists;* for our example scenario, let's say that the **worst-case deadline** for thread B to complete its work is 12 milliseconds.

Now, in terms of relative priorities, how will this work? For simplicity, let's say that the system has a single CPU core. Now, another thread, X (running with the scheduling policy SCHED_OTHER and with a real-time priority of 0, which is the default scheduling policy/priority value), is currently executing code on the CPU. However, if the "event" that any of your real-time threads is waiting upon occurs, it will preempt the currently executing thread and run. This is what's expected; recall that the fundamental rule for real-time scheduling is very simple: *the highest priority runnable thread must be the thread that's running*. Okay; that's good. Now, we need to consider hardware interrupts. A hardware interrupt, as we've seen, has the highest priority. This means it will preempt anything and everything, including your (so-called) real-time thread (see the preceding diagram)!

Let's say that interrupt processing takes 200 microseconds; on a rich OS such as Linux, this isn't considered too bad. However, in this situation, five hardware interrupts will consume 1 millisecond; what if the device becomes busy (many incoming data packets, for example) and emits, say, 20 hardware interrupts in a continuous stream? This will certainly be given priority and will consume (at least) 4 milliseconds! Your real-time thread(s) will definitely be preempted while interrupt processing runs and will be unable to gain the CPU it needs until it's far too late! The (12 ms) deadline will have long expired and the system will fail (if yours is a true real-time app, this could be catastrophic).

The following diagram represents this scenario conceptually (for conciseness and clarity, we have only shown one of our user space SCHED_FIFO real-time threads; that is, thread B at rtprio 45):

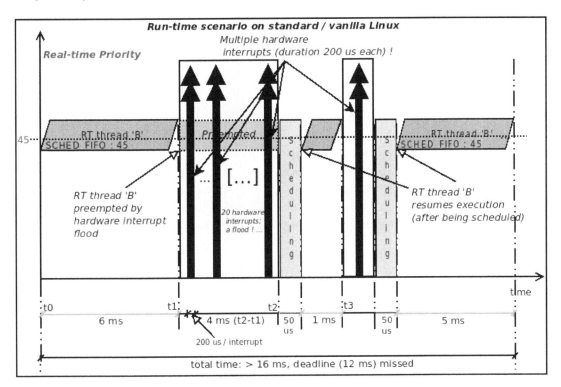

Figure 4.5: The hardirq model – a user mode RT SCHED_FIFO thread interrupted by a hardware interrupt flood; deadline missed

Real-time thread B is depicted as running from time t0 (on the x-axis; the y-axis represents the real-time priority; thread B's rtprio is 45); it has 12 ms (a hard deadline) to complete its work. However, let's say that after 6 ms have elapsed (at time t1), a hardware interrupt fires.

In *Figure 4.5*, we haven't shown the low-level interrupt setup code that executes. Now a hardware interrupt firing at time t1 results in the interrupt handler being invoked; that is, the hardirq (shown as the big black vertical double-arrow in the preceding diagram). Obviously, the hardware interrupt preempts thread B. Now, let's say it takes 200 microseconds to execute; that's not much, but what if a flood of interrupts (say 20 of them, thus eating up 4 ms) arrives! This is depicted in the preceding diagram: the interrupts continue at a rapid rate until time t2; only after they all complete will context be restored. Thus, the scheduling code runs and (let's say) context switches back to thread B, giving it the processor (we take, on a modern Intel CPU, a conservative context switching time of 50 microseconds: https://blog.tsunanet.net/2010/11/how-long-does-it-take-to-make-context.html). However, soon after, at time t3, the hardware interrupt fires once more, preempting B again. This can go on indefinitely; the RT thread will eventually run (when the interrupt storm is complete) but may or may not meet its deadline! This is the main issue.

> The problem that was described in the preceding paragraph doesn't go away by simply raising the real-time priority of your user mode threads; the hardirq hardware interrupts will still always preempt them, regardless of their priority.

By backporting the **threaded interrupt** from the RTL project to mainline Linux, we can **solve** this problem. How? Think about it: with the *threaded interrupt* model, the majority of the interrupt handling work is now performed by a SCHED_FIFO kernel thread running with a real-time priority of 50. So, simply design your user space applications to have, where essential, SCHED_FIFO RT threads with real-time priorities **higher than** 50. **This will ensure that they run in preference to the hardware interrupt handler!**

> The key idea here is that a user mode thread under the SCHED_FIFO policy and a real-time priority 50, can, in effect, preempt the (threaded) hardware interrupt! Quite a thing indeed.

So, for our example scenario, let's now assume we're using threaded interrupts. Next, tweak the user space multithreaded app's design: assign our three real-time threads a policy of SCHED_FIFO and real-time priorities of 60, 65, and 70. The following diagram conceptually depicts this scenario (for clarity, we have only shown one of our user space SCHED_FIFO threads, thread B, this time at rtprio of 65):

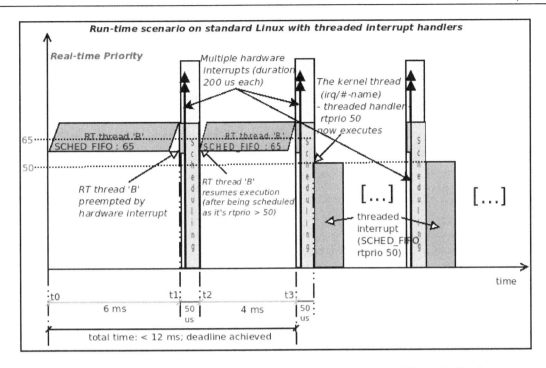

Figure 4.6 – Threaded interrupt model – a user mode RT SCHED_FIFO rtprio 50 thread can preempt the threaded interrupt; deadline achieved

In the preceding diagram, RT thread B is now at the SCHED_FIFO scheduling policy with an rtprio of 65. It has up to 12 ms to complete (reach its deadline). Again, say it executes for 6 ms (t0 to t1); at time t1, a hardware interrupt fires. Here, the low-level setup code and the (kernel default or driver's) hardirq handler will execute immediately, preempting anything on the processor. However, the hardirq or primary handler takes a very short time to execute (a few microseconds at the most). This is, as we have already discussed, the primary handler that is now executing; it will do the bare minimum work required before returning the IRQ_WAKE_THREAD value, which will have the kernel wake up the kernel thread representing the threaded handler. However – and this is the key – the threaded interrupt, which is SCHED_FIFO with a priority of 50, is now competing with other runnable threads for the CPU resource. Since thread B is a SCHED_FIFO real-time thread with an rtprio of 65, **it will beat the threaded handler to the CPU and will run instead!**

To summarize, in the preceding diagram, the following is happening:

- Time t0 to t1: the user mode RT thread (SCHED_FIFO, rtprio 65) is executing its code (for 6 ms)
- At time t1, the thin gray bar represents the hardirq low-level setup/BSP code.
- The thin black double-arrow vertical line represents the primary hardirq handler (both the above take just a few microseconds to complete).
- The blue color bar is the scheduling code.
- The purple bar (at t3 + 50 us) represents the threaded interrupt handler running at rtprio 50.

The upshot of all this is that thread B completes its work well within its deadline (here, as an example, it's met its deadline in just over 10 ms).

Unless time constraints are extremely critical, using the threaded interrupt model to handle your device's interrupts works very well for most devices and drivers. At the time of writing, the devices that tend to remain within the traditional top/bottom half approach (covered in detail in the *Understanding and using top and bottom halves* section) are typically high-performance network, block, and (some) multimedia devices.

Constraints when using a threaded handler

One last thing regarding threaded handlers: the kernel won't blindly allow you to use a threaded handler for any IRQ; it honors some constraints. At the time of registering your thread handler (via the [devm_]request_threaded_irq() APIs), it performs several validity checks, one of which we've mentioned already: IRQF_ONESHOT must be present for a threaded handler.

It also depends on the actual IRQ line; for example, I once tried using a threaded handler for IRQ 1 on x86 (it's typically the i8042 keyboard/mouse controller chip's interrupt line). It failed, with the kernel showing the following:

```
genirq: Flags mismatch irq 1. 00002080 (driver-name) vs. 00000080 (i8042)
```

So, from the preceding output, we can see that the i8042 will only accept the 0x80 bitmask for the IRQ flags, whereas I passed a value of 0x2080; a little checking will show that the 0x2000 flag is indeed the IRQF_ONESHOT flag; apparently, this causes a mismatch and isn't allowed. Not only that, but notice who flagged the error – it was the kernel's generic IRQ layer (genirq) checking things under the hood. (Note that this kind of error checking isn't restricted to threaded interrupts.)

Also, certain critical devices will find that using threaded handlers will actually slow them down; this is pretty typical for modern NICs, block devices, and some multimedia devices. They typically use the hardirq top half and tasklet/softirq bottom half mechanisms (this will be explained in the *Understanding and using top and bottom halves* section).

Working with either hardirq or threaded handlers

Before we conclude this section, there's one more interesting point to take into consideration: the kernel provides an IRQ allocation API that, based on certain circumstances, will either set up your interrupt handler as a traditional hardirq handler or as a threaded handler. This API is called `request_any_context_irq()`; note that it's exported as GPL-only though. Its signature is as follows:

```
int __must_check
request_any_context_irq(unsigned int irq, irq_handler_t handler,
          unsigned long flags, const char *name, void *dev_id);
```

The parameters are identical to that of `request_irq()`. When invoked, this routine will decide whether the interrupt handler function – the `handler` parameter – will run in an atomic hardirq context or in a sleep-capable process context, that of a kernel thread – in other words, as a threaded handler. How will you know which context `handler()` will run in? The return value let's you know based on the context that `handler()` will run in:

- If it's going to run in a hardirq context, it returns a value of `IRQC_IS_HARDIRQ`.
- If it's going to run in a process/threaded context, it returns a value of `IRQC_IS_NESTED`.
- A negative `errno` will be returned on failure (you're expected to check this).

What does this really imply, though? Essentially, there are controllers that are on slow buses (I2C is a great example); they spawn off handlers that use so-called "nested" interrupts, which really means that the handler isn't atomic in nature. It might invoke functions that sleep (again, I2C functions are a good example of this), and thus are required to be preemptible. Using the `request_any_context_irq()` API ensures that if this is the case, the underlying generic IRQ code detects it and gives you an appropriate handling interface. The GPIO-driven matrix keypad driver is another example that makes use of this API (`drivers/input/keyboard/matrix_keypad.c`).

With this coverage, you now understand what threaded interrupts are and why they can be very useful. Now, let's take a look at a shorter topic: how you, as the driver author, can selectively enable/disable IRQ lines.

Enabling and disabling IRQs

Typically, it's the core kernel (and/or arch-specific) code that handles low-level interrupt management. This includes doing things such as masking them as and when required. Nevertheless, some drivers, as well as the OS, require fine-grained control when enabling/disabling hardware interrupts. As your driver or module code runs with kernel privileges, the kernel provides (exported) helper routines that allow you to do exactly this:

Brief comment	API or helper routine
Disable/enable all interrupts on the local processor	
Unconditionally disables all interrupts on the local (current) processor core.	`local_irq_disable()`
Unconditionally enables all interrupts on the local (current) processor core.	`local_irq_enable()`
Saves the state (interrupt mask) of, and then disables all interrupts on the local (current) processor core. The state is saved in the `flags` parameter that's passed.	`local_irq_save(unsigned long flags);`
Restores the state (interrupt mask) that's passed, thus enabling interrupts on the local (current) processor core as per the `flags` parameter.	`local_irq_restore(unsigned long flags);`
Disable/enable a specific IRQ line	
Disables IRQ line `irq`; will wait for – and synchronize – any pending interrupts (on that IRQ line) to complete before returning.	`void disable_irq(unsigned int irq);`
Disables IRQ line `irq`; won't wait for any pending interrupts (on that IRQ line) to complete (`nosync`).	`void disable_irq_nosync(unsigned int irq);`
Disables IRQ line `irq` and waits for the active hardirq handler to complete before returning. It returns `false` if any threaded handlers pertaining to this IRQ line are active (requires GPL).	`bool disable_hardirq(unsigned int irq);`
Enables IRQ line `irq`; undoes the effect of one call to `disable_irq()`.	`void enable_irq(unsigned int irq);`

The `local_irq_disable()` / `local_irq_enable()` helpers are designed to disable/enable all interrupts (except NMI) on the local or current processor core.

 The implementation on x86[_64] of `local_irq_disable()`/`local_irq_enable()` is done via the (in)famous `cli`/`sti` pair of machine instructions; in the bad old days, these used to disable/enable interrupts across the system, on all CPUs. Now, they work on a per-CPU basis.

The `disable_{hard}irq*()`/`enable_irq()` helpers are designed to selectively disable/enable a particular IRQ line and to be called as a pair. A few of the aforementioned routines can be called from an interrupt context, though this should be done with care! it's just safer to ensure you call them from process context. The "with care" statement is there because several of these helpers work by internally invoking non-blocking routines, such as `cpu_relax()`, that wait by repeatedly running some machine instructions on the processor. (`cpu_relax()` is a good example of this "needs to be used with care" case as it works by calling the `nop` machine instruction in an infinite loop; the loop is exited when any hardware interrupt fires, which is exactly what we're waiting for! Now, waiting for a while when in the interrupt context is considered a wrong thing to do; hence the "with care" statement.) The kernel commit for `disable_hardirq()` (link: `https://github.com/torvalds/linux/commit/02cea3958664723a5d2236f0f0058de97c7e4693`) explains that it's there to be used in situations where, *like netpoll, there is a need to disable an interrupt from an atomic context.*

When disabling an interrupt, take care to ensure you're not holding (have locked) any shared resource that the handler might use. This will result in a (self) deadlock! (Locking and its many scenarios will be explained in a lot more detail in the last two chapters of this book.)

The NMI

All the preceding APIs and helpers work on all hardware interrupts except for the **non-maskable interrupt (NMI)**. The NMI is an arch-specific interrupt and is used to implement stuff such as hardware watchdogs and debug features (for example, an unconditional kernel stack dump for all cores; we'll show an example of this very shortly). Also, NMI interrupt lines cannot be shared.

A quick example of exploiting the NMI can be shown with the kernel's so-called **magic SysRq** facility. To see the keyboard hotkeys that are assigned for magic SysRq, you must invoke or trigger it by typing in the [Alt][SysRq][letter] key combination.

magic SysRq triggering: Instead of getting your fingers all twisted typing [Alt][SysRq][letter], there's an easier – and more importantly non-interactive – way to do so: just echo the relevant letter to a proc pseudofile (as root, of course): echo letter/proc/sysrq-trigger.

But which letter do we need to type in? The following output shows a quick way you can find out. This is a kind of quick-help for magic SysRq (I did this on my Raspberry Pi 3B+):

```
rpi # dmesg -C
rpi # echo ? /proc/sysrq-trigger
rpi # dmesg
[ 294.928223] sysrq: HELP : loglevel(0-9) reboot(b) crash(c) terminate-all-
tasks(e) memory-full-oom-kill(f) kill-all-tasks(i) thaw-filesystems(j)
sak(k) show-backtrace-all-active-cpus(l) show-memory-usage(m) nice-all-RT-
tasks(n) poweroff(o) show-registers(p) show-all-timers(q) unraw(r) sync(s)
show-task-states(t) unmount(u) show-blocked-tasks(w) dump-ftrace-buffer(z)
rpi #
```

The one we're currently interested in is shown in bold – the letter l (that's a lowercase L) – show-backtrace-all-active-cpus(l). Once triggered, it literally does as promised – it shows a stack backtrace of the kernel-mode stack on all active CPUs! (This can be a useful debugging aid as you will see what each CPU core is running right now.) How? It does this by sending an NMI to them; that is, to all CPU cores! This is one way we can see exactly what the CPUs are up to at the very moment the command was triggered! This could be very useful when something is hanging the system.

Here, echo l /proc/sysrq-trigger (as root) does the trick! The following partial screenshot shows the output:

```
rpi # dmesg -C
rpi # echo l > /proc/sysrq-trigger
rpi # dmesg
[  439.520548] sysrq: Show backtrace of all active CPUs
[  439.525689] NMI backtrace for cpu 0
[  439.529269] CPU: 0 PID: 633 Comm: bash Tainted: G          C        5.4.51-v7+ #1
[  439.536849] Hardware name: BCM2835
[  439.540331] Backtrace:
[  439.542847] [<8010cb68>] (dump_backtrace) from [<8010ce4c>] (show_stack+0x20/0x24)
[  439.550608]  r6:b1798000 r5:ffffffff r4:00000000 r3:eb02066f
[  439.556411] [<8010ce2c>] (show_stack) from [<8085f21c>] (dump_stack+0xd4/0x120)
[  439.563906] [<8085f148>] (dump_stack) from [<80866394>] (nmi_cpu_backtrace+0xb4/0xc4)
[  439.575537]  r9:00000007 r8:00000000 r7:8010e8b4 r6:00000000 r5:00000000 r4:00000000
[  439.590692] [<808662e0>] (nmi_cpu_backtrace) from [<80866488>] (nmi_trigger_cpumask_backtrace+0xe4/0x130)
[  439.607925]  r5:80d07c8c r4:00000000
[  439.615181] [<808663a4>] (nmi_trigger_cpumask_backtrace) from [<8010f9fc>] (arch_trigger_cpumask_backtrace+0x1c/0x24)
[  439.633362]  r7:0000006c r6:80d6635c r5:80d104ec r4:80d04fdc
[  439.642818] [<8010f9e0>] (arch_trigger_cpumask_backtrace) from [<8059a478>] (sysrq_handle_showallcpus+0x20/0x28)
[  439.660595] [<8059a458>] (sysrq_handle_showallcpus) from [<8059a8c>] (__handle_sysrq+0xa8/0x17c)
[  439.676983] [<8059abe4>] (__handle_sysrq) from [<8059b1c0>] (write_sysrq_trigger+0x48/0x58)
[  439.692990]  r10:00000004 r9:01cf47d8 r8:00000002 r7:b1799f68 r6:00000000 r5:00000000
[  439.708751]  r4:00000002 r3:7f000000
[  439.716174] [<8059b178>] (write_sysrq_trigger) from [<8034ac04>] (proc_reg_write+0x70/0x9c)
[  439.732602]  r4:b6707080 r3:b1799f68
[  439.740164] [<8034ab94>] (proc_reg_write) from [<802c9578>] (__vfs_write+0x38/0x190)
[  439.755832]  r6:b16366c0 r5:00000000 r4:b16366c0 r3:b1799f68
[  439.765562] [<802c9540>] (__vfs_write) from [<802cc1dc>] (vfs_write+0xb0/0x1c8)
[  439.777010]  r8:b1799f68 r7:01cf47d8 r6:00000000 r5:00000000 r4:b16366c0
[  439.787725] [<802cc12c>] (vfs_write) from [<802cc474>] (ksys_write+0x58/0xb8)
[  439.798906]  r8:00000002 r7:b16366c0 r6:b16366c0 r5:00000000 r4:00000000
[  439.809590] [<802cc41c>] (ksys_write) from [<802cc4ec>] (sys_write+0x18/0x1c)
[  439.820591]  r9:b1798000 r8:801011c4 r7:00000004 r6:76f16d90 r5:01cf47d8 r4:00000002
[  439.836052] [<802cc4d4>] (sys_write) from [<80101000>] (ret_fast_syscall+0x0/0x28)
[  439.851513] Exception stack(0xb1799fa8 to 0xb1799ff0)
[  439.860584] 9fa0:                   00000002 01cf47d8 00000001 01cf47d8 00000002 00000000
[  439.876831] 9fc0: 00000002 01cf47d8 76f16d90 00000004 01cf47d8 00000002 001042a8 00000000
[  439.893597] 9fe0: 0000006c 7eb8e328 76e357b8 76e91944
[  439.903144] Sending NMI from CPU 0 to CPUs 1-3:
[  439.912300] NMI backtrace for cpu 1
[  439.912302] CPU: 1 PID: 0 Comm: swapper/1 Tainted: G          C        5.4.51-v7+ #1
[  439.912304] Hardware name: BCM2835
[  439.912305] PC is at tick_nohz_idle_exit+0x108/0x174
[  439.912306] LR is at trace_hardirqs_on+0x54/0x170
```

Figure 4.7 – The output when the NMI is sent to all CPUs, showing the kernel stack backtrace on each of them

In the preceding screenshot, you can see that `bash` PID 633 is running on CPU 0 and that the kernel thread, `swapper/1`, is running on CPU 1 (the kernel stack for each can be seen; read it in a bottom-up fashion).

The magic SysRq facility's code can be found at `drivers/tty/sysrq.c`; it's interesting to browse through. The following is the approximate call graph for what happens on the x86 when the magic SysRq `l` is triggered:

```
include/linux/nmi.h:trigger_all_cpu_backtrace()
arch_trigger_cpumask_backtrace()
    arch/x86/kernel/apic/hw_nmi.c:arch_trigger_cpumask_backtrace()
    nmi_trigger_cpumask_backtrace()
```

The last function actually becomes the generic (not arch-specific) code at `lib/nmi_backtrace.c:nmi_trigger_cpumask_backtrace()`. The code here triggers the CPU backtrace by sending an NMI to each CPU. This is achieved via the `nmi_cpu_backtrace()` function. This function, in turn, displays the information we saw in the preceding screenshot by invoking the `show_regs()` or `dump_stack()` routines, which ultimately become arch-specific code to dump the CPU registers, as well as the kernel-mode stack. The code is also intelligent enough to not attempt to show a backtrace on those CPU cores that are in a low power (idle) state.

 Again, things are not always simple in the real world; see this article by Steven Rostedt on the complex issues people have faced with the x86 NMI and how they've been addressed: *The x86 NMI iret problem*, March 2012: https://lwn.net/Articles/484932/.

So far, we haven't actually seen the kernel view of allocated IRQ lines; the interface is, quite naturally, via the `procfs` filesystem; let's delve into it.

Viewing all allocated interrupt (IRQ) lines

Now that you have understood sufficient details about IRQs and interrupt handling, we can (finally!) leverage the kernel's `proc` filesystem so that we can peek at the currently allocated IRQs. We can do this by reading the content of the `/proc/interrupts` pseudofile. We'll show a couple of screenshots: the first (*Figure 4.8*) shows the IRQ status – the number of interrupts serviced per CPU per I/O device – on my Raspberry Pi ZeroW, while the second (*Figure 4.9*) shows this on our "usual" x86_64 Ubuntu 18.04 VM:

```
rpi0w ~ $ cat /proc/interrupts
          CPU0
 17:       1035  ARMCTRL-level   1 Edge      2000b880.mailbox
 18:         36  ARMCTRL-level   2 Edge      VCHIQ doorbell
 27:      75794  ARMCTRL-level  35 Edge      timer
 40:          0  ARMCTRL-level  48 Edge      bcm2708_fb DMA
 42:       1251  ARMCTRL-level  50 Edge      DMA IRQ
 44:       5652  ARMCTRL-level  52 Edge      DMA IRQ
 56:          1  ARMCTRL-level  64 Edge      dwc_otg, dwc_otg_pcd, dwc_otg_hcd:usb1
 80:       1166  ARMCTRL-level  88 Edge      mmc0
 81:       4145  ARMCTRL-level  89 Edge      uart-pl011
 86:     113854  ARMCTRL-level  94 Edge      mmc1
FIQ:             usb_fiq
Err:          0
rpi0w ~ $
```

Figure 4.8 – IRQ status on a Raspberry Pi ZeroW

In the preceding `/proc/interrupts` output, one line (or record) is emitted for each IRQ line on the system. Let's interpret each column of the output:

- The first column is the IRQ number that's been allocated.
- The second column (onward) shows the number of hardirqs that have been serviced by each CPU core (from system startup until now). The number represents the number of times the interrupt handler ran on that CPU core (the number of columns varies, depending on the number of active cores that are handling IRQs on the system). In the preceding screenshot, the Raspberry Pi Zero has only one CPU core, whereas our x86_64 VM has two (virtualized) CPU cores that interrupts are distributed over and handled (more on this in the *Load balancing interrupts and IRQ affinity* section).
- The third (or later) column shows the interrupt controller chip. On x86 (the fourth column in *Figure 4.9*), the name IO-APIC means that the interrupt controller is an enhanced one that's used on multicore systems to distribute interrupts to various cores or CPU groups (on high-end systems, multiple IO-APICs may be in play).
- The column after that displays the type of interrupt triggering that's being used; that is, level or edge triggering (we discussed this in the *Understanding level- and edge-triggered interrupts* section). Here, `Edge` tells us that the IRQ is edge-triggered. The number that's prefixed to it (for example, `35  Edge` in the preceding screenshot) is very system-dependent. It often represents the interrupt source (that the kernel maps to an IRQ line; many embedded device drivers often use GPIO pins to serve as interrupt sources). It's best not to attempt to interpret it (unless you actually know how to) and just rely on the IRQ number instead (the first column).

- The last column on the right states the current owner of the IRQ line. Typically, this is the name of the device driver or kernel component (that allocated this IRQ line via one of the `*request_*irq()` APIs).

```
$ cat /proc/interrupts
           CPU0       CPU1
  0:         35          0   IO-APIC    2-edge      timer
  1:          9          0   IO-APIC    1-edge      i8042
  4:          0        672   IO-APIC    4-edge      ttyS0
  8:          0          0   IO-APIC    8-edge      rtc0
  9:          0          0   IO-APIC    9-fasteoi   acpi
 12:          0        158   IO-APIC   12-edge      i8042
 14:          0          0   IO-APIC   14-edge      ata_piix
 15:          0       2230   IO-APIC   15-edge      ata_piix
 16:         69       9768   IO-APIC   16-fasteoi   enp0s8
 18:        420         21   IO-APIC   18-fasteoi   vmwgfx
 19:       1049        225   IO-APIC   19-fasteoi   enp0s3
 21:      42670          0   IO-APIC   21-fasteoi   ahci[0000:00:0d.0], snd_intel8x0
 22:         26          0   IO-APIC   22-fasteoi   ohci_hcd:usb1
NMI:          0          0   Non-maskable interrupts
LOC:    1152560    2011317   Local timer interrupts
SPU:          0          0   Spurious interrupts
PMI:          0          0   Performance monitoring interrupts
IWI:          0          0   IRQ work interrupts
```

Figure 4.9 – IRQ status on an x86_64 Ubuntu 18.04 VM (truncated screenshot)

From the 2.6.24 kernel, for x86 and AMD64 systems (or x86_64), even non-device (I/O) interrupts (system interrupts) are displayed here, such as the NMI, **local timer interrupt (LOC)**, PMI, IWI, and so on. You can see in *Figure 4.9*, the last line displays IWI, which is the **Inter-Work Interrupt**.

The kernel procfs code that displays the preceding output of /proc/interrupts – that is, its show method – can be found at kernel/irq/proc.c:show_interrupts() (link: https://elixir.bootlin.com/linux/v5.4/source/kernel/irq/proc.c#L438). First, it prints the header line, then emits a one-line "record" for each IRQ line. The statistics are mainly obtained from within the metadata structure for each IRQ line – struct irq_desc; within each IRQ, it loops over every processor core (via the for_each_online_cpu() helper routine), printing the number of hardirqs that have been served for each of them. Finally (last column), it prints the "owner" of the IRQ line via the name member of struct irqaction. The arch-specific interrupts for the x86 (such as the NMI, LOC, PMI, and IWI IRQs) are displayed via the code at arch/x86/kernel/irq.c:arch_show_interrupts().

On the x86, IRQ 0 is always the **timer interrupt**. In the companion guide *Linux Kernel Programming - Chapter 10, The CPU Scheduler - Part 1*, we learned that, in theory, the timer interrupt fires `HZ` times per second. In practice, for efficiency, this has now been replaced with a per-CPU periodic **high-resolution timer (HRT)**; it shows up as the IRQ named **LOC** (for **LOCal**) for timer interrupts in `/proc/interrupts`. This actually explains why the number of hardware timer interrupts under the `timer` row is very low; check this out (on an x86_64 guest with four (virtual) CPUs):

```
$ egrep "timer|LOC" /proc/interrupts ; sleep 1 ; egrep
"timer|LOC" /proc/interrupts
   0:           33            0            0            0   IO-
APIC    2-edge       timer
LOC:         11038        11809        10058         8848   Local
timer interrupts
   0:           33            0            0            0   IO-
APIC    2-edge       timer
LOC:         11104        11844        10086         8889   Local
timer interrupts
$
```

Notice how IRQ 0 doesn't increment but the `LOC` IRQ does indeed (per CPU core).

The `/proc/stat` pseudofile also provides some information on utilizing servicing interrupts on a per-CPU basis and the number of interrupts that can be serviced (please refer to the man page on `proc(5)` for more details).

Softirqs, as explained in detail in the *Understanding and using top and bottom halves* section, can be viewed via `/proc/softirqs`; more on this later.

With that, you've learned how to view the allocated IRQ lines. However, one major aspect of interrupt handling remains: understanding the so-called top-half/bottom-half dichotomies, why they exist, and how to work with them. We'll look at this in the next section.

Understanding and using top and bottom halves

Much emphasis has been put on the fact that your interrupt handler must complete its work quickly (as explained in the *Keep it fast* section and elsewhere). Having said that, a practical issue does crop up. Let's consider this scenario: you have allocated IRQn and have written the interrupt handler function to handle this interrupt when it arrives. As you may recall, the function we're talking about here, commonly referred to as the **hardirq** or **ISR (Interrupt Service Routine)** or primary handler, is the second parameter to the `request_{threaded}_irq()` API, the third parameter to the `devm_request_irq()` API, and the fourth parameter to the `devm_request_threaded_irq()` API.

As we mentioned previously, there's a quick heuristic to follow: if your hardirq routine's processing consistently exceeds 100 microseconds, then you will need to use alternate strategies. Let's say that your handler finishes well within this time; in this case, there's no issue at all! But what if it does require more time? Perhaps the low-level specification for the peripheral entails that you do a number of things when the interrupt arrives (say there are 10 items to complete). You correctly write the code to do so, but it pretty much always exceeds the time limit (100 microseconds as a thumb rule)! So, what do you do? On the one hand, there are these kernel folks yelling at you to finish fast; on the other, the low-level spec for the peripheral demands that you follow several key steps in order to correctly handle the interrupt! (Talk about being on the horns of a dilemma!)

As we hinted at earlier, there are two broad strategies that are followed in cases like these:

- Employ a thread interrupt to handle the majority of the work; considered the modern approach.
- Use a "bottom half" routine to handle the majority of the work; the traditional approach.

We covered the conceptual understanding, practical usage and the *why* of threaded interrupts in detail in the *Working with the threaded interrupts model* section. In the top-bottom-half model, this is the approach:

- The so-called **top half** is the function that is initially invoked when the hardware interrupt is triggered. This is thus familiar to you - it's nothing but the **hardirq**, ISR, or primary handler routine that you registered via one of the `*request_*irq()` APIs (just for clarity: via one of these APIs: `request_irq()` / `devm_request_irq()` / `request_threaded_irq()` / `devm_request_threaded_irq()`.)

- We also register a so-called **bottom half** routine to perform the majority of the interrupt handling work.

In other words, interrupt handling is **split into two halves** – top and bottom. However, this isn't really a pleasing way to describe it (as the English word half makes you intuitively think that the routines are of approximately the same size); the reality is more like this:

- The top half performs the bare minimum work required (typically, acknowledging the interrupt, perhaps turning it off on the board for the duration of the top half, and then performing any (minimal) hardware-specific work including receiving/sending some data as is required from/to the device).
- The bottom half routine carries out the majority of the interrupt handling work.

So, what is the bottom half? It's just a C function that's appropriately registered with the kernel. The actual registration API you should use depends on the *type* of bottom half you intend to use. There are three types:

- The old **bottom-half** mechanism, which is now deprecated; it's abbreviated as **BH** (you can pretty much ignore it).
- The modern recommended (if you're using this top-bottom-half technology in the first place) mechanism: the **tasklet**.
- The underlying kernel mechanism: the **softirq**.

You will come to see that the tasklet is actually built upon a kernel softirq.

Here's the thing: the top half – the hardirq handler that we've been working with until now – does, as we mentioned previously, the bare minimum work; it then "schedules" its bottom half and exits (returns). The word schedule here does not mean it calls `schedule()`, as that would be ridiculous (we're in an interrupt context, after all!); it's just the word that's used to describe the fact. The kernel will guarantee that the bottom half runs as soon as possible once the top half completes; in particular, no user or kernel thread will ever preempt it.

Hang on a second, though: even if we do all this – splitting the handler into two halves and have them collectively execute the work – then how have we saved any time? That was the original intent, after all. Won't it take an even longer time to complete now with the overhead of invoking two functions as opposed to one? Ah, this brings us to a really key point: **the top half (hardirq) always runs with all interrupts disabled (masked) on the current CPU and the IRQ it's handling disabled (masked) across all CPUs, but the bottom half handler runs with all interrupts enabled.**

Note that the bottom half is still very much running in an atomic or interrupt context! So, the same caveats that apply to the hardirq (top half) handler also apply to the bottom-half handler:

- You cannot transfer data (to or from user kernel spaces).
- You can only allocate memory (if you really must) with the GFP_ATOMIC flag.
- You cannot, ever, directly or indirectly, call schedule().

This bottom-half handling is a subset of what's known as the kernel's *deferred functionality* prowess; the kernel has several of these deferred functionality mechanisms:

- Workqueues (based on kernel threads); context:process
- Bottom half/tasklet (based on softirqs); context:interrupt
- Softirqs; context:interrupt
- kernel timers; context:interrupt

 We will cover kernel timers and workqueues in Chapter 5, *Working with Kernel Timers, Threads, and Workqueues.*

All these mechanisms allows the kernel (or driver) to specify that some work must be carried out later (it's deferred), when it is safe to do so.

At this point, you should be able to understand that the threaded interrupt mechanism we've already discussed is somewhat akin to a deferred functionality mechanism. This is considered the modern approach to use; again, though its performance is acceptable for most peripherals, a few device classes – typically network/block/multimedia – might still require the traditional top-bottom-half mechanisms to provide high enough performance. Also, we emphasize yet again: both top and bottom halves always run in an atomic (interrupt) context, whereas threaded handlers actually run in process context; you can view this as an advantage or disadvantage. The fact is that although the threaded handler is technically within the process context, it's really best to perform fast non-blocking operations within it.

Specifying and using a tasklet

A key difference between a tasklet and the kernel's softirq mechanism is that tasklets are simply easier to work with, making them a good choice for your typical driver. Of course, if you can use a threaded handler instead, just do that; later, we'll show a table that will help you decide what to use and when. One of the key things that makes tasklets easier to use is the fact that (on an SMP system) a particular tasklet will never run in parallel with itself; in other words, a given tasklet will run on exactly one CPU at a time (making it non-concurrent, or serialized, with respect to itself).

The header comment in `linux/interrupt.h` gives us some important properties of the tasklet as well:

```
[...] Properties:
 * If tasklet_schedule() is called, then tasklet is guaranteed
   to be executed on some cpu at least once after this.
 * If the tasklet is already scheduled, but its execution is still not
   started, it will be executed only once.
 * If this tasklet is already running on another CPU (or schedule is
   called from tasklet itself), it is rescheduled for later.
 * Tasklet is strictly serialized wrt itself, but not
   wrt another tasklets. If client needs some intertask synchronization,
   he makes it with spinlocks. [...]
```

We'll show the `tasklet_schedule()` function shortly. The last point in the preceding comment block will be covered in the last two chapters of this book.

So, how can we use a tasklet? First, we have to set it up with the `tasklet_init()` API; then, we have to schedule it for execution. Let's learn how to do this.

Initializing the tasklet

The `tasklet_init()` function initializes a tasklet; its signature is as follows:

```
#include <linux/interrupt.h>
void tasklet_init(struct tasklet_struct *t, void (*func)(unsigned long),
unsigned long data);
```

Let's check out its parameters:

- `struct tasklet_struct *t`: This structure is the metadata representing the tasklet. As you already know, a pointer, by itself, has no memory! Remember to allocate memory to the data structure and then pass the pointer here.
- `void (*func)(unsigned long)`: This is the tasklet function itself – **the "bottom half"** that runs once the hardirq completes; this bottom half function performs the majority of the interrupt handling process.
- `unsigned long data`: Any data item you wish to pass along to the tasklet routine (a cookie).

Where should this initialization work be performed? Typically, this is done within the driver's *probe* (or `init`) function. So, now that it's been initialized and is ready to go, how do we invoke it? Let's find out.

Running the tasklet

The tasklet is the bottom half. Thus, in the top half, which is your hardirq handler routine, the last thing you should do before returning is "schedule" your tasklet to execute:

```
void tasklet_schedule(struct tasklet_struct *t);
```

Simply pass the pointer to your (initialized) tasklet structure to the `tasklet_schedule()` API; the kernel will handle the rest. What does the kernel do? It schedules this tasklet to execute; practically speaking, your tasklet's function code is guaranteed to run before control returns to the task that was interrupted in the first place (be it a user or kernel thread). More details can be found in the *Understanding how the kernel runs softirqs* section.

Regarding the tasklet, there are a few things you need to be clear about:

- The tasklet executes its code in an interrupt (atomic) context; it's actually a softirq context. So, remember, all the restrictions that apply to top halves apply here too! (Check out the *Interrupt context guidelines – what to do and what not to do* section for detailed information on restrictions)
- Synchronization (on an SMP box):
    - A given tasklet will never run in parallel with itself.
    - Different tasklets *can* run in parallel on different CPU cores.
    - Your tasklet can itself be interrupted by a hardirq, including your own IRQ! This is because tasklets, by default, run with all interrupts enabled on the local core, and, of course, hardirq's are the very top priority on the system

- Locking implications really do matter – we'll cover these areas in detail in the last two chapters of this book (particularly when we cover *spinlocks*).

Some (generic driver) sample code is as follows (for clarity, we've avoided showing any error paths):

```
#include <"convenient.h">              // has the PRINT_CTX() macro
static struct tasklet_struct *ts;
[...]
static int __init mydriver_init(void)
{
    struct device *dev;
    [...]
    /* Register the device with the kernel 'misc' driver framework */
    ret = misc_register(&keylog_miscdev);
    dev = keylog_miscdev.this_device;

    ts = devm_kzalloc(dev, sizeof(struct tasklet_struct), GFP_KERNEL);
    tasklet_init(ts, mydrv_tasklet, 0);

    ret = devm_request_irq(dev, MYDRV_IRQ, my_hardirq_handler,
                IRQF_SHARED, OURMODNAME, THIS_MODULE);
    [...]
```

In the preceding code snippet, we declared a global pointer, `ts`, to `struct tasklet_struct`; in the `init` code of the driver, we registered the driver as belonging to the `misc` kernel framework. Next, we allocated RAM to the tasklet structure (via the useful `devm_kzalloc()` API). Next, we initialized the tasklet via the `tasklet_init()` API. Notice that we specified the function name (second parameter) and simply passed `0` as the third parameter, which is the cookie to pass along (many real drivers pass their context/private data structure pointer here). We then allocated an IRQ line (via the `devm_request_irq()` API).

Let's continue looking at the code of this generic driver:

```
/ * Our 'bottom half' tasklet routine */
static void mydrv_tasklet(unsigned long data)
{
    PRINT_CTX();   // from our convenient.h header
    process_it();  // majority of the interrupt work done here
}

/* Our 'hardirq' interrupt handler routine – our 'top half' */
static irqreturn_t my_hardirq_handler(int irq, void *data)
```

```
{
    /* minimal work: ack/disable hardirq, fetch and/or queue data, etc ...
*/
    tasklet_schedule(ts);
    return IRQ_HANDLED;
}
```

In the preceding code, let's imagine we did whatever minimal work was required in our top half (the `my_hardirq_handler()` function). We then primed our tasklet so that it can run by invoking the `tasklet_schedule()` API. You'll find that the tasklet will run almost immediately after the hardirq (in the preceding code, the tasklet function is called `mydrv_tasklet()`). In the tasklet, you are expected to perform the majority of the interrupt processing work. Within it, we called our macro `PRINT_CTX()`; as you will see in the *Fully figuring out the context* section, it prints various details regarding our current context, which is helpful for debugging/learning (you'll find it shows, among other things, that we're currently running in interrupt context).

Instead of the `tasklet_schedule()` API, you can use an alternate routine, via the `tasklet_hi_schedule()` API. This internally makes the tasklet become the *highest priority softirq* (softirq priority 0)! (More information can be found in the *Understanding the kernel softirq mechanism* section.) Note that this is almost never done; the default (softirq) priority that a tasklet enjoys is usually more than sufficient. Setting it to the `hi` level is really only meant for extreme cases; avoid it as far as is possible.

 On version 5.4.0 Linux, there *are* 70-odd instances of the `tasklet_hi_schedule()` function being used by drivers. The drivers are typically high-performance network drivers – a few GPU, crypto, USB, and mmc drivers, as well as a few other drivers.

When it comes to tasklets, the kernel keeps evolving. Recent (as the time of writing, July 2020) patches by *Kees Cook* and others are looking to modernize the tasklet routine (callback). For more information regarding this, please go to `https://www.openwall.com/lists/kernel-hardening/2020/07/16/1`.

Understanding the kernel softirq mechanism

At this point, you understand that the bottom half, the tasklet, is a deferred functionality mechanism that, while running, doesn't mask interrupts. They're designed to allow you to get the best of both worlds: they allow the driver to do fairly lengthy interrupt processing if the situation demands it *and* do it in a deferred safe manner while simultaneously allowing the business of the system (via hardware interrupts) to continue.

You've already learned how to use the tasklet – it's a great example of a deferred functionality mechanism. But how are they internally implemented? The kernel implements tasklets via an underlying facility called the **softirq** (or **software-interrupt**) mechanism. Though on the surface they're analogous to the threaded interrupt we saw earlier, it's really very different in many important ways. The following characteristics of softirqs will help you understand them:

- Softirqs are a pure internal kernel deferred functionality mechanism in the sense that they are statically assigned at kernel compile time (they're all hard-coded into the kernel); you cannot dynamically create a new softirq.
- The kernel (as of version 5.4) provides a total of 10 discrete softirqs:
  - Each softirq is designed to serve a particular need, usually associated with a very particular hardware interrupt or kernel activity. (The exceptions here are perhaps the soft IRQs reserved for the generic tasklet: `HI_SOFTIRQ` and `TASKLET_SOFTIRQ`.)
  - These 10 softirqs have a priority ordering (and will be consumed in that order).
  - The tasklet is, in fact, a thin abstraction on top of a particular softirq (`TASKLET_SOFTIRQ`), one of the 10 available. The tasklet is the only one that can be registered, run, and deregistered at will, making it an ideal choice for many device drivers.
- Softirqs run in interrupt – softirq – context; the `in_softirq()` macro returns `true` here, implying you are in a softirq (or tasklet) context.
- All softirq servicing is considered a high priority on the system. Next to the hardware interrupt (the `hardirq/ISR/primary` handler), the softirq has the highest priority on the system. Pending softirqs are consumed by the kernel *before* the process context that was interrupted in the first place is restored.

The following diagram is a superset of our earlier depiction of priorities on standard Linux; this one includes softirqs (within which is the tasklet):

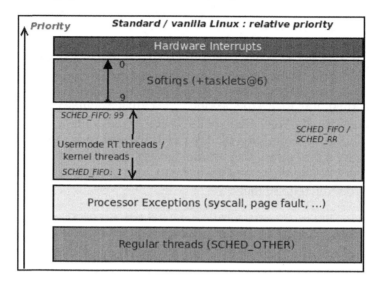

Figure 4.10 – Relative priorities on standard Linux, showing softirqs as well

So, yes, as you can see, softirqs are a very high-priority mechanism on Linux; there are 10 distinct ones at differing priorities. What they are, and what they're meant for, will be covered in the next subsection.

Available softirqs and what they are for

The work that's carried out by a given softirq is statically compiled into the kernel image (it's fixed). This coupling of the softirq and the action it takes (in effect, the code it runs, via the `action` function pointer) is done via the following code:

```
// kernel/softirq.c
void open_softirq(int nr, void (*action)(struct softirq_action *))
{
    softirq_vec[nr].action = action;
}
```

The following diagram is a conceptual representation of the available softirqs and their priority level on Linux (as of kernel version 5.4), with 0 being the highest and 9 the lowest softirq priority level:

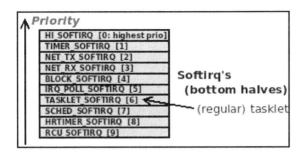

Figure 4.11 – The 10 softirqs on Linux in order of priority (0:highest, 9:lowest)

The following table sums up the individual kernel's softirqs in order of their priority (0: HI_SOFTIRQ being the highest priority one), along with the action or vector, its functionality, and a comment mentioning what its use case is:

Softirq#	Softirq	Comment (what it's used for/does)	"action" or "vector" function
0	HI_SOFTIRQ	**Hi-tasklet**: The highest priority softirq; used when tasklet_hi_schedule() is invoked. It is not recommended for the majority of use cases. Use the regular tasklet instead (softirq #6).	tasklet_hi_action()
1	TIMER_SOFTIRQ	**Timer**: The timer interrupt's bottom half runs expired timers along with other "housekeeping" tasks (including the scheduler CPU runqueue + vruntime updates, increments of the well-known jiffies_64 variable, and so on).	run_timer_softirq()
2	NET_TX_SOFTIRQ	**Net**: Network stack transmit path bottom half (qdisc).	net_tx_action()
3	NET_RX_SOFTIRQ	**Net**: Network stack receive path bottom half (NAPI polling).	net_rx_action()
4	BLOCK_SOFTIRQ	**Block**: Block processing (complete the I/O op; invokes the complete function of block MQ, blk_mq_ops).	blk_done_softirq()
5	IRQ_POLL_SOFTIRQ	**irqpoll**: Implements the kernel's block layer polled IRQ mode (equivalent to the network layer's NAPI processing).	irq_poll_softirq()

6	TASKLET_SOFTIRQ	**Regular tasklet**: Implements the tasklet bottom-half mechanism, the only dynamic (flexible) softirq: can be registered, used, and deregistered by drivers as required.	tasklet_action()
7	SCHED_SOFTIRQ	**sched**: Used for periodic load balancing by the CFS scheduler on SMP; migrates tasks to other runqueues if required.	run_rebalance_domains()
8	HRTIMER_SOFTIRQ	**HRT**: Used for **high-resolution timers** (**HRT**). It was removed in version 4.2 and reentered the kernel in a better form in version 4.16.	hrtimer_run_softirq()
9	RCU_SOFTIRQ	**RCU**: Performs **read copy update** (**RCU**) processing, a form of lock-free technology used within the core kernel.	rcu_core_si() / rcu_process_callbacks()

It's interesting; the network and block stacks are very high priority code paths (as is the timer interrupt), so their code must run as soon as possible. Thus, they have explicit softirqs that service these critical code paths.

Can we see the softirqs that have been fired off so far? Of course, very much like how we can view hardirqs (via its proc/interrupts pseudofile). We have the /proc/softirqs pseudofile for tracking softirqs. Here's a sample screenshot from my native (four-core) x86_64 Ubuntu system:

```
$ cat /proc/softirqs
                CPU0       CPU1       CPU2       CPU3
       HI:        78         34         31         11
    TIMER:  30463160   30718729   30972132   30278757
   NET_TX:    610527        412        696       1214
   NET_RX:   2566186      29323     140033     320436
    BLOCK:    838301      88438     743635    3496658
 IRQ_POLL:         2          0          0          4
  TASKLET:   1818666      87029      46248      48477
    SCHED:  33423812   31244567   30507786   29617786
   HRTIMER:      7514        327       4965       1067
      RCU:   9019635    8959823    9053172    9024646
$
```

Figure 4.12 – Output of /proc/softirqs on a native x86_64 system with 4 CPU cores

Just like with /proc/interrupts, the numbers shown in the preceding screenshot depict the number of times a particular softirq occurred on a particular CPU core from system startup. In addition, FYI, the powerful crash tool has a useful command, irq, that shows information regarding interrupts; irq -b displays the defined softirqs on that kernel.

Understanding how the kernel runs softirqs

The following is the (approximate) call graph that's used on x86 when a hardware interrupt is triggered:

```
do_IRQ() -> handle_irq() -> entering_irq() -> hardirq top-half runs ->
exiting_irq() -> irq_exit() -> invoke_softirq() -> do_softirq() -> ...
bottom half runs: tasklet/softirq ... -> restore context
```

Some of the preceding code paths are arch-dependent. Note that the "marking the context as an interrupt" context is really an artifact. The kernel is marked as having entered this context in the `entering_irq()` function and as having left it once `exiting_irq()` returns (on x86). But hang on! The `exiting_irq()` inline function invokes the `kernel/softirq.c:irq_exit()` function (https://elixir.bootlin.com/linux/v5.4/source/kernel/softirq.c#L403). It's within this routine that the kernel processes, and consumes, all pending softirqs. The basic call graph (from `do_softirq()` onward) is as follows:

```
do_softirq() --  [assembly]do_softirq_own_stack -- __do_softirq()
```

The real work happens in the internal `__do_softirq()` routine (https://elixir.bootlin.com/linux/v5.4/source/kernel/softirq.c#L249). It's here that any pending softirqs are consumed in priority order. Notice that softirq processing is done before context is restored to the interrupted task.

Now, let's briefly focus on some of the internal details of tasklet execution, followed by how to use *ksoftirqd* kernel threads to offload softirq work.

Running tasklets

A word on the internals of tasklet invocation: we understand that the tasklet softirq runs via `tasklet_schedule()`. This API ends up invoking the kernel's internal `__tasklet_schedule_common()` function (https://elixir.bootlin.com/linux/v5.4/source/kernel/softirq.c#L471), which internally calls `raise_softirq_irqoff(softirq_nr)` (https://elixir.bootlin.com/linux/v5.4/source/kernel/softirq.c#L423). This raises the `softirq_nr` softirq; for a regular tasklet, this value is `TASKLET_SOFTIRQ`, whereas when the tasklet is scheduled via the `tasklet_hi_schedule()` API, is value is `HI_SOFTIRQ`, the highest priority softirq! Use it rarely, if ever.

We now know that the "schedule" functionality has set up the softirq; here, the actual execution takes place when the softirqs at that priority level (0 or 6 here) actually run. The function that runs softirqs is called `do_softirq()`; for the regular tasklet, it ends up calling the `tasklet_action()` softirq vector (as shown in the preceding table); this calls `tasklet_action_common()` (https://elixir.bootlin.com/linux/v5.4/source/kernel/softirq.c#L501), which (after some list setup) enables hardware interrupts (via a `local_irq_enable()`) and then loops over the per CPU tasklet list, consuming (running) the tasklet function(s) on it. Did you notice that pretty much all the functions mentioned here are arch-independent? - a good thing.

Employing the ksoftirqd kernel threads

Softirqs can impose an enormous load on the system when there is a flood of them waiting to be processed. This has been repeatedly seen in the network (and to some extent, block) layers, leading to the development of polled mode IRQ handling; it's called NAPI for the network (receive) path and simply interrupt-poll handling for the block layer. But what if, even with polled mode handling, the softirq flood persists? The kernel has one more trick up its sleeve: if softirq processing exceeds 2 milliseconds, the kernel offloads the pending softirq work onto per-CPU kernel threads named `ksoftirqd/n` (where n represents the CPU number, starting from 0). A benefit of this approach is that because kernel threads must compete with other threads for CPU resources, user space doesn't end up getting completely starved of CPU (which could happen with pure hardirq/softirq load).

This sounds like a good solution, but the real world begs to differ. In February 2019, a series of patches to set up softirq vector fine-grained masking looked promising but ultimately seem to have fizzled out (do read the very interesting details provided in the *Further reading* section). The following email from Linus Torvalds clarifies the real problem nicely (https://lore.kernel.org/lkml/CAHk-=wgOZuGZaVOOiC=drG6ykVkOGk8RRXZ_CrPBMXHKjTg0dg@mail.gmail.com/#t):

> ... Note that this is all really fairly independent of the whole masking
> logic. Yes, the masking logic comes into play too (allowing you to run
> a subset of softirq's at a time), but on the whole the complaints I've
> seen have not been "the networking softirq takes so long that it
> delays USB tasklet handling", but they have been along the lines of
> "the networking softirq gets invoked so often that it then floods the
> system and triggers [k]softirqd, and _that_ then makes tasklet handling
> latency go up insanely ..."

The last part of the statement hits the nail on the head.

So, this begs the question: can we *measure* hardirq/softirq instances and latencies? We cover this in the section *Measuring metrics and latency*.

Softirqs and concurrency

As we learned with regard to tasklets, a number of points with regard to *concurrency* must be understood with respect to softirqs:

- As noted with tasklets (on SMP), a tasklet will never run in parallel with itself; this is a feature that makes it easier to use. This isn't true of softirqs: the same softirq vector can indeed run in parallel with itself on another CPU! Thus, the softirq vector code has to be especially careful with the use of locking (and deadlock avoidance).
- A softirq can always be interrupted by a hardirq, including the IRQ that caused it to be raised (this is because, as with tasklets, softirqs run with all interrupts enabled on the local core).
- A softirq cannot preempt another currently executing softirq, even though they have priority levels; they are consumed in priority order.
- The reality is that the kernel provides APIs such as `spin_lock_bh()`, which allow you to disable softirq processing while the lock is held. This is required to prevent deadlock when both the hardirq and the softirq handlers are working on shared data. The locking implications really do matter. We'll cover this in detail in the last two chapters of this book.

Hardirqs, tasklets, and threaded handlers – what to use when

As you already know, the hardirq code is meant to do the bare minimum setup and interrupt handling, leaving the majority of the interrupt processing to be performed in a safe manner via the deferred functionality mechanisms we've been talking about, the tasklet and/or softirq. This 'bottom half' as well as deferred functionality handling is carried out in priority order – first, the softirq kernel timers, then tasklets (both of these are just special cases of the underlying softirq mechanism), then threaded interrupts, and finally workqueues (the latter two use underlying kernel threads).

So, the big question is, when you're writing your driver, which one of these should you use? Should you use a deferred mechanism at all? It really depends on the **amount of time your complete interrupt processing takes** to complete. If your complete interrupt processing can be consistently completed within a few microseconds, then just use the top-half hardirq; nothing else is required.

But what if this isn't the case? Take a look at the following table; the first column specifies the total time it takes for complete interrupt processing, while the other columns provide a few suggestions regarding its use plus pros and cons:

Time: If hardware interrupt handling consistently requires	What to do	Pros/cons
<= 10 microseconds	Use only the hardirq (top half); nothing else is required.	Best case; not typical.
Between 10 and 100 microseconds	Either only hardirq or both hardirq and a tasklet (softirq).	Run stress tests/workloads to see if a tasklet is really required. Its usage is mildly discouraged in favor of threaded handlers or workqueues.
100 microseconds, non-critical device	Use a primary handler (hardirq); that is, either your own handler function (if hardware-specific work is required) or simply use the kernel default and a *threaded* handler. Alternatively, if acceptable, simply use a *workqueue* (covered in the next chapter).	This avoids softirq processing, which helps reduce system latencies but can result in slightly slower handling. This is because the threaded handler competes for CPU time with other threads. Workqueues are also based on kernel threads and have similar characteristics.
100 microseconds, critical device (typically network, block, and some multimedia devices)	Use a primary handler (hardirq/top half) and a tasklet (bottom half).	It prioritizes the device over everything when a flood of interrupts arrive. This is also a downside as this can cause "livelock" issues and long latencies with a softirq "flood"! Test and ascertain.
100 microseconds, extremely critical work/device	Use a primary handler (hardirq/top half) and a hi-tasklet or (possibly) your own (new!) softirq.	This is a rather extreme, unlikely case; to add your own softirq you will need to change the internal (GPL-ed) kernel code. This makes it high maintenance (unless your core kernel changes + driver is contributed upstream!).

The time in microseconds in the first column is, of course, debatable, arch-and-board-dependent, and can (and will) change over time. The suggested value of 100 microseconds as a baseline is merely a heuristic.

As we've already mentioned, softirq processing itself should complete within a few hundred microseconds; a flood of unprocessed softirqs can again lead to a livelock situation. The kernel mitigates (or de-risks) this in two broad ways:

- Threaded interrupts or workqueues (both based on kernel threads)
- Invoking the `ksoftirqd/n` kernel threads to take over softirq processing

The preceding cases run in process context, thus alleviating the issue of starving genuine (user space) threads that require the CPU via the scheduler (as the kernel threads themselves have to compete for the CPU resources).

With regard to the last row of the preceding table, the only way to create a new softirq is to actually dive into the kernel code and modify it. By this, we mean modifying the (GPL licensed) kernel code base. In terms of embedded projects, modifying the kernel source is not uncommon. However, adding softirqs is considered (very) uncommon and not a great idea at all since latencies may already be high without more softirq processing to contend with! This hasn't happened for many years now.

In terms of real time and determinism, in the companion guide *Linux Kernel Programming, Chapter 11, The CPU Scheduler – Part 2*, in the *Viewing the results* section, we mentioned that the *jitter* (the time variance) in interrupt processing on a microprocessor running standard Linux is on the order of +/- 10 microseconds. With the RTL kernel, it's a lot better, yet not a hundred percent deterministic. So, can you be completely deterministic with interrupt handling on Linux? Well, one interesting approach is to use – if enabled and possible – **FIQs**, the so-called *fast interrupt* mechanism that some processors, notably ARM, provide. They work outside the Linux kernel's scope, which is precisely why writing an FIQ interrupt handler would eliminate any kernel-induced jitter. Take a look at this article for more information: `https://bootlin.com/blog/fiq-handlers-in-the-arm-linux-kernel/`.

Finally, it may be worth mentioning that (at the time of writing) a good amount of rethinking is going on here: the opinion of some kernel developers is that the whole top-half bottom-half mechanism isn't required anymore. However, the fact is that this mechanism is deeply embedded into the kernel fabric, making it non-trivial to remove.

Fully figuring out the context

The *Interrupt context guidelines – what to do and what not to do* section made this clear: when you're in any kind of interrupt (or atomic) context, do not invoke any possibly blocking APIs (that end up calling `schedule()`); this really boils down to a few key points (as we saw). One is that you should not make any kernel to user space (or vice versa) data transfers; another, if you must allocate memory, do so with the `GFP_ATOMIC` flag.

This, of course, begs the question: **how do I know if my driver (or module) code is currently running in process or interrupt (atomic) context?** Furthermore, if it's running in interrupt context, is it in a top or bottom half? The short answer to all this is that the kernel provides several macros that you can use to figure this out. These macros are defined in the `linux/preempt.h` header. Instead of unnecessarily duplicating information, we'll show the relevant kernel comment header here; it clearly names and describes these macros:

```
// include/linux/preempt.h
[...]
/*
 * Are we doing bottom half or hardware interrupt processing?
 *
 * in_irq()       - We're in (hard) IRQ context
 * in_softirq()   - We have BH disabled, or are processing softirqs
 * in_interrupt() - We're in NMI,IRQ,SoftIRQ context or have BH disabled
 * in_serving_softirq() - We're in softirq context
 * in_nmi()       - We're in NMI context
 * in_task()      - We're in task context
[...]
```

We covered a subset of this topic in the companion guide *Linux Kernel Programming, Chapter 6, Kernel Internals Essentials – Processes and Threads,* under the *Determining the context* section.

So, it's quite simple; in our `convenient.h` header (https://github.com/PacktPublishing/Linux-Kernel-Programming-Part-2/blob/main/convenient.h), we define a convenience macro called `PRINT_CTX()` that, when invoked, will print the current context to the kernel log. The message is very deliberately formatted. The following is an example of the typical output it emits when invoked:

```
001)  rdwr_drv_secret :29141   |  .N.0   /* read_miscdrv_rdwr() */
```

At first, the format might look strange to you. However, I have simply followed the kernel's Ftrace (latency) output format to show the context (with the exception of the DURATION column; we don't have it here). The Ftrace output format is well supported and understood by developers and kernel users. The following output shows you how to interpret it:

```
The Ftrace 'latency-format'
                                  _------= irqs-off          [d]
                                 / _-----= need-resched      [N]
                                | / _---= hardirq/softirq    [H|h|s] [1]
                                || / _--= preempt-depth      [#]
                                ||| /
  CPU TASK              PID     ||||           FUNCTION CALLS
   |    |                |      ||||            |   |   |   |
  001)  rdwr_drv_secret :29141  | .N.0      /* read_miscdrv_rdwr() */

[1] 'h' = hard irq is running ; 'H' = hard irq occurred inside a softirq
```

This can be very useful as it can help you understand and thus debug difficult situations! You get to see not only what was running (its name and PID, as well as on which CPU core), but also four interesting columns (highlighted in bold (.N.0)). The preceding ASCII art view of these four columns is in fact identical to what Ftrace itself generates. Let's interpret these four columns (in our example here, it's the value .N.0):

- **Column 1**: The IRQ state. It displays . if interrupts are enabled (usually the case) and d if disabled.
- **Column 2**: The TIF_NEED_RESCHED bit state. If 1, the kernel will invoke schedule() at the next opportunity point (return from syscall or return from interrupt, whichever comes first). It displays N if set and . if cleared.
- **Column 3**: If we're in an interrupt context, we can employ more macros to check whether we're in a hardirq (top half) or softirq (bottom half) context. It displays this as follows:
    - .: Process (task) context
    - Interrupt / atomic context:
        - h: Hardirq is running
        - H: Hardirq occurred inside a softirq (that is, a hardirq occurred while a softirq was executing, interrupting it)
        - s: Softirq (or tasklet) context

- **Column 4**: An integer value (derived from a bitmask) called `preempt_depth`. Essentially, it's incremented every time a lock is taken and decremented on every unlock. So, if it's positive, it implies the code is within a critical or atomic section.

The following is (part of) our code implementation for the `convenient.h:PRINT_CTX()` macro (carefully study the code and do use the macro in your code to understand it):

```
// convenient.h
[...]
#define PRINT_CTX() do {                                        \
  int PRINTCTX_SHOWHDR = 0;                                     \
  char intr = '.';                                              \
  if (!in_task()) {                                             \
      if (in_irq() && in_softirq())                             \
          intr = 'H'; /* hardirq occurred inside a softirq */ \
      else if (in_irq())                                        \
          intr = 'h'; /* hardirq is running */                 \
      else if (in_softirq())                                    \
          intr = 's';                                           \
  }                                                             \
  else                                                          \
      intr = '.';                                               \
```

It basically pivots on the `if` condition and checks whether the code is in a process (or task) context or not via the `in_task()` macro, and thus in an interrupt (or atomic) context.

You might have come across the `in_interrupt()` macro being used in situations like this. If it returns `true`, your code is within an interrupt context, while if it returns `false`, it isn't. However, the recommendation for modern code is to *not* rely on this macro (and `in_softirq()`) due to the fact that bottom-half disabling can interfere with its correct working). Hence, we use `in_task()` instead.

Let's continue looking at the code for the `PRINT_CTX()` macro:

```
[...]
if (PRINTCTX_SHOWHDR == 1) \
    pr_debug("CPU) task_name:PID | irqs,need-resched,hard/softirq,preempt-
depth /* func_name() */\n"); \
pr_debug( \
    "%03d) %c%s%c:%d | " \
    "%c%c%c%cu " \
    "/* %s() */\n" \
    , smp_processor_id(), \
    (!current-mm?'[':' '), current-comm, (!current-mm?']':' '), current-
```

```
pid, \
    (irqs_disabled()?'d':'.'), \
    (need_resched()?'N':'.'), \
    intr, \
    (preempt_count() && 0xff), __func__); \
} while (0)
```

If the PRINTCTX_SHOWHDR variable is set to 1, it prints a header line; it's 0 by default. This is where the macro emits the (debug-level) printk (via pr_debug()), which shows the context information in Ftrace (latency) format, as seen in the preceding snippet.

Viewing the context – examples

As an example, in our ch1/miscdrv_rdwr misc driver code (and several others, in fact), we used this very macro (PRINT_CTX()) to display the context. Here's some sample output from when our simple rdwr_drv_secret app read the "secret message" from the driver (for clarity, I removed the dmesg timestamps):

```
CPU) task_name:PID | irqs,need-resched,hard/softirq,preempt-depth /*
func_name() */
001)  rdwr_drv_secret :29141    |   .N.0   /* read_miscdrv_rdwr() */
```

The header line shows how to interpret the output. (In fact, this header line is off by default. I temporarily changed the value of the PRINTCTX_SHOWHDR variable to 1 to show it here.)

The following is another example from an (out of tree) driver while running the code of a (bottom-half) tasklet (we covered tasklets in the *Understanding and using top and bottom halves* section):

```
000)  gnome-terminal- :3075    |   .Ns1   /* mydrv_tasklet() */
```

Let's interpret the preceding output in more detail; from left to right:

- 000): The tasklet ran on CPU core 0.
- The task that was interrupted by this is the gnome-terminal- process with PID 3075. Actually, it was probably interrupted by the hardirq that fired before this tasklet ran, and will only resume execution – best case scenario – once the tasklet's done.

- We can infer the following from the preceding four-column output (the .Ns1 part):

  - .: All interrupts (on the local core, core #0) are enabled.
  - N: The TIF_NEED_RESCHED bit is set (implying that the scheduler code will run when the next scheduling "opportunity point" is hit; realize that it will very likely be run (in process context) by the gnome-terminal- thread).
  - s: The tasklet is an interrupt – more precisely, a softirq – context (to be precise, it's the TASKLET_SOFTIRQ softirq); an atomic context; this is expected - we're running a tasklet!
  - 1: the value of preempt_depth is 1; this implies a (spin)lock is currently being held (again, this implies that we're currently in an atomic context).

- The driver function running in the tasklet context was called mydrv_tasklet().

Often, when viewing a capture like this, in interrupt context, the interrupted task shows up as the swapper/n kernel thread (where n is the CPU core's number). This typically implies that the swapper/n kernel thread was interrupted by the hardirq, further implying that the interrupt triggered while that CPU was in an idle state (since the swapper/n threads only run then), which is a pretty common occurrence on a lightly loaded system.

How Linux prioritizes activities

Now that you have learned about so many areas across the gamut, we can zoom out and see how the Linux kernel prioritizes things. The following (conceptual) diagram - a superset of earlier similar diagrams - neatly sums this up:

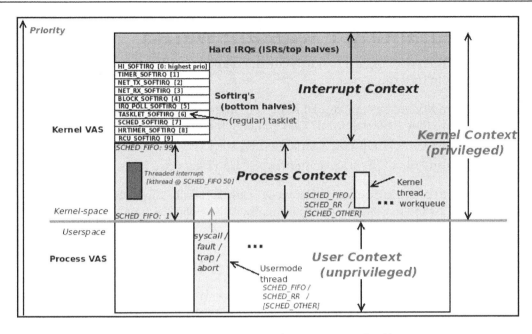

Figure 4.13 – Relative priorities across the full stack - user, kernel process context, and kernel interrupt contexts

This diagram is pretty self-explanatory, so please study it carefully.

In this lengthy section, you have learned about interrupt handling via both the top-half and bottom-half mechanisms, the reasons for them in the first place, and how they are organized and to be used by drivers. You now understand that all bottom-half mechanisms are internally implemented via softirqs; the tasklet is the primary bottom-half mechanism that you, as a driver author, have easy access to use. This, of course, does not imply you must use them – if you can get away with simply using a top-half only, or, even better, just a threaded handler, then that's great. The *Hardirqs, tasklets, and threaded handlers – what to use when* section covered these considerations in detail.

With that, we're almost done! However, some miscellaneous areas still need to be traversed. Let's take a look by jumping into it via the familiar *FAQ* format!

A few remaining FAQs answered

Here are a few FAQs with regard to hardware interrupts and how they are handled. We haven't touched on these areas yet:

- On a multicore system, are all hardware interrupts routed to one CPU? If not, how are they load balanced? Can I change this?
- Does the kernel maintain a separate IRQ stack?
- How can I obtain metrics on interrupts? Can I measure interrupt latency?

The idea here is to provide brief answers; we encourage you to dig deeper and try things out for yourself! At the risk of repetition, remember, the *empirical approach is best!*

Load balancing interrupts and IRQ affinity

First off, on a multicore (SMP) system, the way that hardware interrupts are routed to CPU cores tends to be very board and interrupt controller-specific. Having said that, the generic IRQ layer on Linux provides a very useful abstraction: it allows for (and implements) interrupt load balancing so that no CPUs (of set of CPUs) gets overloaded. There's even frontend utilities, `irqbalance(1)` and `irqbalance-ui(1)`, that allow the admin (or root user) to perform IRQ balancing (`irqbalance-ui` is a `ncurses` frontend to `irqbalance`).

Can you change the interrupts that have been sent to a processor core(s)? Yes, via the `/proc/irq/IRQ/smp_affinity` pseudofile! It's a bitmask specifying the CPUs that this IRQ is allowed to be routed to. **The trouble is** that the default setting is to always allow all CPU cores to handle the interrupt by default. For example, on a system with eight cores, the value of `smp_affinity` for IRQ lines will be `0xff` (which is binary `1111 1111`). Why is this a problem? **CPU caching**. In a nutshell, if multiple cores handle the same interrupt, the caches get trashed and hence many cache invalidations may occur (to keep memory coherent with the CPU caches), leading to all kinds of performance headaches; this is especially true on high-end systems with dozens of cores and multiple NICs.

We cover more on CPU caching issues in `Chapter 7`, *Kernel Synchronization - Part 2* in the section *Cache effects and false sharing*.

It's recommended that you keep a single important IRQ line (such as the Ethernet interrupt) affined to a particular CPU core (or at most, to a physical core that is hyperthreaded). Not only that, but keeping the related network application processes and threads affined to the same core will (probably) result in better performance (we covered process/thread CPU affinity in the companion guide *Linux Kernel Programming - Chapter 11, The CPU Scheduler - Part 2* , in the *Understanding, querying, and setting the CPU affinity mask* section).

Let's go over a couple more points:

- The output of `/proc/interrupts` will reflect the IRQ affinity (and IRQ balancing) and allow you to see exactly how many interrupts have been routed to which CPU core on the system. (We covered interpreting its output in detail in the section *Viewing all allocated interrupt (IRQ) lines*.)
- The `irqbalance` service can actually cause issues as it reverts the IRQ affinity settings to defaults upon startup (`https://unix.stackexchange.com/questions/68812/making-a-irq-smp-affinity-change-permanent`); you might want to disable it if you're carefully tweaking the settings (possibly at boot via an `rc.local` or equivalent `systemd` script.) The newer versions of `irqbalance` allow you to ban IRQ lines and won't (re)set them.

Does the kernel maintain separate IRQ stacks?

In the companion guide *Linux Kernel Programming* in *Chapter 6, Kernel Internals and Essentials – Processes and Threads*, in the *Organizing process, threads, and their stacks – user and kernel space* section, we covered some key points: every single user space thread has two stacks: a user space stack and a kernel space stack. When the thread runs in non-privileged user space, it makes use of the user mode stack, while when it switches to privileged kernel space (via a system call or exception), it works with its kernel-mode stack (refer back to *Figure 6.3* in the companion guide *Linux Kernel Programming*). Next, the kernel-mode stack is very limited and fixed in size – it's only 2 or 4 pages long (depending on whether your arch is 32- or 64-bit, respectively)!

So, imagine your driver code's (let's say, the `ioctl()` method) is running within a deeply nested code path. This implies that the kernel-mode stack for that process context is already pretty loaded up with metadata – the stack frames for each of those functions it's been invoking. Now, a hardware interrupt arrives! This, ultimately, is also code that must run and thus requires a stack. We could have it simply use the existing kernel-mode stack that's already in play, *but* this greatly increases the chances of stack overflow (given that we're deeply nested and the stack is small). A stack overflow within the kernel is disastrous as the system will simply hang/die with no real clues as to the root cause (well, the `CONFIG_VMAP_STACK` kernel config was introduced for mitigating precisely this kind of thing and is set by default on x86_64).

So, long story short, on pretty much all modern architectures, the kernel allocates a *separate kernel space stack per CPU* for hardware interrupt handling. This is known as the **IRQ stack**. When a hardware interrupt arrives, the stack location (via the appropriate CPU stack pointer register) is switched to the IRQ stack of the CPU the interrupt is being processed on (and it's restored on IRQ exit). Some arch's (PPC) have a kernel config called `CONFIG_IRQSTACKS` to enable IRQ stacks. The size of the IRQ stack is fixed as the value is arch-dependent. On the x86_64, it's 4 pages long (16 KB, with a typical 4K page size).

Measuring metrics and latency

We have already discussed, to an extent, what latencies (delays) are and how to measure scheduling latency in the companion guide *Linux Kernel Programming - Chapter 11, The CPU Scheduler – Part 2*, under the *Latency and its measurement* section. Here, we'll look at more aspects of system latencies and their measurement.

As you already know, `procfs` is a rich source of information; we've already seen that both the number of hardirqs and softirqs that are generated per CPU core can be viewed via the `/proc/interrupts` and `/proc/softirqs` (pseudo) files. Similar information is available via `/proc/stat`.

Measuring interrupts with [e]BPF

In the companion guide *Linux Kernel Programming - Chapter 1, Kernel Workspace Setup*, in the *Modern tracing and performance analysis with [e]BPF* section, we pointed out how the modern approach to tracing, performance measurement, and analysis on (recent 4.x) Linux is **[e]BPF**, the **enhanced Berkeley Packet Filter** (just called BPF as well). Among the plethora of tools it stocks (`https://github.com/iovisor/bcc#tools`), two suit our immediate purpose of tracing, measuring, and analyzing interrupts (both hardirqs and softirqs). (The tools are named `toolname-bpfcc` on Ubuntu, where `toolname` is the name of the tool in question, such as `hardirqs-bpfcc` and `softirqs-bpfcc`). These tools dynamically trace interrupts (at the time of writing, they're not based on kernel tracepoints yet). You will require root access to run these [e]BPF tools.

Important: You can install the BCC tools for your regular host Linux distro by reading the installation instructions here: `https://github.com/iovisor/bcc/blob/master/INSTALL.md`. Why not do this on our guest Linux VM? You can do this when you're running a distro kernel (such as an Ubuntu- or Fedora-supplied kernel). The reason you can do this is because the installation of the BCC toolset includes (and depends on) the installation of the `linux-headers-$(uname -r)` package; this `linux-headers` package exists only for distro kernels (and not for our custom 5.4 kernel, which you might be running on the guest).

Measuring time servicing individual hardirqs

The `hardirqs[-bpfcc]` tool displays the total time spent servicing hardirqs (hardware interrupts). The following screenshot shows us running the `hardirqs-bpfcc` tool. Here, you can see the total time that was spent servicing hardirqs every 1 second (first parameter) for 3 seconds (second parameter):

```
~ $ sudo hardirqs-bpfcc 1 3
Tracing hard irq event time... Hit Ctrl-C to end.

HARDIRQ                     TOTAL_usecs
enp0s31f6                             5
iwlwifi                             188
nvidia                             1554

HARDIRQ                     TOTAL_usecs
ahci[0000:00:17.0]                   29
iwlwifi                             126
acpi                                928
nvidia                             1216

HARDIRQ                     TOTAL_usecs
enp0s31f6                            20
iwlwifi                             102
nvidia                             1138
acpi                               4386
~ $
```

Figure 4.14 – hardirqs-bpfcc showing the time that was spent servicing hardirqs every 1 second for 3 seconds

The following screenshot shows us using the same tool to generate a histogram of hard IRQ time distribution (via the −d switch):

```
~ $ sudo hardirqs-bpfcc -d
Tracing hard irq event time... Hit Ctrl-C to end.
^C

hardirq = b'iwlwifi'
    usecs               : count     distribution
       0 -> 1           : 1         |                                        |
       2 -> 3           : 25        |*******************                     |
       4 -> 7           : 48        |****************************************|
       8 -> 15          : 5         |****                                    |
      16 -> 31          : 3         |**                                      |

hardirq = b'ahci[0000:00:17.0]'
    usecs               : count     distribution
       0 -> 1           : 0         |                                        |
       2 -> 3           : 115       |****************************************|
       4 -> 7           : 36        |************                            |
       8 -> 15          : 7         |**                                      |

hardirq = b'i8042'
    usecs               : count     distribution
       0 -> 1           : 0         |                                        |
       2 -> 3           : 0         |                                        |
       4 -> 7           : 0         |                                        |
       8 -> 15          : 0         |                                        |
      16 -> 31          : 2         |****                                    |
      32 -> 63          : 19        |****************************************|
      64 -> 127         : 1         |**                                      |
```

Figure 14.15 – hardirqs-bpfcc -d showing a histogram

Notice how the majority of the network hardirqs (`iwlwifi`, 48 of them) take just between 4 to 7 microseconds to complete, though a few (three of them) take between 16 and 31 usecs.

You can find more examples of how to use the `hardirqs[-bpfcc]` tool at `https:// github.com/iovisor/bcc/blob/master/tools/hardirqs_example.txt`. Looking up its man page would also be beneficial.

Measuring time servicing individual softirqs

Similar to what we did previously with hardirqs, we will now employ the `softirqs[-bpfcc]` tool. It displays the total time spent servicing softirqs (software interrupts). Again, you will require root access to run these [e]BPF tools.

First, let's place our system (native x86_64 running Ubuntu) under some stress (here, it's performing network downloads, network uploads, and disk activity). The following screenshot shows us running the `softirqs-bpfcc` tool, which provides information about the total time spent servicing softirqs every 1 second (first parameter) forever (no second parameter):

```
~ $ sudo softirqs-bpfcc 1
Tracing soft irq event time... Hit Ctrl-C to end.

SOFTIRQ          TOTAL_usecs
rcu                     1032
timer                   1224
sched                   3185
block                   5574

SOFTIRQ          TOTAL_usecs
net_rx                     2
timer                   1280
rcu                     1493
sched                   3705
block                   6182

[...]

SOFTIRQ          TOTAL_usecs
tasklet                   36
rcu                     2684
timer                   3167
block                   7688
sched                   9509

SOFTIRQ          TOTAL_usecs
net_rx                     7
tasklet                   10
rcu                     2011
timer                   2666
block                   7689
sched                   8605
```

Figure 4.16 – softirqs-bpfcc displaying the time that was spent servicing softirqs every 1 second (under some I/O stress)

Notice how the tasklet softirq also comes into play.

Let's look at another example of using the same tool to generate a histogram of soft IRQ time distribution (via the -d switch, again with the system under some I/O – network and disk – stress). The following screenshot shows the output we get after running the sudo softirqs-bpfcc -d command:

```
softirq = block
    usecs               : count     distribution
       0 -> 1           : 157       |***                                      |
       2 -> 3           : 439       |*********                                |
       4 -> 7           : 592       |**************                           |
       8 -> 15          : 1162      |***************************              |
      16 -> 31          : 1604      |*****************************************|
      32 -> 63          : 879       |********************                     |
      64 -> 127         : 591       |**************                           |
     128 -> 255         : 262       |******                                   |
     256 -> 511         : 280       |******                                   |
     512 -> 1023        : 13        |                                         |
    1024 -> 2047        : 5         |                                         |

softirq = timer
    usecs               : count     distribution
       0 -> 1           : 12957     |*****************************************|
       2 -> 3           : 8084      |*************************                |
       4 -> 7           : 3652      |***********                              |
       8 -> 15          : 912       |**                                       |
      16 -> 31          : 246       |                                         |
      32 -> 63          : 96        |                                         |
      64 -> 127         : 1         |                                         |

softirq = tasklet
    usecs               : count     distribution
       0 -> 1           : 27        |**********************                   |
       2 -> 3           : 36        |*****************************            |
       4 -> 7           : 48        |*****************************************|
       8 -> 15          : 5         |****                                     |
      16 -> 31          : 0         |                                         |
      32 -> 63          : 1         |                                         |
      64 -> 127         : 2         |*                                        |

softirq = net_rx
    usecs               : count     distribution
       0 -> 1           : 3         |******                                   |
       2 -> 3           : 12        |*************************                |
       4 -> 7           : 18        |*****************************************|
       8 -> 15          : 8         |*****************                        |
      16 -> 31          : 2         |****                                     |
```

Figure 4.17 – softirqs-bpfcc -d showing a histogram (under some I/O stress)

Again, within this small sample set, the majority of NET_RX_SOFTIRQ instances have taken just between 4 and 7 microseconds, whereas the majority of BLOCK_SOFTIRQ instances have taken between 16 and 31 microseconds to complete.

These [e]BPF tools have man pages as well (again, with examples). I recommend that you install these [e]BPF on a native Linux system (see the companion guide *Linux Kernel Programming - Chapter 1, Kernel Workspace Setup,* the *Modern tracing and performance analysis with [e]BPF* section). Take a look and try out the tools for yourself.

Using Ftrace to get a handle on system latencies

Linux has a very powerful tracing engine built into the kernel itself called **Ftrace**. Just as you can trace system calls via the (oh so useful) `strace(1)` (and library APIs via `ltrace(1)`) utility in user space, you can also trace pretty much every function running in kernel space via Ftrace. Ftrace, though, is much more than simply a function tracer – it's a framework, a linchpin of the kernel's underlying tracing infrastructure.

> Steven Rostedt is the original author of Ftrace. His paper entitled *Finding Origins of Latencies Using Ftrace* is a very good read. You can find it here: `https://static.lwn.net/images/conf/rtlws11/papers/proc/p02.pdf`.
>
> In this section, we don't intend to cover how to use Ftrace in an in-depth manner as it's really not part of the subject matter here. Learning to use Ftrace isn't difficult, and is a valuable weapon in your kernel debug armory! If you're unfamiliar with it, please go through the links we've provided on Ftrace in the *Further reading* section at the end of this chapter.

Latency is the delay between the time when something is supposed to happen and when it actually does happen (the tongue in cheek difference between theory and practice). System latencies in an OS can be the underlying cause of performance issues. Among them are interrupt and scheduling latencies. But what's the actual cause of these latencies? Borrowing from Steve Rostedt's paper (mentioned previously), four *events* cause these latencies:

- **Interrupts disabled**: If IRQs are off, interrupts cannot be serviced until they're turned on (here, we shall focus on measuring this one.)
- **Preemption disabled**: If this is the case, a thread that has been woken up cannot run until preemption is enabled.
- **Scheduling latency**: The delay between a thread being scheduled to run and it actually running on a core (we covered measuring this in the companion guide *Linux Kernel Programming - Chapter 11, The CPU Scheduler - Part 2* in the section *Latency and its measurement.*)

- **Interrupt inversion**: When an interrupt runs in preference to a task that has higher priority (similar to priority inversion, this can happen in hard real-time; of course, as you learned, this is exactly why threaded handlers are key).

Ftrace can record all but the last one. Here, we shall focus on learning how to leverage Ftrace to find (or sample, really) the worst-case time for which hardware interrupts are disabled. This is referred to as `irqsoff` latency tracing. Let's go!

Finding the interrupts disabled worst-case time latency with Ftrace

Ftrace has a number of plugins (or tracers) that it works with. First, you need to ensure that the `irqsoff` latency tracer (or plugin of Ftrace) is actually enabled within the kernel. You can check this in two different ways:

- Check the kernel config file (`grep` for `CONFIG_IRQSOFF_TRACER` within it).
- Check the available tracers (or plugins) via Ftrace infrastructure.

We'll go with the latter option here:

```
$ sudo cat /sys/kernel/debug/tracing/available_tracers
hwlat blk mmiotrace function_graph wakeup_dl wakeup_rt wakeup
function nop
```

In the preceding output, the `irqsoff` tracer – the one we require – is missing! This is usually the case and implies that you will have to configure the kernel (turning it on) and (re)build your custom 5.4 kernel. (This will be provided as an exercise in the *Questions* section at the end of this chapter.) We also recommend that you install a very useful frontend to Ftrace known as the `trace-cmd(1)` utility (we mentioned this utility in the companion guide *Linux Kernel Programming - Chapter 1, Kernel Workspace Setup* and used it in *Chapter 11, The CPU Scheduler - Part 2* in the section *Visualizing with trace-cmd*).

 Lockdep can cause issues here: if enabled, it's really best to disable the kernel's lockdep feature when you're performing latency tracing (it could add too much overhead). We'll discuss lockdep in some detail in `Chapter` `7`, *Kernel Synchronization - Part 2*.

Once you have `CONFIG_IRQSOFF_TRACER` enabled (and `trace-cmd` installed), follow these steps to let Ftrace's latency tracer figure out the **worst-case *interrupts-off* latency**. Needless to say, these steps must be carried out as root:

1. Get yourself a root shell (you will need root privileges to do this):

   ```
   sudo /bin/bash
   ```

2. Reset the Ftrace framework (this can be done with the `trace-cmd(1)` frontend to Ftrace):

   ```
   trace-cmd reset
   ```

3. Change directories to the one for ftrace:

   ```
   cd /sys/kernel/debug/tracing
   ```

   It's can usually be found here. If you have the `debugfs` pseudo filesystem mounted under a different directory, then please `cd` there (and to the `tracing` directory under it).

4. Turn off all tracing using `echo 0 tracing_on` (ensure you leave a space between the 0 and the > symbol).

5. Set the `irqsoff` tracer as the current tracer:

   ```
   echo irqsoff current_tracer
   ```

6. Now, turn tracing on:

   ```
   echo 1 tracing_on
   ... it runs! ...
   ```

7. The following output shows the worst-case `irqsoff latency` (this is typically shown in microseconds; worry not, we'll show a sample run shortly):

   ```
   cat tracing_max_latency
   [...]
   ```

8. Fetch and read the full report. All Ftrace output is held within the `trace` pseudofile:

   ```
   cp trace /tmp/mytrc.txt
   cat /tmp/mytrc.txt
   ```

9. Reset the Ftrace framework:

```
trace-cmd reset
```

The output we obtain will look like this:

```
# cat /tmp/mytrc.txt
# tracer: irqsoff
#
# irqsoff latency trace v1.1.5 on 5.4.0-llkd01
# --------------------------------------------------------------
---
# latency: 234 us, #53/53, CPU#1 | (M:desktop VP:0, KP:0, SP:0 HP:0
#P:2)
#    -----------------
#    | task: sshd-25311 (uid:1000 nice:0 policy:0 rt_prio:0)
#    -----------------
# = started at: schedule
# = ended at: finish_task_switch
[...]
```

Here, the worst-case `irqsoff` latency turned out to be 234 microseconds (experienced while the `sshd` task with PID 25311 was executing), implying that hardware interrupts were off for this period of time. For your convenience, I have provided a simple wrapper Bash script (`ch4/irqsoff_latency_ftrc.sh`) that does the same job.

Now, we will mention a few other useful tools you can use to measure system latencies.

Other tools

The following are a few tools worth mentioning with regard to capturing and analyzing system latencies (and more):

- You can learn how to set up and use the powerful **Linux Tracing Toolkit – next generation (LTTng)** toolset to record traces of the system in action. I highly recommend using the superb **Trace Compass** GUI to analyze it. In fact, in the companion guide *Linux Kernel Programming - Chapter 1, Kernel Workspace Setup*, in the *Linux Tracing Toolkit next generation (LTTng)* section, we showed an interesting screenshot (*Figure 1.9*) of the Trace Compass GUI being used to display and analyze IRQ lines 1 and 130 (the interrupt lines for the i8042 and Wi-Fi chipset on my native x86_64 system, respectively).
- You can also try using the `latencytop` tool to determine which kernel ops what user space threads are blocking on. You will have to turn on `CONFIG_LATENCYTOP` in the kernel config to do this.

- Besides latency metrics, you can use `dstat(1)`, `mpstat(1)`, `watch(1)`, and so on to gain a "top"-like view of interrupts (`https://unix.stackexchange.com/questions/8699/is-there-a-utility-that-interprets-proc-interrupts-data-in-time`).

With that, we've completed this section and this chapter.

Summary

Congratulations! This chapter has been long but worthwhile. You will have learned a lot regarding how to work with hardware interrupts. We started by briefly looking at how the OS handles interrupts before learning how you, as a driver author, must work with them. To do so you learned how to, via several methods, allocate IRQ lines (and free them) and implement the hardware interrupt routine. Here, several limitations and caveats, essentially boiling down to the fact that it's an atomic activity, were discussed. The hows and whys of the "threaded interrupt" model were then covered; it's often regarded as the modern recommended way to handle interrupts. After that, we understood and learned how to work with hardirqs/softirqs and top/bottom halves. Finally, we covered, in typical FAQ style, information which taught you about load balancing interrupts, IRQ stacks, and how to employ some useful frameworks and tools that can measure interrupt metrics and latencies.

All of this is essential knowledge when it comes to engineering a well-written driver that must work with hardware interrupts!

The next chapter covers the areas of working with time: delays and timeouts within the kernel space, creating and managing kernel threads, and using kernel workqueues. I suggest that you diligently work on this chapter's exercises, browse the numerous resources in the *Further reading* section, and then take a break (hey, all work and no play makes Jack a dull boy, right!?) before diving back in! See you there!

Questions

1. On an x86 system (a VM is fine), show that while the number of timer interrupts (IRQ 0) remains the same, another periodic system interrupt is actually continually incrementing (hence keeping track of time on a per-CPU basis). *Hint:* use a `proc` pseudo-file associated with interrupts.

2. *keylogger_simple ; native x86 only [use only for ethical hacking; may not work on a VM]*

(A bit more advanced) Write a simple keyboard logger driver using the "misc" kernel framework. Trap it inside the i8042's IRQ 1 in order to "trap" it inside the keyboard press/release and read the key scancode. Use a `kfifo` data structure to hold the keyboard scancode in kernel space memory. Have a user mode process (or thread) periodically read the data items from your driver's `kfifo` into a user space buffer and write them into a log file. Write an app (or use another thread) to interpret the keyboard keys.

Tips:

1. Can you ensure that it runs only on x86 (as it should)? Yes; use `#ifdef CONFIG_X86` at the very beginning of your code!

2. Can you ensure that it runs only on a native system and not within a VM? Yes, you can use the `virt-what` script within a wrapper script to load up the driver; only perform `insmod` (or `modprobe`) if you're not on a VM.

3. Writing a driver is actually a difficult (and quite unnecessary!) way to implement a key logger (here, you're just doing so as a learning exercise so that you know how to work with hardware interrupts within a device driver). It's really simpler and better to work at higher level abstractions – basically, by querying the kernel's `events` layer for keystrokes. A simple way you can do this is by using an event monitoring and capture tool – `evtest(1)` is great! (run it as root; `https://www.kernel.org/doc/html/latest/input/input_uapi.html`).

References for this assignment:

- *Using the kernel kfifo*: `https://elixir.bootlin.com/linux/latest/source/samples/kfifo/bytestream-example.c`

- *US keyboard map and interpretation*: `http://www.philipstorr.id.au/pcbook/book3/scancode.htm`; `http://www.osdever.net/bkerndev/Docs/keyboard.htm`

4. The kernel provides "deferred functionality" mechanisms often called _____; they're deliberately designed to get the best of both worlds: (i) _____ and (ii) _____.

    1. Top halves; run the hardirq as soon as possible; immediately restore the interrupted context after that.

    2. Bottom halves; to allow the driver author to do fairly lengthy interrupt processing if the situation demands it. Do this in a deferred, safe manner while allowing the business of the system to continue.

    3. Better half; do more work in the interrupt context so that you don't have to pay for it later.

4. Bottom halves; run interrupt code with interrupts disabled and let it run for a long time.

5. Use a code browsing tool (`cscope(1)` is a good choice) to find drivers that are using the `tasklet_hi_schedule()` API.

6. Use the Ftrace `irqsoff` latency tracer plugin to find the maximum time for which interrupts have been turned off.
    Tip: This will involve using the `irqsoff` plugin (`CONFIG_IRQSOFF_TRACER`); if it's not turned on by default, you will have to configure the kernel so that it includes it (and other tracers as required; you can find them under `make menuconfig : Kernel Hacking / Tracers`). Then, you must build the kernel and turn off it.
    Tip: When measuring things such as system latencies (interrupts-off, interrupts-and-preemption-off, scheduling latency), it's best to disable `lockdep`.
    Reference: Finding Origins of Latencies Using Ftrace, Steven Rostedt, RedHat: `https://static.lwn.net/images/conf/rtlws11/papers/proc/p02.pdf`.

 Solutions to some of the preceding questions could be found at `https://github.com/PacktPublishing/Linux-Kernel-Programming-Part-2/tree/main/solutions_to_assgn`.

Further reading

- Kernel documentation: *Linux generic IRQ handling*: `https://www.kernel.org/doc/html/latest/core-api/genericirq.html#linux-generic-irq-handling`
- LWN kernel index on interrupts: `https://lwn.net/Kernel/Index/#Interrupts`

- Interrupt triggering at the level/edge:
    - *Edge Triggered versus Level Triggered interrupts*, Mar '13: `http://venkateshabbarapu.blogspot.com/2013/03/edge-triggered-vs-level-triggered.html`
    - *Level-triggered versus Edge-triggered Interrupts*, Nov '08: `https://www.garystringham.com/level-triggered-vs-edge-triggered-interrupts/`

- *How do I disable non-maskable interrupts programmatically?*: `https://stackoverflow.com/questions/55394608/how-do-i-disable-non-maskable-interrupts-programmatically`
- *Threadable NAPI polling, softirqs, and proper fixes*, Jon Corbet, May 2016, LWN: `https://lwn.net/Articles/687617/`

- Possible future directions: softirq vector fine-grained masking:
  - *Per-vector software-interrupt masking*, Jon Corbet, Feb 2019, LWN: `https://lwn.net/Articles/779738/`
  - *Soft-interruptible softirqs (or per vector masking)*, Frederic Weisbecker, SuSe: `https://linuxplumbersconf.org/event/4/contributions/420/attachments/375/609/lpc_softirq.pdf`
- IRQ balancing and affinity:
  - *IRQ Balancing*, ntop project: `https://www.ntop.org/pf_ring/irq-balancing/`
  - *Setting interrupt affinity systems*, RHEL8: `https://access.redhat.com/documentation/en-us/red_hat_enterprise_linux/8/html/monitoring_and_managing_system_status_and_performance/configuring-an-operating-system-to-optimize-cpu-utilization_monitoring-and-managing-system-status-and-performance#setting-interrupt-affinity-systems_configuring-an-operating-system-to-optimize-cpu-utilization`
- The modern approach to performance measurement and analysis with eBPF:
  - *Linux bcc/eBPF tracing tools*, Brendan Gregg: `https://github.com/iovisor/bcc#tools`
  - *bcc Tutorial*: `https://github.com/iovisor/bcc/blob/master/docs/tutorial.md#bcc-tutorial`
- Ftrace:
  - Kernel doc: *ftrace – Function Tracer*: `https://www.kernel.org/doc/Documentation/trace/ftrace.txt`
  - The following is a collection of links to articles on Ftrace on LWN (some of which are mentioned here): `https://lwn.net/Kernel/Index/#Ftrace`
  - *Debugging the kernel using ftrace - part 1*, Steven Rostedt, LWN, Dec 2009: `https://lwn.net/Articles/365835/`
  - *Secrets of the ftrace function tracer*, Steven Rostedt, LWN, Jan 2010: `https://lwn.net/Articles/370423/`
  - *trace-cmd: a frontend for ftrace*, Steven Rostedt, LWN, Oct 2010: `https://lwn.net/Articles/410200/`
  - *Finding Origins of Latencies Using Ftrace*, Steven Rostedt, Oct 2011: `https://static.lwn.net/images/conf/rtlws11/papers/proc/p02.pdf`
- *LWN Kernel index on Latency*: `https://lwn.net/Kernel/Index/#Latency`

5
Working with Kernel Timers, Threads, and Workqueues

What if the low-level specification for your device driver demands that, between the execution of `func_a()` and `func_b()`, there should be a 50-millisecond delay? Furthermore, depending on your circumstances, the delay should work when you're running in either process or interrupt contexts. What if, in another part of the driver, you require a monitoring function of some sort to be executed asynchronously and periodically (say, every second)? Or do you need to have a thread (or several threads) silently performing work in the background but within the kernel?

These are very common requirements in all kinds of software, including our corner of the universe – Linux kernel module (and driver) development! In this chapter, you will learn how to set up, understand, and use delays while running in kernel space, as well as how to work with kernel timers, kernel threads, and workqueues.

In this chapter, you will learn how to optimally perform these tasks. In a nutshell, we will cover the following topics:

- Delaying for a given time in the kernel
- Setting up and using kernel timers
- Creating and working with kernel threads
- Using kernel workqueues

Let's get started!

Technical requirements

I assume that you have gone through the Preface section To get the most out of this book and have appropriately prepared a guest VM running Ubuntu 18.04 LTS (or a later stable release) and installed all the required packages. If not, I highly recommend you do this first. To get the most out of this book, I strongly recommend you first set up the workspace environment, including cloning this book's GitHub repository for the code, and work on it in a hands-on fashion. The repository can be found here: `https://github.com/PacktPublishing/Linux-Kernel-Programming-Part-2`.

Delaying for a given time in the kernel

Often, your kernel or driver code will need to wait for a given time before moving on to the next instruction. This can be achieved within the Linux kernel space via a set of delay APIs. Right from the outset, a key point to understand is that you can enforce a delay in two broad ways:

- Delay via non-blocking or atomic APIs that will never cause a sleep process to occur (in other words, it will never schedule out)
- Delay via blocking APIs that cause the current process context to sleep (in other words, by scheduling out)

(As we covered in detail in the companion guide *Linux Kernel Programming*, our chapters on CPU scheduling *Chapter 10, The CPU Scheduler – Part 1*, and *Chapter 11, The CPU Scheduler – Part 2*), putting a process context to sleep internally implies that the kernel's core `schedule()` function is invoked at some point, ultimately causing a context switch to occur. This leads up to a really important point (one we've mentioned previously!): you must never, ever invoke `schedule()` while running in an atomic or interrupt context of any sort.

Often, as is our case here with inserting delays, you have to figure out what context the code where you intend to insert a delay is running in. We covered this in the companion guide *Linux Kernel Programming - Chapter 6, Kernel Internals Essentials – Processes and Threads*, in the *Determining the context* section; please refer back to it if you're unclear. (We went into even more detail on this in `Chapter 4`, *Handling Hardware Interrupts*.)

Next, think about this carefully: if you are indeed in an atomic (or interrupt) context, is there really a need to delay? The whole point of an atomic or interrupt context is that the execution within it is limited to an as-brief-as-possible duration; it is strongly recommended that you design it in this way. This implies that you don't insert delays into atomic code unless you can't avoid doing so.

- **Use the first type**: These are the non-blocking or atomic APIs that will never cause a sleep to occur. You should use this when your code is in an atomic (or interrupt) context and you really do require a non-blocking delay with a short duration; but how short is that? As a rule of thumb, use these APIs for non-blocking atomic delays that are 1 millisecond or less. Even if you need to delay for longer than a millisecond in an atomic context – say, within the code of an interrupt handler (*but why delay in an interrupt!?*) – use these `*delay()` APIs (the `*` character implies a wildcard; here, as you will see, it implies the `ndelay()`, `delay()`, and `mdelay()` routines).
- **Use the second type**: These are the blocking APIs that cause the current process context to sleep. You should use this when your code is in a process (or task) context, for delays that are blocking in nature and of a longer duration; in effect, for delays over a millisecond. These kernel APIs follow the form `*sleep()`. (Again, without going into too much detail, think about this: if you are in a process context *but* within the critical section of a spinlock, it's an atomic context – if you must incorporate a delay, then you must use the `*delay()` APIs! We'll cover spinlocks and much more in the last two chapters of this book.)

Now, let's look at these kernel APIs and see how they're used. We'll begin by looking at `*delay()` atomic APIs.

Understanding how to use the *delay() atomic APIs

Without further ado, let's take a look at a table that quickly summarizes the available (to us module authors) non-blocking or atomic *delay() kernel APIs; *they're meant to be used in any kind of atomic or interrupt context where you cannot block or sleep* (or invoke schedule()):

API	Comment
ndelay(ns);	Delay for ns nanoseconds.
udelay(us);	Delay for us microseconds.
mdelay(ms);	Delay for ms milliseconds.

Table 5.1 – The *delay() non-blocking APIs

There are a few points to note regarding these APIs, their internal implementation, and their usage:

- Always include the <linux/delay.h> header when using these macros/APIs.
- You are expected to call an appropriate routine based on the time you must delay for; for example, if you need to perform an atomic non-blocking delay of, say, 30 milliseconds, you should call mdelay(30) and not udelay(30*1000). The kernel code mentions this very point: linux/delay.h – *"Using udelay() for intervals greater than a few milliseconds can risk overflow for high loops_per_jiffy (high bogomips) machines ..."*.
- The internal implementation of these APIs, like many on Linux, is nuanced: there is a higher-level abstracted implementation for these functions (or macros, as the case may be) in the <linux/delay.h> header; there is often a low-level arch-specific implementation within an arch-specific header (<asm-<arch>/delay.h> *or* <asm-generic/delay.h>; where arch, of course, means CPU) that will automatically override the high-level version at call time (the linker will ensure this).

- In the current implementation, these APIs ultimately boil down to wrappers over `udelay()`; this function itself boils down to a tight assembly loop that performs what's called "busy looping"! (for x86, the code can be found in `arch/x86/lib/delay.c:__const_udelay()`). Without going into the gory details, early in the boot process, the kernel calibrates a couple of values: the so-called **bogomips** – bogus MIPS – and **loops per jiffy (lpj)** values. Essentially, the kernel figures out, on that particular system, how many times a loop must be iterated over in order for 1 timer tick or a jiffy to elapse. This value is known as the system's bogomips value and can be seen in the kernel log. For example, on my Core-i7 laptop, it's as follows:

```
Calibrating delay loop (skipped), value calculated using timer
frequency.. 5199.98 BogoMIPS (lpj=10399968)
```

- For delays over `MAX_UDELAY_MS` (set to 5 ms), the kernel will internally call the `udelay()` function in a loop.

Remember the `*delay()` APIs must be used when you require a delay in any type of atomic context, such as an interrupt handler (top or bottom half), as they guarantee that no sleep – and thus no call to `schedule()` – ever occurs. A reminder (we mentioned this point in *Chapter 4, Handling Hardware Interrupts*): `might_sleep()` is used as a debug aid; the kernel (and drivers) internally uses the `might_sleep()` macro in places in the code base where the code runs in the process context; that is, where it can sleep. Now, if `might_sleep()` is ever invoked within an atomic context, that's just plain wrong – a noisy printk stack trace is then emitted, thus helping you catch these issues early and fix them. You can use these `*delay()` APIs in the process context as well.

In these discussions, you will often come across the `jiffies` kernel variable; essentially, think of `jiffies` as a global unsigned 64-bit value that is incremented on every timer interrupt (or timer tick; it's internally protected against overflow). Thus, the continually incrementing variable is used as a way to measure uptime, as well as a means of implementing simple timeouts and delays.

Now, let's look at the second type of delay APIs available – the blocking type.

Understanding how to use the *sleep() blocking APIs

Let's look at another table that quickly summarizes the available (to us module authors) blocking `*sleep*()` kernel APIs; these are *only meant to be used in the process context when it's safe to sleep*; that is, where the invocation of `schedule()` is not a problem. In other words, the delay is implemented by the process context actually going to sleep for the duration of the delay and is then woke up when it's done:

API	Internally "backed by"	Comment
`usleep_range(umin, umax);`	`hrtimers` (high-resolution timers)	Sleep for between `umin` and `umax` microseconds. Use where the wakeup time is flexible. This is the **recommended API** to use.
`msleep(ms);`	`jiffies/legacy_timers`	Sleep for `ms` milliseconds. Typically meant for a sleep with a duration of 10 ms or more.
`msleep_interruptible(ms);`	`jiffies/legacy_timers`	An interruptible variant of `msleep(ms);`.
`ssleep(s);`	`jiffies/legacy_timers`	Sleep for `s` seconds. This is meant for sleeps > 1 s (wrapper over `msleep()`).

Table 5.2 – The *sleep*() blocking APIs

There's a few points to note regarding these APIs, their internal implementation, and their usage:

- Ensure you include the `<linux/delay.h>` header when using these macros/APIs.
- All these `*sleep()` APIs are internally implemented in such a manner that they *cause the current process context to sleep* (that is, by internally invoking `schedule()`); thus, of course, they must only ever be invoked in the process context when it's "safe to sleep". Again, just because your code is in the process context does not necessarily mean it's safe to sleep; for example, the critical section of a spinlock is atomic; thus, you must not invoke the aforementioned `*sleep()` APIs there!

- We mentioned that `usleep_range()` is the **preferred/recommended API** to use when you want a short sleep – but why? This will become clearer in the *Let's try it – how long do delays and sleeps really take?* section.

As you are aware, sleeps on Linux can be of two types: interruptible and uninterruptible. The latter means that no signal task can "disturb" the sleep. So, when you invoke `msleep(ms);`, it puts the current process context to sleep for `ms` by internally invoking the following:

```
__set_current_state(TASK_UNINTERRUPTIBLE);
return schedule_timeout(timeout);
```

The `schedule_timeout()` routine works by setting up a kernel timer (our next topic!) that will expire in the desired time, then immediately putting the process to sleep by calling `schedule()`! (For the curious, have a peek at its code here: `kernel/time/timer.c:schedule_timeout()`.) The `msleep_interruptible()` implementation is very similar, except that it calls `__set_current_state(TASK_INTERRUPTIBLE);`. As a design heuristic, follow the UNIX paradigm of *provide mechanism, not policy*; this way, calling `msleep_interruptible()` might be a good idea in situations where, if the userspace app aborts the work (by the user pressing ^C perhaps), the kernel or driver obediently releases the task: its process context is awoken, it runs the appropriate signal handler, and life continues. In situations where it's important that the kernel space is not disturbed by user-generated signals, use the `msleep()` variant.

Again, as a rule of thumb, use the following APIs, depending on the duration of the delay:

- **For delays of over 10 milliseconds**: `msleep()` or `msleep_interruptible()`
- **For delays of over 1 second**: `ssleep()`

As you might expect, `ssleep()` is a simple wrapper over `msleep();` and becomes `msleep(seconds * 1000);`.

One simple way to implement the (approximate) equivalent of the user space `sleep(3)` API can be seen in our `convenient.h` header; at heart, it employs the `schedule_timeout()` API:

```
#ifdef __KERNEL__
void delay_sec(long);
/*------------ delay_sec -------------------------------------------------
 * Delays execution for @val seconds.
 * If @val is -1, we sleep forever!
 * MUST be called from process context.
```

```
 * (We deliberately do not inline this function; this way, we can see it's
 * entry within a kernel stack call trace).
 */
void delay_sec(long val)
{
    asm (""); // force the compiler to not inline it!
    if (in_task()) {
        set_current_state(TASK_INTERRUPTIBLE);
        if (-1 == val)
            schedule_timeout(MAX_SCHEDULE_TIMEOUT);
        else
            schedule_timeout(val * HZ);
    }
}
#endif /* #ifdef __KERNEL__ */
```

Now that you've learned how to delay (yes, smile please), let's move on and learn a useful skill: timestamping kernel code. This allows you to quickly calculate how long a particular piece of code takes to execute.

Taking timestamps within kernel code

It's important to be able to take an accurate timestamp as kernels open employ this facility. For example, the `dmesg(1)` utility shows the time since the system booted in `seconds.microseconds` format; Ftrace traces typically show the time a function takes to execute. When in user mode, we often employ the `gettimeofday(2)` system call to take a timestamp. Within the kernel, several interfaces exist; commonly, the `ktime_get_*()` family of routines is employed for the purpose of obtaining accurate timestamps. For our purposes, the following routine is useful:

```
u64 ktime_get_real_ns(void);
```

This routine internally queries the wall (clock) time via the `ktime_get_real()` API and then converts the result into a nanosecond quantity. We won't bother with the internal details here. Also, several variants of this API are available; for example, `ktime_get_real_fast_ns()`, `ktime_get_real_ts64()`, and so on. The former is both fast and NMI-safe.

Now that you know how to get a timestamp, you can calculate how long some code takes to execute to a good degree of accuracy, with nanosecond resolution no less! You can use the following pseudocode to achieve this:

```
#include <linux/ktime.h>
t1 = ktime_get_real_ns();
foo();
bar();
t2 = ktime_get_real_ns();
time_taken_ns = (t2 -> t1);
```

Here, the time taken for the (fictional) `foo()` and `bar()` functions to execute is calculated, and the result – in nanoseconds – is available in the `time_taken_ns` variable. The `<linux/ktime.h>` kernel header itself includes the `<linux/timekeeping.h>` header, which is where the `ktime_get_*()` family of routines is defined.

> A macro to help you calculate the time taken between two timestamps has been provided in our `convenient.h` header file: `SHOW_DELTA(later, earlier);`. Ensure that you pass the later timestamp as the first parameter and the first timestamp as the second parameter.

The code example in the next section will help us employ this kind of approach.

Let's try it – how long do delays and sleeps really take?

By now, you know how to use the `*delay()` and `*sleep()` APIs to construct delays and sleeps (non-blocking and blocking, respectively). Hang on, though – we haven't really tried it out in a kernel module. Not only that, are the delays and sleeps as accurate as we have been led to believe? Let's, as usual, be *empirical* (this is important!) and not make any assumptions. Let's actually try it out for ourselves!

The demo kernel module we'll be looking at in this subsection performs two kinds of delays, in order:

- First, it employs the `*delay()` routines (which you learned about in the *Understanding how to use the *delay() atomic APIs* section) to implement atomic non-blocking delays of 10 ns, 10 us, and 10 ms.
- Next, it employs the `*sleep()` routines (which you learned about in the *Understanding how to use the *sleep() blocking APIs* section) to implement blocking delays of 10 us, 10 ms, and 1 second.

We call the code for this like so:

```
DILLY_DALLY("udelay() for    10,000 ns", udelay(10));
```

Here, `DILLY_DALLY()` is a custom macro. Its implementation is as follows:

```
// ch5/delays_sleeps/delays_sleeps.c
/*
 * DILLY_DALLY() macro:
 * Runs the code @run_this while measuring the time it takes; prints the
string
 * @code_str to the kernel log along with the actual time taken (in ns, us
 * and ms).
 * Macro inspired from the book 'Linux Device Drivers Cookbook', PacktPub.
 */
#define DILLY_DALLY(code_str, run_this) do {     \
    u64 t1, t2;                                  \
    t1 = ktime_get_real_ns();                    \
    run_this;                                    \
    t2 = ktime_get_real_ns();                    \
    pr_info(code_str "-> actual: %11llu ns = %7llu us = %4llu ms\n", \
        (t2-t1), (t2-t1)/1000, (t2-t1)/1000000);\
} while(0)
```

Here, we have implemented the time delta calculation trivially; a good implementation will involve checking that the value of `t2` is greater than `t1`, that no overflow occurs, and so on.

We invoke it, for various delays and sleeps, within our kernel module's `init` function, like this:

```
[ ... ]
/* Atomic busy-loops, no sleep! */
pr_info("\n1. *delay() functions (atomic, in a delay loop):\n");
DILLY_DALLY("ndelay() for        10 ns", ndelay(10));
/* udelay() is the preferred interface */
DILLY_DALLY("udelay() for     10,000 ns", udelay(10));
DILLY_DALLY("mdelay() for 10,000,000 ns", mdelay(10));

/* Non-atomic blocking APIs; causes schedule() to be invoked */
pr_info("\n2. *sleep() functions (process ctx, sleeps/schedule()'s
out):\n");
    /* usleep_range(): HRT-based, 'flexible'; for approx range [10us -
20ms] */
    DILLY_DALLY("usleep_range(10,10) for 10,000 ns", usleep_range(10, 10));
    /* msleep(): jiffies/legacy-based; for longer sleeps (> 10ms) */
    DILLY_DALLY("msleep(10) for      10,000,000 ns", msleep(10));
    DILLY_DALLY("msleep_interruptible(10)         ",
msleep_interruptible(10));
```

```
    /* ssleep() is a wrapper over msleep(): = msleep(ms*1000); */
    DILLY_DALLY("ssleep(1)                        ", ssleep(1));
```

Here's some sample output when the kernel module is run on our trusty x86_64 Ubuntu
VM:

```
                1. *delay() functions (atomic, in a delay loop):
[80360.847699] ndelay() for          10 ns-> actual:           98 ns =        0 us =     0 ms
[80360.848225] udelay() for      10,000 ns-> actual:         9967 ns =        9 us =     0 ms
[80360.858657] mdelay() for 10,000,000 ns-> actual:       9920943 ns =     9920 us =     9 ms
[80360.859229]
                2. *sleep() functions (process ctx, sleeps/schedule()'s out):
[80360.859817] usleep_range(10,10) for 10,000 ns-> actual:        56206 ns =       56 us =     0 ms
[80360.878300] msleep(10) for       10,000,000 ns-> actual:     17786899 ns =    17786 us =    17 ms
[80360.898538] msleep_interruptible(10)          -> actual:     19537145 ns =    19537 us =    19 ms
[80361.911452] ssleep(1)                         -> actual:   1009815171 ns =  1009815 us =  1009 ms
```

Figure 5.1 – A partial screenshot showing the output of our delays_sleeps.ko kernel module

Carefully study the preceding output; it's peculiar that both the udelay(10) and
mdelay(10) routines seem to complete their execution *before* the desired delay period has
expired (in our sample output, in 9 us and 9 ms, respectively)! How come? The reality is
that **the *delay() routines tend to finish earlier**. This fact is documented within the
kernel source. Let's take a look at the relevant portion of code here (it's self-explanatory):

```
// include/linux/delay.h
/*
 [ ... ]
 * Delay routines, using a pre-computed "loops_per_jiffy" value.
 *
 * Please note that ndelay(), udelay() and mdelay() may return early for
 * several reasons:
 * 1. computed loops_per_jiffy too low (due to the time taken to
 * execute the timer interrupt.)
 * 2. cache behavior affecting the time it takes to execute the
 * loop function.
 * 3. CPU clock rate changes.
 *
 * Please see this thread:
 * http://lists.openwall.net/linux-kernel/2011/01/09/56
```

The *sleep() routines have the reverse characteristic; they pretty much always tend to
sleep for *longer* than asked. Again, these are expected issues in a non-real-time OS such as
standard Linux.

You can **mitigate these issues** in a few ways:

- On standard Linux, in user mode, do the following:
    - First of all, it's best to use the **High-Resolution Timer (HRT)** interfaces for high accuracy. This, again, is code that's been merged from the RTL project into mainstream Linux (way back in 2006). It supports timers that require a resolution of less than a single *jiffy* (which, as you know, is tightly coupled to the timer "tick", the kernel `CONFIG_HZ` value); for example, with the `HZ` value being 100, a jiffy is 1000/100 = 10 ms; with `HZ` being 250, a jiffy is 4 ms, and so on.
    - Once you've done this, why not employ the soft RT scheduling features of Linux? Here, you can specify a scheduling policy of `SCHED_FIFO` or `SCHED_RR` and a high priority for your user mode thread (the range is 1 to 99; we covered these details in the companion guide *Linux Kernel Programming - Chapter 10, The CPU Scheduler – Part 1*).

Most modern Linux systems will have HRT support. However, how do you exploit it? This is simple: you're recommended to write your timer code *in user space* and employ standard POSIX timer APIs (such as the `timer_create(2)` and `timer_settime(2)` system calls). Since this book is concerned with kernel development, we won't delve into these user space APIs here. In fact, this topic was covered in some detail in my earlier book, *Hands-On System Programming with Linux*, in *Chapter 13, Timers*, in the *The newer POSIX (interval) timers mechanism* section.

- The kernel developers have taken the trouble to clearly document some excellent recommendations for when you're using these delay and sleep APIs within the kernel. It's really important that you browse through this document within the official kernel documentation: `https://www.kernel.org/doc/Documentation/timers/timers-howto.rst`.
- Configure and build the Linux OS as an RTOS; this will significantly reduce scheduling "jitter" (we covered this topic in detail in the companion guide *Linux Kernel Programming - Chapter 11, The CPU Scheduler – Part 2*, in the *Converting mainline Linux into an RTOS* section).

Interestingly, using our "better" Makefile's checkpatch target can be a real boon. Let's take a look at what it (the kernel's checkpatch Perl script) has caught (first ensure you're in the correct source directory):

```
$ cd <...>/ch5/delays_sleeps
$ make checkpatch
make clean
[ ... ]
--- cleaning ---
[ ... ]
--- kernel code style check with checkpatch.pl ---

/lib/modules/5.4.0-58-generic/build/scripts/checkpatch.pl --no-tree -f --
max-line-length=95 *.[ch]
[ ... ]
WARNING: usleep_range should not use min == max args; see
Documentation/timers/timers-howto.rst
#63: FILE: delays_sleeps.c:63:
+ DILLY_DALLY("XXXXXXXXXXXXXXXXXXXXXXXXXXXXXXXX", usleep_range(10, 10));

total: 0 errors, 2 warnings, 79 lines checked
[ ... ]
```

That's really good! Ensure that you use the targets in our "better" `Makefile` (we covered this in detail in the companion guide *Linux Kernel Programming - Chapter 5, Writing Your First Kernel Module LKMs – Part 2*, in the *A "better" Makefile template for your kernel modules* section).

With that, we've finished looking at kernel delays and sleeping within the kernel. With this as a base, you shall now learn how to set up and use kernel timers, kernel threads, and workqueues in the remaining sections of this chapter.

The "sed" drivers – to demo kernel timers, kthreads, and workqueues

To make this chapter more interesting and hands-on, we shall begin evolving a miscellaneous class character "driver" called a **simple encrypt decrypt** – or **sed** for short – driver (not to be confused with the well-known `sed(1)` utility). No, you won't get a grand prize for guessing that it provides some kind of – very simplistic – text encryption/decryption support.

The point here is that we shall imagine that in the specification for this driver, one clause demands that the work (practically speaking, the encryption/decryption functionality) is carried out within a given time interval – in effect, *within a given deadline*. In order to check this, we shall design our driver so that it has a kernel timer that will expire in the given time interval; the driver will check that the functionality does indeed complete within this time constraint!

We shall evolve a series of sed drivers and their user space counterparts (apps):

- The first driver – the sed1 driver and user mode app (ch5/sed1) – will perform what we just described: the demo user mode app will employ ioctl system calls to interface with the driver and get the encrypt/decrypt message functionality going. The driver will focus on a kernel timer that we will set up to expire by the given deadline. If it does expire, we deem the operation to have failed; if not, the timer is canceled and the operation is a success.
- The second version, sed2 (ch5/sed2), will do the same as sed1, except that the actual encrypt/decrypt message functionality here will be carried out in the context of a separately created kernel thread! This changes the design of the project.
- The third version, sed3 (ch5/sed3), will again do the same as sed1 and sed2, except that this time the actual encrypt/decrypt message functionality will be carried out by a kernel workqueue!

Now that you have learned how to perform delays (both atomic and blocking) and capture timestamps, let's learn how to set up and use kernel timers.

Setting up and using kernel timers

A **timer** provides software with a means of being asynchronously notified when a designated amount of time has passed. All kinds of software, both in user and kernel space, require timers; this commonly includes network protocol implementations, block layer code, device drivers, and various kernel subsystems. This timer provides a means of asynchronous notification, thus allowing the driver to execute work in parallel with the running timer. An important question that arises is, *how will I know when the timer expires?* In user space apps, typically, the kernel sends a signal to the relevant process (the signal is typically SIGALRM).

In kernel space, it's a bit nuanced. As you will know from our discussion on top and bottom halves for hardware interrupts (see *Chapter 4, Handling Hardware Interrupts,* the *Understanding and using top and bottom halves* section), after the timer interrupt's top half (or ISR) completes, the kernel will ensure it runs the timer interrupt bottom half or timer softirq (as we showed in the table in `Chapter 4`, *Handling Hardware Interrupts* section *Available softirqs and what they are for*). This is a very high priority softirq called `TIMER_SOFTIRQ`. This softirq is what consumes expired timers! In effect – and this is very important to understand – your timer's "callback" function – the function that will run when the timer expires – is run by the timer softirq *and thus runs in atomic (interrupt) context.* Thus, it's limited in what it can and cannot do (again, this was explained in detail in *Chapter 4, Handling Hardware Interrupts*).

In the following section, you will learn how to set up and use a kernel timer.

Using kernel timers

In order to use a kernel timer, you must follow a few steps. Here's what to do in a nutshell (we'll discuss this in more detail afterward):

1. Initialize the timer metadata structure (`struct timer_list`) with the `timer_setup()` macro. The key items that get initialized here are as follows:
   - The time to expire by (that value that `jiffies` should reach for the timer to expire)
   - The function to invoke when the timer expires – in effect, the timer "callback" function
2. Write the code for your timer callback routine.
3. When appropriate, "arm" the timer – that is, have it start – by invoking the `add_timer()` (or `mod_timer()`) function.
4. When the timer times out (expires), the OS will automatically invoke your timer's callback function (the one you set up in *step 2*); remember, it will be running in the timer softirq or an atomic or interrupt context.
5. (Optional) *Timers are not cyclic, they are one-time by default.* To have your timer run again, you will have to invoke the `mod_timer()` API; this is how you can set up an interval timer – one that times out at a given fixed time interval. If you don't perform this step, your timer will be a one-shot timer - it will count down and expire exactly once.

6. When you are done, delete the timer with `del_timer[_sync]()`; this can also be used to cancel the timeout. It returns a value denoting whether a pending timer has been deactivated or not; that is, it returns 1 for an active timer or 0 for an inactive timer being canceled.

The `timer_list` data structure is the one that's relevant to our work here; within it, the relevant members (the module/driver authors) are shown:

```
// include/linux/timer.h
struct timer_list {[ ... ]
    unsigned long expires;
    void (*function)(struct timer_list *);
    u32 flags;
[ ...] };
```

Use the `timer_setup()` macro to initialize it:

```
timer_setup(timer, callback, flags);
```

The parameters of `timer_setup()` are as follows:

- `@timer`: The pointer to the `timer_list` data structure (this should be allocated memory first; also, prefixing the formal parameter name with an @ is a common convention).
- `@callback`: The pointer to the callback function. This is the function that the OS invokes (in the softirq context) when the timer expires. Its signature is `void (*function)(struct timer_list *);`. The parameter you receive in the callback function is the pointer to the `timer_list` data structure. So, how can we pass and access some arbitrary data within our timer callback? We'll answer this question shortly.
- `@flags`: These are the timer flags. We typically pass this as 0 (implying no special behavior). The flags you can specify are `TIMER_DEFERRABLE`, `TIMER_PINNED`, and `TIMER_IRQSAFE`. Let's look at both in the kernel source code:

```
// include/linux/timer.h
/**
 * @TIMER_DEFERRABLE: A deferrable timer will work normally when
the
 * system is busy, but will not cause a CPU to come out of idle
just
 * to service it; instead, the timer will be serviced when the CPU
 * eventually wakes up with a subsequent non-deferrable timer.
 [ ... ]
```

```
 * @TIMER_PINNED: A pinned timer will not be affected by any timer
 * placement heuristics (like, NOHZ) and will always expire on the
CPU
 * on which the timer was enqueued.
```

Using the `TIMER_DEFERRABLE` flag is useful when power consumption must be watched (such as on a battery-backed device). The third flag, `TIMER_IRQSAFE`, is special-purpose only; avoid using it.

Next, use the `add_timer()` API to arm, or start, the timer. Once called, the timer is "live" and starts counting down:

```
void add_timer(struct timer_list *timer);
```

Its parameter is the pointer to the `timer_list` structure that you just initialized (via the `timer_setup()` macro).

Our simple kernel timer module – code view 1

Without further ado, let's dive into the code of a simple kernel timer, written using the **Loadable Kernel Module (LKM)** framework (this can be found at `ch5/timer_simple`). As with most drivers, we keep a context or private data structure containing the information required while running; here, we call it `st_ctx`. We instantiate it as the `ctx` variable. We also specify the time to expire (as 420 ms) in a global named `exp_ms`:

```
// ch5/timer_simple/timer_simple.c
#include <linux/timer.h>
[ ... ]
static struct st_ctx {
    struct timer_list tmr;
    int data;
} ctx;
static unsigned long exp_ms = 420;
```

Now, let's check out the first portion of our *init* code:

```
static int __init timer_simple_init(void)
{
    ctx.data = INITIAL_VALUE;

    /* Initialize our kernel timer */
    ctx.tmr.expires = jiffies + msecs_to_jiffies(exp_ms);
    ctx.tmr.flags = 0;
    timer_setup(&ctx.tmr, ding, 0);
```

This is pretty straightforward. First, we initialize the `ctx` data structure, setting a `data` member to the value 3. The one key point here is that the `timer_list` structure is within our `ctx` structure, so we must initialize it. Now, setting the timer callback function (the `function` parameter) and the `flags` parameter values is simple; what about setting the time to expire? You must set the `timer_list.expires` member to the value that the `jiffies` variable (macro, actually) in the kernel must reach; at that point, the timer will expire! So, we prime it to have the timer expire 420 milliseconds in the future by adding the current value of jiffies to the jiffies value that the 420 ms elapsed time will take, like this:

```
ctx.tmr.expires = jiffies + msecs_to_jiffies(exp_ms);
```

The `msecs_to_jiffies()` convenience routine helps us out here as it converts the millisecond value that's passed to `jiffies`. Adding this result to the current value of `jiffies` will give us the value that `jiffies` will be in the future, in 420 ms from now, which is when we want our kernel timer to expire.

> This code is an inline function in `include/linux/jiffies.h:msecs_to_jiffies()`; the comments help us understand how it works. In a similar fashion, the kernel contains the `usecs_to_jiffies()`, `nsecs_to_jiffies()`, `timeval_to_jiffies()`, and `jiffies_to_timeval()` (inline) function helper routines.

The next portion of the *init* code is as follows:

```
    pr_info("timer set to expire in %ld ms\n", exp_ms);
    add_timer(&ctx.tmr); /* Arm it; let's get going! */
    return 0;    /* success */
}
```

As we can see, by invoking the `add_timer()` API, we have armed (start) our kernel timer. It's now live and counting down... in (approximately) 420 ms, it will expire. (Why approximately? As you saw in the *Let's try it – how long do delays and sleeps really take?* section, delay and sleep APIs aren't all that precise. In fact, a suggested exercise for you to work on later is to test the accuracy of the timeout; you can find this in the *Questions/kernel_timer_check* section. Also, in a sample solution for this exercise, we will show how using the `time_after()` macro is a good idea; it performs a validity check to ensure that the second timestamp is actually later than the first. Similar macros can be found in `include/linux/jiffies.h`; see the comment preceding this line: `include/linux/jiffies.h:#define time_after(a,b)`).

Our simple kernel timer module – code view 2

`add_timer()` started our kernel timer. As you just saw, it will soon expire. Internally, as we mentioned earlier, the kernel's timer softirq will run our timer's callback function. In the preceding section, we initialized the callback function to the `ding()` function (ha, *onomatopoeia* – a word that suggests the sound it describes – in action!) via the `timer_setup()` API. Hence, this code will run when the timer expires:

```
static void ding(struct timer_list *timer)
{
    struct st_ctx *priv = from_timer(priv, timer, tmr);
    /* from_timer() is in fact a wrapper around the well known
     * container_of() macro! This allows us to retrieve access to our
     * 'parent' driver context structure */
    pr_debug("timed out... data=%d\n", priv->data--);
    PRINT_CTX();

    /* until countdown done, fire it again! */
    if (priv->data)
        mod_timer(&priv->tmr, jiffies + msecs_to_jiffies(exp_ms));
}
```

There are a few things to keep in mind regarding this function:

- The timer callback handler code (`ding()` here) runs in atomic (interrupt, softirq) context; thus, you aren't allowed to invoke any perform any blocking APIs, memory allocation other than with the `GFP_ATOMIC` flag, or any kind of data transfer between kernel and user space (we covered this in detail in the previous chapter in the *Interrupt context guidelines – what to do and what not to do* section).
- The callback function receives, as a parameter, the pointer to the `timer_list` structure. Since we have (very deliberately) kept `struct timer_list` within our context or private data structure, we can usefully employ the `from_timer()` macro to retrieve the pointer to our private structure; that is, `struct st_ctx`). The first line of code shown previous does this. How does this work? Let's look at its implementation:

  ```
  // include/linux/timer.h
  #define from_timer(var, callback_timer, timer_fieldname) \
          container_of(callback_timer, typeof(*var), timer_fieldname)
  ```

It's really a wrapper over the `container_of()` macro!

- We then print and decrement our `data` value.
- We then issue our `PRINT_CTX()` macro (recall that it's defined in our `convenient.h` header file). It will show that we're running in softirq context.
- Next, as long as our data member is positive, we force another timeout (of the same period) by invoking the `mod_timer()` API:

```
int mod_timer(struct timer_list *timer, unsigned long expires);
```

As you can see, with `mod_timer()`, when the timer triggers again is completely up to you; it's considered an efficient way of updating a timer's expiry date. By using `mod_timer()`, you can even arm an inactive timer (the job that `add_timer()` does); in this case, the return value is 0, else it's 1 (implying that we've modified an existing active timer).

Our simple kernel timer module – running it

Now, let's test our kernel timer module. On our x86_64 Ubuntu VM, we will use our `lkm` convenience script to load up the kernel module. The following screenshot shows a partial view of this and the kernel log:

```
-----------------------------------------
sudo insmod ./timer_simple.ko && lsmod|grep timer_simple
-----------------------------------------
timer_simple            20480  0
-----------------------------------------
dmesg
-----------------------------------------
[ 4233.401948] timer_simple:timer_simple_init(): timer set to expire in 420 ms
$
$ dmesg
[ 4233.401948] timer_simple:timer_simple_init(): timer set to expire in 420 ms
[ 4233.841358] timer_simple:ding(): timed out... data=3
[ 4233.842162] timer_simple:ding(): 001) [swapper/1]:0    | ..s1   /* ding() */
[ 4234.289334] timer_simple:ding(): timed out... data=2
[ 4234.290177] timer_simple:ding(): 001) [swapper/1]:0    | ..s1   /* ding() */
[ 4234.737346] timer_simple:ding(): timed out... data=1
[ 4234.738096] timer_simple:ding(): 001) [swapper/1]:0    | ..s1   /* ding() */
$
```

Figure 5.2 – A partial screenshot of running our timer_simple.ko kernel module

Study the `dmesg` (kernel log) output shown here. Since we've set the initial value of our private structure's `data` member to `3`, the kernel timer expires three times (just as our logic demands). Check out the timestamps in the left-most column; you can see that the second timer expiry occurred at `4234.289334` (sec.us) and the third at `4234.737346`; a quick subtraction reveals that the time difference is 448,012 microseconds; that is, about 448 milliseconds. This is reasonable since we asked for a 420 ms timeout (its a bit over that; the overheads of the printks do matter as well).

The `PRINT_CTX()` macro's output is revealing as well; let's look at the second one shown in the preceding screenshot:

```
[ 4234.290177] timer_simple:ding(): 001) [swapper/1]:0   |  ..s1    /*
ding() */
```

This shows that (as explained in detail in *Chapter 4, Handling Hardware Interrupts*) the code ran on CPU 1 (the `001)`) in softirq context (`s` in `..s1`). Furthermore, the process context that got interrupted – by the timer interrupt and softirq – is the `swapper/1` kernel thread; this is the CPU idle thread running on CPU 1 when it's idle. This makes sense and is quite typical on an idle or lightly loaded system. The system (or at least CPU 1) was idle when the timer interrupt was initiated and a subsequent softirq came along and ran our timer callback.

sed1 – implementing timeouts with our demo sed1 driver

In this section, we'll write a bit of a more interesting driver (the code's for this can be found at `ch5/sed1/sed1_driver`). We'll design it so that it encrypts and/or decrypts a given message (very trivially, of course). The basic idea is that a user mode app (this can be found in `ch5/userapp_sed`) serves as its user interface. When run, it opens our `misc` character driver's device file (`/dev/sed1_drv`) and issues an `ioctl(2)` system call upon it.

> We have provided material online to help you understand how to interface a kernel module or device driver to a user space process via several common methods: via procfs, sysfs, debugfs, netlink sockets, and the `ioctl()` system call (`https://github.com/PacktPublishing/Learn-Linux-Kernel-Development/blob/master/User_kernel_communication_pathways.pdf`)!

The `ioctl()` call passes a data structure that encapsulates the data being passed, its length, the operation (or transform) to perform upon it, and a `timed_out` field (to figure out if it failed due to it missing its deadline). The valid ops are as follows:

- Encrypt: `XF_ENCRYPT`
- Decrypt: `XF_DECRYPT`

Due to lack of space, we don't intend to show the code in great detail here – after all, having read so much of this book, you're now in a good position to browse and try and understand the code on your own! Nevertheless, certain key details relevant to this section will be shown.

Let's take a look at its overall design:

- Our `sed1` driver (`ch5/sed1/sed1_driver/sed1_drv.c`) is really a pseudo driver, in the sense that it doesn't operate on any peripheral hardware controller or chip but on memory; nevertheless, it's a full-fledged `misc` class character device driver.
- It registers itself as a `misc` device; in the process, a device node is auto-created by the kernel (here, we will call it `/dev/sed1_drv`).
- We arrange for it to have a driver "context" structure (`struct stMyCtx`) containing key members that it uses throughout; one of them is a `struct timer_list` structure for a kernel timer, which we initialize in the init code path (with the `timer_setup()` API).
- A user space app (`ch5/sed1/userapp_sed/userapp_sed1.c`) opens the device file of our `sed1` driver (it's passed as a parameter to it, along with the message to encrypt). It invokes an `ioctl(2)` system call – the command being to encrypt – and the `arg` parameter, which is a pointer to a duly populated structure containing all the required information (including the message payload to encrypt). Let's take a look at it in brief:

```
kd->data_xform = XF_ENCRYPT;
ioctl(fd, IOCTL_LLKD_SED_IOC_ENCRYPT_MSG, kd);
```

- Our `sed1` driver's `ioctl` method takes over. After performing validity checks, it copies the metadata structure (via the usual `copy_from_user()`) and fires off our `process_it()` function, which then invokes our `encrypt_decrypt_payload()` routine.
- `encrypt_decrypt_payload()` is the key routine here. It does the following:
    - Starts our kernel timer (with the `mod_timer()` API), setting it to expire in `TIMER_EXPIRE_MS` milliseconds from now (here, we've set `TIMER_EXPIRE_MS` to 1).
    - Grabs a timestamp, `t1 = ktime_get_real_ns();`.
    - Kicks off the actual work – it's either an encrypt or decrypt operation (we've kept it very simplistic: a mere `XOR` operation followed by an increment for each byte of the payload; the reverse for decryption).
    - As soon as the work's complete, do two things: grab a second timestamp, `t2 = ktime_get_real_ns();`, and cancel the kernel timer (with the `del_timer()` API).
    - Show the time taken to complete (via our `SHOW_DELTA()` macro).
- The user space app then sleeps for 1 second (to gather itself) and runs the `ioctl` decryption, resulting in our driver decrypting the message.
- Finally, it terminates.

The following is the relevant code from the `sed1` driver:

```
// ch5/sed1/sed1_driver/sed1_drv.c
[ ... ]
static void encrypt_decrypt_payload(int work, struct sed_ds *kd, struct
sed_ds *kdret)
{
        int i;
        ktime_t t1, t2;    // a s64 qty
        struct stMyCtx *priv = gpriv;
        [ ... ]
        /* Start - the timer; set it to expire in TIMER_EXPIRE_MS ms */
        mod_timer(&priv->timr, jiffies +
msecs_to_jiffies(TIMER_EXPIRE_MS));
        t1 = ktime_get_real_ns();

        // perform the actual processing on the payload
        memcpy(kdret, kd, sizeof(struct sed_ds));
        if (work == WORK_IS_ENCRYPT) {
                for (i = 0; i < kd->len; i++) {
                        kdret->data[i] ^= CRYPT_OFFSET;
```

```
                                kdret->data[i] += CRYPT_OFFSET;
                        }
                } else if (work == WORK_IS_DECRYPT) {
                        for (i = 0; i < kd->len; i++) {
                                kdret->data[i] -= CRYPT_OFFSET;
                                kdret->data[i] ^= CRYPT_OFFSET;
                        }
                }
                kdret->len = kd->len;
                // work done!
                [ ... // code to miss the deadline here! (explained below) ... ]
                t2 = ktime_get_real_ns();

                // work done, cancel the timeout
                if (del_timer(&priv->timr) == 0)
                        pr_debug("cancelled the timer while it's inactive!
(deadline missed?)\n");
                else
                        pr_debug("processing complete, timeout cancelled\n");
                SHOW_DELTA(t2, t1);
        }
```

That's pretty much it! To get a feel for how it works, let's see it in action. First, we must insert our kernel driver (LKM):

```
$ sudo insmod ./sed1_drv.ko
$ dmesg
[29519.684832] misc sed1_drv: LLKD sed1_drv misc driver (major # 10)
registered, minor# = 55,
                dev node is /dev/sed1_drv
[29519.689403] sed1_drv:sed1_drv_init(): init done (make_it_fail is off)
[29519.690358] misc sed1_drv: loaded.
$
```

The following screenshot shows a sample run of it encrypting and decrypting (here, we deliberately run the **Address Sanitizer** (**ASan**) debug version of this app; it might just reveal bugs, so why not!):

```
$ ../userapp_sed/userapp_sed1_dbg_asan
Usage: ../userapp_sed/userapp_sed1_dbg_asan device_file message
$ ../userapp_sed/userapp_sed1_dbg_asan /dev/sed1_drv "EncrypT ThiS plEaSe"
device opened: fd=3
msg before encrypt: EncrypT ThiS plEaSe
ioctl IOCTL_LLKD_SED_IOC_ENCRYPT_MSG done; len=19
msg after encrypt: ▓▓▓▓▓▓^▓▓▓▓^▓▓▓▓▓▓

msg before decrypt: ▓▓▓▓▓▓▓^▓▓▓▓^▓▓▓▓▓▓
ioctl IOCTL_LLKD_SED_IOC_DECRYPT_MSG done; len=19
msg after decrypt: EncrypT ThiS plEaSe
$
$ dmesg
[29519.684832] misc sed1_drv: LLKD sed1_drv misc driver (major # 10) registered, minor# = 55,
               dev node is /dev/sed1_drv
[29519.689403] sed1_drv:sed1_drv_init(): init done (make_it_fail is off)
[29519.690358] misc sed1_drv: loaded.
[29586.300784] sed1_drv:open_miscdrv(): 000)  userapp_sed1_db :22180    |  ...0   /* open_miscdrv() */
[29586.305511] sed1_drv:open_miscdrv(): opening "sed1_drv" now
[29586.306471] sed1_drv:ioctl_miscdrv(): In ioctl cmd option: encrypt
               arg=0x616000000080
[29586.308160] sed1_drv:ioctl_miscdrv(): xform=2, len=19
[29586.309011] payload: 00000000: 45 6e 63 72 79 70 54 20 54 68 69 53 20 70 6c 45  EncrypT ThiS plE
[29586.310084] payload: 00000010: 61 53 65                                         aSe
[29586.311075] sed1_drv:process_it(): data transform type: XF_ENCRYPT
[29586.311959] sed1_drv:encrypt_decrypt_payload(): starting timer + processing now ...
[29586.312977] sed1_drv:encrypt_decrypt_payload(): processing complete, timeout cancelled
[29586.313986] sed1_drv:encrypt_decrypt_payload(): delta: 99 ns (= 0 us = 0 ms)
[29586.314923] ret payload: 00000000: b9 90 9b 8c 85 8e aa 5e aa 96 95 ab 5e 8e 92 b9  .......^....^...
[29586.316458] ret payload: 00000010: 9d ab 99                                          ...
[29587.353483] sed1_drv:ioctl_miscdrv(): In ioctl cmd option: decrypt
               arg=0x616000000380
[29587.358744] sed1_drv:ioctl_miscdrv(): xform=1, len=19
[29587.359444] payload: 00000000: b9 90 9b 8c 85 8e aa 5e aa 96 95 ab 5e 8e 92 b9  .......^....^...
[29587.360408] payload: 00000010: 9d ab 99                                          ...
[29587.361281] sed1_drv:process_it(): data transform type: XF_DECRYPT
[29587.362056] sed1_drv:encrypt_decrypt_payload(): starting timer + processing now ...
[29587.362934] sed1_drv:encrypt_decrypt_payload(): processing complete, timeout cancelled
[29587.363893] sed1_drv:encrypt_decrypt_payload(): delta: 86 ns (= 0 us = 0 ms)
[29587.364788] ret payload: 00000000: 45 6e 63 72 79 70 54 20 54 68 69 53 20 70 6c 45  EncrypT ThiS plE
[29587.366134] ret payload: 00000010: 61 53 65                                         aSe
[29587.367070] sed1_drv:close_miscdrv(): closing "sed1_drv"
$ █
```

Figure 5.3 – Our sed1 mini-project encrypting and decrypting a message within the prescribed deadline

Everything went well here.

Let's take a look at the code of our kernel timer's callback function. Here, in our simple `sed1` driver, we merely have it do the following:

- Atomically set an integer in our private structure, `timed_out`, to a value of `1`, indicating failure. As we copy the data structure back to our user mode app (over `ioctl()`), this allows it to easily detect the failure and report/log it (the details on using atomic operators and much more will be covered in the last two chapters of this book).
- Emit a `printk` to the kernel log (at the `KERN_NOTICE` level), indicating that we timed out.
- Invoke our `PRINT_CTX()` macro to show the context details.

The code for our kernel timer's callback function is as follows:

```
static void timesup(struct timer_list *timer)
{
    struct stMyCtx *priv = from_timer(priv, timer, timr);

    atomic_set(&priv->timed_out, 1);
    pr_notice("*** Timer expired! ***\n");
    PRINT_CTX();
}
```

Can we see this code – the `timesup()` timer expiry function – run? We arrange to do just this next.

Deliberately missing the bus

The part I left out earlier is an interesting wrinkle: just before the second timestamp is taken, we insert a bit of code to deliberately miss the sacrosanct deadline! How? It's really very simple:

```
static void encrypt_decrypt_payload(int work, struct sed_ds *kd, struct
sed_ds *kdret)
{
    [ ... ]
    // work done!
    if (make_it_fail == 1)
        msleep(TIMER_EXPIRE_MS + 1);
    t2 = ktime_get_real_ns();
```

`make_it_fail` is a module parameter that is set to 0 by default; thus, only if you want to live dangerously (yes, a bit exaggerated!) should you pass it as 1. Let's try it out and see our kernel timer expire. The user mode app will detect this and report the failure as well:

```
$ sudo rmmod sed1_drv
$ sudo dmesg -C
$ sudo insmod ./sed1_drv.ko make_it_fail=1
$ dmesg
[30090.202904] misc sed1_drv: LLKD sed1_drv misc driver (major # 10) registered, minor# = 56,
               dev node is /dev/sed1_drv
[30090.207537] sed1_drv:sed1_drv_init(): init done (make_it_fail is *on*)
[30090.208413] misc sed1_drv: loaded.
$
$
$ ../userapp_sed/userapp_sed1_dbg_asan /dev/sed1_drv "EncrypT ThiS plEaSe"
device opened: fd=3
msg before encrypt: EncrypT ThiS plEaSe
*** Operation Timed Out ***
$
$ dmesg
[30090.202904] misc sed1_drv: LLKD sed1_drv misc driver (major # 10) registered, minor# = 56,
               dev node is /dev/sed1_drv
[30090.207537] sed1_drv:sed1_drv_init(): init done (make_it_fail is *on*)
[30090.208413] misc sed1_drv: loaded.
[30103.759259] sed1_drv:open_miscdrv(): 000)  userapp_sed1_db :22264   |  ...0  /* open_miscdrv() */
[30103.768031] sed1_drv:open_miscdrv(): opening "sed1_drv" now
[30103.769119] sed1_drv:ioctl_miscdrv(): In ioctl cmd option: encrypt
               arg=0x616000000080
[30103.770727] sed1_drv:ioctl_miscdrv(): xform=2, len=19
[30103.771504] payload: 00000000: 45 6e 63 72 79 70 54 20 54 68 69 53 20 70 6c 45  EncrypT ThiS plE
[30103.772650] payload: 00000010: 61 53 65                                         aSe
[30103.773646] sed1_drv:process_it(): data transform type: XF_ENCRYPT
[30103.774578] sed1_drv:encrypt_decrypt_payload(): starting timer + processing now ...
[30103.780372] sed1_drv:timesup(): *** Timer expired! ***
[30103.783770] sed1_drv:timesup(): 000) [swapper/0]:0   |  ..s1  /* timesup() */
[30103.790158] sed1_drv:encrypt_decrypt_payload(): cancelled the timer while it's inactive! (deadline missed?)
[30103.793372] sed1_drv:encrypt_decrypt_payload(): delta: 14580905 ns (= 14580 us = 14 ms)
[30103.794353] sed1_drv:ioctl_miscdrv(): ** timed out **
[30103.795117] ret payload: 00000000: b9 90 9b 8c 85 8e aa 5e aa 96 95 ab 5e 8e 92 b9  .......^....^...
[30103.796635] ret payload: 00000010: 9d ab 99                                         ...
[30103.801124] sed1_drv:close_miscdrv(): closing "sed1_drv"
$
```

Figure 5.4 – Our sed1 mini-project running with the make_it_fail module parameter set to 1, causing the deadline to be missed

This time, the deadline is exceeded before the timer is canceled, thus causing it to expire and fire. Its `timesup()` callback function then runs (highlighted in the preceding screenshot). I highly recommend that you take the time to read the code of the driver and user mode app in detail and try it out on your own.

The `schedule_timeout()` function that we briefly used earlier is a great example of using kernel timers! Its internal implementation can be seen here: `kernel/time/timer.c:schedule_timeout()`.

 Additional information on timers can be found within the `proc` filesystem; among the relevant (pseudo) files is `/proc/[pid]/timers` (per-process POSIX timers) and the `/proc/timer_list` pseudofile (this contains information about all pending high-resolution timers, as well as all clock event sources. Note that the `/proc/timer_stats` pseudo-file disappeared after kernel version 4.10). You can find out more information about them on the man page about `proc(5)` at https://man7.org/linux/man-pages/man5/proc.5.html.

In the next section, you will learn how to create and use kernel threads to your benefit. Read on!

Creating and working with kernel threads

A thread is an execution path; it's purely concerned with executing a given function. That function is its life and scope; once it returns from that function, it's dead. In user space, a thread is an execution path within a process; processes can be single or multi-threaded. Kernel threads are very similar to user mode threads in many respects. In kernel space, a thread is also an execution path, except that it runs within the kernel VAS, with kernel privilege. This means that kernels are also multi-threaded. A quick look at the output of `ps(1)` (run with the **Berkeley Software Distribution** (**BSD**) style `aux` option switches) shows us the kernel threads – they're the ones whose names are enclosed in square brackets:

```
$ ps aux
USER          PID %CPU %MEM    VSZ    RSS TTY      STAT START    TIME
COMMAND
root            1  0.0  0.5 167464 11548 ?        Ss   06:20   0:00
/sbin/init splash 3
root            2  0.0  0.0      0     0 ?        S    06:20   0:00
[kthreadd]
root            3  0.0  0.0      0     0 ?        I<   06:20   0:00
[rcu_gp]
root            4  0.0  0.0      0     0 ?        I<   06:20   0:00
[rcu_par_gp]
root            6  0.0  0.0      0     0 ?        I<   06:20   0:00
[kworker/0:0H-kblockd]
root            9  0.0  0.0      0     0 ?        I<   06:20   0:00
```

```
[mm_percpu_wq]
root            10  0.0  0.0     0     0 ?          S    06:20   0:00
[ksoftirqd/0]
root            11  0.0  0.0     0     0 ?          I    06:20   0:05
[rcu_sched]
root            12  0.0  0.0     0     0 ?          S    06:20   0:00
[migration/0]
[ ... ]
root            18  0.0  0.0     0     0 ?          S    06:20   0:00
[ksoftirqd/1]
[ ... ]
```

The majority of the kernel threads have been created for a definite purpose; often, they're created at system startup and run forever (in an infinite loop). They put themselves into a sleep state, and, when some work is required to be done, wake up, perform it, and go right back to sleep. A good example is that of the `ksoftirqd/n` kernel thread(s) (there's typically one per CPU core; that's what the n signifies – it's the core number); when the softirq load gets too heavy, they're woken up by the kernel to help consume the pending softirqs and thus help out (we discussed this in `Chapter 4`, *Handling Hardware Interrupts,* in the *Employing the ksoftirqd kernel threads* section; in the preceding `ps` output, you can see them on a dual-core VM; they have PID 10 and 18). Similarly, the kernel also employs *"kworker" worker threads,* which are dynamic – they come and go as work is required (a quick `ps aux | grep kworker` should reveal several of them).

Let's take a look at a few characteristics of kernel threads:

- They always execute in kernel VAS, in kernel mode with kernel privilege.
- They always run in process context (refer to the companion guide *Linux Kernel Programming - Chapter 6, Kernel Internals Essentials – Processes and Threads,* the *Understanding process and interrupt contexts* section) and they have a task structure (and thus a PID and all other typical thread attributes, though their *credentials* always are set to 0, implying root access).
- They compete for the CPU resource with other threads (including user mode threads) via the CPU scheduler; kernel threads (often abbreviated as **kthreads**) do get a slight bump in priority.
- Since they run purely in kernel VAS, they're blind to user VAS; thus, their `current->mm` value is always NULL (indeed, it's a quick way to identify a kthread).

- All kernel threads descend from the kernel thread named `kthreadd`, which has a PID of 2. This is created by the kernel (technically, the first `swapper/0` kthread with a PID of 0) during early boot; you can verify this by doing `pstree -t -p 2` (look up the man page on `pstree(1)` for usage details).
- They have naming conventions. kthreads are named differently, though some conventions are followed. Often, the name ends in `/n`; this signifies that it's a per-CPU kernel thread. The number specifies the CPU core it's been affined to run upon (we covered CPU affinity in the companion guide *Linux Kernel Programming - Chapter 11, The CPU Scheduler – Part 2*, in the *Understanding, querying, and setting the CPU affinity mask* section). Furthermore, kernel threads are used for specific purposes and their name reflects that; for example, `irq/%d-%s` (where `%d` is the PID and `%s` is the name) is a threaded interrupt handler (covered in *Chapter 4, Handling Hardware Interrupts*). You can learn how to find out the kthread name and about many practical uses of kthreads (and how to tune them to reduce jitter) by reading the kernel documentation, *Reducing OS jitter due to per-cpu kthreads*, at `https://www.kernel.org/doc/Documentation/kernel-per-CPU-kthreads.txt`.

The bit we're interested in is that the kernel modules and device drivers often need to run a certain code path in the background, in parallel with other work that it and the kernel routinely performs. Let's say you need to block upon an asynchronous event that's occurring, or need to, upon some event, execute a user mode process from within the kernel, which is time-consuming. The kernel thread is just the ticket here; thus, we shall focus on how you, as a module author, can create and manage kernel threads.

Yes, you can execute a user mode process or app from within the kernel! The kernel provides some **user mode helper** (**umh**) APIs to do so, with a common one being `call_usermode_helper()`. You can view its implementation here: `kernel/umh.c:int call_usermodehelper(const char *path, char **argv, char **envp, int wait)`. Be careful, though; you are not meant to abuse this API to invoke just any app from the kernel – that's simply bad design! There are very few actual use cases of using this API in the kernel; use `cscope(1)` to check it out.

Great; with that, let's learn how to create and work with a kernel thread.

A simple demo – creating a kernel thread

The primary API for creating kernel threads (that's exposed to us module/driver authors) is
`kthread_create()`; it's a macro that invokes the `kthread_create_on_node()` API. The
fact is, calling `kthread_create()` alone isn't sufficient to have your kernel thread do
anything useful; this is because, while this macro does create the kernel thread, you need
to make it a candidate for the scheduler by setting it's stated to running and waking it up.
This can be done with the `wake_up_process()` API (once successful, it's enqueued onto a
CPU runqueue, which makes it schedulable so that it runs in the near future). The good
news is that the `kthread_run()` helper macro can be used to invoke both
`kthread_create()` and `wake_up_process()` in one go. Let's take a look at its
implementation in the kernel:

```
// include/linux/kthread.h
/**
 * kthread_run - create and wake a thread.
 * @threadfn: the function to run until signal_pending(current).
 * @data: data ptr for @threadfn.
 * @namefmt: printf-style name for the thread.
 *
 * Description: Convenient wrapper for kthread_create() followed by
 * wake_up_process(). Returns the kthread or ERR_PTR(-ENOMEM).
 */
#define kthread_run(threadfn, data, namefmt, ...) \
({ \
    struct task_struct *__k \
        = kthread_create(threadfn, data, namefmt, ## __VA_ARGS__); \
    if (!IS_ERR(__k)) \
        wake_up_process(__k); \
    __k; \
})
```

The comments in the preceding code snippet make the parameters and return value
of `kthread_run()` clear.

To demonstrate how to create and use a kernel thread, we will write a kernel module
called `kthread_simple`. The following is the relevant code of its `init` method:

```
// ch5/kthread_simple/kthread_simple.c
static int kthread_simple_init(void)
{   [ ... ]
    gkthrd_ts = kthread_run(simple_kthread, NULL, "llkd/%s", KTHREAD_NAME);
    if (IS_ERR(gkthrd_ts)) {
        ret = PTR_ERR(gkthrd_ts); // it's usually -ENOMEM
        pr_err("kthread creation failed (%d)\n", ret);
        return ret;
```

```
    }
        get_task_struct(gkthrd_ts); // inc refcnt, marking the task struct as
    in use
        [ ... ]
```

The first parameter to `kthread_run()` is the new kthread's lifeblood – its function! Here, we don't intend to pass any data to our newborn kthread, which is why the second parameter is `NULL`. The remaining parameters are the printf-style format string specifying its name. Once successful, it returns the pointer to the new kthread's task structure (we covered the task structures in some detail in the companion guide *Linux Kernel Programming - Chapter 6, Kernel Internals Essentials – Processes and Threads*, in the *Understanding and accessing the kernel task structure* section). Now, the `get_task_struct()` inline function is important – it increments the reference count of the task structure passed to it. This marks the task as being in use (later, in the cleanup code, we will issue the `kthread_stop()` helper routine; it will perform the converse operation, thus decrementing (and ultimately freeing up) the task structure's reference count).

Now, let's look at our kernel thread itself (we'll only show the relevant code snippets):

```
static int simple_kthread(void *arg)
{
    PRINT_CTX();
    if (!current->mm)
        pr_info("mm field NULL, we are a kernel thread!\n");
```

The moment `kthread_run()` succeeds in creating the kernel thread, it will begin running its code in parallel with the rest of the system: it's now a schedulable thread! Our `PRINT_CTX()` macro reveals that it runs in process context and is indeed a kernel thread. (We have mimicked the tradition of enclosing its name in square brackets to show just this. The check to verify that the current mm pointer is `NULL` confirms the same.) You can see the output in *Figure 5.5*. All the code in your kernel thread routine is going to be running in the *process context*; hence, you can perform blocking operations (unlike with interrupt context).

Next, by default, the kernel thread runs with root ownership and all signals are masked. However, as a simple test case, we can turn on a couple of signals via the `allow_signal()` helper routine. After that, we simply loop (we'll get to the `kthread_should_stop()` routine shortly); in the loop body, we put ourselves to sleep by setting our task's state to `TASK_INTERRUPTIBLE` (implying that the sleep can be interrupted by signals) and invoking `schedule()`:

```
        allow_signal(SIGINT);
        allow_signal(SIGQUIT);
```

```
    while (!kthread_should_stop()) {
        pr_info("FYI, I, kernel thread PID %d, am going to sleep now...\n",
            current->pid);
        set_current_state(TASK_INTERRUPTIBLE);
        schedule(); // yield the processor, go to sleep...
        /* Aaaaaand we're back! Here, it's typically due to either the
         * SIGINT or SIGQUIT signal hitting us! */
        if (signal_pending(current))
            break;
    }
```

Thus, only when we're awoken– which will happen when you send the kernel thread either the `SIGINT` or `SIGQUIT` signal – will we resume execution. When this occurs, we break out of the loop (notice how we first verify that this is indeed the case with the `signal_pending()` helper routine!). Now, our kthread resumes execution outside the loop, only to (deliberately, and quite dramatically) die:

```
    set_current_state(TASK_RUNNING);
    pr_info("FYI, I, kernel thread PID %d, have been rudely awoken; I
shall"
            " now exit... Good day Sir!\n", current->pid);
    return 0;
}
```

The cleanup code of the kernel module is as follows:

```
static void kthread_simple_exit(void)
{
    kthread_stop(gkthrd_ts);    /* waits for our kthread to terminate;
                                 * it also internally invokes
                                 * the put_task_struct() to decrement task's
                                 * reference count
                                 */
    pr_info("kthread stopped, and LKM removed.\n");
}
```

Here, within the cleanup code path, you're expected to call `kthread_stop()`, which performs the necessary cleanup. Internally, it actually waits for the kthread to die (via the `wait_for_completion()` routine). So, if you call the `rmmod` without having killed the kthread by sending it the `SIGINT` or `SIGQUIT` signal, the `rmmod` process will appear to hang here; it's (the `rmmod` process, that is) waiting (well, `kthread_stop()` is really the one waiting) for the kthread to die! This is why, if the kthread hasn't been signaled yet, this could cause a problem.

There should be a better way to deal with stopping a kernel thread than sending it signals from user space. Indeed there is: the correct way is to employ the `kthread_should_stop()` routine as the (inverse) condition of the `while` loop it runs, so this is exactly what we'll do! In the preceding code, we have the following:

```
while (!kthread_should_stop()) {
```

The `kthread_should_stop()` routine returns a Boolean value that's true if the kthread should stop (terminate) now! Calling `kthread_stop()` in the cleanup code path will cause `kthread_should_stop()` to return true, thus causing our kthread to break out of the `while` loop and terminate via a simple `return 0;`. This value (0) is passed back to `kthread_stop()`. Due to this, the kernel module is successfully unloaded, *even if no signal is ever sent to our kernel thread*. We will leave testing this case as a simple exercise for you!

Note that the return value of `kthread_stop()` can be useful: it's an integer and the result of the thread function that ran – in effect, it states whether your kthread succeeded (0 returned) in its work or not. It will be the value `-EINTR` if your kthread was never woken up.

Running the kthread_simple kernel thread demo

Now, let's try it out (`ch5/kthread_simple`)! We can perform module insertion via `insmod(8)`; the module gets inserted into the kernel as planned. The kernel log shown in the following screenshot, as well as a quick `ps`, proves that our brand new kernel thread has indeed been created. Also, as you can see from the code (`ch5/kthread_simple/kthread_simple.c`), our kthread puts itself to sleep (by setting its state to `TASK_INTERRUPTIBLE` and then calling `schedule()`):

```
[23963.688367] kthread_simple:kthread_simple_init(): Lets now create a kernel thread...
[23963.689536] kthread_simple:kthread_simple_init(): Initialized, kernel thread task ptr is 0xffff8d1638b35d00 (
actual=0xffff8d1638b35d00)
           See the new kernel thread 'llkd/kt_simple' with ps (and kill it with SIGINT or SIGQUIT)
[23963.691646] kthread_simple:simple_kthread(): 000) [llkd/kt_simple]:11372   | ...0   /* simple_kthread() */
[23963.694989] kthread_simple:simple_kthread(): mm field NULL, we are a kernel thread!
[23963.696102] kthread_simple:simple_kthread(): FYI, I, kernel thread PID 11372, am going to sleep now...
```

Figure 5.5 – A partial screenshot showing that our kernel thread is born, alive – and, well, asleep

Quickly running `ps(1)` `grep` for our kernel thread by name shows that our kthread is alive and well (and asleep):

```
$ ps -e |grep kt_simple
 11372    ?           00:00:00 llkd/kt_simple
$
```

Let's shake things up a bit and send the `SIGQUIT` signal to our kthread. This has it wake up (since we've set its signal mask to allow the `SIGINT` and `SIGQUIT` signals), set its state to `TASK_RUNNING`, and then, well, simply exit. We then use `rmmod(8)` to remove the kernel module, as shown in the following screenshot:

```
$ sudo kill -SIGQUIT 11372
$ sudo rmmod kthread_simple ; dmesg
[23963.688367] kthread_simple:kthread_simple_init(): Lets now create a kernel thread...
[23963.689536] kthread_simple:kthread_simple_init(): Initialized, kernel thread task ptr is 0xffff8d1638b35d00 (
actual=0xffff8d1638b35d00)
              See the new kernel thread 'llkd/kt_simple' with ps (and kill it with SIGINT or SIGQUIT)
[23963.691646] kthread_simple:simple_kthread(): 000) [llkd/kt_simple]:11372   |  ...0   /* simple_kthread() */
[23963.694989] kthread_simple:simple_kthread(): mm field NULL, we are a kernel thread!
[23963.696102] kthread_simple:simple_kthread(): FYI, I, kernel thread PID 11372, am going to sleep now...
[24037.034934] kthread_simple:simple_kthread(): FYI, I, kernel thread PID 11372, have been rudely awoken; I shal
l now exit... Good day Sir!
[24052.609663] kthread_simple:kthread_simple_exit(): kthread stopped, and LKM removed.
$
```

Figure 5.6 – A partial screenshot showing our kernel thread waking up and the module successfully unloaded

Now that you have understood how to create and work with kernel threads, let's move on and design and implement the second version of our `sed` driver.

The sed2 driver – design and implementation

In this section (as mentioned in the *The "sed" drivers – to demo kernel timers, kthreads, and workqueues* section), we will write the next evolution of the `sed1` driver, called `sed2`.

sed2 – the design

Our `sed` v2 (`sed2`; code: `ch5/sed2/`) mini-project is very similar to our `sed1` project. The key difference is that this time, we'll carry out the "work" via a kernel thread created by the driver for just this purpose. The key differences between this version and the previous one are as follows:

- There's just one global shared memory buffer for holding the metadata, along with the payload; that is, the message to encrypt/decrypt. This is the `struct sed_ds->shmem` member within our driver context structure, `struct stMyCtx`.

- The work of encryption/decryption is now performed within a kernel thread (that this driver spawns); we keep the kernel thread asleep. Only when work arises does the driver wake up the kthread and have it consume (execute) the work.
- We now run the kernel timer within the kthread's context and show if it expires prematurely (indicating that the deadline wasn't met).
- A quick test reveals that eliminating the several `pr_debug()` printks within the kernel thread's critical section goes a long way toward reducing the time taken to complete the work! (You can always change the Makefile's `EXTRA_CFLAGS` variable to undefine the `DEBUG` symbol if you wish to eliminate this overhead (by using `EXTRA_CFLAGS += -UDEBUG`)!). Hence, here, the deadline is longer (10 ms).

So, in a nutshell, the whole idea here is to primarily demonstrate using a custom kernel thread, along with a kernel timer, to timeout an operation. A key point to understand that changes the overall design (especially the way that the user space app interacts with our `sed2` driver) is that since we're running the work in the context of a kernel thread, it's not the same context as that of the process that `ioctl()` is issued to. Due to this, it's very important to realize the following things:

- You cannot simply transfer data from the kernel thread's process context to the user space process – they're completely different (they run in different virtual address spaces: the user mode process has its own complete VAS and PID, and so on; the kernel thread literally lives within the kernel VAS with its own PID and kernel mode stack). Due to this, using the `copy_{from|to}_user()` (and similar) routine is out of question for communicating from the kthread to the user mode app.
- The potential for dangerous *races* is significant; the kernel thread runs asynchronously with respect to the user process context; thus, we can end up creating concurrency-related bugs if we're not careful. This is the entire reason for the last two chapters of this book, where we'll cover kernel synchronization, locking (and related) concepts, and technologies. For now, bear with us – we keep things as simple as possible by using some simple polling tricks in place of proper synchronization.

We have four operations inside our `sed2` project:

- **Encrypt** the message (this also gets the message from user space into the driver; thus, this has to be done first).
- **Decrypt** the message.

- **Retrieve** the message (sent from the driver to the user space app).
- **Destroy** the message (in effect, it's reset – the memory and metadata are wiped clean within the driver).

It's important to realize that due to the potential for races, we *cannot simply* transfer data directly from the kthread to the user space app. Due to this, we must do the following:

- We must carry out the retrieve and destroy operations in the process context of the user space process by issuing the `ioctl()` system calls.
- We must carry out the encrypt and decrypt operations in the process context of our kernel thread, asynchronously with respect to the user space app (we run it within a kernel thread, not because we *have to* but because we want to; this is, after all, the point of this topic!).

This design can be summarized by a simple ASCII-art diagram:

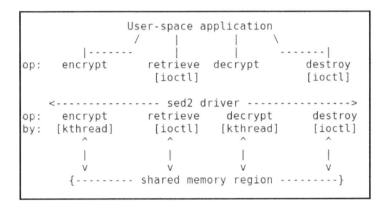

Figure 5.7 – The high-level design of our sed2 mini-project

Right, let's now check out the relevant code implementation for `sed2`.

sed2 driver – code implementation

In terms of code, the `ioctl()` method's code within the `sed2` driver for the encrypt operation is as follows (for clarity, we won't show all the error checking code here; we will show only the most relevant parts). You can find the full code at `ch5/sed2/`:

```
// ch5/sed2/sed2_driver/sed2_drv.c
[ ... ]
#if LINUX_VERSION_CODE >= KERNEL_VERSION(2, 6, 36)
static long ioctl_miscdrv(struct file *filp, unsigned int cmd, unsigned
```

```
long arg)
#else
static int ioctl_miscdrv(struct inode *ino, struct file *filp, unsigned int
cmd, unsigned long arg)
#endif
{
    struct stMyCtx *priv = gpriv;

[ ... ]
switch (cmd) {
    case IOCTL_LLKD_SED_IOC_ENCRYPT_MSG: /* kthread: encrypts the msg
passed in */
        [ ... ]
        if (atomic_read(&priv->msg_state) == XF_ENCRYPT) { // already
encrypted?
            pr_notice("encrypt op: message is currently encrypted; aborting
op...\n");
            return -EBADRQC; /* 'Invalid request code' */
        }
        if (copy_from_user(priv->kdata, (struct sed_ds *)arg, sizeof(struct
sed_ds))) {
            [ ... ]

        POLL_ON_WORK_DONE(1);
        /* Wake up our kernel thread and have it encrypt the message ! */
        if (!wake_up_process(priv->kthrd_work))
            pr_warn("worker kthread already running when awoken?\n");
        [ ... ]
```

The driver, after performing several validity checks in its ioctl() method, gets down to
work: for the encryption operation, we check if the current payload is already encrypted
(obviously, we have a state member within our context structure that is updated to hold
this information; that is, priv->msg_state). If everything is fine, it copies in the message
(along with the required metadata in struct sed_ds) from the user space app. Then, it
wakes up our kernel thread (via the wake_up_process() API; the parameter is the pointer to
its task structure, which is the return value from the kthread_create() API). This causes
the kernel thread to resume execution!

In the init code, we created the kthread with the kthread_create()
API (and not the kthread_run() macro) as we do *not* want the kthread
to run immediately! Instead, we prefer to keep it asleep, only awakening it
when work is required of it. This is the typical approach we should follow
when employing a worker thread (the so-called manager-worker model).

The following code within our `init` method creates the kernel thread:

```
static int __init sed2_drv_init(void)
{
    [ ... ]
    gpriv->kthrd_work = kthread_create(worker_kthread, NULL, "%s/%s",
DRVNAME, KTHREAD_NAME);
    if (IS_ERR(gpriv->kthrd_work)) {
        ret = PTR_ERR(gpriv->kthrd_work); // it's usually -ENOMEM
        dev_err(dev, "kthread creation failed (%d)\n", ret);
        return ret;
    }
    get_task_struct(gpriv->kthrd_work); // inc refcnt, marking the task
struct as in use
    pr_info("worker kthread created... (PID %d)\n",
task_pid_nr(gpriv->kthrd_work));
    [ ... ]
```

After this, the timer is initialized (via the `timer_setup()` API). The (truncated) code of our worker thread looks as follows:

```
static int worker_kthread(void *arg)
{
    struct stMyCtx *priv = gpriv;

    while (!kthread_should_stop()) {
        /* Start - the timer; set it to expire in TIMER_EXPIRE_MS ms */
        if (mod_timer(&priv->timr, jiffies +
msecs_to_jiffies(TIMER_EXPIRE_MS)))
            pr_alert("timer already active?\n");
        priv->t1 = ktime_get_real_ns();

        /*--------------- Critical section begins -----------------------
-*/
        atomic_set(&priv->work_done, 0);
        switch (priv->kdata->data_xform) {
        [ ... ]
        case XF_ENCRYPT:
            pr_debug("data transform type: XF_ENCRYPT\n");
            encrypt_decrypt_payload(WORK_IS_ENCRYPT, priv->kdata);
            atomic_set(&priv->msg_state, XF_ENCRYPT);
            break;
        case XF_DECRYPT:
            pr_debug("data transform type: XF_DECRYPT\n");
            encrypt_decrypt_payload(WORK_IS_DECRYPT, priv->kdata);
            atomic_set(&priv->msg_state, XF_DECRYPT);
            break;
        [ ... ]
```

```
priv->t2 = ktime_get_real_ns();
// work done, cancel the timeout
if (del_timer(&priv->timr) == 0)
[ ... ]
```

Here, you can see the timer being started (mod_timer()), the actual encrypt/decrypt functions being invoked as required, the timestamps being captured, and then the kernel timer being canceled. This is what happened in sed1 except that, this time (sed2), the work happens in the context of our kernel thread! The kernel thread function then makes itself go to sleep while yielding the processor by (as was covered in the companion guide *Linux Kernel Programming - Chapter 10, The CPU Scheduler – Part 1*, and *Chapter 11, The CPU Scheduler – Part 2*) setting the task state to a sleep state (TASK_INTERRUPTIBLE) and invoking schedule().

Hang on a minute – within the ioctl() method, did you notice the call to the POLL_ON_WORK_DONE(1); macro just before the kernel thread was woken up? Take a look at the following code:

```
[ ... ]
POLL_ON_WORK_DONE(1);
/* Wake up our kernel thread
 * and have it encrypt the message !
 */
if (!wake_up_process(priv->kthrd_work))
    pr_warn("worker kthread already running when awoken?\n");
/*
 * Now, our kernel thread is doing the 'work';
 * it will either be done, or it will miss it's
 * deadline and fail. Attempting to lookup the payload
 * or do anything more here would be a
 * mistake, a race! Why? We're currently running in
 * the ioctl() process context; the kernel thread runs
 * in it's own process context! (If we must look it up,
 * then we really require a (mutex) lock; we shall
 * discuss locking in detail in the book's last two chapters.
 */
break;
```

The poll is used to circumvent a possible race: what if one (user mode) thread invokes ioctl() to, say, encrypt a given message, and simultaneously on another CPU core, another user mode thread invokes ioctl() to, say, decrypt a given message? This will cause concurrency issues! Again, the last two chapters of this book are devoted to understanding and handling these; but here and now, what can we do? Let's implement a poor man's synchronization solution: *polling*.

This is not ideal but will have to do. We'll make use of the fact that the driver sets an atomic variable in the driver's context structure, named `work_done`, to 1 when the work is done; its value is 0 otherwise. We poll for this within this macro:

```
/*
 * Is our kthread performing any ongoing work right now? poll...
 * Not ideal (but we'll live with it); ideally, use a lock (we cover
locking in
 * this book's last two chapters)
 */
#define POLL_ON_WORK_DONE(sleep_ms) do { \
        while (atomic_read(&priv->work_done) == 0) \
            msleep_interruptible(sleep_ms); \
} while (0)
```

To keep this code somewhat palatable, we aren't hogging the processor; if the work isn't done (yet), we sleep for a millisecond (via the `msleep_interruptible()` API) and try again.

So far, we've covered the relevant code for the encrypt and decrypt functionality of `sed2` (both of which run in our worker kthread's context). Now, let's look at the remaining two pieces of functionality – retrieving and destroying messages. These are carried out in the original user space process context – the process (or thread) that issues the `ioctl()` system calls. Here's the relevant code for them:

```
// ch5/sed2/sed2_driver/sed2_drv.c : ioctl() method
[ ... ]
case IOCTL_LLKD_SED_IOC_RETRIEVE_MSG: /* ioctl: retrieves the encrypted msg
*/
        if (atomic_read(&priv->timed_out) == 1) {
            pr_debug("the encrypt op had timed out! returning -
ETIMEDOUT\n");
            return -ETIMEDOUT;
        }
        if (copy_to_user((struct sed_ds *)arg, (struct sed_ds
*)priv->kdata, sizeof(struct sed_ds))) {
            //  [ ... error handling ... ]
        break;
    case IOCTL_LLKD_SED_IOC_DESTROY_MSG: /* ioctl: destroys the msg */
        pr_debug("In ioctl 'destroy' cmd option\n");
        memset(priv->kdata, 0, sizeof(struct sed_ds));
        atomic_set(&priv->msg_state, 0);
        atomic_set(&priv->work_done, 1);
        atomic_set(&priv->timed_out, 0);
```

```
            priv->t1 = priv->t2 = 0;
            break;
   [ ... ]
```

Now that you've seen the (relevant) sed2 code, let's try it out!

sed2 – trying it out

Let's take a look at a sample run of our sed2 mini project over a couple of screenshots; ensure that you look at them carefully:

```
$ lsmod |grep sed2
sed2_drv               20480  0
$ dmesg
[41050.801737] misc sed2_drv: LLKD sed2_drv misc driver (major # 10) registered, minor# = 56,
               dev node is /dev/sed2_drv
[41050.803594] sed2_drv:sed2_drv_init(): worker kthread created... (PID 24117)
[41050.804482] sed2_drv:sed2_drv_init(): init done (make_it_fail is off)
[41050.805298] misc sed2_drv: loaded.
$ ../userapp_sed/userapp_sed2_dbg_asan
Usage: ../userapp_sed/userapp_sed2_dbg_asan device_file message_to_encrypt
$ ../userapp_sed/userapp_sed2_dbg_asan /dev/sed2_drv "Hello sed2!"
device opened: fd=3
---< Welcome to the SED (Simple Encrypt Decrypt) v2 User mode app >---
((c) 'Learn Linux Kernel Development', Kaiwan N Billimoria, Packt)

The message we shall work with is:
"Hello sed2!"

   *** Menu ***
   --- Message Control ---
1. Encrypt the message
2. Retrieve the message (from the driver)
3. Decrypt the message (that was encrypted in (1))
4. Destroy the message
      --- Kernel Logs ---
5. View the kernel log (via dmesg(1))
6. Clear the kernel log (via sudo)
7. Quit
> 1

---> Message ENCRYPTED in the kernel driver; retrieve to see <---
     (ioctl IOCTL_LLKD_SED_IOC_ENCRYPT_MSG successful)

   *** Menu ***
   --- Message Control ---
1. Encrypt the message
2. Retrieve the message (from the driver)
3. Decrypt the message (that was encrypted in (1))
4. Destroy the message
      --- Kernel Logs ---
5. View the kernel log (via dmesg(1))
6. Clear the kernel log (via sudo)
7. Quit
>
```

Figure 5.8 – Our sed2 mini-project showing off an interactive menu system. Here, a message has been successfully encrypted

So, we have encrypted a message, but how do we view it? Simple: we use the menu! Select option 2 to retrieve the (encrypted) message (it will be displayed for your leisurely perusal), option 3 to decrypt it, option 2 once more to view it, and option 5 to see the kernel log – quite useful! Some of these options are shown in the following screenshot:

```
>  5
---> View kernel log : dmesg(1) <---
[41050.801737] misc sed2_drv: LLKD sed2_drv misc driver (major # 10) registered, minor# = 56,
               dev node is /dev/sed2_drv
[41050.803594] sed2_drv:sed2_drv_init(): worker kthread created... (PID 24117)
[41050.804482] sed2_drv:sed2_drv_init(): init done (make_it_fail is off)
[41050.805298] misc sed2_drv: loaded.
[41168.793377] sed2_drv:open_miscdrv(): 001)  userapp_sed2_db :24190   |  ...0  /* open_miscdrv() */
[41168.797793] sed2_drv:open_miscdrv(): opening "sed2_drv" now
[41168.798689] sed2_drv:ioctl_miscdrv(): In ioctl 'retrieve' cmd option; arg=0x616000000080
[41178.868959] sed2_drv:ioctl_miscdrv(): In ioctl 'encrypt' cmd option; arg=0x616000000380
[41178.876847] sed2_drv:ioctl_miscdrv(): xform=2, len=11
[41178.882135] payload: 00000000: 48 65 6c 6c 6f 20 73 65 64 32 21            Hello sed2!
[41178.883655] sed2_drv:worker_kthread(): starting timer + processing now ...
[41178.884591] sed2_drv:worker_kthread(): [24117] worker kthread ready to execute work!
[41178.885577] sed2_drv:worker_kthread(): 001) [sed2_drv/worker]:24117   |  ...0  /* worker_kthread() */
[41178.887014] sed2_drv:worker_kthread(): data transform type: XF_ENCRYPT
[41178.887866] kdata->shmem: 00000000: 48 65 6c 6c 6f 20 73 65 64 32 21            Hello sed2!
[41178.888875] sed2_drv:worker_kthread(): processing complete, timeout cancelled
[41178.889749] sed2_drv:worker_kthread(): delta: 4284080 ns (= 4284 us = 4 ms)
[41178.890658] sed2_drv:worker_kthread(): [24117] FYI, work done, going to sleep now...
[41329.579674] sed2_drv:ioctl_miscdrv(): In ioctl 'retrieve' cmd option; arg=0x616000000680
[41355.080593] sed2_drv:ioctl_miscdrv(): In ioctl 'decrypt' cmd option
[41355.088162] sed2_drv:worker_kthread(): starting timer + processing now ...
[41355.090647] sed2_drv:worker_kthread(): [24117] worker kthread ready to execute work!
[41355.091676] sed2_drv:worker_kthread(): 001) [sed2_drv/worker]:24117   |  ...0  /* worker_kthread() */
[41355.093201] sed2_drv:worker_kthread(): data transform type: XF_DECRYPT
[41355.094073] kdata->shmem: 00000000: b6 99 92 92 8f 5e 8b 99 9a 4c 5d            .....^...L]
[41355.095075] sed2_drv:worker_kthread(): processing complete, timeout cancelled
[41355.095960] sed2_drv:worker_kthread(): delta: 4427745 ns (= 4427 us = 4 ms)
[41355.096913] sed2_drv:worker_kthread(): [24117] FYI, work done, going to sleep now...
[41361.884472] sed2_drv:ioctl_miscdrv(): In ioctl 'retrieve' cmd option; arg=0x616000000c80


    ***  Menu  ***
  --- Message Control ---
1. Encrypt the message
2. Retrieve the message (from the driver)
3. Decrypt the message (that was encrypted in (1))
4. Destroy the message
      --- Kernel Logs ---
5. View the kernel log (via dmesg(1))
6. Clear the kernel log (via sudo)
7. Quit
>  █
```

Figure 5.9 – Our sed2 mini-project showing off an interactive menu system. Here, a message has been successfully encrypted

As shown in the kernel log, our user mode app (`userapp_sed2_dbg_asan`) has opened the device and issued the retrieve operation, followed by the encrypt operation a few seconds later (the timestamps in the bottom-left corner of the preceding screenshot help you figure this out). Then, the driver wakes up the kernel thread; you can see its printk output, as well as the output of `PRINT_CTX()`, here:

```
[41178.885577] sed2_drv:worker_kthread(): 001) [sed2_drv/worker]:24117   |
...0   /* worker_kthread() */
```

The encrypt operation then completes (successfully and within the deadline; the timer is canceled):

```
[41178.888875] sed2_drv:worker_kthread(): processing complete, timeout
cancelled
```

Similarly, other operations are carried out. We shall refrain from showing the user space app's code here since it's a simple user mode "C" program. This time (unusually), it's an interactive app with a simple menu (as shown in the screenshots); do check it out. I'll leave it to you to read and understand the `sed2` code in detail and try it out for yourself.

Querying and setting the scheduling policy/priority of a kernel thread

In closing, how can you query and/or change the scheduling policy and (real-time) priority of a kernel thread? The kernel provides APIs for this (the `sched_setscheduler_nocheck()` API is often used within the kernel). As a practical example, the kernel will require kernel threads for the purpose of servicing interrupts – the *threaded interrupt* model, which we covered in Chapter 4, *Handling Hardware Interrupts*, in the *Internally implementing the threaded interrupt* section).

It creates these threads (via `kthread_create()`) and changes their scheduling policy and real-time priority via the `sched_setscheduler_nocheck()` API. We won't explicitly cover their usage here as we covered this in the companion guide *Linux Kernel Programming - Chapter 11, The CPU Scheduler – Part 2*. It's interesting:
the `sched_setscheduler_nocheck()` API is just a simple wrapper over the underlying `_sched_setscheduler()` routine. Why? The `_sched_setscheduler()` API isn't exported at all and is thus unavailable to module authors;
the `sched_setscheduler_nocheck()` wrapper is exported via the `EXPORT_SYMBOL_GPL()` macro (implying that only GPL licensed code can actually make use of it!).

What about querying and/or changing the scheduling policy and (real-time) priority of **user space threads**? The Pthreads library provides wrapper APIs to do just this; the `pthread_[get|set]schedparam(3)` pair can be used here since they're wrappers around system calls such as `sched_[get|set]scheduler(2)` and `sched_[get|set]attr(2)`. They require root access and, for security purposes, have the `CAP_SYS_NICE` capability bit set in the binary executable file.

 Though this book only covers kernel programming, I've mentioned this here as it's a really powerful thing: in effect, the user space app designer/developer has the ability to create and deploy application threads perfectly suited to their purpose: real-time threads at differing scheduling policies, real-time priorities between 1 and 99, non-RT threads (with the base nice value of 0), and so on. Indiscriminately creating kernel threads is frowned upon, and the reason is clear – every additional kernel thread adds overhead, both in terms of memory and CPU cycles. When you're in the design phase, pause and think: do you really require one or more kernel threads? Or is there a better way of doing things? Workqueues are often exactly that – a better way!

Now, let's look at workqueues!

Using kernel workqueues

A **workqueue** is an abstraction layer over the creation and management of kernel worker threads. They help solve a crucial problem: directly working with kernel threads, especially when several are involved, is not only difficult but can quite easily result in dangerous bugs such as races (and thus the potential for deadlock), as well as poor thread management, resulting in efficiency losses. Workqueues are *bottom-half* mechanisms that are employed within the Linux kernel (along with tasklets and softirqs).

The modern workqueue implementation in the Linux kernel – called the **concurrency managed work queue (cmwq)** – is really a pretty elaborate framework, with various strategies for dynamically and efficiently provisioning kernel threads based on specific requirements.

In this book, we prefer to focus on the *usage* of the kernel-global workqueue rather than its internal design and implementation. If you'd like to learn more about the internals, I recommend that you read the "official" kernel documentation here: `https://www.kernel.org/doc/Documentation/core-api/workqueue.rst`. The *Further reading* section also contains some useful resources.

The key characteristics of the workqueue are as follows:

- The workqueue task(s) (callbacks) always execute in a preemptible process context. This is obvious once you realize that they are executed by kernel (worker) threads, which run in a preemptible process context.
- By default, all interrupts are enabled and no locks are taken.
- The aforementioned points imply that you can do lengthy, blocking, I/O-bound work within your workqueue function(s) (this is diametrically opposite to an atomic context such as a hardirq, tasklet, or softirq!).
- Just as you learned about kernel threads, transferring data to and from user space (via the typical `copy_[to|from]_user()` and similar routines) is *not* possible; this is because your workqueue handler (function) executes within its own process context – that of a kernel thread. As we know, kernel threads have no user mapping.
- The kernel workqueue framework maintains worker pools. These are literally several kernel worker threads organized in differing ways according to their needs. The kernel handles all the complexity of managing them, as well as concurrency concerns. The following screenshot shows several workqueue kernel worker threads (this was taken on my x86_64 Ubuntu 20.04 guest VM):

```
$ ps -e|egrep --color=auto "events|kworker|_wq"
      6 ?        00:00:00 kworker/0:0H-kblockd
      9 ?        00:00:00 mm_percpu_wq
     20 ?        00:00:00 kworker/1:0H-kblockd
     80 ?        00:00:00 tpm_dev_wq
     84 ?        00:00:00 devfreq_wq
    111 ?        00:00:00 kworker/u5:0
    172 ?        00:00:01 kworker/0:1H-kblockd
    192 ?        00:00:00 kworker/1:1H-kblockd
  46204 ?        00:00:09 kworker/0:3-events
  50536 ?        00:00:00 kworker/0:1-events
  55177 ?        00:00:00 kworker/u4:0-events_unbound
  55200 ?        00:00:02 kworker/1:0-events
  55771 ?        00:00:00 kworker/1:1-events
  56290 ?        00:00:00 kworker/u4:2-events_unbound
  56302 ?        00:00:00 kworker/u4:1-events_power_efficient
$
```

Figure 5.10 – Several kernel threads serving the kernel workqueue's bottom-half mechanism

As we mentioned in the *Creating and working with kernel threads* section, one way to figure out the kthread's name and learn about the many practical uses of kthreads (and how to tune them to reduce jitter) is by reading the relevant kernel documentation; that is, *Reducing OS jitter due to per-cpu kthreads* (`https://www.kernel.org/doc/Documentation/kernel-per-CPU-kthreads.txt`).

> In terms of how to use workqueues (and the other bottom-half mechanisms), refer back to `Chapter 4`, *Handling Hardware Interrupts*, the *Hardirqs, tasklets, and threaded handlers – what to use when* section, especially the table there.

It's important to understand that the kernel has an always-ready default workqueue available for use; it's known as the **kernel-global workqueue** or **system workqueue**. To avoid stressing the system, it's highly recommended that you use it. We shall use the kernel-global workqueue, enque our work task(s) on it, and have it consume our work.

You can even use and create other kinds of workqueues! The kernel provides the elaborate *cmwq* framework, along with a set of APIs, to help you create specific types of workqueues. We'll look at this in more detail in the next section.

The bare minimum workqueue internals

We don't go into too much depth about the internals of the workqueue here; in fact, we will merely scratch the surface (as we mentioned previously, our purpose here is to only focus on using the kernel-global workqueue).

It's always recommended that you use the default kernel-global (system) workqueue to consume your asynchronous background work. If this is deemed to be insufficient, don't worry – certain interfaces are exposed that let you create your workqueues. (Keep in mind that doing so will increase stress on the system!) To allocate a new workqueue instance, you can use the `alloc_workqueue()` API; this is the primary API that's used for creating (allocating) workqueues (via the modern *cmwq* framework):

```
include/linux/workqueue.h
struct workqueue_struct *alloc_workqueue(const char *fmt, unsigned int
flags, int max_active, ...);
```

Note that it's exported via `EXPORT_SYMBOL_GPL()`, which means it's only available to modules and drivers that use the GPL license. `fmt` (and the parameters following `max_active`) specifies how to name the workqueue threads in the pool. The `flags` parameter specifies a bitmask of special behavioral values or other characteristics, such as the following:

- Use the `WQ_MEM_RECLAIM` flag when the workqueue needs forward progress guarantees under memory pressure.
- Use the `WQ_HIGHPRI` flag when work items are to be serviced by a worker pool of kthreads at an elevated priority level.
- Use the `WQ_SYSFS` flag to make some of the workqueue details visible to user space via sysfs (practically, look under `/sys/devices/virtual/workqueue/`).
- Similarly, there are several other flags. Take a look at the official kernel documentation for more details (https://www.kernel.org/doc/Documentation/core-api/workqueue.rst; it provides some interesting coverage on reducing "jitter" due to workqueue execution within the kernel).

The `max_active` parameter is used to specify the maximum number of kernel threads per CPU that can be assigned to a work item.

Broadly speaking, there are two types of workqueues:

- **Single-threaded (ST) workqueues or ordered workqueues**: Here, only one thread can be active at any given point in time across the system. They can be created with `alloc_ordered_workqueue()` (it's really just a wrapper over `alloc_workqueue()` specifying the ordered flags with `max_active` set to exactly 1).
- **Multi-threaded (MT) workqueues**: This is the default option. The exact `flags` specify the behavior; `max_active` specifies the maximum number of worker kernel threads the work item can possibly have per CPU.

All workqueues can be created via the `alloc_workqueue()` API. The code for creating them is as follows:

```
// kernel/workqueue.c
int __init workqueue_init_early(void)
{
    [ ... ]
    system_wq = alloc_workqueue("events", 0, 0);
    system_highpri_wq = alloc_workqueue("events_highpri", WQ_HIGHPRI, 0);
    system_long_wq = alloc_workqueue("events_long", 0, 0);
    system_unbound_wq = alloc_workqueue("events_unbound", WQ_UNBOUND,
```

```
WQ_UNBOUND_MAX_ACTIVE);
    system_freezable_wq = alloc_workqueue("events_freezable", WQ_FREEZABLE,
0);
    system_power_efficient_wq = alloc_workqueue("events_power_efficient",
WQ_POWER_EFFICIENT, 0);
    system_freezable_power_efficient_wq =
alloc_workqueue("events_freezable_power_efficient",
                        WQ_FREEZABLE | WQ_POWER_EFFICIENT, 0);
[ ... ]
```

This happens early in the boot process (literally in the early init kernel code path). The first is highlighted in bold; this is the kernel-global workqueue or the system workqueue being created. Its worker pool is named `events`. (The name of the kernel threads that belong to this pool follow this naming convention and have the word `events` in their name; see *Figure 5.10* again. The same happens with kthreads belonging to other worker pools.)

The underlying framework has evolved a great deal; an earlier *legacy* workqueue framework (prior to 2010) used to use the `create_workqueue()` and friends APIs; however, these are now considered deprecated. The modern **concurrency managed workqueue (cmwq)** framework (around 2010 onward) is, interestingly, backward compatible with the old one. The following table summarizes the mapping of the older workqueue APIs to the modern cmwq ones:

Legacy (old and deprecated) workqueue API	Modern (cmwq) workqueue API
`create_workqueue(name)`	`alloc_workqueue(name,WQ_MEM_RECLAIM, 1)`
`create_singlethread_workqueue(name)`	`alloc_ordered_workqueue(name, WQ_MEM_RECLAIM)`
`create_freezable_workqueue(name)`	`alloc_workqueue(name, WQ_FREEZABLE | WQ_UNBOUND | WQ_MEM_RECLAIM, 1)`

Table 5.3 – Mapping of the older workqueue APIs to the modern cmwq ones

The following diagram summarizes (in a simple, conceptual manner) the kernel workqueue subsystem:

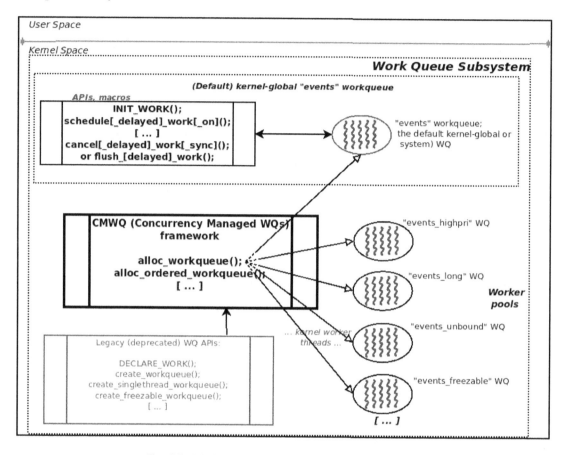

Figure 5.11 – A simple conceptual view of the workqueue subsystem within the kernel

The kernel's workqueue framework dynamically maintains these worker pools (of kernel threads); some, such as the `events` workqueue (corresponding to the kernel-global workqueue) are general-purpose, while others are created and maintained for a specific purpose (in terms of the names given to their kernel threads, such as block I/O, `kworker*blockd`, memory control, `kworker*mm_percpu_wq`, device-specific ones such as tpm, `tpm_dev_wq`, CPU frequency governor drivers, `devfreq_wq`, and so on).

Note that the kernel workqueue subsystem maintains all these workqueues (and their associated worker pools of kernel threads) automatically, elegantly, and efficiently.

So, how do you actually make use of the workqueue? The next section will show you how to use the kernel-global workqueue. This will be followed by a demo kernel module that clearly demonstrates its usage.

Using the kernel-global workqueue

In this section, we shall learn how exactly to use the kernel-global (also known as the system or events workqueue, which is the default) workqueue. This typically involves initializing the workqueue with your work task, having it consume your work, and finally, performing cleanup.

Initializing the kernel-global workqueue for your task – INIT_WORK()

Enqueuing work onto this workqueue is actually very easy: use the INIT_WORK() macro! This macro takes two parameters:

```
#include <linux/workqueue.h>
INIT_WORK(struct work_struct *_work, work_func_t _func);
```

The work_struct structure is the workhorse structure for work queues (from the module/driver author's point of view, at least); you are to allocate memory to it and pass the pointer as the first parameter. The second parameter to INIT_WORK() is a pointer to the workqueue callback function – the function that will be consumed by the worker thread(s) of the workqueue! work_func_t is a typedef that specifies the signature for this function, which is void (*work_func_t)(struct work_struct *work).

Having your work task execute – schedule_work()

Calling `INIT_WORK()` registers the specified work structure and function with the in-house default kernel-global workqueue. But it doesn't execute it – yet! You have to tell it when to execute your "work" by calling the `schedule_work()` API at the appropriate moment:

```
bool schedule_work(struct work_struct *work);
```

Clearly, the parameter to `schedule_work()` is the pointer to the `work_struct` structure (which you initialized earlier via the `INIT_WORK()` macro). It returns a Boolean (quoting directly from the source): `%false if @work was already on the kernel-global workqueue and %true otherwise` True. In effect, `schedule_work()` checks if the function that was specified (via the work structure) is already on the kernel-global workqueue; if not, it enqueues it there; if it already was there, it leaves it alone in the same position (it doesn't add one more instance). It then marks the work item for execution. This typically happens as soon as the underlying kernel thread(s) corresponding to the workqueue get scheduled, thus giving you a chance to run your work.

To have two work items (functions) within your module or driver execute via the (default) kernel-global workqueue, simply call the `INIT_WORK()` macro twice, each time passing different work structures and functions. Similarly, for more work items, call `INIT_WORK()` for each of them... (For example, take this kernel block driver (`drivers/block/mtip32xx/mtip32xx.c`): apparently, for Micron PCIe SSDs, it calls `INIT_WORK()` eight times in a row (!) with its probe method, using arrays to hold all the items).

Note that you can call `schedule_work()` in an atomic context! The call is non-blocking; it merely schedules the work item to be consumed at a later, deferred (and safe) point in time, when it will run in process context.

Variations of scheduling your work task

There are a few variations of the `schedule_work()` API we just described, all of which are available via the `schedule[_delayed]_work[_on]()` APIs. Let's briefly enumerate them. First, let's look at the `schedule_delayed_work()` inline function, whose signature is as follows:

```
bool schedule_delayed_work(struct delayed_work *dwork, unsigned long
delay);
```

Use this routine when you want to delay the execution of the workqueue handler function by a specified amount of time; the second parameter, `delay`, is the number of `jiffies` you want to wait for. Now, we know that the `jiffies` variable increments by `HZ` jiffies per second; thus, to have your work task delayed by n seconds, specify n * `jiffies`. Similarly, you could always pass the `msecs_to_jiffies(n)` value as the second parameter to have it execute n milliseconds from now.

Next, notice that the first parameter to `schedule_delayed_work()` is different; it's a `delayed_work` structure, which itself contains the now-familiar `work_struct` structure as a member, along with other housekeeping members (a kernel timer, a pointer to the workqueue structure, and a CPU number). To initialize it, just allocate memory to it and then make use of the `INIT_DELAYED_WORK()` macro (the syntax remains identical to `INIT_WORK()`); it will take care of all initialization.

Another slight variation on the theme is the `schedule[_delayed]_work_on()` routine; `on` in the name allows you to specify which CPU core your work task will be scheduled upon when it executes. Here's the signature of the `schedule_delayed_work_on()` inline function:

```
bool schedule_delayed_work_on(int cpu, struct delayed_work *dwork, unsigned
long delay);
```

The first parameter specifies the CPU core to execute the work task upon, while the remaining two parameters are identical to the `schedule_delayed_work()` routine's parameters. (You can employ the `schedule_delayed_work()` routine to schedule your task – immediately – on a given CPU core).

Cleaning up – canceling or flushing your work task

At some point, you will want to ensure that your work task(s) have actually completed execution. You may wish to do this before destroying your workqueue (assuming it's a custom created one and not the kernel-global one) or, more likely, when using the kernel-global workqueue in the cleanup method of your LKM or driver. The typical API to use here is `cancel_[delayed_]work[_sync]()`. Its variations and signatures are as follows:

```
bool cancel_work_sync(struct work_struct *work);
bool cancel_delayed_work(struct delayed_work *dwork);
bool cancel_delayed_work_sync(struct delayed_work *dwork);
```

It's quite simple, really: use `cancel_work_sync()` once you have used the `INIT_WORK()` and `schedule_work()` routines; use the latter two when you've delayed your work task. Notice that two of the routines are suffixed with `_sync`; this implies that the cancellation is *synchronous* – the kernel will wait until your work tasks have completed execution before these functions return! This is usually what we want. These routines return a boolean: `True` if there was work pending and `False` otherwise.

> Within a kernel module, not canceling (or flushing) your work task(s) in your cleanup (`rmmod`) code path is a sure-fire way to cause serious issues; ensure you do so!

The kernel workqueue subsystem also provides a few `flush_*()` routines (including `flush_scheduled_work()`, `flush_workqueue()`, and `flush_[delayed_]work()`). The kernel documentation (https://www.kernel.org/doc/html/latest/core-api/workqueue.html) clearly warns us that these routines are not the easiest to use as you can easily cause deadlock issues with them. It's recommended that you use the aforementioned `cancel_[delayed_]work[_sync]()` APIs instead.

A quick summary of the workflow

When using the kernel-global workqueue, a simple pattern (workflow) emerges:

1. *Initialize* the work task.
2. At the appropriate point in time, *schedule* it to execute (perhaps with a delay and/or on a particular CPU core).
3. Clean up. Typically, in the kernel module (or driver's) cleanup code path, *cancel* it. (Preferably, do this with synchronization so that any pending work tasks are completed first. Here, we will stick to employing the recommended `cancel*work*()` routines, avoiding the `flush_*()` ones).

Let's summarize this using a table:

Using the kernel-global workqueue	Regular work task	Delayed work task	Execute work task on given CPU
1. Initialization	`INIT_WORK()`	`INIT_DELAYED_WORK()`	*< either immediate or delayed's fine >*
2. Schedule work task to execute	`schedule_work()`	`schedule_delayed_work()`	`schedule_delayed_work_on()`
3. Cancel (or flush) it; *foo_sync()* to ensure it's complete	`cancel_work_sync()`	`cancel_delayed_work_sync()`	*< either immediate or delayed's fine >*

Table 5.4 – Using the kernel-global workqueue – summary of the workflow

In the next few sections, we'll write a simple kernel module using the kernel-default workqueue in order to execute a work task.

Our simple work queue kernel module – code view

Let's get hands-on with a work queue! In the following sections, we will write a simple demo kernel module (`ch5/workq_simple`) that demonstrates using the kernel-default workqueue to execute a work task. It's actually built upon our earlier LKM, which we used to demonstrate kernel timers (`ch5/timer_simple`). Let's check it out code-wise (as usual, we won't show the full code here, only the most relevant portions). We'll begin by looking at its private context data structure and *init* method:

```
static struct st_ctx {
    struct work_struct work;
    struct timer_list tmr;
    int data;
} ctx;
[ ... ]
static int __init workq_simple_init(void)
{
    ctx.data = INITIAL_VALUE;
    /* Initialize our work queue */
    INIT_WORK(&ctx.work, work_func);
    /* Initialize our kernel timer */
    ctx.tmr.expires = jiffies + msecs_to_jiffies(exp_ms);
    ctx.tmr.flags = 0;
```

```
        timer_setup(&ctx.tmr, ding, 0);
        add_timer(&ctx.tmr); /* Arm it; let's get going! */
        return 0;
}
```

A key point to ponder: how will we manage to pass along some useful data items to our work function? The `work_struct` structure only has an atomic long integer that's used for internal purposes. A good (and very typical!) trick is to have your `work_struct` structure embedded within your driver's context structure; then, within the work task callback function, use the `container_of()` macro to gain access to the parent context data structure! This is a strategy that's often employed. (The `container_of()` is a powerful macro, but not really easy to decipher! We've provided a couple of useful links for this in the *Further reading* section.) So, in the preceding code, we have our driver's context structure embed a `struct work_struct` within it. You can see the initialization of our work task within the `INIT_WORK()` macro.

Once the timer's been armed (`add_timer()` does the trick here), it will expire in approximately 420 milliseconds and the timer callback function will run in the timer softirq context (this is very much an atomic context):

```
static void ding(struct timer_list *timer)
{
    struct st_ctx *priv = from_timer(priv, timer, tmr);
    pr_debug("timed out... data=%d\n", priv->data--);
    PRINT_CTX();
    /* until countdown done, fire it again! */
    if (priv->data)
        mod_timer(&priv->tmr, jiffies + msecs_to_jiffies(exp_ms));
    /* Now 'schedule' our work queue function to run */
    if (!schedule_work(&priv->work))
        pr_notice("our work's already on the kernel-global workqueue!\n");
}
```

After decrementing the `data` variable, it sets up the timer to fire again (in 420 ms, via `mod_timer()`), after which, via the `schedule_work()` API, it schedules our work queue callback to run! The kernel will recognize that the work queue function must now be executed (consumed) as soon as is viable. But hang on – the work queue callback must and will run *only in the process context, via a global kernel worker thread* – the so-called events thread(s). Thus, only once we're out of this softirq context and (one of) the "events" kernel worker threads is on a CPU runqueue and actually runs will our work queue callback function be invoked.

Relax – it will happen soon enough... the whole point of using workqueues is that not only is the thread management completely taken care of by the kernel, but the function runs in the process context, where it's then possible to perform lengthy blocking or I/O operations.

Again, how soon is soon? Let's attempt to measure this: we take a timestamp (via the usual `ktime_get_real_ns()` inline function) immediately after `schedule_work()` as the first line of code in the work queue function. Our trusty `SHOW_DELTA()` macro shows the difference in time. As expected, it's small, typically within a few hundredths of a microsecond's range (of course, this depends on several factors, including the hardware platform, kernel version, and so on). A highly loaded system would result in it taking longer to context switch to the events kernel thread(s), which could cause a delay in your work queue's functionality executing. You will see it in a sample run within a screenshot capture (*Figure 5.12*) in the following section.

The following code is of our work task function. This is where we employ the `container_of()` macro to gain access to our module's context structure:

```
/* work_func() - our workqueue callback function! */
static void work_func(struct work_struct *work)
{
    struct st_ctx *priv = container_of(work, struct st_ctx, work);

    t2 = ktime_get_real_ns();
    pr_info("In our workq function: data=%d\n", priv->data);
    PRINT_CTX();
    SHOW_DELTA(t2, t1);
}
```

Furthermore, our `PRINT_CTX()` macro's output conclusively shows that this function runs in the process context.

> Be careful when you're using `container_of()` within a *delayed* work task callback function – you'll have to specify the third parameter as a `work` member of `struct delayed_work` (one of our exercise questions has you try out this very thing! There's a solution provided as well...). I suggest that you master the basics first before trying this out for yourself.

In the next section, we will run our kernel module.

Our simple work queue kernel module – running it

Let's take it for a spin! Take a look at the following screenshot:

```
--------------------------------
sudo insmod ./workq_simple.ko && lsmod|grep workq_simple
--------------------------------
workq_simple          20480  0
--------------------------------
dmesg
--------------------------------
[74829.407661] workq_simple:workq_simple_init(): Work queue initialized, timer set to expire in 420 ms
$
$
$ dmesg
[74829.407661] workq_simple:workq_simple_init(): Work queue initialized, timer set to expire in 420 ms
[74829.840749] workq_simple:ding(): timed out... data=3
[74829.843076] workq_simple:ding(): 001) [swapper/1]:0    |  .Ns1    /* ding() */
[74829.844040] workq_simple:work_func(): In our workq function: data=2
[74829.844853] workq_simple:work_func(): 001) [kworker/1:0]:55200    |  ...0    /* work_func() */
[74829.845758] workq_simple:work_func(): delta: 175038 ns (= 175 us = 0 ms)
[74830.288314] workq_simple:ding(): timed out... data=2
[74830.291991] workq_simple:ding(): 001) [swapper/1]:0    |  .Ns1    /* ding() */
[74830.296725] workq_simple:work_func(): In our workq function: data=1
[74830.300663] workq_simple:work_func(): 001) [kworker/1:0]:55200    |  ...0    /* work_func() */
[74830.302103] workq_simple:work_func(): delta: 600495 ns (= 600 us = 0 ms)
[74830.748178] workq_simple:ding(): timed out... data=1
[74830.750019] workq_simple:ding(): 001) [swapper/1]:0    |  .Ns1    /* ding() */
[74830.752278] workq_simple:work_func(): In our workq function: data=0
[74830.753679] workq_simple:work_func(): 001) [kworker/1:0]:55200    |  ...0    /* work_func() */
[74830.754549] workq_simple:work_func(): delta: 307562 ns (= 307 us = 0 ms)
$
```

Figure 5.12 – Our workq_simple.ko LKM with the work queue function execution highlighted

Let's take a look at this code in more detail:

- Via our `lkm` helper script, we build and then `insmod(8)` the kernel module; that is, `workq_simple.ko`.
- The kernel log is displayed via `dmesg(1)`:
  - Here, the workqueue and kernel timer are initialized and armed within the init method.
  - The timer expires (in approximately 420 ms); you can see its printks (showing `timed out...` and the value of our `data` variable).

- It invokes the `schedule_work()` API, causing our workqueue function to run.
- As highlighted in the preceding screenshot, our work queue function, `work_func()`, indeed runs; it displays the data variable's current value, proving that it correctly gained access to our "context" or private data structure.

Note that we used our `PRINT_CTX()` macro in this LKM (it's within our `convenient.h` header) to reveal something interesting:

- When it runs in the context of the timer callback function, its status bits contain the `s` character (the third character within the four-character field – `.Ns1` or similar), showing that it's running in *softirq* (an interrupt, atomic) context.
- When it runs in the context of the work queue callback function, its status bit's third character will *never* contain the `s` character; it will always be a `.`, *proving that the workqueue always executes in the process context!*

Next, the `SHOW_DELTA()` macro calculates and spits out the time difference between the workqueue being scheduled and actually executing. As you can see (here, at least, on our lightly loaded x86_64 guest VM), it's in the range of a few hundred microseconds.

Why not look up the actual kernel worker thread that was used to consume our work queue? A simple `ps(1)` on the PID is all that's required here. In this particular case, it happens to be one of the kernel's per CPU core generic workqueue consumer threads – a kernel worker (`kworker/...`) thread:

```
$ ps -el | grep -w 55200
  1 I     0  55200      2  0  80  0 -      0 -      ?        00:00:02
kworker/1:0-mm_percpu_wq
  $
```

Of course, the kernel code base is littered with workqueue usage (especially many device drivers). Please use `cscope(1)` to find and browse through instances of such code.

The sed3 mini project – a very brief look

Let's conclude this chapter by taking a very brief look at the evolution of our `sed2` project to `sed3`. This mini-project is identical to `sed2` except that it's simpler! The (en/de)crypt work **is now carried out by our work task (function) via the kernel's workqueue functionality** or bottom-half mechanism. We use a workqueue – the default kernel-global workqueue – to get the work done instead of manually creating and managing kthreads (as we did in `sed2`)!

The following screenshot shows us accessing the kernel log of a sample run; in the run, we had the user mode app encrypt, then decrypt, and then retrieve the message for viewing. We've highlighted the interesting bit here – the execution of our work task via the kernel-global workqueue's worker threads – in the two red rectangles:

```
--- Message Control ---
1. Encrypt the message
2. Retrieve the message (from the driver)
3. Decrypt the message (that was encrypted in (1))
4. Destroy the message
   --- Kernel Logs ---
5. View the kernel log (via dmesg(1))
6. Clear the kernel log (via sudo)
7. Quit
> 5
---> View kernel log : dmesg(1) <---
[ 6942.413924] misc sed3_drv: LLKD sed3_drv misc driver (major # 10) registered, minor# = 56,
               dev node is /dev/sed3_drv
[ 6942.416249] sed3_drv:sed3_drv_init(): Our work task on the kernel-global workqueue is initialized
[ 6942.417238] sed3_drv:sed3_drv_init(): init done (make_it_fail is off)
[ 6942.418041] misc sed3_drv: loaded.
[ 6961.239178] sed3_drv:open_miscdrv(): 001) userapp_sed2 :10611   | ...0  /* open_miscdrv() */
[ 6961.242642] sed3_drv:open_miscdrv(): opening "sed3_drv" now
[ 6961.243865] sed3_drv:ioctl_miscdrv(): In ioctl 'retrieve' cmd option; arg=0x5653408508c0
[ 6964.117949] sed3_drv:ioctl_miscdrv(): In ioctl 'encrypt' cmd option; arg=0x565340850ef0
[ 6964.119064] sed3_drv:ioctl_miscdrv(): xform=2, len=12
[ 6964.119765] payload: 00000000: 68 65 6c 6c 6f 6f 6f 20 31 32 33          hellooo 123
[ 6964.120791] sed3_drv:sed3_worker(): starting timer + processing now ...
[ 6964.122074] sed3_drv:sed3_worker(): [9812] work task about to execute work!
[ 6964.123193] sed3_drv:sed3_worker(): 001) [kworker/1:0]:9812   | .N.0  /* sed3_worker() */
[ 6964.124309] sed3_drv:sed3_worker(): data transform type: XF_ENCRYPT
[ 6964.125276] kdata->shmem: 00000000: 68 65 6c 6c 6f 6f 6f 20 31 32 33         helloooo 123
[ 6964.126416] sed3_drv:sed3_worker(): processing complete, timeout cancelled
[ 6964.127365] sed3_drv:sed3_worker(): delta: 4342250 ns (= 4342 us = 4 ms)
[ 6964.128397] sed3_drv:sed3_worker(): [9812] FYI, work task done, leaving...
[ 6971.182545] sed3_drv:ioctl_miscdrv(): In ioctl 'retrieve' cmd option; arg=0x565340851110
[ 6973.503980] sed3_drv:ioctl_miscdrv(): In ioctl 'decrypt' cmd option
[ 6973.508518] sed3_drv:sed3_worker(): starting timer + processing now ...
[ 6973.509984] sed3_drv:sed3_worker(): [9791] work task about to execute work!
[ 6973.510695] sed3_drv:sed3_worker(): 000) [kworker/0:2]:9791   | ...0  /* sed3_worker() */
[ 6973.511629] sed3_drv:sed3_worker(): data transform type: XF_DECRYPT
[ 6973.512408] kdata->shmem: 00000000: 96 99 92 92 8f 8f 8f 8f 5e 4d 4c 4b       ........^MLK
[ 6973.513373] sed3_drv:sed3_worker(): processing complete, timeout cancelled
[ 6973.514159] sed3_drv:sed3_worker(): delta: 3468902 ns (= 3468 us = 3 ms)
[ 6973.515034] sed3_drv:sed3_worker(): [9791] FYI, work task done, leaving...
[ 6974.523902] sed3_drv:ioctl_miscdrv(): In ioctl 'retrieve' cmd option; arg=0x565340851550

*** Menu ***
```

Figure 5.13 – Kernel log when running our sed3 driver; the work task running via the default kernel-global workqueue is highlighted

By the way, the user mode app is identical to the one we used in sed2. The preceding screenshot shows (via our trusty PRINT_CTX() macro) the actual kernel worker threads that the kernel-global workqueue employed to run our encrypt and decrypt work; in this particular case, it's [kworker/1:0] PID 9812 for the encrypt work and [kworker/0:2] PID 9791 for the decrypt work. Note how they both run in the process context. We shall leave it to you to browse through the code of sed3 (ch5/sed3).

This brings this section to a close. Here, you learned how the kernel workqueue infrastructure is indeed a blessing for module/driver authors as it helps you add a powerful abstraction layer over the underlying details regarding kernel threads, their creation, and intricate management and manipulation. It makes it very easy for you to perform work in the kernel – especially by employing the pre-existing kernel-global (default) workqueue – without having to worry about the gory details.

Summary

Well done! We covered a lot of ground in this chapter. First, you learned how to create delays in kernel space, both the atomic and the blocking types (via the *delay() and *sleep() routines, respectively). Next, you learned how to set up and use kernel timers within your LKM (or driver) – a very common and required task. Directly creating and working with kernel threads can be a heady (and even difficult) experience, which is why you learned the basics of doing so. After that, you looked at the kernel workqueue subsystem, which solves complexity (and concurrency) issues. You learned what it is and how to practically make use of the kernel-global (default) workqueue to make your work task(s) execute when required.

The series of three sed (simple encrypt decrypt) demo drivers we designed and implemented showed you a bit of a more sophisticated use case for these interesting technologies: sed1 with the timeout implementation, sed2 adding to the kernel thread to perform work, and sed3 using the kernel-global workqueue to have work consumed when required.

Please take some time to work on the following *Questions*/exercises for this chapter and browse through the *Further reading* resources. When you're done, I suggest that you take a well-deserved break and jump back in. We're almost there: the final two chapters cover a really key topic – kernel synchronization!

Questions

1. Spot the bug(s) in the following pseudocode:

```
static my_chip_tasklet(void)
{
    // ... process data
    if (!copy_to_user(to, from, count)) {
        pr_warn("..."); [...]
    }
}
static irqreturn_t chip_hardisr(int irq, void *data)
{
    // ack irq
    // << ... fetch data into kfifo ... >>
    // << ... call func_a(), delay, then call func_b() >>
    func_a();
    usleep(100); // 100 us delay required here! see datasheet pg
...
    func_b();
    tasklet_schedule(...);
    return IRQ_HANDLED;
}
my_chip_probe(...)
{
    // ...
    request_irq(CHIP_IRQ, chip_hardisr, ...);
    // ...
    tasklet_init(...);
}
```

2. `timer_simple_check`: Enhance the `timer_simple` kernel module so that it checks the amount of time that elapsed between setting up a timeout and it actually being serviced.

3. `kclock`: Write a kernel module that sets up a kernel timer so that it times out every second. Then, use this to print the timestamp to the kernel log to get, in effect, a simple "clock app" in the kernel.

4. `mutlitime`: Develop a kernel module that takes the number of seconds to issue a timer callback in as a parameter. Have it default to zero (implying no timer and thus a validity error). Here's how it should work: if the number that's passed is 3, it should create three kernel timers; the first one will expire in 3 seconds, the second in 2 seconds, and the last in 1 second. In other words, if the number passed is "n", it should create "n" kernel timers; the first one will expire in "n" seconds, the second in "n-1" seconds, the third in "n-2" seconds, and so on until the count hits zero.

5. Build and run the `sed[123]` mini-projects provided in this chapter and verify (by looking at the kernel logs) that they work the way they should.

6. `workq_simple2`: The `ch5/workq_simple` LKM we provided sets up and "consumes" one work item (function) via the kernel-global workqueue; enhance it so that it sets up and executes two "work" tasks. Verify that it works correctly.

7. `workq_delayed`: Build upon the previous assignment (`workq_simple2`) to execute two work tasks, plus one more task (from the init code path). This one (the third one) should be delayed; the amount of time to delay by should be passed as a module parameter named `work_delay_ms` (in milliseconds; the default should be 500 ms).
[*Tip:* Be careful when using `container_of()` within the delayed work task callback function; you'll have to specify the third parameter as a `work` member of `struct delayed_work`; check out a solution we've provided].

You will find some of the questions answered in the book's GitHub repo: `https://github.com/PacktPublishing/Linux-Kernel-Programming-Part-2/tree/main/solutions_to_assgn`.

Further reading

- Kernel documentation: *Delays, sleep mechanisms*: `https://www.kernel.org/doc/Documentation/timers/timers-howto.tx`
- Kernel Timer Systems: `https://elinux.org/Kernel_Timer_Systems#Timer_information`

- Workqueues:
    - This is a very good presentation: *Async execution with workqueues*, Bhaktipriya Shridhar: `https://events.static.linuxfound.org/sites/events/files/slides/Async%20execution%20with%20wqs.pdf`
    - Kernel documentation: *Concurrency Managed Workqueue (cmwq)*: `https://www.kernel.org/doc/html/latest/core-api/workqueue.html#concurrency-managed-workqueue-cmwq`

- The `container_of()` macro explained:
    - *The Magical container_of() Macro*, November 2012: `https://radek.io/2012/11/10/magical-container_of-macro/`
    - *Understanding of container_of macro in Linux kernel*: `https://embetronicx.com/tutorials/linux/c-programming/understanding-of-container_of-macro-in-linux-kernel/`

Section 2: Delving Deeper

Here you will learn about an advanced and critical topic: the concepts behind, the need for, and the usage of kernel synchronization technologies and APIs.

This section comprises the following chapters:

Kernel Synchronization - Part 1

6

As any developer familiar with programming in a multithreaded environment (or even a single-threaded one where multiple processes work on shared memory, or where interrupts are a possibility) is well aware, there is a need for **synchronization** whenever two or more threads (code paths in general) may race; that is, their outcome cannot be predicted. Pure code itself is never an issue as its permissions are read/execute (r-x); reading and executing code simultaneously on multiple CPU cores is not only perfectly fine and safe, but it's encouraged (it results in better throughput and is why multithreading is a good idea). However, the moment you're working on shared writeable data is the moment you need to start being very careful!

The discussions around concurrency and its control – synchronization – are varied, especially in the context of a complex piece of software such as a Linux kernel (its subsystems and related regions, such as device drivers), which is what we're dealing with in this book. Thus, for convenience, we will split this large topic into two chapters, this one and the next.

In this chapter, we will cover the following topics:

- Critical sections, exclusive execution, and atomicity
- Concurrency concerns within the Linux kernel
- Mutex or spinlock? Which to use when
- Using the mutex lock
- Using the spinlock
- Locking and interrupts

Let's get started!

Critical sections, exclusive execution, and atomicity

Imagine you're writing software for a multicore system (well, nowadays, it's typical that you will work on multicore systems, even on most embedded projects). As we mentioned in the introduction, running multiple code paths in parallel is not only safe, it's desirable (why spend those dollars otherwise, right?). On the other hand, concurrent (parallel and simultaneous) code paths within which **shared writeable data** (also known as **shared state**) **is accessed** in any manner is where you are required to guarantee that, at any given point in time, only one thread can work on that data at a time! This is really key; why? Think about it: if you allow multiple concurrent code paths to work in parallel on shared writeable data, you're literally asking for trouble: **data corruption** (a "race") can occur as a result.

What is a critical section?

A code path that can execute in parallel and that works on (reads and/or writes) shared writeable data (shared state) is called a critical section. They require protection from parallelism. Identifying and protecting critical sections from simultaneous execution is an implicit requirement for correct software that you – the designer/architect/developer – must handle.

A critical section is a piece of code that must run either exclusively; that is, alone (serialized), or atomically; that is, indivisibly, to completion, without interruption.

By exclusively, we're implying that at any given point in time, one thread is running the code of the critical section; this is obviously required for data safety reasons.

This notion also brings up the important concept of *atomicity*: a single atomic operation is one that is indivisible. On any modern processor, two operations are considered to always be **atomic**; that is, they cannot be interrupted and will run to completion:

- The execution of a single machine language instruction.
- Reads or writes to an aligned primitive data type that is within the processor's word size (typically 32 or 64 bits); for example, reading or writing a 64-bit integer on a 64-bit system is guaranteed to be atomic. Threads reading that variable will never see an in-between, torn, or dirty result; they will either see the old or the new value.

So, if you have some lines of code that work upon shared (global or static) writeable data, it cannot – in the absence of any explicit synchronization mechanism – be guaranteed to run exclusively. Note that at times, running the critical section's code *atomically*, as well as exclusively, is required, but not all the time.

When the code of the critical section is running in a safe-to-sleep process context (such as typical file operations on a driver via a user app (open, read, write, ioctl, mmap, and so on), or the execution path of a kernel thread or workqueue), it might well be acceptable to not have the critical section being truly atomic. However, when its code is running in a non-blocking atomic context (such as a hardirq, tasklet, or softirq), *it must run atomically as well as exclusively* (we shall cover these points in more detail in the *Mutex or spinlock? Which to use when* section).

A conceptual example will help clarify things. Let's say that three threads (from user space app(s)) attempt to open and read from your driver more or less simultaneously on a multicore system. Without any intervention, they may well end up running the critical section's code in parallel, thus working on the shared writable data in parallel, thus very likely corrupting it! For now, let's look at a conceptual diagram to see how non-exclusive execution within a critical section's code path is wrong (we won't even talk about atomicity here):

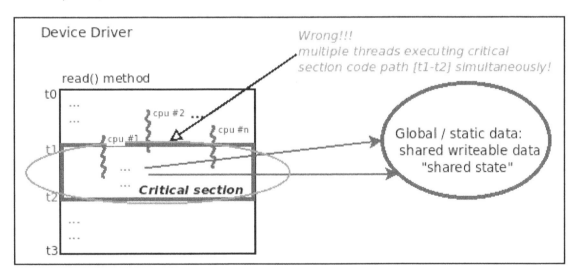

Figure 6.1 – A conceptual diagram showing how a critical section code path is violated by having >1 thread running within it simultaneously

As shown in the preceding diagram, in your device driver, within its (say) read method, you're having it run some code in order to perform its job (reading some data from the hardware). Let's take a more in-depth look at this diagram *in terms of data accesses being made* at different points in time:

- From time $t0$ to $t1$: None or only local variable data is accessed. This is concurrent-safe, with no protection required, and can run in parallel (since each thread has its own private stack).
- From time $t1$ to $t2$: Global/static shared writeable data is accessed. This is *not* concurrent-safe; it's **a critical section** and thus must be **protected** from concurrent access. It should only contain code that runs exclusively (alone, exactly one thread at a time, serialized) and, perhaps, atomically.
- From time $t2$ to $t3$: None or only local variable data is accessed. This is concurrent-safe, with no protection required, and can run in parallel (since each thread has its own private stack).

In this book, we assume that you are already aware of the need to synchronize critical sections; we will not discuss this particular topic any further. Those of you who are interested may refer to my earlier book, *Hands-On System Programming with Linux (Packt, October 2018)*, which covers these points in detail (especially *Chapter 15, Multithreading with Pthreads Part II – Synchronization*).

So, knowing this, we can now restate the notion of a critical section while also mentioning when the situation arises (shown in square brackets and italics in the bullet points). A critical section is code that must run as follows:

- **(Always) Exclusively**: Alone (serialized)
- **(When in an atomic context) Atomically**: Indivisibly, to completion, without interruption

In the next section, we'll look at a classic scenario – the increment of a global integer.

A classic case – the global i ++

Think of this classic example: a global i integer is being incremented within a concurrent code path, one within which multiple threads of execution can simultaneously execute. A naive understanding of computer hardware and software will lead you to believe that this operation is obviously atomic. However, the reality is that modern hardware and software (the compiler and OS) are much more sophisticated than you may imagine, thus causing all kinds of invisible (to the app developer) performance-driven optimizations.

We won't attempt to delve into too much detail here, but the reality is that modern processors are extremely complex: among the many technologies they employ toward better performance, a few are superscalar and super-pipelined execution in order to execute multiple independent instructions and several parts of various instructions in parallel (respectively), performing on-the-fly instruction and/or memory reordering, caching memory in complex hierarchical on-CPU caches, false sharing, and so on! We will delve into some of these details in Chapter 7, *Kernel Synchronization – Part 2*, in the *Cache effects – false sharing* and *Memory barriers* sections.

The paper *What every systems programmer should know about concurrency* by *Matt Kline, April 2020*, (https://assets.bitbashing.io/papers/concurrency-primer.pdf) is superb and a must-read on this subject; do read it!

All of this makes for a situation that's more complex than it appears to be at first glance. Let's continue with the classic i ++:

```
static int i = 5;
[ ... ]
foo()
{
    [ ... ]
    i ++;      // is this safe? yes, if truly atomic... but is it truly
atomic??
}
```

Is this increment safe by itself? The short answer is no, you must protect it. Why? It's a critical section – we're accessing shared writeable data for a read and/or write operation. The longer answer is that it really depends on whether the increment operation is truly atomic (indivisible); if it is, then i ++ poses no danger in the presence of parallelism – if not, it does! So, how do we know whether i ++ is truly atomic or not? Two things determine this:

- The processor's **Instruction Set Architecture (ISA)**, which determines (among several things related to the processor at a low level) the machine instructions that execute at runtime.
- The compiler.

If the ISA has the facility to employ a single machine instruction to perform an integer increment, *and* the compiler has the intelligence to use it, *then* it's truly atomic – it's safe and doesn't require locking. Otherwise, it's not safe and requires locking!

Try this out: Navigate your browser to this wonderful compiler explorer website: https://godbolt.org/. Select C as the programming language and then, in the left pane, declare the global i integer and increment within a function. Compile in the right pane with an appropriate compiler and compiler options. You'll see the actual machine code generated for the C high-level i ++; statement. If it's indeed a single machine instruction, then it will be safe; if not, you will require locking. By and large, you will find that you can't really tell: in effect, you *cannot* afford to assume things – you will have to assume it's unsafe by default and protect it! This can be seen in the following screenshot:

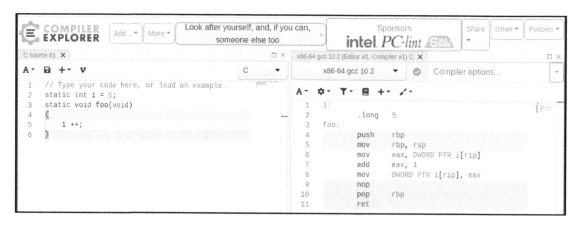

Figure 6.2 – Even with the latest stable gcc version but no optimization, the x86_64 gcc produces multiple instructions for the i ++

The preceding screenshot clearly shows this: the yellow background regions in the left- and right-hand panes is the C source and the corresponding assembly generated by the compiler, respectively (based on the x86_64 ISA and the compiler's optimization level). By default, with no optimization, i ++ becomes three machine instructions. This is exactly what we expect: it corresponds to the *fetch* (memory to register), the *increment*, and the *store* (register to memory)! Now, this is *not* atomic; it's entirely possible that, after one of the machine instructions executes, the control unit interferes and switches the instruction stream to a different point. This could even result in another process or thread being context switched in!

The good news is that with a quick -O2 in the Compiler options... window, i ++ becomes just one machine instruction – truly atomic! However, we can't predict these things in advance; one day, your code may execute on a fairly low-end ARM (RISC) system, increasing the chance that multiple machine instructions are required for i ++. (Worry not – we shall cover an optimized locking technology specifically for integers in the *Using the atomic integer operators* section).

Modern languages provide native atomic operators; for C/C++, it's fairly recent (from 2011); the ISO C++11 and the ISO C11 standards provide ready-made and built-in atomic variables for this. A little googling will quickly reveal them to you. Modern glibc also makes use of them. As an example, if you've worked with signaling in user space, you will know to use the volatile sig_atomic_t data type to safely access and/or update an atomic integer within signal handlers. What about the kernel? In the next chapter, you'll learn about the Linux kernel's solution to this key issue. We'll cover this in the *Using the atomic integer operators* and *Using the atomic bit operators* sections.

The Linux kernel is, of course, a concurrent environment: multiple threads of execution run in parallel on multiple CPU cores. Not only that, but even on uni-processor (UP/single CPU) systems, the presence of hardware interrupts, traps, faults, exceptions, and software signals can cause data integrity issues. Needless to say, protecting against concurrency at required points in the code path is easier said than done; identifying and protecting critical sections using technologies such as locking – as well as other synchronization primitives and technologies – is absolutely essential, which is why this is the core subject matter of this chapter and the next.

Concepts – the lock

We require synchronization because of the fact that, without any intervention, threads can concurrently execute critical sections where shared writeable data (shared state) is being worked upon. To defeat concurrency, we need to get rid of parallelism, and we need to *serialize* code that's within the critical section – the place where the shared data is being worked upon (for reading and/or writing).

To force a code path to become serialized, a common technique is to use a **lock**. Essentially, a lock works by guaranteeing that precisely one thread of execution can "take" or own the lock at any given point in time. Thus, using a lock to protect a critical section in your code will give you what we're after – running the critical section's code exclusively (and perhaps atomically; more on this to come):

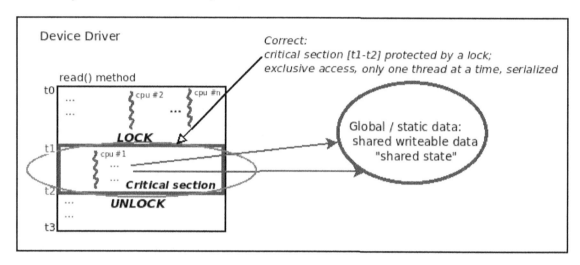

Figure 6.3 – A conceptual diagram showing how a critical section code path is honored, given exclusivity, by using a lock

The preceding diagram shows one way to fix the situation mentioned previously: using a lock to protect the critical section! How does the lock (and unlock) work, conceptually?

The basic premise of a lock is that whenever there is contention for it – that is, when multiple competing threads (say, n threads) attempt to acquire the lock (the LOCK operation) – exactly one thread will succeed. This is called the "winner" or the "owner" of the lock. It sees the *lock* API as a non-blocking call and thus continues to run happily – and exclusively – while executing the code of the critical section (the critical section is effectively the code between the *lock* and the *unlock* operations!). What happens to the n−1 "loser" threads? They (perhaps) see the lock API as a blocking call; they, to all practical effect, wait. Wait upon what? The *unlock* operation, of course, which is performed by the owner of the lock (the "winner" thread)! Once unlocked, the remaining n−1 threads now compete for the next "winner" slot; of course, exactly one of them will "win" and proceed forward; in the interim, the n−2 losers will now wait upon the (new) winner's *unlock*; this repeats until all n threads (finally and sequentially) acquire the lock.

Now, locking works of course, but – and this should be quite intuitive – it results in (pretty steep!) **overhead, as it defeats parallelism and serializes** the execution flow! To help you visualize this situation, think of a funnel, with the narrow stem being the critical section where only one thread can fit at a time. All other threads get choked; locking creates bottlenecks:

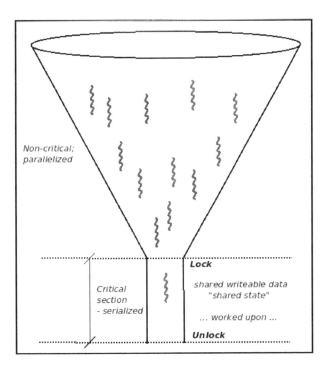

Figure 6.4 – A lock creates a bottleneck, analogous to a physical funnel

Another oft-mentioned physical analog is a highway with several lanes merging into one very busy – and choked with traffic – lane (a poorly designed toll booth, perhaps). Again, parallelism – cars (threads) driving in parallel with other cars in different lanes (CPUs) – is lost, and serialized behavior is required – cars are forced to queue one behind the other.

Thus, it is imperative that we, as software architects, try and design our products/projects so that locking is minimally required. While completely eliminating global variables is not practically possible in most real-world projects, optimizing and minimizing their usage is required. We shall cover more regarding this, including some very interesting lockless programming techniques, later.

Another really key point is that a newbie programmer might naively assume that performing reads on a shared writeable data object is perfectly safe and thus requires no explicit protection (with the exception of an aligned primitive data type that is within the size of the processor's bus); this is untrue. This situation can lead to what's called **dirty or torn reads**, a situation where possibly stale data can be read as another writer thread is simultaneously writing while you are – incorrectly, without locking – reading the very same data item.

Since we're on the topic of atomicity, as we just learned, on a typical modern microprocessor, the only things guaranteed to be atomic are a single machine language instruction or a read/write to an aligned primitive data type within the processor bus's width. So, how can we mark a few lines of "C" code so that they're truly atomic? In user space, this isn't even possible (we can come close, but cannot guarantee atomicity).

How do you "come close" to atomicity in user space apps? You can always construct a user thread to employ a SCHED_FIFO policy and a real-time priority of 99. This way, when it wants to run, pretty much nothing besides hardware interrupts/exceptions can preempt it. (The old audio subsystem implementation heavily relied on this.)

In kernel space, we can write code that's truly atomic. How, exactly? The short answer is that we can use spinlocks! We'll learn about spinlocks in more detail shortly.

A summary of key points

Let's summarize some key points regarding critical sections. It's really important to go over these carefully, keep these handy, and ensure you use them in practice:

- A **critical section** is a code path that can execute in parallel and that works upon (reads and/or writes) shared writeable data (also known as "shared state").
- Because it works on shared writable data, the critical section requires protection from the following:
    - Parallelism (that is, it must run alone/serialized/in a mutually exclusive fashion)
    - When running in an atomic (interrupt) non-blocking context – atomically: indivisibly, to completion, without interruption. Once protected, you can safely access your shared state until you "unlock".
- Every critical section in the code base must be identified and protected:
    - Identifying critical sections is critical! Carefully review your code and make sure you don't miss them.
    - Protecting them can be achieved via various technologies; one very common technique is *locking* (there's also lock-free programming, which we'll look at in the next chapter).
    - A common mistake is only protecting critical sections that *write* to global writeable data; you must also protect critical sections that *read* global writeable data; otherwise, you risk a **torn or dirty read!** To help make this key point clear, visualize an unsigned 64-bit data item being read and written on a 32-bit system; in such a case, the operation can't be atomic (two load/store operations are required). Thus, what if, while you're reading the value of the data item in one thread, it's being simultaneously written to by another thread!? The writer thread takes a "lock" of some sort but because you thought reading is safe, the lock isn't taken by the reader thread; due to an unfortunate timing coincidence, you can end up performing a partial/torn/dirty read! We will learn how to overcome these issues by using various techniques in the coming sections and the next chapter.
    - Another deadly mistake is not using the same lock to protect a given data item.

- Failing to protect critical sections leads to a **data race**, a situation where the outcome – the actual value of the data being read/written – is "racy", which means it varies, depending on runtime circumstances and timing. This is known as a bug. (A bug that, once in "the field", is extremely difficult to see, reproduce, determine its root cause, and fix. We will cover some very powerful stuff to help you with this in the next chapter, in the *Lock debugging within the kernel* section; be sure to read it!)

- **Exceptions**: You are safe (implicitly, without explicit protection) in the following situations:

  - When you are working on local variables. They're allocated on the private stack of the thread (or, in the interrupt context, on the local IRQ stack) and are thus, by definition, safe.

  - When you are working on shared writeable data in code that cannot possibly run in another context; that is, it's serialized by nature. In our context, the *init* and *cleanup* methods of an LKM qualify (they run exactly once, serially, on `insmod` and `rmmod` only).

  - When you are working on shared data that is truly constant and read-only (don't let C's `const` keyword fool you, though!).

- Locking is inherently complex; you must carefully think, design, and implement this to avoid *deadlocks*. We'll cover this in more detail in the *Locking guidelines and deadlocks* section.

Concurrency concerns within the Linux kernel

Recognizing critical sections within a piece of kernel code is of critical importance; how can you protect it if you can't even see it? The following are a few guidelines to help you, as a budding kernel/driver developer, recognize where concurrency concerns – and thus critical sections – may arise:

- The presence of **Symmetric Multi-Processor (SMP)** systems (`CONFIG_SMP`)
- The presence of a preemptible kernel
- Blocking I/O
- Hardware interrupts (on either SMP or UP systems)

These are critical points to understand, and we will discuss each in this section.

Multicore SMP systems and data races

The first point is pretty obvious; take a look at the pseudocode shown in the following screenshot:

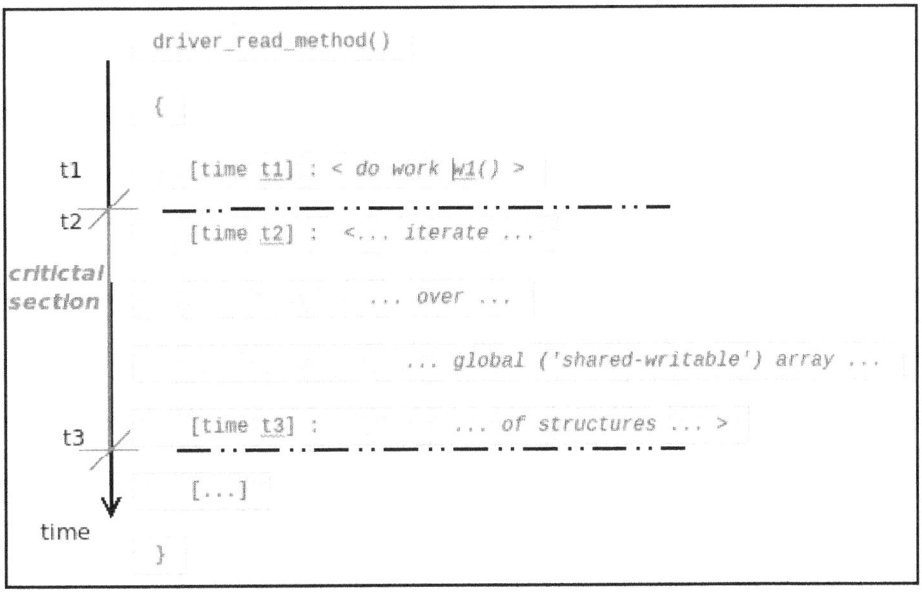

Figure 6.5 – Pseudocode – a critical section within a (fictional) driver's read method: it's wrong as there's no locking

It's a similar situation to what we showed in *Figures 6.1* and *6.3*; it's just that here, we're showing the concurrency in terms of pseudocode. Clearly, from time t2 to time t3, the driver is working on some global shared writeable data, thus making this a critical section.

Now, visualize a system with, say, four CPU cores (an SMP system); two user space processes, P1 (running on, say, CPU 0) and P2 (running on, say, CPU 2), can concurrently open the device file and simultaneously issue a read(2) system call. Now, both processes will be concurrently executing the driver read "method", thus simultaneously working on shared writeable data! This (the code between t2 and t3) is a critical section, and since we are in violation of the fundamental exclusivity rule – critical sections must be executed by only a single thread at any point in time – we can very well end up corrupting the data, the application, or worse.

In other words, this is now a **data race**; depending on delicate timing coincidences, we may or may not generate an error (a bug). This very uncertainty – the delicate timing coincidence – is what makes finding and fixing errors like this extremely difficult (it can escape your testing effort).

> This aphorism is all too unfortunately true: *Testing can detect the presence of errors, not their absence.* Adding to this, you're worse off if your testing fails to catch races (and bugs), allowing them free rein in the field.

You might feel that since your product is a small embedded system running on one CPU core (UP), this discussion regarding controlling concurrency (often, via locking) does not apply to you. We beg to differ: pretty much all modern products, if they haven't already, will move to multicore (in their next-generation phases, perhaps). More importantly, even UP systems have concurrency concerns, as we shall explore.

Preemptible kernels, blocking I/O, and data races

Imagine you're running your kernel module or driver on a Linux kernel that's been configured to be preemptible (that is, CONFIG_PREEMPT is on; we covered this topic in the companion guide *Linux Kernel Programming, Chapter 10, The CPU Scheduler – Part 1*). Consider that a process, P1, is running the driver's read method code in the process context, working on the global array. Now, while it's within the critical section (between time t2 and t3), what if the kernel *preempts* process P1 and context switches to another process, P2, which is just waiting to execute this very code path? It's dangerous, and again, a data race. This could well happen on even a UP system!

Another scenario that's somewhat similar (and again, could occur on either a single core (UP) or multicore system): process P1 is running through the critical section of the driver method (between time t2 and t3; again, see *Figure 6.5*). This time, what if, within the critical section, it hits a blocking call?

A **blocking call** is a function that causes the calling process context to be put to sleep, waiting upon an event; when that event occurs, the kernel will "wake up" the task, and it will resume execution from where it left off. This is also known as blocking on I/O and is very common; many APIs (including several user space library and system calls, as well as several kernel APIs, are blocking by nature). In such a case, process P1 is effectively context switches off the CPU and goes to sleep, which means that the code of schedule() runs and enqueues it onto a wait queue.

In the interim, before P1 gets switched back, what if another process, P2, is scheduled to run? What if that process is also running this particular code path? Think about it – by the time P1 is back, the shared data could have changed "underneath it", causing all kinds of errors; again, a data race, a bug!

Hardware interrupts and data races

Finally, envision this scenario: process P1 is, again, innocently running the driver's read method code; it enters the critical section (between time t2 and t3; again, see *Figure 6.5*). It makes some progress but then, alas, a hardware interrupt triggers (on the same CPU)! On the Linux OS, hardware (peripheral) interrupts have the highest priority; they preempt any code (including kernel code) by default. Thus, process (or thread) P1 will be at least temporarily shelved, thus losing the processor; the interrupt handling code will preempt it and run.

Well, you might be wondering, so what? Indeed, this is a completely commonplace occurrence! Hardware interrupts fire very frequently on modern systems, effectively (and literally) interrupting all kinds of task contexts (do a quick vmstat 3 on your shell; the column under system labeled in shows the number of hardware interrupts that fired on your system in the last 1 second!). The key question to ask is this: is the interrupt handling code (either the hardirq top half or the so-called tasklet or softirq bottom half, whichever occurred), *sharing and working upon the same shared writable data of the process context that it just interrupted?*

If this is true, then, *Houston, we have a problem* – a data race! If not, then your interrupted code is not a critical section with respect to the interrupt code path, and that's fine. The fact is that the majority of device drivers do handle interrupt(s); thus, it is the driver author's (your!) responsibility to ensure that no global or static data – in effect, no critical sections – are shared between the process context and interrupt code paths. If they are (which does happen), you must somehow protect that data from data races and possible corruption.

These scenarios might leave you feeling that protecting against these concurrency concerns is a really tall order; how exactly can you accomplish data safety in the face of critical sections existing, along with various possible concurrency concerns? Interestingly, the actual APIs are not hard to learn to use; again, we emphasize that **recognizing critical sections** is the key thing to do.

Again, the basics regarding how a lock (conceptually) works, locking guidelines (very important; we'll recap on them shortly), and the types of and how to prevent deadlocks, are all dealt with in my earlier book, *Hands-On System Programming with Linux (Packt, Oct 2018)*. This books covers these points in detail in *Chapter 15, Multithreading with Pthreads Part II – Synchronization*.

Without further ado, let's dive into the primary synchronization technology that will serve to protect our critical sections – locking.

Locking guidelines and deadlocks

Locking, by its very nature, is a complex beast; it tends to give rise to complex interlocking scenarios. Not understanding it well enough can lead to both performance headaches and bugs – deadlocks, circular dependencies, interrupt-unsafe locking, and more. The following locking guidelines are key to ensuring correctly written code when using locking:

- **Locking granularity**: The 'distance' between the lock and the unlock (in effect, the length of the critical section) should not be coarse (too long a critical section) it should be 'fine enough'; what does this mean? The points below explain this:
  - You need to be careful here. When you're working on large projects, keeping too few locks is a problem, as is keeping too many! Too few locks can lead to performance issues (as the same locks are repeatedly used and thus tend to be highly contended).
  - Having a lot of locks is actually good for performance, but not good for complexity control. This also leads to another key point to understand: with many locks in the code base, you should be very clear on which lock protects which shared data object. It's completely meaningless if you use, say, `lockA` to protect `mystructX`, but in a code path far away (perhaps an interrupt handler) you forget this and try and use some other lock, `lockB`, for protection when working on the same structure! Right now, these things might sound obvious, but (as experienced developers know), under sufficient pressure, even the obvious isn't always obvious!
  - Try and balance things out. In large projects, using one lock to protect one global (shared) data structure is typical. (*Naming* the lock variable well can become a big problem in itself! This is why we place the lock that protects a data structure within it as a member.)

- **Lock ordering** is critical; **locks must be taken in the same order throughout**, and their order should be documented and followed by all the developers working on the project (annotating locks is useful too; more on this in the section on *lockdep* in the next chapter). Incorrect lock ordering often leads to deadlocks.
- Avoid recursive locking as much as possible.
- Take care to prevent starvation; verify that a lock, once taken, is indeed released "quickly enough".
- **Simplicity is key**: Try to avoid complexity or over-design, especially with regard to complex scenarios involving locks.

On the topic of locking, the (dangerous) issue of deadlocks arises. A **deadlock** is the inability to make any progress; in other words, the app and/or kernel component(s) appear to hang indefinitely. While we don't intend to delve into the gory details of deadlocks here, I will quickly mention some of the more common types of deadlock scenarios that can occur:

- Simple case, single lock, process context:
    - We attempt to acquire the same lock twice; this results in a **self-deadlock**.

- Simple case, multiple (two or more) locks, process context – an example:
    - On CPU 0, thread A acquires lock A and then wants lock B.
    - Concurrently, on CPU 1, thread B acquires lock B and then wants lock A.
    - The result is a deadlock, often called the **AB-BA deadlock**.
    - It can be extended; for example, the AB-BC-CA **circular dependency** (A-B-C lock chain) results in a deadlock.
- Complex case, single lock, and process and interrupt contexts:
    - Lock A takes in an interrupt context.
    - What if an interrupt occurs (on another core) and the handler attempts to take lock A? Deadlock is the result! Thus, locks acquired in the interrupt context must always be used with interrupts disabled. (How? We will look at this in more detail when we cover spinlocks.)
- More complex cases, multiple locks, and process and interrupt (hardirq and softirq) contexts

In simpler cases, always following the *lock ordering guideline* is sufficient: always obtain and release locks in a well-documented order (we will provide an example of this in kernel code in the *Using the mutex lock* section). However, this can get very complex; complex deadlock scenarios can trip up even experienced developers. Luckily for us, *lockdep* – the Linux kernel's runtime lock dependency validator – can catch every single deadlock case! (Don't worry – we shall get there: we'll cover lockdep in detail in the next chapter). When we cover spinlocks (the *Using the spinlock* section), we'll come across process and/or interrupt context scenarios similar to the ones mentioned previously; the type of spinlock to use is made clear there.

> With regard to deadlocks, a pretty detailed presentation on lockdep was given by Steve Rostedt at a Linux Plumber's Conference (back in 2011); the relevant slides are informative and explore both simple and complex deadlock scenarios, as well as how lockdep can detect them (https://blog.linuxplumbersconf.org/2011/ocw/sessions/153).

> Also, the reality is that not just deadlock, but even **livelock** situations, can be just as deadly! Livelock is essentially a situation similar to deadlock; it's just that the state of the participating task is running and not waiting. An example, an interrupt "storm" can cause a livelock; modern network drivers mitigate this effect by switching off interrupts (under interrupt load) and resorting to a polling technique called **New API; Switching Interrupts (NAPI)** (switching interrupts back on when appropriate; well, it's more complex than that, but we leave it at that here).

For those of you who've been living under a rock, you will know that the Linux kernel has two primary types of locks: the mutex lock and the spinlock. Actually, there are several more types, including other synchronization (and "lockless" programming) technology, all of which will be covered in the course of this chapter and the next.

Mutex or spinlock? Which to use when

The exact semantics of learning to use the mutex lock and the spinlock are quite simple (with appropriate abstraction within the kernel API set, making it even easier for the typical driver developer or module author). The critical question in this situation is a conceptual one: what really is the difference between the two locks? More to the point, under which circumstances should you use which lock? You will learn the answers to these questions in this section.

Taking our previous driver read method's pseudocode (*Figure 6.5*) as a base example, let's say that three threads – **tA**, **tB**, and **tC** – are running in parallel (on an SMP system) through this code. We shall solve this concurrency issue, while avoiding any data races, by taking or acquiring a lock prior to the start of the critical section (time **t2**), and release the lock (unlock) just after the end of the critical section code path (time **t3**). Let's take a look at the pseudocode once more, this time with locking to ensure it's correct:

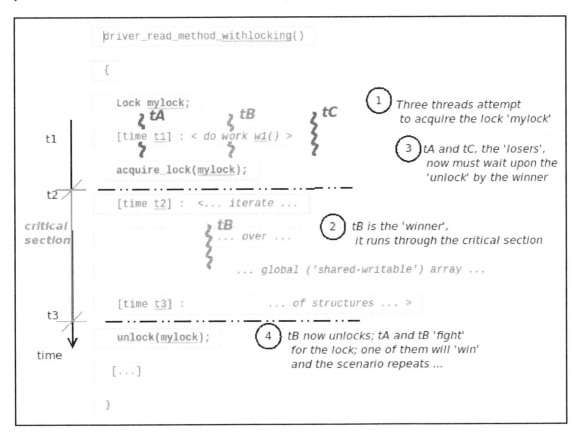

Figure 6.6 – Pseudocode – a critical section within a (fictional) driver's read method: correct, with locking

When the three threads attempt to simultaneously acquire the lock, the system guarantees that only exactly one of them will get it. Let's say that **tB** (thread B) gets the lock: it's now the "winner" or "owner" thread. This means that threads **tA** and **tC** are the "losers"; what do they do? They wait upon the unlock! The moment the "winner" (**tB**) completes the critical section and unlocks the lock, the battle resumes between the previous losers; one of them will be the next winner and the process repeats.

The key difference between the two lock types – the mutex and the spinlock – is based on how the losers wait upon the unlock. With the mutex lock, the loser threads are put to sleep; that is, they wait by sleeping. The moment the winner performs the unlock, the kernel awakens the losers (all of them) and they run, again competing for the lock. (In fact, mutexes and semaphores are sometimes referred to as sleeplocks.)

With the **spinlock**, however, there is no question of sleeping; the losers wait by spinning upon the lock until it is unlocked. Conceptually, this looks as follows:

```
while (locked) ;
```

Note that this is *only conceptual*. Think about it a moment – this is actually polling. However, as a good programmer, you will understand, that polling is usually considered a bad idea. Why, then, does the spinlock work this way? Well, it doesn't; it has only been presented in this manner for conceptual purposes. As you will soon understand, spinlocks only really have meaning on multicore (SMP) systems. On such systems, while the winner thread is away and running the critical section code, the losers wait by spinning on other CPU cores! In reality, at the implementation level, the code that's used to implement the modern spinlock is highly optimized (and arch-specific) and does not work by trivially "spinning" (for example, many spinlock implementations for ARM use the **wait for event** (**WFE**) machine language instruction, which has the CPU optimally wait in a low power state; see the *Further reading* section for several resources on the internal implementation of spinlocks).

Determining which lock to use – in theory

How the spinlock is implemented is really not our concern here; the fact that the spinlock has a lower overhead than the mutex lock is of interest to us. How so? It's simple, really: for the mutex lock to work, the loser thread has to go to sleep. To do so, internally, the schedule() function gets called, which means the loser sees the mutex lock API as a blocking call! A call to the scheduler will ultimately result in the processer being context-switched off. Conversely, when the owner thread unlocks the lock, the loser thread(s) must be woken up; again, it will be context-switched back onto the processor. Thus, the minimal "cost" of the mutex lock/unlock operation is the time it takes to perform two context switches on the given machine. (See the *Information Box* in the next section.) By relooking at the preceding screenshot once more, we can determine a few things, including the time spent in the critical section (the "locked" code path); that is, t_locked = t3 - t2.

Let's say that `t_ctxsw` represents the time to context switch. As we've learned, the minimal cost of the mutex lock/unlock operation is `2 * t_ctxsw`. Now, let's say that the following expression is true:

```
t_locked < 2 * t_ctxsw
```

In other words, what if the time spent within the critical section is less than the time taken for two context switches? In this case, using the mutex lock is just wrong as this is far too much overhead; more time is being spent performing metawork than actual work – a phenomenon known as **thrashing**. It's this precise use case – the presence of very short critical sections – that's often the case on modern OSes such as Linux. So, in conclusion, for short non-blocking critical sections, using a spinlock is (far) superior to using a mutex lock.

Determining which lock to use – in practice

So, operating under the `t_locked < 2 * t_ctxsw` "rule" might be great in theory, but hang on: are you really expected to precisely measure the context switch time and the time spent in the critical section of each and every case where one (critical section) exists? No, of course not – that's pretty unrealistic and pedantic.

Practically speaking, think about it this way: the mutex lock works by having the loser threads sleep upon the unlock; the spinlock does not (the losers "spin"). Let's recall one of our golden rules of the Linux kernel: a kernel cannot sleep (call `schedule()`) in any kind of atomic context. Thus, we can never use the mutex lock in an interrupt context, or indeed in any context where it isn't safe to sleep; using the spinlock, however, would be fine. (Remember, a blocking API is one that puts the calling context to sleep by calling `schedule()`.) Let's summarize this:

- **Is the critical section running in an atomic (interrupt) context, or, in a process context, where it cannot sleep?** Use the spinlock.
- **Is the critical section running in a process context and sleep in the critical section is necessary?** Use the mutex lock.

Of course, using the spinlock is considered lower overhead than using the mutex; thus, you can even use the spinlock in the process context (such as our fictional driver's read method), as long as the critical section does not block (sleep).

[1] The time taken for a context switch is varied; it largely depends on the hardware and the OS quality. Recent (September 2018) measurements show that context switching time is in the region of 1.2 to 1.5 **us** (**microseconds**) on a pinned-down CPU, and around 2.2 us without pinning (`https://eli.thegreenplace.net/2018/measuring-context-switching-and-memory-overheads-for-linux-threads/`).

Both hardware and the Linux OS have improved tremendously, and because of that, so has the average context switching time. An old (December 1998) Linux Journal article determined that on an x86 class system, the average context switch time was 19 us (microseconds), and that the worst-case time was 30 us.

This brings up the question, how do we know if the code is currently running in a process or interrupt context? Easy: our `PRINT_CTX()` macro (within our `convenient.h` header) shows us this:

```
if (in_task())
    /* we're in process context (usually safe to sleep / block) */
else
    /* we're in an atomic or interrupt context (cannot sleep / block) */
```

Now that you understand which one – mutex or spinlock – to use and when, let's get into the actual usage. We'll begin with how to use the mutex lock!

Using the mutex lock

Mutexes are also called sleepable or blocking mutual exclusion locks. As you have learned, they are used in the process context if the critical section can sleep (block). They must not be used within any kind of atomic or interrupt context (top halves, bottom halves such as tasklets or softirqs, and so on), kernel timers, or even the process context where blocking is not allowed.

Initializing the mutex lock

A mutex lock "object" is represented in the kernel as a `struct mutex` data structure. Consider the following code:

```
#include <linux/mutex.h>
struct mutex mymtx;
```

To use a mutex lock, it *must* be explicitly initialized to the unlocked state. Initialization can be performed statically (declare and initialize the object) with the `DEFINE_MUTEX()` macro, or dynamically via the `mutex_init()` function (this is actually a macro wrapper over the `__mutex_init()` function).

For example, to declare and initialize a mutex object called `mymtx`, we can use `DEFINE_MUTEX(mymtx);`.

We can also do this dynamically. Why dynamically? Often, the mutex lock is a member of the (global) data structure that it protects (clever!). For example, let's say we have the following global context structure in our driver code (note that this code is fictional):

```
struct mydrv_priv {
    <member 1>
    <member 2>
    [...]
    struct mutex mymtx; /* protects access to mydrv_priv */
    [...]
};
```

Then, in your driver's (or LKM's) `init` method, do the following:

```
static int init_mydrv(struct mydrv_priv *drvctx)
{
    [...]
    mutex_init(drvctx-mymtx);
    [...]
}
```

Keeping the lock variable as a member of the (parent) data structure it protects is a common (and clever) pattern that's used within Linux; this approach has the added benefit of avoiding namespace pollution and is unambiguous about which mutex protects which shared data item (a bigger problem than it might appear to be at first, especially in enormous projects such as the Linux kernel!).

Keep the lock protecting a global or shared data structure as a member within that data structure.

Correctly using the mutex lock

Typically, you can find very insightful comments within the kernel source tree. Here's a great one that neatly summarizes the rules you must follow to correctly use a mutex lock; please read this carefully:

```
// include/linux/mutex.h
/*
 * Simple, straightforward mutexes with strict semantics:
 *
 * - only one task can hold the mutex at a time
 * - only the owner can unlock the mutex
 * - multiple unlocks are not permitted
 * - recursive locking is not permitted
 * - a mutex object must be initialized via the API
 * - a mutex object must not be initialized via memset or copying
 * - task may not exit with mutex held
 * - memory areas where held locks reside must not be freed
 * - held mutexes must not be reinitialized
 * - mutexes may not be used in hardware or software interrupt
 * contexts such as tasklets and timers
 *
 * These semantics are fully enforced when DEBUG_MUTEXES is
 * enabled. Furthermore, besides enforcing the above rules, the mutex
 * [ ... ]
```

As a kernel developer, you must understand the following:

- A critical section causes the code path *to be serialized, defeating parallelism*. Due to this, it's imperative that you keep the critical section as short as possible. A corollary to this is **lock data, not code**.
- Attempting to reacquire an already acquired (locked) mutex lock – which is effectively recursive locking – is *not* supported and will lead to a self-deadlock.

- **Lock ordering**: This is a very important rule of thumb for preventing dangerous deadlock situations. In the presence of multiple threads and multiple locks, it is critical that *the order in which locks are taken is documented and strictly followed by all the developers working on the project.* The actual lock ordering itself isn't sacrosanct, but the fact that once it's been decided on it must be followed, is. While browsing through the kernel source tree, you will come across many places where the kernel developers ensure this is done, and they (usually) write a comment regarding this for other developers to see and follow. Here's a sample comment from the slab allocator code (mm/slub.c):

```
/*
 * Lock order:
 * 1. slab_mutex (Global Mutex)
 * 2. node-list_lock
 * 3. slab_lock(page) (Only on some arches and for debugging)
```

Now that we understand how mutexes work from a conceptual standpoint (and we understand their initialization), let's learn how to make use of the lock/unlock APIs.

Mutex lock and unlock APIs and their usage

The actual locking and unlocking APIs for the mutex lock are as follows. The following code shows how to lock and unlock a mutex, respectively:

```
void __sched mutex_lock(struct mutex *lock);
void __sched mutex_unlock(struct mutex *lock);
```

(Ignore __sched here; it's just a compiler attribute that has this function disappear in the WCHAN output, which shows up in procfs and with certain option switches to ps(1) (such as -l)).

Again, the comments within the source code in kernel/locking/mutex.c are very detailed and descriptive; I encourage you to take a look at this file in more detail. We've only shown some of its code here, which has been taken directly from the 5.4 Linux kernel source tree:

```
// kernel/locking/mutex.c
[ ... ]
/**
 * mutex_lock - acquire the mutex
 * @lock: the mutex to be acquired
 *
 * Lock the mutex exclusively for this task. If the mutex is not
 * available right now, it will sleep until it can get it.
```

```
*
* The mutex must later on be released by the same task that
* acquired it. Recursive locking is not allowed. The task
* may not exit without first unlocking the mutex. Also, kernel
* memory where the mutex resides must not be freed with
* the mutex still locked. The mutex must first be initialized
* (or statically defined) before it can be locked. memset()-ing
* the mutex to 0 is not allowed.
*
* (The CONFIG_DEBUG_MUTEXES .config option turns on debugging
* checks that will enforce the restrictions and will also do
* deadlock debugging)
*
* This function is similar to (but not equivalent to) down().
*/
void __sched mutex_lock(struct mutex *lock)
{
    might_sleep();

    if (!__mutex_trylock_fast(lock))
        __mutex_lock_slowpath(lock);
}
EXPORT_SYMBOL(mutex_lock);
```

`might_sleep()` is a macro with an interesting debug property; it catches code that's supposed to execute in an atomic context but doesn't! So, think about it: `might_sleep()`, which is the first line of code in `mutex_lock()`, implies that this code path should not be executed by anything that's in an atomic context since it might sleep. This means that you should only use the mutex in the process context when it's safe to sleep!

A quick and important reminder: The Linux kernel can be configured with a large number of debug options; in this context, the `CONFIG_DEBUG_MUTEXES` config option will help you catch possible mutex-related bugs, including deadlocks. Similarly, under the **Kernel Hacking** menu, you will find a large number of debug-related kernel config options. We discussed this in the companion guide *Linux Kernel Programming - Chapter 5, Writing Your First Kernel Module – LKMs Part 2*. There are several very useful kernel configs with regard to lock debugging; we shall cover these in the next chapter, in the *Lock debugging within the kernel* section.

Mutex lock – via [un]interruptible sleep?

As usual, there's more to the mutex than what we've seen so far. You already know that a Linux process (or thread) cycles through various states of a state machine. On Linux, sleeping has two discrete states – an interruptible sleep and an uninterruptible sleep. A process (or thread) in an interruptible sleep is sensitive, which means it will respond to user space signals, whereas a task in an uninterruptible sleep is not sensitive to user signals.

In a human-interactive application with an underlying driver, as a general rule of thumb, you should typically put a process into an interruptible sleep (while it's blocking upon the lock), thus leaving it up to the end user as to whether to abort the application by pressing *Ctrl + C* (or some such mechanism involving signals). There is a design rule that's often followed on Unix-like systems: **provide mechanism, not policy**. Having said this, on non-interactive code paths, it's often the case that you must wait on the lock to wait indefinitely, with the semantic that a signal that's been delivered to the task should not abort the blocking wait. On Linux, the uninterruptible case turns out to be the most common one.

So, here's the thing: the `mutex_lock()` API always puts the calling task into an uninterruptible sleep. If this is not what you want, use the `mutex_lock_interruptible()` API to put the calling task into an interruptible sleep. There is one difference syntax-wise; the latter returns an integer value of 0 on success and –`EINTR` (remember the 0/-E return convention) on failure (due to signal interruption).

In general, using `mutex_lock()` is faster than using `mutex_lock_interruptible()`; use it when the critical section is short (thus pretty much guaranteeing that the lock is held for a short while, which is a very desirable characteristic).

The 5.4.0 kernel contains over 18,500 and just over 800 instances of calling the `mutex_lock()` and `mutex_lock_interruptible()` APIs, respectively; you can check this out via the powerful `cscope(1)` utility on the kernel source tree.

In theory, the kernel provides a `mutex_destroy()` API as well. This is the opposite of `mutex_init()`; its job is to mark the mutex as being unusable. It must only be invoked once the mutex is in the unlocked state, and once invoked, the mutex cannot be used. This is a bit theoretical because, on regular systems, it just reduces to an empty function; only on a kernel with `CONFIG_DEBUG_MUTEXES` enabled does it become actual (simple) code. Thus, we should use this pattern when working with the mutex, as shown in the following pseudocode:

```
DEFINE_MUTEX(...);          // init: initialize the mutex object
/* or */ mutex_init();
[ ... ]
```

```
/* critical section: perform the (mutex) locking, unlocking */
mutex_lock[_interruptible]();
<< ... critical section ... >>
mutex_unlock();
mutex_destroy();          // cleanup: destroy the mutex object
```

Now that you have learned how to use the mutex lock APIs, let's put this knowledge to use. In the next section, we will build on top of one of our earlier (poorly written – no protection!) "misc" drivers by employing the mutex object to lock critical sections as required.

Mutex locking – an example driver

We have created a simple device driver code example in *Chapter 1 - Writing a Simple misc Character Device Driver*; that is, ch1/miscdrv_rdwr. There, we wrote a simple misc class character device driver and used a user space utility program (ch12/miscdrv_rdwr/rdwr_drv_secret.c) to read and write a (so-called) secret from and to the device driver's memory.

However, what we glaringly (egregiously is the right word here!) failed to do in that code is protect shared (global) writeable data! This will cost us dearly in the real world. I urge you to take some time to think about this: it isn't viable that two (or three or more) user mode processes open the device file of this driver, and then concurrently issue various I/O reads and writes. Here, the global shared writable data (in this particular case, two global integers and the driver context data structure) could easily get corrupted.

So, let's learn from and correct our mistakes by making a copy of this driver (we will now call it ch12/1_miscdrv_rdwr_mutexlock/1_miscdrv_rdwr_mutexlock.c) and rewriting some portions of it. The key point is that we must use mutex locks to protect all critical sections. Instead of displaying the code here (it's in this book's GitHub repository at https://github.com/PacktPublishing/Linux-Kernel-Programming, after all, please do git clone it!), let's do something interesting: let's look at a "diff" (the differences – the delta generated by diff(1)) between the older unprotected version and the newer protected code version. The output here has been truncated:

```
$ pwd
<.../ch12/1_miscdrv_rdwr_mutexlock
$ diff -u ../../ch12/miscdrv_rdwr/miscdrv_rdwr.c miscdrv_rdwr_mutexlock.c>>
miscdrv_rdwr.patch
$ cat miscdrv_rdwr.patch
[ ... ]
+#include <linux/mutex.h> // mutex lock, unlock, etc
 #include "../../convenient.h"
```

```
[ ... ]
-#define OURMODNAME "miscdrv_rdwr"
+#define OURMODNAME "miscdrv_rdwr_mutexlock"

+DEFINE_MUTEX(lock1); // this mutex lock is meant to protect the integers
ga and gb
[ ... ]
+       struct mutex lock; // this mutex protects this data structure
 };
[ ... ]
```

Here, we can see that in the newer safe version of the driver, we have declared and initialized a mutex variable called `lock1`; we shall use it to protect the (just for demonstration purposes) two global integers, `ga` and `gb`, within our driver. Next, importantly, we declared a mutex lock named `lock` within the "driver context" data structure; that is, `drv_ctx`. This will be used to protect any and all access to members of that data structure. It is initialized within the `init` code:

```
+       mutex_init(&ctx->lock);
+
+       /* Initialize the "secret" value :-) */
        strscpy(ctx->oursecret, "initmsg", 8);
-       dev_dbg(ctx->dev, "A sample print via the dev_dbg(): driver
initialized\n");
+       /* Why don't we protect the above strscpy() with the mutex lock?
+        * It's working on shared writable data, yes?
+        * Yes, BUT this is the init code; it's guaranteed to run in exactly
+        * one context (typically the insmod(8) process), thus there is
+        * no concurrency possible here. The same goes for the cleanup
+        * code path.
+        */
```

This detailed comment clearly explains why we don't need to lock/unlock around `strscpy()`. Again, this should be obvious, but local variables are implicitly private to each process context (as they reside in that process or thread's kernel mode stack) and therefore require no protection (each thread/process has a separate *instance* of the variable, so no one steps on anyone's toes!). Before we forget, the *cleanup* code path (which is invoked via the `rmmod(8)` process context), must destroy the mutexes:

```
-static void __exit miscdrv_rdwr_exit(void)
+static void __exit miscdrv_exit_mutexlock(void)
 {
+       mutex_destroy(&lock1);
+       mutex_destroy(&ctx->lock);
        misc_deregister(&llkd_miscdev);
 }
```

Now, let's look at the diff of the driver's open method:

```
+
+       mutex_lock(&lock1);
+       ga++; gb--;
+       mutex_unlock(&lock1);
+
+       dev_info(dev, " filename: \"%s\"\n"
        [ ... ]
```

This is where we manipulated the global integers, *making this a critical section*; unlike the previous version of this program, here, we *do protect this critical section* with the `lock1` mutex. So, there it is: the critical section here is the code `ga++; gb--;`: the code between the (mutex) lock and unlock operations.

But (there's always a but, isn't there?), all is not well! Take a look at the `printk` function (`dev_info()`) following the `mutex_unlock()` line of code:

```
+ dev_info(dev, " filename: \"%s\"\n"
+           " wrt open file: f_flags = 0x%x\n"
+           " ga = %d, gb = %d\n",
+           filp->f_path.dentry->d_iname, filp->f_flags, ga, gb);
```

Does this look okay to you? No, look carefully: we are *reading* the value of the global integers, `ga` and `gb`. Recall the fundamentals: in the presence of concurrency (which is certainly a possibility here in this driver's *open* method), *even reading shared writeable data without the lock is potentially unsafe*. If this doesn't make sense to you, please think: what if, while one thread is reading the integers, another is simultaneously updating (writing) them; what then? This kind of situation is called a **dirty read** (or a **torn read**); we might end up reading stale data and must be protected against. (The fact is that this isn't really a great example of a dirty read as, on most processors, reading and writing single integer items does tend to be an atomic operation. However, we must not assume such things – we must simply do our job and protect it.)

In fact, there's another similar bug-in-waiting: we have read data from the open file structure (the `filp` pointer) without bothering to protect it (indeed, the open file structure has a lock; we're supposed to use it! We shall do so later).

 The precise semantics of how and when things such as *dirty reads* occur does tend to be very arch (machine)-dependent; nevertheless, our job as module or driver authors is clear: we must ensure that we protect all critical sections. This includes reads upon shared writable data.

For now, we shall just flag these as potential errors (bugs). We will take care of this in the *Using the atomic integer operators* section, in a more performance-friendly manner. Looking at the diff of the driver's read method reveals something interesting (ignore the line numbers shown here; they might change):

```
 static ssize_t read_miscdrv_rdwr(struct file *filp, char __user *ubuf,
-                size_t count, loff_t *off)
+                size_t count, loff_t *off)
 {
-    int ret = count, secret_len = strnlen(ctx->oursecret, MAXBYTES);
+    int ret = count, secret_len;
     struct device *dev = ctx->dev;

+    mutex_lock(&ctx->lock);
+    secret_len = strlen(ctx->oursecret);
+    mutex_unlock(&ctx->lock);
+
     PRINT_CTX();
     dev_info(dev, "%s wants to read (upto) %zd bytes\n", current->comm, count);

@@ -134,17 +140,20 @@
     * member to userspace.
     */
     ret = -EFAULT;
+    mutex_lock(&ctx->lock);
     if (copy_to_user(ubuf, ctx->oursecret, secret_len)) {
         dev_warn(dev, "copy_to_user() failed\n");
-        goto out_notok;
+        goto out_ctu;
     }
     ret = secret_len;

     // Update stats
-    ctx->tx += secret_len;   // our 'transmit' is wrt this driver
+    ctx->tx += secret_len;   // our 'transmit' is wrt this driver
     dev_info(dev, " %d bytes read, returning... (stats: tx=%d, rx=%d)\n",
-        secret_len, ctx->tx, ctx->rx);
- out_notok:
+            secret_len, ctx->tx, ctx->rx);
+out_ctu:
+    mutex_unlock(&ctx->lock);
+out_notok:
     return ret;
```

Figure 6.7 – The diff of the driver's read() method: see the usage of the mutex lock in the newer version

We have now used the driver context structure's mutex lock to protect the critical sections. The same goes for both the *write* and *close* (release) methods of the device driver (generate the patch for yourself and take a look).

Note that the user mode app remains unchanged, which means for us to test the new safer version, we must continue using the user mode app at `ch12/miscdrv_rdwr/rdwr_drv_secret.c`. Running and testing code such as this driver code on a debug kernel, which contains various locking errors and deadlock detection capabilities, is crucial (we'll return to these "debug" capabilities in the next chapter, in the *Lock debugging within the kernel* section).

In the preceding code, we took the mutex lock just before the `copy_to_user()` routine; that's fine. However, we only release it after `dev_info()`. Why not release it before this `printk`, thus shortening the critical section?

A closer look at `dev_info()` reveals why it's *within* the critical section. We are printing the values of three variables here: the number of bytes read by `secret_len` and the number of bytes that are "transmitted" and "received" by `ctx->tx` and `ctx->rx`, respectively. `secret_len` is a local variable and does not require protection, but the other two variables are within the global driver context structure and thus do require protection, even from (possibly dirty) reads.

The mutex lock – a few remaining points

In this section, we will cover a few additional points regarding mutexes.

Mutex lock API variants

First, let's take a look at a few variants of the mutex lock API; besides the interruptible variant (described in the *Mutex lock – via [un]interruptible sleep?* section), we have the *trylock*, *killable*, and *io* variants.

The mutex trylock variant

What if you would like to implement a **busy-wait** semantic; that is, test for the availability of the (mutex) lock and, if available (meaning it's currently unlocked), acquire/lock it and continue with the critical section code path? If this is not available (it's currently in the locked state), do not wait for the lock; instead, perform some other work and retry. In effect, this is a non-blocking mutex lock variant and is called the trylock; the following flowchart shows how it works:

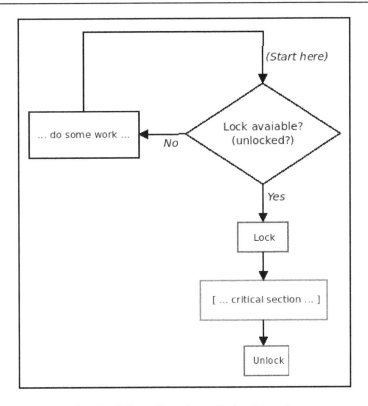

Figure 6.8 – The "busy wait" semantic, a non-blocking trylock operation

The API for this trylock variant of the mutex lock is as follows:

```
int mutex_trylock(struct mutex *lock);
```

This API's return value signifies what transpired at runtime:

- A return value of 1 indicates that the lock has been successfully acquired.
- A return value of 0 indicates that the lock is currently contended (locked).

Though it might sound tempting to, do *not* attempt to use the `mutex_trylock()` API to figure out if a mutex lock is in a locked or unlocked state; this is inherently "racy". Next, note that using this trylock variant in a highly contended lock path may well reduce your chances of acquiring the lock. The trylock variant has been traditionally used in deadlock prevention code that might need to back out of a certain lock order sequence and be retried via another sequence (ordering).

Also, with respect to the trylock variant, even though the literature uses the term *try and acquire the mutex atomically*, it does not work in an atomic or interrupt context – it *only* works in the process context (as with any type of mutex lock). As usual, the lock must be released by `mutex_unlock()` being invoked by the owner context.

I suggest that you try working on the trylock mutex variant as an exercise. See the *Questions* section at the end of this chapter for an assignment!

The mutex interruptible and killable variants

As you have already learned, the `mutex_lock_interruptible()` API is used when the driver (or module) is willing to acknowledge any (user space) signal interrupting it (and returns `-ERESTARTSYS` to tell the kernel VFS layer to perform signal handling; the user space system call will fail with `errno` set to `EINTR`). An example can be found in the module handling code in the kernel, within the `delete_module(2)` system call (which `rmmod(8)` invokes):

```
// kernel/module.c
[ ... ]
SYSCALL_DEFINE2(delete_module, const char __user *, name_user,
        unsigned int, flags)
{
    struct module *mod;
    [ ... ]
    if (!capable(CAP_SYS_MODULE) || modules_disabled)
        return -EPERM;
    [ ... ]
    if (mutex_lock_interruptible(&module_mutex) != 0)
        return -EINTR;
    mod = find_module(name);
    [ ... ]
out:
    mutex_unlock(&module_mutex);
    return ret;
}
```

Notice how the API returns `-EINTR` on failure. (The `SYSCALL_DEFINEn()` macro becomes a system call signature; n signifies the number of parameters this particular system call accepts. Also, notice the capability check – unless you are running as root or have the `CAP_SYS_MODULE` capability (or module loading is completely disabled), the system call just returns a failure (`-EPERM`).)

If, however, your driver is only willing to be interrupted by fatal signals (those that *will kill* the user space context), then use the `mutex_lock_killable()` API (the signature is identical to that of the interruptible variant).

The mutex io variant

The `mutex_lock_io()` API is identical in syntax to the `mutex_lock()` API; the only difference is that the kernel thinks that the wait time of the loser thread(s) is the same as waiting for I/O (the code comment in `kernel/locking/mutex.c:mutex_lock_io()` clearly documents this; take a look). This can matter accounting-wise.

 You can find fairly exotic APIs such as `mutex_lock[_interruptible]_nested()` within the kernel, with the emphasis here being on the `nested` suffix. However, note that the Linux kernel does not prefer developers to use nested (or recursive) locking (as we mentioned in the *Correctly using the mutex lock* section). Also, these APIs only get compiled in the presence of the `CONFIG_DEBUG_LOCK_ALLOC` config option; in effect, the nested APIs were added to support the kernel lock validator mechanism. They should only be used in special circumstances (where a nesting level must be incorporated between instances of the same lock type).

In the next section, we will answer a typical FAQ: what's the difference between the mutex and semaphore objects? Does Linux even have a semaphore object? Read on to find out!

The semaphore and the mutex

The Linux kernel does provide a semaphore object, along with the usual operations you can perform on a (binary) semaphore:

- A semaphore lock acquire via the `down[_interruptible]()` (and variations) APIs
- A semaphore unlock via the `up()` API.

 In general, the semaphore is an older implementation, so it's advised that you use the mutex lock in place of it.

An FAQ worth looking at, though, is this: *what is the difference between a mutex and a semaphore?* They appear to be conceptually similar, but are actually quite different:

- A semaphore is a more generalized form of a mutex; a mutex lock can be acquired (and subsequently released or unlocked) exactly once, while a semaphore can be acquired (and subsequently released) multiple times.
- A mutex is used to protect a critical section from simultaneous access, while a semaphore should be used as a mechanism to signal another waiting task that a certain milestone has been reached (typically, a producer task posts a signal via the semaphore object, which a consumer task is waiting to receive, in order to continue with further work).
- A mutex has the notion of ownership of the lock and only the owner context can perform the unlock; there is no ownership for a binary semaphore.

Priority inversion and the RT-mutex

A word of caution when using any kind of locking is that you should carefully design and code to prevent the dreaded *deadlock* scenarios that could arise (more on this in the next chapter in the *The lock validator lockdep – catch locking issues early* section).

Aside from deadlocks, there is another risky scenario that arises when using the mutex: that of priority inversion (again, we will not delve into the details in this book). Suffice it to say that the unbounded **priority inversion** case can be a deadly one; the end result is that the product's high(est) priority thread is kept off the CPU for too long.

 As I covered in some detail in my earlier book, *Hands-on System Programming with Linux*, it's precisely this priority inversion issue that struck NASA's Mars Pathfinder robot, on the Martian surface no less, back in July 1997! See the *Further reading* section of this chapter for interesting resources about this, something that every software developer should be aware of!

The userspace Pthreads mutex implementation certainly has **priority inheritance (PI)** semantics available. But what about within the Linux kernel? For this, Ingo Molnar provided the PI-futex-based RT-mutex (a real-time mutex; in effect, a mutex extended to have PI capabilities. futex(2) is a sophisticated system call that provides a fast userspace mutex). These become available when the CONFIG_RT_MUTEXES config option is enabled. Quite similar to the "regular" mutex semantics, RT-mutex APIs are provided to initialize, (un)lock, and destroy the RT-mutex object. (This code has been merged into the mainline kernel from Ingo Molnar's -rt tree). As far as actual usage is concerned, the RT-mutex is used for internally implementing the PI futex (the futex(2) system call itself internally implements the userspace Pthreads mutex). Besides this, the kernel locking self-test code and the I2C subsystem uses the RT-mutex directly.

Thus, for a typical module (or driver) author, these APIs are not going to be used very frequently. The kernel does provide some documentation on the internal design of the RT-mutex at https://www.kernel.org/doc/Documentation/locking/rt-mutex-design. rst (covering priority inversion, priority inheritance, and more).

Internal design

A word on the reality of the internal implementation of the mutex lock deep within the kernel fabric: Linux tries to implement a *fast path* approach when possible.

 A **fast path** is the most optimized high-performance type of code path; for example, one with no locks and no blocking. The intent is to have code follow this fast path as far as possible. Only when it really isn't possible does the kernel fall back to a (possible) "mid path", and then a "slow path", approach; it still works but is slow(er).

This fast path is taken in the absence of contention for the lock (that is, the lock is in an unlocked state to begin with). So, the lock is locked with no fuss, pretty much immediately. If, however, the mutex is already locked, then the kernel typically uses a mid path optimistic spinning implementation, making it more of a hybrid (mutex/spinlock) lock type. If even this isn't possible, the "slow path" is followed – the process context attempting to get the lock may well enter the sleep state. If you're interested in its internal implementation, more details can be found within the official kernel documentation: https://www.kernel.org/doc/Documentation/locking/mutex-design.rst.

LDV (Linux Driver Verification) project: in the companion guide *Linux Kernel Programming - Chapter 1, Kernel Workspace Setup*, in the section *The LDV – Linux Driver Verification – project*, we mentioned that this project has useful "rules" with respect to various programming aspects of Linux modules (drivers, mostly) as well as the core kernel.

With regard to our current topic, here's one of the rules: *Locking a mutex twice or unlocking without prior locking* (`http://linuxtesting.org/ldv/online?action=show_rulerule_id=0032`). It mentions the kind of things you cannot do with the mutex lock (we have already covered this in the *Correctly using the mutex lock* section). The interesting thing here: you can see an actual example of a bug – a mutex lock double-acquire attempt, leading to (self) deadlock – in a kernel driver (as well as the subsequent fix).

Now that you've understood how to use the mutex lock, let's move on and look at the other very common lock within the kernel – the spinlock.

Using the spinlock

In the *Mutex or spinlock? Which to use when* section, you learned when to use the spinlock instead of the mutex lock and vice versa. For convenience, we have reproduced the key statements we provided previously here:

- **Is the critical section running in an atomic (interrupt) context or in a process context where it cannot sleep?** Use the spinlock.
- **Is the critical section running in a process context and sleep in the critical section is necessary?** Use the mutex lock.

In this section, we shall consider that you've now decided to use the spinlock.

Spinlock – simple usage

For all the spinlock APIs, you must include the relevant header file; that is, `include <linux/spinlock.h>`.

Similar to the mutex lock, you *must* declare and initialize the spinlock to the unlocked state before use. The spinlock is an "object" that's declared via the `typedef` data type named `spinlock_t` (internally, it's a structure defined in `include/linux/spinlock_types.h`). It can be initialized dynamically via the `spin_lock_init()` macro:

```
spinlock_t lock;
spin_lock_init(&lock);
```

Alternatively, this can be performed statically (declared and initialized) with `DEFINE_SPINLOCK(lock);`.

As with the mutex, declaring a spinlock within the (global/static) data structure is meant to protect against concurrent access, and is typically a very good idea. As we mentioned earlier, this very idea is made use of within the kernel often; as an example, the data structure representing an open file on the Linux kernel is called `struct file`:

```
// include/linux/fs.h
struct file {
    [...]
    struct path f_path;
    struct inode *f_inode; /* cached value */
    const struct file_operations *f_op;
    /*
     * Protects f_ep_links, f_flags.
     * Must not be taken from IRQ context.
     */
    spinlock_t f_lock;
    [...]
    struct mutex f_pos_lock;
    loff_t f_pos;
    [...]
```

Check it out: for the `file` structure, the spinlock variable named `f_lock` is the spinlock that protects the `f_ep_links` and `f_flags` members of the `file` data structure (it also has a mutex lock to protect another member; that is, the file's current seek position – `f_pos`).

How do you actually lock and unlock the spinlock? There are quite a few variations on the API that are exposed by the kernel to us module/driver authors; the simplest form of the spin(un)lock APIs are as follows:

```
void spin_lock(spinlock_t *lock);
<< ... critical section ... >>
void spin_unlock(spinlock_t *lock);
```

Note that there is no spinlock equivalent of the `mutex_destroy()` API.

Now, let's see the spinlock APIs in action!

Spinlock – an example driver

Similar to what we did with our mutex locking sample driver (the *Mutex locking – an example driver* section), to illustrate the simple usage of a spinlock, we shall make a copy of our earlier `ch12/1_miscdrv_rdwr_mutexlock` driver as a starting template and then place it in a new kernel driver; that is, `ch12/2_miscdrv_rdwr_spinlock`. Again, here, we'll only show small parts of the diff (the differences, the delta generated by `diff(1)`) between that program and this one (we won't show every line of the diff, only the relevant portions):

```
// location: ch12/2_miscdrv_rdwr_spinlock/
+#include <linux/spinlock.h>
[ ... ]
-#define OURMODNAME "miscdrv_rdwr_mutexlock"
+#define OURMODNAME "miscdrv_rdwr_spinlock"
[ ... ]
static int ga, gb = 1;
-DEFINE_MUTEX(lock1); // this mutex lock is meant to protect the integers
ga and gb
+DEFINE_SPINLOCK(lock1); // this spinlock protects the global integers ga
and gb
[ ... ]
+/* The driver 'context' data structure;
+ * all relevant 'state info' reg the driver is here.
  */
 struct drv_ctx {
    struct device *dev;
@@ -63,10 +66,22 @@
    u64 config3;
 #define MAXBYTES 128
    char oursecret[MAXBYTES];
- struct mutex lock; // this mutex protects this data structure
+ struct mutex mutex; // this mutex protects this data structure
+ spinlock_t spinlock; // ...so does this spinlock
 };
 static struct drv_ctx *ctx;
```

This time, to protect the members of our `drv_ctx` global data structure, we have both the original mutex lock and a new spinlock. This is quite common; the mutex lock protects member usage in a critical section where blocking can occur, while the spinlock is used to protect members in critical sections where blocking (sleeping – recall that it might sleep) cannot occur.

Of course, we must ensure that we initialize all the locks so that they're in the unlocked state. We can do this in the driver's `init` code (continuing with the patch output):

```
-     mutex_init(&ctx->lock);
+     mutex_init(&ctx->mutex);
+     spin_lock_init(&ctx->spinlock);
```

In the driver's `open` method, we replace the mutex lock with the spinlock to protect the increments and decrements of the global integers:

```
  * open_miscdrv_rdwr()
@@ -82,14 +97,15 @@

      PRINT_CTX(); // displays process (or intr) context info

-     mutex_lock(&lock1);
+     spin_lock(&lock1);
      ga++; gb--;
-     mutex_unlock(&lock1);
+     spin_unlock(&lock1);
```

Now, within the driver's `read` method, we use the spinlock instead of the mutex to protect some critical sections:

```
  static ssize_t read_miscdrv_rdwr(struct file *filp, char __user *ubuf,
  size_t count, loff_t  *off)
  {
-     int ret = count, secret_len;
+     int ret = count, secret_len, err_path = 0;
      struct device *dev = ctx->dev;

-     mutex_lock(&ctx->lock);
+     spin_lock(&ctx->spinlock);
      secret_len = strlen(ctx->oursecret);
-     mutex_unlock(&ctx->lock);
+     spin_unlock(&ctx->spinlock);
```

However, that's not all! Continuing with the driver's `read` method, carefully take a look at the following code and comment:

```
[ ... ]
@@ -139,20 +157,28 @@
     * member to userspace.
     */
    ret = -EFAULT;
-   mutex_lock(&ctx->lock);
+   mutex_lock(&ctx->mutex);
+   /* Why don't we just use the spinlock??
+    * Because - VERY IMP! - remember that the spinlock can only be used
when
+    * the critical section will not sleep or block in any manner; here,
+    * the critical section invokes the copy_to_user(); it very much can
+    * cause a 'sleep' (a schedule()) to occur.
+    */
    if (copy_to_user(ubuf, ctx->oursecret, secret_len)) {
[ ... ]
```

When protecting data where the critical section has possibly blocking APIs – such as in `copy_to_user()` – we *must* only use a mutex lock! (Due to lack of space, we haven't displayed more of the code diff here; we expect you to read through the spinlock sample driver code and try it out for yourself.)

Test – sleep in an atomic context

You have already learned that the one thing we should *not do is sleep (block) in any kind of atomic or interrupt context*. Let's put this to the test. As always, the empirical approach – where you test things for yourself rather than relying on other's experiences – is key!

How exactly can we test this? Easy: we shall use a simple integer module parameter, `buggy`, that, when set to `1` (the default value being `0`), executes a code path within our spinlock's critical section that violates this rule. We shall invoke the `schedule_timeout()` API (which, as you learned in Chapter 5, *Working with Kernel Timers, Threads, and Workqueues*, in the *Understanding how to use the *sleep() blocking APIs* section) internally invokes `schedule()`; it's how we go to sleep in the kernel space). Here's the relevant code:

```
// ch12/2_miscdrv_rdwr_spinlock/2_miscdrv_rdwr_spinlock.c
[ ... ]
static int buggy;
module_param(buggy, int, 0600);
MODULE_PARM_DESC(buggy,
```

```
"If 1, cause an error by issuing a blocking call within a spinlock critical
section");
[ ... ]
static ssize_t write_miscdrv_rdwr(struct file *filp, const char __user
*ubuf,
                size_t count, loff_t *off)
{
    int ret, err_path = 0;
    [ ... ]
    spin_lock(&ctx->spinlock);
    strscpy(ctx->oursecret, kbuf, (count > MAXBYTES ? MAXBYTES : count));
    [ ... ]
    if (1 == buggy) {
        /* We're still holding the spinlock! */
        set_current_state(TASK_INTERRUPTIBLE);
        schedule_timeout(1*HZ); /* ... and this is a blocking call!
                * Congratulations! you've just engineered a bug */
    }
    spin_unlock(&ctx->spinlock);
    [ ... ]
}
```

Now, for the interesting part: let's test this (buggy) code path in two kernels: first, in our custom 5.4 "debug" kernel (the kernel where we have enabled several kernel debug configuration options (mostly from the Kernel Hacking menu in make menuconfig), as explained in the companion guide *Linux Kernel Programming - Chapter 5, Writing Your First Kernel Module – LKMs Part 2*), and second, on a generic distro (we usually run on Ubuntu) 5.4 kernel without any relevant kernel debug options enabled.

Testing on a 5.4 debug kernel

First of all, ensure you've built the custom 5.4 kernel and that all the required kernel debug config options enabled (again, look back to the companion guide *Linux Kernel Programming - Chapter 5, Writing Your First Kernel Module – LKMs Part 2*, the *Configuring a debug kernel* section if you need to). Then, boot off your debug kernel (here, it's named 5.4.0-llkd-dbg). Now, build the driver (in ch12/2_miscdrv_rdwr_spinlock/) against this debug kernel (the usual make within the driver's directory should do this; you might find that, on the debug kernel, the build is noticeably slower!):

```
$ lsb_release -a 2>/dev/null | grep "^Description" ; uname -r
Description: Ubuntu 20.04.1 LTS
5.4.0-llkd-dbg
$ make
[ ... ]
$ modinfo ./miscdrv_rdwr_spinlock.ko
```

```
filename:
/home/llkd/llkd_src/ch12/2_miscdrv_rdwr_spinlock/./miscdrv_rdwr_spinlock.ko
[ ... ]
description: LLKD book:ch12/2_miscdrv_rdwr_spinlock: simple misc char
driver rewritten with spinlocks
[ ... ]
parm: buggy:If 1, cause an error by issuing a blocking call within a
spinlock critical section (int)
$ sudo virt-what
virtualbox
kvm
$
```

As you can see, we're running our custom 5.4.0 "debug" kernel on our x86_64 Ubuntu 20.04 guest VM.

> How do you know whether you're running on a **virtual machine** (**VM**) or on the "bare metal" (native) system? virt-what (1) is a useful little script that shows this (you can install it on Ubuntu with sudo apt install virt-what).

To run our test case, insert the driver into the kernel and set the buggy module parameter to 1. Invoking the driver's read method (via our user space app; that is, ch12/miscdrv_rdwr/rdwr_test_secret) isn't an issue, as shown here:

```
$ sudo dmesg -C
$ sudo insmod ./miscdrv_rdwr_spinlock.ko buggy=1
$ ../../ch12/miscdrv_rdwr/rdwr_test_secret
Usage: ../../ch12/miscdrv_rdwr/rdwr_test_secret opt=read/write device_file
["secret-msg"]
 opt = 'r' => we shall issue the read(2), retrieving the 'secret' form the
driver
 opt = 'w' => we shall issue the write(2), writing the secret message
<secret-msg>
   (max 128 bytes)
$
$ ../../ch12/miscdrv_rdwr/rdwr_test_secret r
/dev/llkd_miscdrv_rdwr_spinlock
Device file /dev/llkd_miscdrv_rdwr_spinlock opened (in read-only mode):
fd=3
../../ch12/miscdrv_rdwr/rdwr_test_secret: read 7 bytes from
/dev/llkd_miscdrv_rdwr_spinlock
The 'secret' is:
 "initmsg"
$
```

Next, we issue a `write(2)` to the driver via the user mode app; this time, our buggy code path gets executed. As you saw, we issued a `schedule_timeout()` within a spinlock critical section (that is, between the lock and unlock). The debug kernel detects this as a bug and spawns (impressively large) debug diagnostics into the kernel log (note that bugs like this can quite possibly hang your system, so test this on a VM first):

```
[28853.172825] miscdrv_rdwr_spinlock:write_miscdrv_rdwr(): 004)  rdwr_test_secre :23578   |  ...0   /* write_mi
scdrv_rdwr() */
[28853.178231] misc llkd_miscdrv_rdwr_spinlock: rdwr_test_secre wants to write 24 bytes
[28853.181539] misc llkd_miscdrv_rdwr_spinlock:  24 bytes written, returning... (stats: tx=7, rx=24)
[28853.184243] BUG: scheduling while atomic: rdwr_test_secre/23578/0x00000002
[28853.187489] 1 lock held by rdwr_test_secre/23578:
[28853.189904]  #0: ffff8880285c2d60 (&(&ctx->spinlock)->rlock){+.+.}, at: write_miscdrv_rdwr.cold+0xde/0x247 [
miscdrv_rdwr_spinlock]
[28853.195078] Modules linked in: miscdrv_rdwr_spinlock(OE) vboxsf(OE) vboxvideo(OE) crct10dif_pclmul crc32_pcl
mul ghash_clmulni_intel vmwgfx snd_intel8x0 snd_ac97_codec ac97_bus snd_pcm aesni_intel glue_helper crypto_simd
 cryptd joydev snd_seq snd_timer drm_kms_helper snd_seq_device input_leds serio_raw snd syscopyarea sysfillrect
 sysimgblt fb_sys_fops ttm video mac_hid vboxguest(OE) soundcore drm sch_fq_codel parport_pc ppdev lp parport i
p_tables x_tables autofs4 hid_generic usbhid hid psmouse e1000 ahci libahci i2c_piix4 pata_acpi [last unloaded:
 miscdrv_rdwr_spinlock]
[28853.211613] CPU: 4 PID: 23578 Comm: rdwr_test_secre Tainted: G           OE     5.4.0-llkd-dbg #2
[28853.214596] Hardware name: innotek GmbH VirtualBox/VirtualBox, BIOS VirtualBox 12/01/2006
[28853.217244] Call Trace:
[28853.219461]  dump_stack+0xc2/0x11a
[28853.221692]  __schedule_bug.cold+0x2b/0x3c
[28853.223893]  __schedule+0xd4d/0x1090
[28853.226207]  ? firmware_map_remove+0xe9/0xe9
[28853.228428]  ? _raw_spin_unlock_irqrestore+0x51/0x60
[28853.230741]  ? schedule_timeout+0x2b4/0x8c0
[28853.232891]  ? lockdep_hardirqs_on+0x1a2/0x280
[28853.235050]  schedule+0x75/0x140
[28853.237118]  schedule_timeout+0x2b9/0x8c0
[28853.239207]  ? __dev_printk+0xd6/0xf3
[28853.241276]  ? usleep_range+0x100/0x100
[28853.243310]  ? _dev_info+0xcd/0xfb
[28853.245421]  ? __next_timer_interrupt+0xe0/0xe0
[28853.247475]  write_miscdrv_rdwr.cold+0x1ea/0x247 [miscdrv_rdwr_spinlock]
[28853.249726]  ? display_stats+0x80/0x80 [miscdrv_rdwr_spinlock]
[28853.251802]  ? apparmor_file_permission+0x1a/0x20
[28853.253814]  ? security_file_permission+0x65/0x190
[28853.255871]  __vfs_write+0x4f/0x90
[28853.257885]  vfs_write+0x14b/0x2d0
[28853.259744]  ksys_write+0xd9/0x180
[28853.261612]  ? __ia32_sys_read+0x50/0x50
[28853.263388]  ? mark_held_locks+0x29/0xb0
[28853.265119]  ? do_syscall_64+0x19/0x2c0
[28853.266842]  ? entry_SYSCALL_64_after_hwframe+0x49/0xbe
```

Figure 6.9 – Kernel diagnostics being triggered by the "scheduling in atomic context" bug we've deliberately hit here

The preceding screenshot shows part of what transpired (follow along while viewing the driver code in ch12/2_miscdrv_rdwr_spinlock/2_miscdrv_rdwr_spinlock.c):

1. First, we have our user mode app's process context (rdwr_test_secre; notice how the name is truncated to the first 16 characters, including the NULL byte), which enters the driver's write method; that is, write_miscdrv_rdwr(). This can be seen in the output of our useful PRINT_CTX() macro (we've reproduced this line here):

   ```
   miscdrv_rdwr_spinlock:write_miscdrv_rdwr(): 004) rdwr_test_secre
   :23578 | ...0 /*  write_miscdrv_rdwr() */
   ```

2. It copies in the new 'secret' from the user space writer process and writes it, for 24 bytes.
3. It then "takes" the spinlock, enters the critical section, and copies this data to the oursecret member of our driver's context structure.
4. After this, if (1 == buggy) { evaluates to true.
5. Then, it calls schedule_timeout(), which is a blocking API (as it internally calls schedule()), triggering the bug, which is helpfully highlighted in red:

   ```
   BUG: scheduling while atomic: rdwr_test_secre/23578/0x00000002
   ```

6. The kernel now dumps a good deal of the diagnostic output. Among the first things to be dumped is the **call stack**.

The call stack or stack backtrace (or "call trace") of the kernel mode stack of the process – here, it's our user space app, rdwr_drv_secret, which is running our (buggy) driver's code in the process context – can be clearly seen in *Figure 6.9*. Each line after the Call Trace: header is essentially a call frame on the kernel stack.

As a tip, ignore the stack frames that begin with the ? symbol; they are literally questionable call frames, in all likelihood "leftovers" from previous stack usage in the same memory region. It's worth taking a small memory-related diversion here: this is how stack allocation really works; stack memory isn't allocated and freed on a per-call frame basis as that would be frightfully expensive. Only when a stack memory page is exhausted is a new one automatically *faulted in*! (Recall our discussions in the companion guide *Linux Kernel Programming - Chapter 9, Kernel Memory Allocation for Module Authors – Part 2*, in the *A brief note on memory allocations and demand paging* section.) So, the reality is that, as code calls and returns from functions, the same stack memory page(s) tend to keep getting reused.

Not only that, but for performance reasons, the memory isn't wiped each time, leading to leftovers from previous frames often appearing. (They can literally "spoil" the picture. However, fortunately, the modern stack call frame tracing algorithms are usually able to do a superb job in figuring out the correct stack trace.)

Following the stack trace bottom-up (*always read it bottom-up*), we can see that, as expected, our user space `write(2)` system call (it often shows up as (something like) `SyS_write` or, on the x86, as `__x64_sys_write`, though not visible in *Figure 6.9*) invokes the kernel's VFS layer code (you can see `vfs_write()` here, which calls `__vfs_write()`), which further invokes our driver's write method; that is, `write_miscdrv_rdwr()`! This code, as we well know, invokes the buggy code path where we call `schedule_timeout()`, which, in turn, invokes `schedule()` (and `__schedule()`), causing the whole `BUG: scheduling while atomic` bug to trigger.

The format of the `scheduling while atomic` code path is retrieved from the following line of code, which can be found in `kernel/sched/core.c`:

```
printk(KERN_ERR "BUG: scheduling while atomic: %s/%d/0x%08x\n", prev->comm,
prev->pid, preempt_count());
```

Interesting! Here, you can see that it printed the following string:

```
BUG: scheduling while atomic: rdwr_test_secre/23578/0x00000002
```

After `atomic:`, it prints the process name – the PID – and then invokes the `preempt_count()` inline function, which prints the *preempt depth*; the preempt depth is a counter that's incremented every time a lock is taken and decremented on every unlock. So, if it's positive, this implies that the code is within a critical or atomic section; here, it shows as the value 2.

Note that this bug gets neatly served up during this test run precisely because the `CONFIG_DEBUG_ATOMIC_SLEEP` debug kernel config option is turned on. It's on because we're running a custom "debug kernel" (kernel version 5.4.0)! The config option details (you can interactively find and set this option in `make menuconfig`, under the `Kernel Hacking` menu) are as follows:

```
// lib/Kconfig.debug
[ ... ]
config DEBUG_ATOMIC_SLEEP
    bool "Sleep inside atomic section checking"
    select PREEMPT_COUNT
    depends on DEBUG_KERNEL
    depends on !ARCH_NO_PREEMPT
    help
```

```
     If you say Y here, various routines which may sleep will become very
noisy if they are called inside atomic sections: when a spinlock is
held, inside an rcu read side critical section, inside preempt disabled
sections, inside an interrupt, etc...
```

Testing on a 5.4 non-debug distro kernel

As a contrasting test, we will now perform the very same thing on our Ubuntu 20.04 LTS VM, which we'll boot via its default generic 'distro' 5.4 Linux kernel that is typically *not configured as a 'debug' kernel* (here, the CONFIG_DEBUG_ATOMIC_SLEEP kernel config option hasn't been set).

First, we insert our (buggy) driver. Then, when we run our rdwr_drv_secret process in order to write the new secret to the driver, the buggy code path gets executed. However, this time, the kernel *does not crash, nor does it report any issues at all* (looking at the dmesg(1) output validates this):

```
$ uname -r
5.4.0-56-generic
$ sudo insmod ./miscdrv_rdwr_spinlock.ko buggy=1
$ ../../ch12/miscdrv_rdwr/rdwr_test_secret w
/dev/llkd_miscdrv_rdwr_spinlock "passwdcosts500bucksdude"
Device file /dev/llkd_miscdrv_rdwr_spinlock opened (in write-only mode):
fd=3
../../ch12/miscdrv_rdwr/rdwr_test_secret: wrote 24 bytes to
/dev/llkd_miscdrv_rdwr_spinlock
$ dmesg
[ ... ]
[ 65.420017] miscdrv_rdwr_spinlock:miscdrv_init_spinlock(): LLKD misc
driver (major # 10) registered, minor# = 56, dev node is
/dev/llkd_miscdrv_rdwr
[ 81.665077] miscdrv_rdwr_spinlock:miscdrv_exit_spinlock():
miscdrv_rdwr_spinlock: LLKD misc driver deregistered, bye
[ 86.798720] miscdrv_rdwr_spinlock:miscdrv_init_spinlock(): VERMAGIC_STRING
= 5.4.0-56-generic SMP mod_unload
[ 86.799890] miscdrv_rdwr_spinlock:miscdrv_init_spinlock(): LLKD misc
driver (major # 10) registered, minor# = 56, dev node is
/dev/llkd_miscdrv_rdwr
[ 130.214238] misc llkd_miscdrv_rdwr_spinlock: filename:
"llkd_miscdrv_rdwr_spinlock"
                wrt open file: f_flags = 0x8001
                ga = 1, gb = 0
```

```
[ 130.219233] misc llkd_miscdrv_rdwr_spinlock: stats: tx=0, rx=0
[ 130.219680] misc llkd_miscdrv_rdwr_spinlock: rdwr_test_secre wants to
write 24 bytes
[ 130.220329] misc llkd_miscdrv_rdwr_spinlock: 24 bytes written,
returning... (stats: tx=0, rx=24)
[ 131.249639] misc llkd_miscdrv_rdwr_spinlock: filename:
"llkd_miscdrv_rdwr_spinlock"
                ga = 0,  gb = 1
[ 131.253511] misc llkd_miscdrv_rdwr_spinlock: stats: tx=0, rx=24
$
```

We know that our write method has a deadly bug, yet it doesn't seem to fail in any manner! This is really bad; it's this kind of thing that can erroneously lead you to conclude that your code is just fine when there's actually a nasty bug silently lying in wait to pounce one fine day!

To help us investigate what exactly is going on under the hood, let's run our test app (the `rdwr_drv_secret` process) once more, but this time via the powerful `trace-cmd(1)` tool (a very useful wrapper over the Ftrace kernel infrastructure; the following is its truncated output:

The Linux kernel's **Ftrace** infrastructure is the kernel's primary tracing infrastructure; it provides a detailed trace of pretty much every function that's been executed in the kernel space. Here, we are leveraging Ftrace via a convenient frontend: the `trace-cmd(1)` utility. These are indeed very powerful and useful debug tools; we've mentioned several others in the companion guide *Linux Kernel Programming - Chapter 1, Kernel Workspace Setup*, but unfortunately, the details are beyond the scope of this book. Check out the man pages to learn more.

```
$ sudo trace-cmd record -p function_graph -F
../../ch12/miscdrv_rdwr/rdwr_test_secret w /dev/llkd_miscdrv_rdwr_spinlock
"passwdcosts500bucks"
$ sudo trace-cmd report -I -S -l > report.txt
$ sudo less report.txt
[ ... ]
```

The output can be seen in the following screenshot:

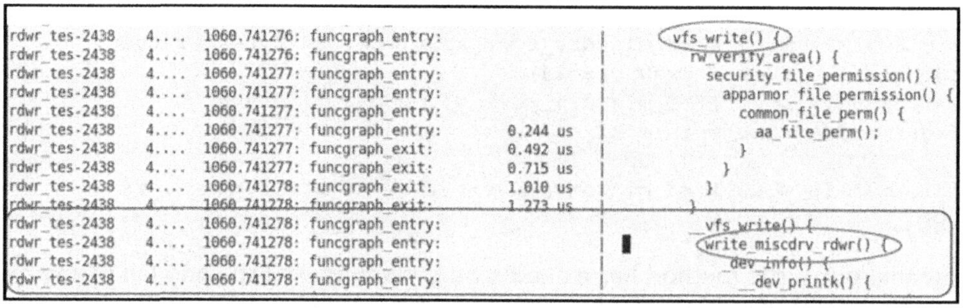

```
rdwr_tes-2438   4....  1060.741276: funcgraph_entry:              |  vfs_write() {
rdwr_tes-2438   4....  1060.741276: funcgraph_entry:              |    rw_verify_area() {
rdwr_tes-2438   4....  1060.741277: funcgraph_entry:              |      security_file_permission() {
rdwr_tes-2438   4....  1060.741277: funcgraph_entry:              |        apparmor_file_permission() {
rdwr_tes-2438   4....  1060.741277: funcgraph_entry:              |          common_file_perm() {
rdwr_tes-2438   4....  1060.741277: funcgraph_entry:    0.244 us  |            aa_file_perm();
rdwr_tes-2438   4....  1060.741277: funcgraph_exit:     0.492 us  |          }
rdwr_tes-2438   4....  1060.741277: funcgraph_exit:     0.715 us  |        }
rdwr_tes-2438   4....  1060.741278: funcgraph_exit:     1.010 us  |      }
rdwr_tes-2438   4....  1060.741278: funcgraph_exit:     1.273 us  |    }
rdwr_tes-2438   4....  1060.741278: funcgraph_entry:              |    __vfs_write() {
rdwr_tes-2438   4....  1060.741278: funcgraph_entry:              |      write_miscdrv_rdwr() {
rdwr_tes-2438   4....  1060.741278: funcgraph_entry:              |        dev_info() {
rdwr_tes-2438   4....  1060.741278: funcgraph_entry:              |          _dev_printk() {
```

Figure 6.10 – A partial screenshot of the trace-cmd(1) report output

As you can see, the `write(2)` system call from our user mode app becomes, as expected, `vfs_write()`, which itself (after security checks) invokes `__vfs_write()`, which, in turn, invokes our driver's write method – the `write_miscdrv_rdwr()` function!

In the (large) Ftrace output stream, we can see that the `schedule_timeout()` function has indeed been invoked:

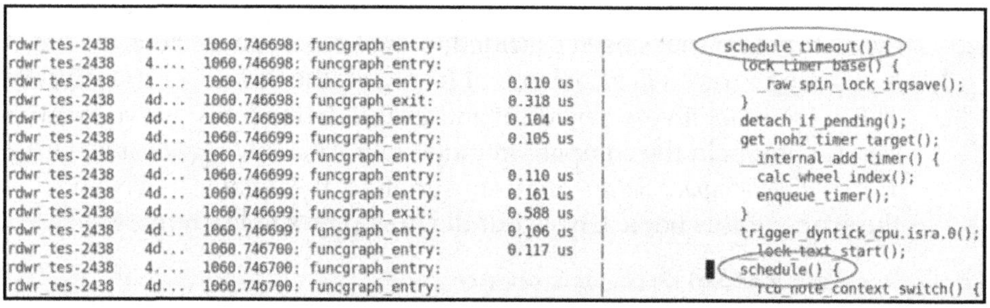

```
rdwr_tes-2438   4....  1060.746698: funcgraph_entry:              |  schedule_timeout() {
rdwr_tes-2438   4....  1060.746698: funcgraph_entry:              |    lock_timer_base() {
rdwr_tes-2438   4....  1060.746698: funcgraph_entry:    0.110 us  |      _raw_spin_lock_irqsave();
rdwr_tes-2438   4d...  1060.746698: funcgraph_exit:     0.318 us  |    }
rdwr_tes-2438   4d...  1060.746698: funcgraph_entry:    0.104 us  |    detach_if_pending();
rdwr_tes-2438   4d...  1060.746699: funcgraph_entry:    0.105 us  |    get_nohz_timer_target();
rdwr_tes-2438   4d...  1060.746699: funcgraph_entry:              |    __internal_add_timer() {
rdwr_tes-2438   4d...  1060.746699: funcgraph_entry:    0.110 us  |      calc_wheel_index();
rdwr_tes-2438   4d...  1060.746699: funcgraph_entry:    0.161 us  |      enqueue_timer();
rdwr_tes-2438   4d...  1060.746699: funcgraph_exit:     0.588 us  |    }
rdwr_tes-2438   4d...  1060.746699: funcgraph_entry:    0.106 us  |    trigger_dyntick_cpu.isra.0();
rdwr_tes-2438   4d...  1060.746700: funcgraph_entry:    0.117 us  |    __lock_text_start();
rdwr_tes-2438   4....  1060.746700: funcgraph_entry:              |    schedule() {
rdwr_tes-2438   4d...  1060.746700: funcgraph_entry:              |      rcu_note_context_switch() {
```

Figure 6.11 – A partial screenshot of the trace-cmd(1) report output, showing the (buggy!) calls to schedule_timeout() and schedule() within an atomic context

A few lines of output after `schedule_timeout()`, we can clearly see `schedule()` being invoked! So, there we have it: our driver has (deliberately, of course) performed something buggy – calling `schedule()` in an atomic context. But again, the key point here is that on this Ubuntu system, we are *not* running a "debug" kernel, which is why we have the following:

```
$ grep DEBUG_ATOMIC_SLEEP /boot/config-5.4.0-56-generic
# CONFIG_DEBUG_ATOMIC_SLEEP is not set
$
```

This is why the bug isn't being reported! This proves the usefulness of running test cases – and indeed performing kernel development – on a "debug" kernel, a kernel with many debug features enabled. (As an exercise, if you haven't done so already, prepare a "debug" kernel and run this test case on it.)

> **Linux Driver Verification (LDV) project**: In the companion guide *Linux Kernel Programming - Chapter 1, Kernel Workspace Setup*, in the section *The LDV – Linux Driver Verification – project*, we mentioned that this project has useful "rules" with respect to various programming aspects of Linux modules (drivers, mostly) as well as the core kernel.
>
> With regard to our current topic, here's one of the rules: *Usage of spin lock and unlock functions* (`http://linuxtesting.org/ldv/online?action=show_rulerule_id=0039`). It mentions key points with regard to the correct usage of spinlocks; interestingly, here, it shows an actual bug instance in a driver where a spinlock was attempted to be released twice – a clear violation of the locking rules, leading to an unstable system.

Locking and interrupts

So far, we have learned how to use the mutex lock and, for the spinlock, the basic `spin_[un]lock()` APIs. A few other API variations on the spinlock exist, and we shall examine the more common ones here.

To understand exactly why you may need other APIs for spinlocks, let's go over a scenario: as a driver author, you find that the device you're working on asserts a hardware interrupt; accordingly, you write the interrupt handler for it. Now, while implementing a `read` method for your driver, you find that you have a non-blocking critical section within it. This is easy to deal with: as you have learned, you should use a spinlock to protect it. Great! But what if, while in the `read` method's critical section, the device's hardware interrupt fires? As you're aware, *hardware interrupts preempt anything and everything*; thus, control will go to the interrupt handler code preempting the driver's `read` method.

The key question here: is this an issue? That answer depends both on what your interrupt handler and your `read` method were doing and how they were implemented. Let's visualize a few scenarios:

- The interrupt handler (ideally) uses only local variables, so even if the `read` method were in a critical section, it really doesn't matter; the interrupt handling will complete very quickly and control will be handed back to whatever was interrupted (again, there's more to it than this; as you know, any existing bottom-half, such as a tasklet or softirq, may also need to execute). In other words, as such, there is really no race in this case.
- The interrupt handler is working on (global) shared writeable data but *not* on the data items that your read method is using. Thus, again, there is no conflict and no race with the read code. What you should realize, of course, is that the interrupt code *does have a critical section and that it must be protected* (perhaps with another spinlock).
- The interrupt handler is working on the same global shared writeable data that your `read` method is using. In this case, we can see that the potential for a race definitely exists, so we need locking!

Let's focus on the third case. Obviously, we should use a spinlock to protect the critical section within the interrupt handling code (recall that using a mutex is disallowed when we're in any kind of interrupt context). Also, *unless we use the very same spinlock* in both the `read` method and the interrupt handler's code path, they will not be protected at all! (Be careful when working with locks; take the time to think through your design and code in detail.)

Let's try and make this a bit more hands-on (with pseudocode for now): let's say we have a global (shared) data structure named `gCtx`; we're operating on it in both the `read` method as well as the interrupt handler (hardirq handler) within our driver. Since it's shared, it's a critical section and therefore requires protection; since we are running in an atomic (interrupt) context, we *can't use a mutex*, so we must use a spinlock instead (here, the spinlock variable is called `slock`). The following pseudocode shows some timestamps (`t1`, `t2`, ...) for this situation:

```
// Driver read method ; WRONG !
driver_read(...)                    << time t0 >>
{
    [ ... ]
    spin_lock(&slock);
    <<--- time t1 : start of critical section >>
... << operating on global data object gCtx >> ...
    spin_unlock(&slock);
    <<--- time t2 : end of critical section >>
```

```
    [ ... ]
}                                    << time t3 >>
```

The following pseudocode is for the device driver's interrupt handler:

```
handle_interrupt(...)              << time t4; hardware interrupt fires!
>>
{
    [ ... ]
    spin_lock(&slock);
    <<--- time t5: start of critical section >>
    ... << operating on global data object gCtx >> ...
    spin_unlock(&slock);
    <<--- time t6 : end of critical section >>
    [ ... ]
}                                    << time t7 >>
```

This can be summed up with the following diagram:

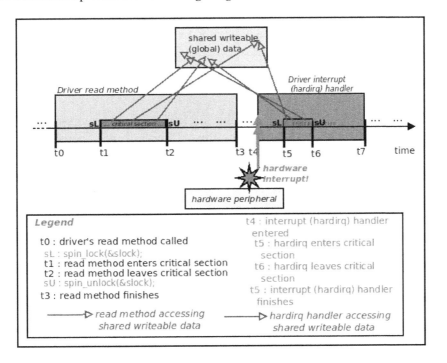

Figure 6.12 – Timeline – the driver's read method and hardirq handler run sequentially when working on global data: there's no issues here

Luckily, everything has gone well – "luckily" because the hardware interrupt fired *after* the `read` function's critical section completed. Surely we can't count on luck as the exclusive safety stamp of our product! The hardware interrupt is asynchronous; what if it fired at a less opportune time (for us) – say, while the `read` method's critical section is running between time t1 and t2? Well, isn't the spinlock going to do its job and protect our data?

At this point, the interrupt handler's code will attempt to acquire the same spinlock (`&slock`). Wait a minute – it cannot "get" it as it's currently locked! In this situation, it "spins", in effect waiting on the unlock. But how can it be unlocked? It cannot, and there we have it: a **(self) deadlock**.

Interestingly, the spinlock is more intuitive and makes sense on an SMP (multicore) system. Let's assume that the `read` method is running on CPU core 1; the interrupt can be delivered on another CPU core, say core 2. The interrupt code path will "spin" on the lock on CPU core 2, while the `read` method, on core 1, completes the critical section and then unlocks the spinlock, thus unblocking the interrupt handler. But what about on **UP** (**uniprocessor**, with only one CPU core)? How will it work then? Ah, so here's the solution to this conundrum: when "racing" with interrupts, *regardless of uniprocessor or SMP, simply use the `_irq` variant of the spinlock API*:

```
#include <linux/spinlock.h>
void spin_lock_irq(spinlock_t *lock);
```

The `spin_lock_irq()` API internally disables interrupts on the processor core that it's running on; that is, the local core. So, by using this API in our `read` method, interrupts will be disabled on the local core, thus making any possible "race" impossible via interrupts. (If the interrupt does fire on another CPU core, the spinlock technology will simply work as advertised, as discussed previously!)

> The `spin_lock_irq()` implementation is pretty nested (as with most of the spinlock functionality), yet fast; down the line, it ends up invoking the `local_irq_disable()` and `preempt_disable()` macros, disabling both interrupts and kernel preemption on the local processor core that it's running on. (Disabling hardware interrupts has the (desirable) side effect of disabling kernel preemption as well.)

`spin_lock_irq()` pairs off with the corresponding `spin_unlock_irq()` API. So, the correct usage of the spinlock for this scenario (as opposed to what we saw previously) is as follows:

```
// Driver read method ; CORRECT !
driver_read(...)                        << time t0 >>
{
```

```
    [ ... ]
    spin_lock_irq(&slock);
    <<--- time t1 : start of critical section >>
[now all interrupts + preemption on local CPU core are masked (disabled)]
... << operating on global data object gCtx >> ...
    spin_unlock_irq(&slock);
    <<--- time t2 : end of critical section >>
    [ ... ]
}                                        << time t3 >>
```

Before patting ourselves solidly on the back and taking the rest of the day off, let's consider another scenario. This time, on a more complex product (or project), it's quite possible that, among the several developers working on the code base, one has deliberately set the interrupt mask to a certain value, thus blocking some interrupts while allowing others. For the sake of our example, let's say that this has occurred earlier, at some point in time t0. Now, as we described previously, another developer (you!) comes along, and in order to protect a critical section within the driver's read method, uses the spin_lock_irq() API. Sounds correct, yes? Yes, but this API has the power *to turn off (mask) all hardware interrupts* (and kernel preemption, which we'll ignore for now) on the local CPU core. It does so by manipulating, at a low level, the (very arch-specific) hardware interrupt mask register. Let's say that setting a bit corresponding to an interrupt to 1 enables that interrupt, while clearing the bit (to 0) disables or masks it. Due to this, we may end up with the following scenario:

- time t0: The interrupt mask is set to some value, say, 0x8e (10001110b), enabling some and disabling some interrupts. This is important to the project (here, for simplicity, we're assuming there's an 8-bit mask register) *[... time elapses ...].*
- time t1: Just before entering the driver read method's critical section, call spin_lock_irq(&slock);. This API will have the internal effect of clearing all the bits in the interrupt mask registered to 0, thus disabling all interrupts (as we *think* we desire).
- time t2: Now, hardware interrupts cannot fire on this CPU core, so we go ahead and complete the critical section. Once we're done, we call spin_unlock_irq(&slock);. This API will have the internal effect of setting all the bits in the interrupt mask register to 1, reenabling all interrupts.

However, the interrupt mask register has now been wrongly "restored" to a value of `0xff` (11111111b), *not the value* `0x8e` as the original developer wants, requires, and assumes! This can (and probably will) break something in the project.

The solution is quite straightforward: don't assume anything, **simply save and restore the interrupt mask**. This can be achieved with the following API pair:

```
#include <linux/spinlock.h>>
 unsigned long spin_lock_irqsave(spinlock_t *lock, unsigned long flags);
 void spin_unlock_irqrestore(spinlock_t *lock, unsigned long flags);
```

The first parameter to both the lock and unlock functions is the spinlock variable to use. The second parameter, `flags`, *must be a local variable* of the `unsigned long` type. This will be used to save and restore the interrupt mask:

```
spinlock_t slock;
spin_lock_init(&slock);
[ ... ]
driver_read(...)
{
    [ ... ]
    spin_lock_irqsave(&slock, flags);
    << ... critical section ... >>
    spin_unlock_irqrestore(&slock, flags);
    [ ... ]
}
```

 To be pedantic, `spin_lock_irqsave()` is not an API, but a macro; we've shown it as an API for readability. Also, although the return value of this macro is not void, it's an internal detail (the `flags` parameter variable is updated here).

What about if a tasklet or a softirq (a bottom-half interrupt mechanism) has a critical section that "races" with your process-context code paths? In such situations, using the `spin_lock_bh()` routine is likely what's required since it can disable bottom halves on the local processor and then take the spinlock, thus safeguarding the critical section (similar to the way that `spin_lock_irq[save]()` protects the critical section in the process context by disabling hardware interrupts on the local core):

```
void spin_lock_bh(spinlock_t *lock);
```

Of course, *overhead* does matter in highly performance-sensitive code paths (the network stack being a great example). Thus, using the simplest form of spinlocks will help with more complex variants. Having said that, though, there are certainly going to be occasions that demand the use of the stronger forms of the spinlock API. For example, on the 5.4.0 Linux kernel, this is an approximation of the number of usage instances of different forms of the spinlock APIs we have seen: `spin_lock()`: over 9,400 usage instances; `spin_lock_irq()`: over 3,600 usage instances; `spin_lock_irqsave()`: over 15,000 usage instances; and `spin_lock_bh()`: over 3,700 usage instances. (We don't draw any major inference from this; it's just that we wish to point out that using the stronger form of spinlock APIs is quite widespread in the Linux kernel).

Finally, let's provide a very brief note on the internal implementation of the spinlock: in terms of under-the-hood internals, the implementation tends to be very arch-specific code, often comprised of atomic machine language instructions that execute very fast on the microprocessor. On the popular x86[_64] architecture, for example, the spinlock ultimately boils down to an *atomic test-and-set* machine instruction on a member of the spinlock structure (typically implemented via the `cmpxchg` machine language instruction). On ARM machines, as we mentioned earlier, it's often the `wfe` (Wait For Event, as well as the **SetEvent (SEV)**) machine instruction at the heart of the implementation. (You will find resources regarding its internal implementation in the *Further reading* section). Regardless, as a kernel or driver author, you should only use the exposed APIs (and macros) when using spinlocks.

Using spinlocks – a quick summary

Let's quickly summarize spinlocks:

- **Simplest, lowest overhead**: Use the non-irq spinlock primitives, `spin_lock()`/`spin_unlock()`, when protecting critical sections in the process context (there's either no interrupts to deal with or there are interrupts, but we do not race with them at all; in effect, use this when interrupts don't come into play or don't matter).
- **Medium overhead**: Use the irq-disabling (as well as kernel preemption disabling) versions, `spin_lock_irq()` / `spin_unlock_irq()`, when interrupts are in play and do matter (the process and interrupt contexts can "race"; that is, they share global data).

- **Strongest (relatively), high overhead**: This is the safest way to use a spinlock. It does the same as the medium overhead, except it performs a save-and-restore on the interrupt mask via the `spin_lock_irqsave()` / `spin_unlock_irqrestore()` pair, so as to guarantee that the previous interrupt mask settings aren't inadvertently overwritten, which could happen with the previous case.

As we saw earlier, the spinlock – in the sense of "spinning" on the processor it's running on when awaiting the lock – is impossible on UP (how can you spin on the one CPU that's available while another thread runs simultaneously on the very same CPU?). Indeed, on UP systems, the only real effect of the spinlock APIs is that it can disable hardware interrupts and kernel preemption on the processor! On SMP (multicore) systems, however, the spinning logic actually comes into play, and thus the locking semantics work as expected. But hang on – this should not stress you, budding kernel/driver developer; in fact, the whole point is that you should simply use the spinlock APIs as described and you will never have to worry about UP versus SMP; the details of what is done and what isn't are all hidden by the internal implementation.

 Though this book is based on the 5.4 LTS kernel, a new feature was added to the 5.8 kernel from the **Real-Time Linux** (**RTL**, previously called PREEMPT_RT) project, which deserves a quick mention here: "**local locks**". While the main use case for local locks is for (hard) real-time kernels, they help with non-real-time kernels too, mainly for lock debugging via static analysis, as well as runtime debugging via lockdep (we cover lockdep in the next chapter). Here's the LWN article on the subject: `https://lwn.net/Articles/828477/`.

With this, we complete the section on spinlocks, an extremely common and key lock used in the Linux kernel by virtually all its subsystems, including drivers.

Summary

Congratulations on completing this chapter!

Understanding concurrency and its related concerns is absolutely critical for any software professional. In this chapter, you learned key concepts regarding critical sections, the need for exclusive execution within them, and what atomicity means. You then learned *why* we need to be concerned with concurrency while writing code for the Linux OS. After that, we delved into the actual locking technologies – mutex locks and spinlocks – in detail. You also learned what lock you should use and when. Finally, learning how to handle concurrency concerns when hardware interrupts (and their possible bottom halves) are in play was covered.

But we aren't done yet! There are many more concepts and technologies we need to learn about, which is just what we will do in the next, and final, chapter of this book. I suggest that you digest the content of this chapter well first by browsing through it, as well as the resources in the *Further reading* section and the exercises provided, before diving into the last chapter!

Questions

As we conclude, here is a list of questions for you to test your knowledge regarding this chapter's material: `https://github.com/PacktPublishing/Linux-Kernel-Programming/tree/master/questions`. You will find some of the questions answered in the book's GitHub repo: `https://github.com/PacktPublishing/Linux-Kernel-Programming/tree/master/solutions_to_assgn`.

Further reading

To help you delve deeper into the subject with useful materials, we provide a rather detailed list of online references and links (and at times, even books) in a Further reading document in this book's GitHub repository. The *Further reading* document is available here: `https://github.com/PacktPublishing/Linux-Kernel-Programming/blob/master/Further_Reading.md`.

Kernel Synchronization - Part 2

7

This chapter continues the discussion from the previous chapter, on the topic of kernel synchronization and dealing with concurrency within the kernel in general. I suggest that if you haven't already, first read the previous chapter, and then continue with this one.

Here, we shall continue our learning with respect to the vast topic of kernel synchronization and handling concurrency when in kernel space. As before, the material is targeted at kernel and/or device driver developers. In this chapter, we shall cover the following:

- Using the atomic_t and refcount_t interfaces
- Using the RMW atomic operators
- Using the reader-writer spinlock
- Cache effects and false sharing
- Lock-free programming with per-CPU variables
- Lock debugging within the kernel
- Memory barriers – an introduction

Using the atomic_t and refcount_t interfaces

In our simple demo misc character device driver
program's (`miscdrv_rdwr/miscdrv_rdwr.c`) open method (and elsewhere), we defined
and manipulated two static global integers, `ga` and `gb`:

```
static int ga, gb = 1;
[...]
ga++; gb--;
```

By now, it should be obvious to you that this – the place where we operate on these integers
– is a potential bug if left as is: it's shared writable data (in a shared state) and therefore *a
critical section, thus requiring protection against concurrent access*. You get it; so, we
progressively improved upon this. In the previous chapter, understanding the issue, in our
`ch12/1_miscdrv_rdwr_mutexlock/1_miscdrv_rdwr_mutexlock.c` program, we first
used a *mutex lock* to protect the critical section. Later, you learned that using a *spinlock* to
protect non-blocking critical sections such as this one would be (far) superior to using a
mutex in terms of performance; so, in our next
driver, `ch12/2_miscdrv_rdwr_spinlock/2_miscdrv_rdwr_spinlock.c`, we used a
spinlock instead:

```
spin_lock(&lock1);
ga++; gb--;
spin_unlock(&lock1);
```

That's good, but we can do better still! Operating upon global integers turns out to be
such a common occurrence within the kernel (think of reference or resource counters
getting incremented and decremented, and so on) that the kernel provides a class of
operators called the **refcount** and **atomic integer operators** or interfaces; these are very
specifically designed to atomically (safely and indivisibly) operate on **only integers**.

The newer refcount_t versus older atomic_t interfaces

At the outset of this topic area, it's important to mention this: from the 4.11 kernel, there is
a newer and better set of interfaces christened the `refcount_t` APIs, meant for a kernel
space object's reference counters. It greatly improves the security posture of the kernel (via
much-improved **Integer OverFlow (IoF)** and **Use After Free (UAF)** protection as well as
memory ordering guarantees, which the older `atomic_t` APIs lack). The `refcount_t`
interfaces, like several other security technologies used on Linux, have their origins in work
done by The PaX Team – `https://pax.grsecurity.net/` (it was called `PAX_REFCOUNT`).

Having said that, the reality is that (as of the time of writing) the older atomic_t interfaces are still very much in use within the kernel core and drivers (they are slowly being converted, with the older atomic_t interfaces being moved to the newer refcount_t model and the API set). Thus, in this topic, we cover both, pointing out differences and mentioning which refcount_t API supersedes an atomic_t API wherever applicable. Think of the refcount_t interfaces as a variant of the (older) atomic_t interfaces, which are specialized toward reference counting.

A key difference between the atomic_t operators and the refcount_t ones is that the former works upon signed integers whereas the latter is essentially designed to work upon only an unsigned int quantity; more specifically, and this is important, it works only within a strictly specified range: 1 to UINT_MAX-1 (or [1..INT_MAX] when !CONFIG_REFCOUNT_FULL). The kernel has a config option named CONFIG_REFCOUNT_FULL; if set, it performs a (slower and more thorough) "full" reference count validation. This is beneficial for security but can result in slightly degraded performance (the typical default is to keep this config turned off; it's the case with our x86_64 Ubuntu guest).

Attempting to set a refcount_t variable to 0 or negative, or to [U]INT_MAX or above, is impossible; this is good for preventing integer underflow/overflow issues and thus preventing the use-after-free class bug in many cases! (Well, it's not impossible; it results in a (noisy) warning being fired via the WARN() macro.) Think about it, refcount_t variables are meant to be used *only for kernel object reference counting, nothing else*.

Thus, this is indeed the required behavior; the reference counter must start at a positive value (typically 1 when the object is newly instantiated), is incremented (or added to) whenever the code gets or takes a reference, and is decremented (or subtracted from) whenever the code puts or leaves a reference on the object. You are expected to carefully manipulate the reference counter (matching your gets and puts), always keeping its value within the legal range.

Quite non-intuitively, at least for the generic arch-independent refcount implementation, the refcount_t APIs are internally implemented over the atomic_t API set. For example, the refcount_set() API – which atomically sets a refcount's value to the parameter passed – is implemented like this within the kernel:

```
// include/linux/refcount.h
/**
 * refcount_set - set a refcount's value
 * @r: the refcount
 * @n: value to which the refcount will be set
 */
static inline void refcount_set(refcount_t *r, unsigned int n)
```

```
{
        atomic_set(&r->refs, n);
}
```

It's a thin wrapper over `atomic_set()` (which we will cover very shortly). The obvious FAQ here is: why use the refcount API at all? There are a few reasons:

- The counter saturates at the `REFCOUNT_SATURATED` value (which is set to `UINT_MAX` by default) and will not budge once there. This is critical: it avoids wrapping the counter, which could cause weird and spurious UAF bugs; this is even considered as a key security fix (`https://kernsec.org/wiki/index.php/Kernel_Protections/refcount_t`).
- Several of the newer refcount APIs do provide **memory ordering** guarantees; in particular the `refcount_t` APIs – as compared to their older `atomic_t` cousins – and the memory ordering guarantees they provide are clearly documented at `https://www.kernel.org/doc/html/latest/core-api/refcount-vs-atomic.html#refcount-t-api-compared-to-atomic-t` (do have a look if you're interested in the low-level details).
- Also, realize that arch-dependent refcount implementations (when they exist; for example, x86 does have it, while ARM doesn't) can differ from the previously-mentioned generic one.

 What exactly is *memory ordering* and how does it affect us? The fact is, it's a complex topic and, unfortunately, the inner details on this are beyond the scope of this book. It's worth knowing the basics: I suggest you read up on the **Linux-Kernel Memory Model (LKMM)**, which includes coverage on processor memory ordering and more. We refer you to good documentation on this here: *Explanation of the Linux-Kernel Memory Model* (`https://github.com/torvalds/linux/blob/master/tools/memory-model/Documentation/explanation.txt`).

The simpler atomic_t and refcount_t interfaces

Regarding the `atomic_t` interfaces, we should mention that all the following `atomic_t` constructs are for 32-bit integers only; of course, with 64-bit integers now being commonplace, 64-bit atomic integer operators are available as well. Typically, they are semantically identical to their 32-bit counterparts with the difference being in the name (`atomic_foo()` becomes `atomic64_foo()`). So the primary data type for 64-bit atomic integers is called `atomic64_t` (AKA `atomic_long_t`). The `refcount_t` interfaces, on the other hand, cater to both 32 and 64-bit integers.

The following table shows how to declare and initialize an `atomic_t` and `refcount_t` variable, side by side so that you can compare and contrast them:

	(Older) atomic_t (32-bit only)	**(Newer) refcount_t (both 32- and 64-bit)**
Header file to include	`<linux/atomic.h>`	`<linux/refcount.h>`
Declare and initialize a variable	`static atomic_t gb = ATOMIC_INIT(1);`	`static refcount_t gb = REFCOUNT_INIT(1);`

Table 17.1 – The older atomic_t versus the newer refcount_t interfaces for reference counting: header and init

The complete set of all the `atomic_t` and `refcount_t` APIs available within the kernel is pretty large; to help keep things simple and clear in this section, we only list some of the more commonly used (atomic 32-bit) and `refcount_t` interfaces in the following table (they operate upon a generic `atomic_t` or `refcount_t` variable, v):

Operation	**(Older) atomic_t interface**	**(Newer) refcount_t interface [range: 0 to [U]INT_MAX]**
Header file to include	`<linux/atomic.h>`	`<linux/refcount.h>`
Declare and initialize a variable	`static atomic_t v = ATOMIC_INIT(1);`	`static refcount_t v = REFCOUNT_INIT(1);`
Atomically read the current value of v	`int atomic_read(atomic_t *v)`	`unsigned int refcount_read(const refcount_t *v)`
Atomically set v to the value i	`void atomic_set(atomic_t *v, i)`	`void refcount_set(refcount_t *v, int i)`
Atomically increment the v value by 1	`void atomic_inc(atomic_t *v)`	`void refcount_inc(refcount_t *v)`
Atomically decrement the v value by 1	`void atomic_dec(atomic_t *v)`	`void refcount_dec(refcount_t *v)`
Atomically add the value of i to v	`void atomic_add(i, atomic_t *v)`	`void refcount_add(int i, refcount_t *v)`
Atomically subtract the value of i from v	`void atomic_sub(i, atomic_t *v)`	`void refcount_sub(int i, refcount_t *v)`

Atomically add the value of i to v and return the result	`int atomic_add_return(i, atomic_t *v)`	`bool refcount_add_not_zero(int i, refcount_t *v)` (not a precise match; adds i to v unless it's 0.)
Atomically subtract the value of i from v and return the result	`int atomic_sub_return(i, atomic_t *v)`	`bool refcount_sub_and_test(int i, refcount_t *r)` (not a precise match; subtracts i from v and tests; returns `true` if resulting refcount is 0, else `false`.)

Table 17.2 – The older atomic_t versus the newer refcount_t interfaces for reference counting: APIs

You've now seen several `atomic_t` and `refcount_t` macros and APIs; let's quickly check out a few examples of their usage in the kernel.

Examples of using refcount_t within the kernel code base

In one of our demo kernel modules regarding kernel threads (in `ch15/kthread_simple/kthread_simple.c`), we created a kernel thread and then employed the `get_task_struct()` inline function to mark the kernel thread's task structure as being in use. As you can now guess, the `get_task_struct()` routine increments the task structure's reference counter – a `refcount_t` variable named `usage` – via the `refcount_inc()` API:

```
// include/linux/sched/task.h
static inline struct task_struct *get_task_struct(struct task_struct *t)
{
    refcount_inc(&t->usage);
    return t;
}
```

The converse routine, `put_task_struct()`, performs the subsequent decrement on the reference counter. The actual routine employed by it internally, `refcount_dec_and_test()`, tests whether the new refcount value has dropped to 0; if so, it returns `true`, and if this is the case, it implies that the task structure isn't being referenced by anyone. The call to `__put_task_struct()` frees it up:

```
static inline void put_task_struct(struct task_struct *t)
{
    if (refcount_dec_and_test(&t->usage))
```

```
            __put_task_struct(t);
}
```

Another example of the refcounting APIs in use within the kernel is found in `kernel/user.c` (which helps track the number of processes, files, and so on that a user has claimed via a per-user structure):

```
linux-5.4 $ grep -iHnA1 refcount kernel/user.c
kernel/user.c:100:        .__count        = REFCOUNT_INIT(1),
kernel/user.c-101-        .processes      = ATOMIC_INIT(1),
:
kernel/user.c:127:                        refcount_inc(&user->__count);
kernel/user.c-128-                        return user;
:
kernel/user.c:171:        if (refcount_dec_and_lock_irqsave(&up->__count, &uidhash_lock, &flags))
kernel/user.c-172-                free_user(up, flags);
:
kernel/user.c:190:                        refcount_set(&new->__count, 1);
kernel/user.c-191-                        ratelimit_state_init(&new->ratelimit, HZ, 100);
linux-5.4 $
```

Figure 7.1 – Screenshot showing the usage of the refcount_t interfaces in kernel/user.c

Look up the `refcount_t` API interface documentation (`https://www.kernel.org/doc/html/latest/driver-api/basics.html#reference-counting`); `refcount_dec_and_lock_irqsave()` returns `true` and withholds the spinlock with interrupts disabled if able to decrement the reference counter to 0, and `false` otherwise.

As an exercise for you, convert our earlier `ch16/2_miscdrv_rdwr_spinlock/miscdrv_rdwr_spinlock.c` driver code to use refcount; it has the integers `ga` and `gb`, which, when being read or written, were protected via a spinlock. Now, make them refcount variables and use the appropriate `refcount_t` APIs when working on them.

Careful! Don't allow their values to go out of the allowed range, [0..[U]INT_MAX]! (Recall that the range is [1..UINT_MAX-1] for full refcount validation (CONFIG_REFCOUNT_FULL being on) and [1..INT_MAX] when it's not full validation (the default)). Doing so typically leads to the WARN() macro being invoked (the code for this demo seen in *Figure 7.1* isn't included in our GitHub repository):

```
$ dmesg
[ 7890.344169] miscdrv_rdwr_refcount:miscdrv_init_refcount(): LLKD misc driver (major # 10) registered, minor#
= 55, dev node is llkd_miscdrv_rdwr_refcount
[ 7890.345642] misc llkd_miscdrv_rdwr_refcount: A sample print via the dev_dbg(): driver initialized
[ 7904.871029] miscdrv_rdwr_refcount:open_miscdrv_rdwr(): 001)  rdwr_test_secre :8519    |  ...0   /* open_miscd
rv_rdwr() */
[ 7904.879384] ------------[ cut here ]------------
[ 7904.879735] refcount_t hit zero at open_miscdrv_rdwr+0x194/0x2b0 [miscdrv_rdwr_refcount] in rdwr_test_secre[
8519], uid/euid: 1001/1001
[ 7904.880685] WARNING: CPU: 1 PID: 8519 at kernel/panic.c:677 refcount_error_report+0xf1/0x103
[ 7904.881301] Modules linked in: miscdrv_rdwr_refcount(OE) vboxsf(OE) vboxvideo(OE) snd_intel8x0 vmwgfx snd_ac
97_codec ac97_bus snd_pcm crct10dif_pclmul crc32_pclmul ghash_clmulni_intel snd_seq aesni_intel glue_helper cry
pto_simd cryptd drm_kms_helper snd_timer snd_seq_device input_leds snd joydev syscopyarea serio_raw sysfillrect
 sysimgblt fb_sys_fops ttm soundcore vboxguest(OE) video mac_hid sch_fq_codel drm parport_pc ppdev lp parport i
p_tables x_tables autofs4 hid_generic usbhid hid psmouse e1000 ahci libahci i2c_piix4 pata_acpi [last unloaded:
 miscdrv_rdwr_refcount]
[ 7904.885282] CPU: 1 PID: 8519 Comm: rdwr_test_secre Tainted: G      W  OE     5.4.1-try1 #1
[ 7904.886040] Hardware name: innotek GmbH VirtualBox/VirtualBox, BIOS VirtualBox 12/01/2006
[ 7904.886668] RIP: 0010:refcount_error_report+0xf1/0x103
```

Figure 7.2 – (Partial) screenshot showing the WARN() macro firing when we wrongly attempt to set a refcount_t variable to <= 0

The kernel has an interesting and useful test infrastructure called the **Linux Kernel Dump Test Module (LKDTM)**; see drivers/misc/lkdtm/refcount.c for many test cases being run on the refcount interfaces, which you can learn from... FYI, you can also use LKDTM via the kernel's fault injection framework to test and evaluate the kernel's reaction to faulty scenarios (see the documentation here: *Provoking crashes with Linux Kernel Dump Test Module (LKDTM)* – https://www.kernel.org/doc/html/latest/fault-injection/provoke-crashes.html#provoking-crashes-with-linux-kernel-dump-test-module-lkdtm).

The atomic interfaces covered so far all operate on 32-bit integers; what about on 64-bit? That's what follows.

64-bit atomic integer operators

As mentioned at the start of this topic, the set of `atomic_t` integer operators we have dealt with so far all operate on traditional 32-bit integers (this discussion doesn't apply to the newer `refcount_t` interfaces; they anyway operate upon both 32 and 64-bit quantities). Obviously, with 64-bit systems becoming the norm rather than the exception nowadays, the kernel community provides an identical set of atomic integer operators for 64-bit integers. The difference is as follows:

- Declare the 64-bit atomic integer as a variable of type `atomic64_t` (that is, `atomic_long_t`).
- For all operators, in place of the `atomic_` prefix, use the `atomic64_` prefix.

So, take the following examples:

- In place of `ATOMIC_INIT()`, use `ATOMIC64_INIT()`.
- In place of `atomic_read()`, use `atomic64_read()`.
- In place of `atomic64_dec_if_positive()`, use `atomic64_dec_if_positive()`.

> Recent C and C++ language standards – C11 and C++11 – provide an atomic operations library that helps developers implement atomicity in an easier fashion due to the implicit language support; we won't delve into this aspect here. A reference can be found here (C11 also has pretty much the same equivalents): `https://en.cppreference.com/w/c/atomic`.

Note that all these routines – both the 32- and 64-bit atomic `_operators` – are **arch-independent**. A key point worth repeating is that any and all operations performed upon an atomic integer must be done by declaring the variable as `atomic_t` and via the methods provided. This includes initialization and even a (integer) read operation.

In terms of internal implementation, a `foo()` atomic integer operator is typically a macro that becomes an inline function, which in turn invokes the arch-specific `arch_foo()` function. As usual, glancing through the official kernel documentation on atomic operators is always a good idea (within the kernel source tree, it's here: `Documentation/atomic_t.txt`; go to `https://www.kernel.org/doc/Documentation/atomic_t.txt`). It neatly categorizes the numerous atomic integer APIs into distinct sets. FYI, arch-specific *memory ordering issues* do affect the internal implementation. Here, we won't delve into the internals. If interested, refer to this page on the official kernel documentation site at `https://www.kernel.org/doc/html/v4.16/core-api/refcount-vs-atomic.html#refcount-t-api-compared-to-atomic-t` (also, details on memory ordering go beyond the scope of this book; check out the kernel documentation at `https://www.kernel.org/doc/Documentation/memory-barriers.txt` for more on this).

We haven't attempted to show all the atomic and refcount APIs here (it's really not necessary); the official kernel documentation covers it:

- `atomic_t` interfaces:
    - *Semantics and Behavior of Atomic and Bitmask Operations* (`https://www.kernel.org/doc/html/v5.4/core-api/atomic_ops.html#semantics-and-behavior-of-atomic-and-bitmask-operations`)
    - API ref: Atomics (`https://www.kernel.org/doc/html/latest/driver-api/basics.html#atomics`)

- (Newer) `refcount_t` interfaces for kernel object reference counting:
    - `refcount_t` API compared to `atomic_t` (`https://www.kernel.org/doc/html/latest/core-api/refcount-vs-atomic.html#refcount-t-api-compared-to-atomic-t`)
    - API ref: Reference counting (`https://www.kernel.org/doc/html/latest/driver-api/basics.html#reference-counting`)

Let's move on to the usage of a typical construct when working on drivers – **Read Modify Write (RMW)**. Read on!

Using the RMW atomic operators

A more advanced set of atomic operators called the RMW APIs is available as well. Among its many uses (we show a list in the coming section) is that of performing atomic RMW operations on bits, in other words, performing bitwise operations atomically (safely, indivisibly). As a device driver author operating upon device or peripheral *registers*, this is indeed something you will find yourself using.

> The material in this section assumes you have at least a basic understanding of accessing peripheral device (chip) memory and registers; we have covered this in detail in Chapter 3, *Working with Hardware I/O Memory*. Please ensure you understand it before moving further.

Very often, you'll need to perform bit operations (with the bitwise AND & and bitwise OR | being the most commonplace operators) on registers; this is done to modify its value, setting and/or clearing some bits within it. The thing is, merely performing some C manipulation to query or set device registers isn't quite enough. No, sir: don't forget about concurrency issues! Read on for the full story.

RMW atomic operations – operating on device registers

Let's quickly go over some basics first: a byte consists of 8 bits, numbered from bit 0, the **Least Significant Bit (LSB)**, to bit 7, the **Most Significant Bit (MSB)**. (This is actually formally defined as the BITS_PER_BYTE macro in include/linux/bits.h, along with a few other interesting definitions.)

A **register** is basically a small piece of memory within the peripheral device; typically, its size, the register bit width, is one of 8, 16, or 32 bits. The device registers provide control, status, and other information and are often programmable. This, in fact, is largely what you as a driver author will do – program the device registers appropriately to make the device do something, and query it.

To flesh out this discussion, let's consider a hypothetical device that has two registers: a status register and a control register, each 8 bits wide. (In the real world, every device or chip has a *datasheet* that will provide a detailed specification of the chip and register-level hardware; this becomes an essential document for the driver author). Hardware folks usually design devices in such a way that several registers are sequentially clubbed together in a larger piece of memory; this is called register banking. By having the base address of the first register and the offset to each following one, it becomes easy to address any given register (here, we won't delve into how exactly registers are "mapped" into the virtual address space on an OS such as Linux). For example, the (purely hypothetical) registers may be described like this in a header file:

```
#define REG_BASE        0x5a00
#define STATUS_REG      (REG_BASE+0x0)
#define CTRL_REG        (REG_BASE+0x1)
```

Now, say that in order to turn on our fictional device, the datasheet informs us we can do so by setting bit 7 (the MSB) of the control register to 1. As every driver author quickly learns, there is a hallowed sequence for modifying registers:

1. **Read** the register's current value into a temporary variable.
2. **Modify** the variable to the desired value.
3. **Write** back the variable to the register.

This is often called the **RMW sequence**; so, great, we write the (pseudo)code like this:

```
turn_on_dev()
{
    u8 tmp;

    tmp = ioread8(CTRL_REG);    /* read: current register value into tmp */
    tmp |= 0x80;                /* modify: set bit 7 (MSB) */
    iowrite8(tmp, CTRL_REG);    /* write: new tmp value into register */
}
```

(FYI, the actual routines used on Linux **MMIO – memory-mapped I/O** – are `ioread[8|16|32]()` and `iowrite[8|16|32]()`.)

A key point here: *this isn't good enough*; the reason is **concurrency, data races!** Think about it: a register (both CPU and device registers) is in fact a *global shared writable memory location*; thus, accessing it *constitutes a critical section*, which you have to take care to protect from concurrent access! The how is easy; we could just use a spinlock (for now at least). It's trivial to modify the preceding pseudocode to insert the `spin_[un]lock()` APIs in the critical section – the RMW sequence.

However, there is an even better way to achieve data safety when dealing with small quantities such as integers; we have already covered it: *atomic operators*! Linux, however, goes further, providing a set of atomic APIs for both of the following:

- **Atomic non-RMW operations** (the ones we saw earlier, in the *Using the atomic_t and refcount_t interfaces* section)
- **Atomic RMW operations**; these include several types of operators that can be categorized into a few distinct classes: arithmetic, bitwise, swap (exchange), reference counting, miscellaneous, and barriers

Let's not reinvent the wheel; the kernel documentation (https://www.kernel.org/doc/Documentation/atomic_t.txt) has all the information required. We'll show just a relevant portion of this document as follows, quoting directly from the Documentation/atomic_t.txt kernel code base:

```
// Documentation/atomic_t.txt
[ ... ]
Non-RMW ops:
  atomic_read(), atomic_set()
  atomic_read_acquire(), atomic_set_release()


RMW atomic operations:


Arithmetic:
  atomic_{add,sub,inc,dec}()
  atomic_{add,sub,inc,dec}_return{,_relaxed,_acquire,_release}()
  atomic_fetch_{add,sub,inc,dec}{,_relaxed,_acquire,_release}()


Bitwise:
  atomic_{and,or,xor,andnot}()
  atomic_fetch_{and,or,xor,andnot}{,_relaxed,_acquire,_release}()


Swap:
  atomic_xchg{,_relaxed,_acquire,_release}()
  atomic_cmpxchg{,_relaxed,_acquire,_release}()
  atomic_try_cmpxchg{,_relaxed,_acquire,_release}()


Reference count (but please see refcount_t):
  atomic_add_unless(), atomic_inc_not_zero()
  atomic_sub_and_test(), atomic_dec_and_test()
```

```
Misc:
   atomic_inc_and_test(), atomic_add_negative()
   atomic_dec_unless_positive(), atomic_inc_unless_negative()
[ ... ]
```

Good; now that you're aware of these RMW (and non-RMW) operators, let's get practical – we'll check out how to use the RMW operators for bit operations next.

Using the RMW bitwise operators

Here, we'll focus on employing the RMW bitwise operators; we'll leave it to you to explore the others (refer to the kernel docs mentioned). So, let's think again about how to more efficiently code our pseudocode example. We can set (to 1) any given bit in any register or memory item using the set_bit() API:

```
void set_bit(unsigned int nr, volatile unsigned long *p);
```

This atomically – safely and indivisibly – sets the nrth bit of p to 1. (The reality is that the device registers (and possibly device memory) are mapped into kernel virtual address space and thus appear to be visible as though they are RAM locations – such as the address p here. This is called MMIO and is the common way by which driver authors map in and work with device memory.)

Thus, with the RMW atomic operators, we can safely achieve what we've (incorrectly) attempted previously – turning on our (fictional) device – with a single line of code:

```
set_bit(7, CTRL_REG);
```

The following table summarizes common RMW bitwise atomic APIs:

RMW bitwise atomic API	Comment
void set_bit(unsigned int nr, volatile unsigned long *p);	Atomically set (set to 1) the nrth bit of p.
void clear_bit(unsigned int nr, volatile unsigned long *p)	Atomically clear (set to 0) the nrth bit of p.
void change_bit(unsigned int nr, volatile unsigned long *p)	Atomically toggle the nrth bit of p.
The following APIs return the previous value of the bit being operated upon (nr)	

`int test_and_set_bit(unsigned int nr, volatile unsigned long *p)`	Atomically set the n r th bit of p returning the previous value (kernel API doc at `https://www.kernel.org/doc/htmldocs/kernel-api/API-test-and-set-bit.html`).
`int test_and_clear_bit(unsigned int nr, volatile unsigned long *p)`	Atomically clear the n r th bit of p returning the previous value.
`int test_and_change_bit(unsigned int nr, volatile unsigned long *p)`	Atomically toggle the n r th bit of p returning the previous value.

Table 17.3 – Common RMW bitwise atomic APIs

Careful: these atomic APIs are not just atomic with respect to the CPU core they're running upon, but now with respect to all/other cores. In practice, this implies that if you're performing atomic operations in parallel on multiple CPUs, that is, if they (can) race, then it's a critical section and you must protect it with a lock (typically a spinlock)!

Trying out a few of these RMW atomic APIs will help build your confidence in using them; we do so in the section that follows.

Using bitwise atomic operators – an example

Let's check out a quick kernel module that demonstrates the usage of the Linux kernel's RMW atomic bit operators (ch13/1_rmw_atomic_bitops). You should realize that these operators can work on *any memory*, both a (CPU or device) register or RAM; here, we operate on a simple static global variable (named mem) within the example LKM. It's very simple; let's check it out:

```
// ch13/1_rmw_atomic_bitops/rmw_atomic_bitops.c
[ ... ]
#include <linux/spinlock.h>
#include <linux/atomic.h>
#include <linux/bitops.h>
#include "../../convenient.h"
[ ... ]
static unsigned long mem;
static u64 t1, t2;
static int MSB = BITS_PER_BYTE - 1;
DEFINE_SPINLOCK(slock);
```

We include the required headers and declare and initialize a few global variables (notice how our MSB variable uses BIT_PER_BYTE). We employ a simple macro, SHOW(), to display the formatted output with the printk. The init code path is where the actual work is done:

```
[ ... ]
#define SHOW(n, p, msg) do {                                             \
    pr_info("%2d:%27s: mem : %3ld = 0x%02lx\n", n, msg, p, p); \
} while (0)
[ ... ]
static int __init atomic_rmw_bitops_init(void)
{
    int i = 1, ret;

    pr_info("%s: inserted\n", OURMODNAME);
    SHOW(i++, mem, "at init");

    setmsb_optimal(i++);
    setmsb_suboptimal(i++);

    clear_bit(MSB, &mem);
    SHOW(i++, mem, "clear_bit(7,&mem)");

    change_bit(MSB, &mem);
    SHOW(i++, mem, "change_bit(7,&mem)");

    ret = test_and_set_bit(0, &mem);
    SHOW(i++, mem, "test_and_set_bit(0,&mem)");
    pr_info(" ret = %d\n", ret);

    ret = test_and_clear_bit(0, &mem);
    SHOW(i++, mem, "test_and_clear_bit(0,&mem)");
    pr_info(" ret (prev value of bit 0) = %d\n", ret);

    ret = test_and_change_bit(1, &mem);
    SHOW(i++, mem, "test_and_change_bit(1,&mem)");
    pr_info(" ret (prev value of bit 1) = %d\n", ret);

    pr_info("%2d: test_bit(%d-0,&mem):\n", i, MSB);
    for (i = MSB; i >= 0; i--)
        pr_info(" bit %d (0x%02lx) : %s\n", i, BIT(i), test_bit(i,
&mem)?"set":"cleared");

    return 0; /* success */
}
```

The RMW atomic operators we use here are highlighted in bold font. A key part of this demo is to show that using the RMW bitwise atomic operators is not only much easier but also much faster than using the traditional approach where we manually perform the RMW operation within the confines of a spinlock. Here are the two functions for both of these approaches:

```
/* Set the MSB; optimally, with the set_bit() RMW atomic API */
static inline void setmsb_optimal(int i)
{
    t1 = ktime_get_real_ns();
    set_bit(MSB, &mem);
    t2 = ktime_get_real_ns();
    SHOW(i, mem, "set_bit(7,&mem)");
    SHOW_DELTA(t2, t1);
}
/* Set the MSB; the traditional way, using a spinlock to protect the RMW
 * critical section   */
static inline void setmsb_suboptimal(int i)
{
    u8 tmp;

    t1 = ktime_get_real_ns();
    spin_lock(&slock);
    /* critical section: RMW : read, modify, write */
    tmp = mem;
    tmp |= 0x80; // 0x80 = 1000 0000 binary
    mem = tmp;
    spin_unlock(&slock);
    t2 = ktime_get_real_ns();

    SHOW(i, mem, "set msb suboptimal: 7,&mem");
    SHOW_DELTA(t2, t1);
}
```

We call these functions early in our `init` method; notice that we take timestamps (via the `ktime_get_real_ns()` routine) and display the time taken via our `SHOW_DELTA()` macro (defined in our `convenient.h` header). Right, here's the output:

```
[15186.312399] 2_rmw_atomic_bitops: inserted
[15186.314690]    1:                        at init: mem :   0 = 0x00
[15186.315936]    2:               set_bit(7,&mem): mem : 128 = 0x80
[15186.317155] delta: 415 ns (= 0 us = 0 ms)
[15186.318746]    3: set msb suboptimal: 7,&mem: mem : 128 = 0x80
[15186.320096] delta: 110101 ns (= 110 us = 0 ms)
[15186.321285]    4:             clear_bit(7,&mem): mem :   0 = 0x00
[15186.323010]    5:            change_bit(7,&mem): mem : 128 = 0x80
[15186.324379]    6:     test_and_set_bit(0,&mem): mem : 129 = 0x81
[15186.325785]             ret = 0
[15186.327019]    7: test_and_clear_bit(0,&mem): mem : 128 = 0x80
[15186.328396]           ret (prev value of bit 0) = 1
[15186.329868]    8:test_and_change_bit(1,&mem): mem : 130 = 0x82
[15186.331487]           ret (prev value of bit 1) = 0
[15186.333013]    9: test_bit(7-0,&mem):
[15186.334436]    bit 7 (0x80) : set
[15186.335747]    bit 6 (0x40) : cleared
[15186.337013]    bit 5 (0x20) : cleared
[15186.338401]    bit 4 (0x10) : cleared
[15186.339648]    bit 3 (0x08) : cleared
[15186.340825]    bit 2 (0x04) : cleared
[15186.342129]    bit 1 (0x02) : set
[15186.343285]    bit 0 (0x01) : cleared
```

Figure 7.3 – Screenshot of output from our ch13/1_rmw_atomic_bitops LKM, showing off some of the atomic RMW operators at work

(I ran this demo LKM on my x86_64 Ubuntu 20.04 guest VM.) The modern approach – via the `set_bit()` RMW atomic bitwise API – took, in this sample run, just 415 nanoseconds to execute; the traditional approach was about 265 times slower! The code (via `set_bit()`) is so much simpler as well...

On a somewhat related note to the atomic bitwise operators, the following section is a very brief look at the highly efficient APIs available within the kernel for searching a bitmask – a fairly common operation in the kernel, as it turns out.

Efficiently searching a bitmask

Several algorithms depend on performing a really fast search of a bitmask; several scheduling algorithms (such as SCHED_FIFO and SCHED_RR, which you learned about in the companion guide *Linux Kernel Programming - Chapter 10, The CPU Scheduler – Part 1, and Chapter 11, The CPU Scheduler – Part 2*) often internally require this. Implementing this efficiently becomes important (especially for OS-level performance-sensitive code paths). Hence, the kernel provides a few APIs to scan a given bitmask (these prototypes are found in include/asm-generic/bitops/find.h):

- unsigned long find_first_bit(const unsigned long *addr, unsigned long size): Finds the first set bit in a memory region; returns the bit number of the first set bit, else (no bits are set) returns @size.
- unsigned long find_first_zero_bit(const unsigned long *addr, unsigned long size): Finds the first cleared bit in a memory region; returns the bit number of the first cleared bit, else (no bits are cleared) returns @size.
- Other routines include find_next_bit(), find_next_and_bit(), find_last_bit().

Looking through the <linux/bitops.h> header reveals other quite interesting macros as well, such as for_each_{clear,set}_bit{_from}().

Using the reader-writer spinlock

Visualize a piece of kernel (or driver) code wherein a large, global, doubly linked circular list (with a few thousand nodes) is being searched. Now, since the data structure is global (shared and writable), accessing it constitutes a critical section that requires protection.

Assuming a scenario where searching the list is a non-blocking operation, you'd typically use a spinlock to protect the critical section. A naive approach might propose not using a lock at all since we're *only reading data* within the list, not updating it. But, of course (as you have learned), even a read on shared writable data has to be protected to protect against an inadvertent write occurring simultaneously, thus resulting in a dirty or torn read.

So, we conclude that we require the spinlock; we imagine the pseudocode might look something like this:

```
spin_lock(mylist_lock);
for (p = &listhead; (p = next_node(p)) != &listhead; ) {
    << ... search for something ...
        found? break out ... >>
}
spin_unlock(mylist_lock);
```

So, what's the problem? Performance, of course! Imagine several threads on a multicore system ending up at this code fragment more or less at the same time; each will attempt to take the spinlock, but only one winner thread will get it, iterate over the entire list, and then perform the unlock, allowing the next thread to proceed. In other words, as expected, execution is now *serialized*, dramatically slowing things down. But it can't be helped; or can it?

Enter the **reader-writer spinlock**. With this locking construct, it's required that all threads performing reads on the protected data will ask for a **read lock**, whereas any thread requiring write access to the list will ask for an **exclusive write lock**. A read lock will be granted immediately to any thread that asks as long as no write lock is currently in play. In effect, this construct *allows all readers concurrent access to the data, meaning, in effect, no real locking at all*. This is fine, as long as there are only readers. The moment a writer thread comes along, it requests a write lock. Now, normal locking semantics apply: the writer **will have to wait** for all readers to unlock. Once that happens, the writer gets an exclusive write lock and proceeds. So now, if any readers or writers attempt access, they will be forced to wait to spin upon the writer's unlock.

 Thus, for those situations where the access pattern to data is such that reads are performed very often and writes are rare, and the critical section is a fairly long one, the reader-writer spinlock is a performance-enhancing one.

Reader-writer spinlock interfaces

Having used spinlocks, using the reader-writer variant is straightforward; the lock data type is abstracted as the `rwlock_t` structure (in place of `spinlock_t`) and, in terms of API names, simply substitute `read` or `write` in place of `spin`:

```
#include <linux/rwlock.h>
rwlock_t mylist_lock;
```

The most basic APIs of the reader-writer spinlock are as follows:

```
void read_lock(rwlock_t *lock);
void write_lock(rwlock_t *lock);
```

As an example, the kernel's `tty` layer has code to handle a **Secure Attention Key (SAK)**; the SAK is a security feature, a means to prevent a Trojan horse-type credentials hack by killing all processes associated with the TTY device. This will happen when the user presses the SAK (`https://www.kernel.org/doc/html/latest/security/sak.html`). When this actually happens (that is, when the user presses the SAK, mapped to the `Alt-SysRq-k` sequence by default), within its code path, it has to iterate over all tasks, killing the entire session and any threads that have the TTY device open. To do so, it must take, in read mode, a reader-writer spinlock called `tasklist_lock`. The (truncated) relevant code is seen as follows, with `read_[un]lock()` on `tasklist_lock` highlighted:

```
// drivers/tty/tty_io.c
void __do_SAK(struct tty_struct *tty)
{
    [...]
    read_lock(&tasklist_lock);
    /* Kill the entire session */
    do_each_pid_task(session, PIDTYPE_SID, p) {
        tty_notice(tty, "SAK: killed process %d (%s): by session\n",
task_pid_nr(p), p->comm);
        group_send_sig_info(SIGKILL, SEND_SIG_PRIV, p, PIDTYPE_SID);
    } while_each_pid_task(session, PIDTYPE_SID, p);
    [...]
    /* Now kill any processes that happen to have the tty open */
    do_each_thread(g, p) {
        [...]
    } while_each_thread(g, p);
    read_unlock(&tasklist_lock);
```

As an aside, in the companion guide *Linux Kernel Programming - Chapter 6, Kernel Internals Essentials* section *Processes and Threads Iterating over the task list*, we did something kind of similar: we wrote a kernel module (`https://github.com/PacktPublishing/Linux-Kernel-Programming/blob/master/ch6/foreach/thrd_showall/thrd_showall.c`) that iterated over all threads in the task list, spewing out a few details about each thread. So, now that we understand the deal regarding concurrency, shouldn't we have taken this very lock – `tasklist_lock` – the reader-writer spinlock protecting the task list? Yes, but it didn't work (`insmod(8)` failed with the message `thrd_showall: Unknown symbol tasklist_lock (err -2)`). The reason, of course, is that this `tasklist_lock` variable is *not* exported and thus is unavailable to our kernel module.

As another example of a reader-writer spinlock within the kernel code base, the `ext4` filesystem uses one when working with its extent status tree. We don't intend to delve into the details here; we will simply mention the fact that a reader-writer spinlock (within the inode structure, `inode->i_es_lock`) is quite heavily used here to protect the extent status tree against data races (`fs/ext4/extents_status.c`).

There are many such examples within the kernel source tree; many places in the network stack including the ping code (`net/ipv4/ping.c`) use `rwlock_t`, routing table lookup, neighbor, PPP code, filesystems, and so on.

Just as with regular spinlocks, we have the typical variations on the reader-writer spinlock APIs: `{read,write}_lock_irq{save}()` paired with the corresponding `{read,write}_unlock_irq{restore}()`, as well as the `{read,write}_{un}lock_bh()` interfaces. Note that even the read IRQ lock disables kernel preemption.

A word of caution

Issues do exist with reader-writer spinlocks. One typical issue with it is that, unfortunately, **writers can starve** when blocking on several readers. Think about it: let's say that three reader threads currently have the reader-writer lock. Now, a writer comes along wanting the lock. It has to wait until all three readers perform the unlock. But what if, in the interim, more readers come along (which is entirely possible)? This becomes a disaster for the writer, who has to now wait even longer – in effect, starve. (Carefully instrumenting or profiling the code paths involved might be necessary to figure out whether this is indeed the case.)

Not only that, *cache effects* – known as cache ping-pong – can and do occur quite often when several reader threads on different CPU cores are reading the same shared state in parallel (while holding the reader-writer lock); we in fact discuss this in the *Cache effects and false sharing* section). The kernel documentation on spinlocks (`https://www.kernel.org/doc/Documentation/locking/spinlocks.txt`) says pretty much the same thing. Here's a quote directly from it: "*NOTE! reader-writer locks require more atomic memory operations than simple spinlocks. Unless the reader critical section is long, you are better off just using spinlocks.*" In fact, the kernel community is working toward removing reader-writer spinlocks as far as is possible, moving them to superior lock-free techniques (such as **RCU - Read Copy Update**, an advanced lock-free technology). Thus, gratuitous use of reader-writer spinlocks is ill advised.

The neat and simple kernel documentation on the usage of spinlocks (written by Linus Torvalds himself), which is well worth reading, is available here: `https://www.kernel.org/doc/Documentation/locking/spinlocks.txt`.

The reader-writer semaphore

We earlier mentioned the semaphore object (`Chapter 6`, *Kernel Synchronization – Part 1*, in the *The semaphore and the mutex* section), contrasting it with the mutex. There, you understood that it's preferable to simply use a mutex. Here, we point out that within the kernel, just as there exist reader-writer spinlocks, so do there exist *reader-writer semaphores*. The use cases and semantics are similar to that of the reader-writer spinlock. The relevant macros/APIs are (within `<linux/rwsem.h>`) `{down,up}_{read,write}_{trylock,killable}()`. A common example within the `struct mm_struct` structure (which is itself within the task structure) is that one of the members is a reader-writer semaphore: `struct rw_semaphore mmap_sem;`.

Rounding off this discussion, we'll merely mention a couple of other related synchronization mechanisms within the kernel. A synchronization mechanism that is heavily used in user space application development (we're thinking particularly of the Pthreads framework in Linux user space) is the **Condition Variable** (**CV**). In a nutshell, it provides the ability for two or more threads to synchronize with each other based on the value of a data item or some specific state. Its equivalent within the Linux kernel is called the *completion mechanism*. Please find details on its usage within the kernel documentation at `https://www.kernel.org/doc/html/latest/scheduler/completion.html#completions-wait-for-completion-barrier-apis`.

The *sequence lock* is used in mostly write situations (as opposed to the reader-write spinlock/semaphore locks, which are suitable in mostly read scenarios), where the writes far exceed the reads on the protected variable. As you can imagine, this isn't a very common occurrence; a good example of using sequence locks is the update of the `jiffies_64` global.

For the curious, the `jiffies_64` global's update code begins here: `kernel/time/tick-sched.c:tick_do_update_jiffies64()`. This function figures out whether an update to jiffies is required, and if so, calls `do_timer(++ticks);` to actually update it. All the while, the `write_seq[un]lock(&jiffies_lock);` APIs provide protection over the mostly write-critical section.

Cache effects and false sharing

Modern processors make use of several levels of parallel cache memory within them, in order to provide a very significant speedup when working on memory (we briefly touched upon this in the companion guide *Linux Kernel Programming - Chapter 8, Kernel Memory Allocation for Module Authors – Part 1*, in the *Allocating slab memory* section). We realize that modern CPUs do *not* really read and write RAM directly; no, when the software indicates that a byte of RAM is to be read starting at some address, the CPU actually reads several bytes – a whole **cacheline** of bytes (typically 64 bytes) from the starting address into all the CPU caches (say, L1, L2, and L3: levels 1, 2, and 3). This way, accessing the next few elements of sequential memory results in a tremendous speedup as it's first checked for in the caches (first in L1, then L2, then L3, and a cache hit becomes likely). The reason it's (much) faster is simple: accessing CPU cache memory takes typically one to a few (single-digit) nanoseconds, whereas accessing RAM can take anywhere between 50 and 100 nanoseconds (of course, this depends on the hardware system in question and the amount of money you're willing to shell out!).

Software developers take advantage of such phenomena by doing things such as the following:

- Keeping important members of a data structure together (hopefully, within a single cacheline) and at the top of the structure
- Padding a structure member such that we don't fall off a cacheline (again, these points have been covered in the companion guide *Linux Kernel Programming - Chapter 8, Kernel Memory Allocation for Module Authors – Part 1*, in the *Data structures – a few design tips* section)

However, risks are involved and things do go wrong. As an example, consider two variables declared like so: u16 ax = 1, bx = 2; (u16 denotes an unsigned 16-bit integer value).

Now, as they have been declared adjacent to each other, they will, in all likelihood, occupy the same CPU cacheline at runtime. To understand what the issue is, let's take an example: consider a multicore system with two CPU cores, with each core having two CPU caches, L1 and L2, as well as a common or unified L3 cache. Now, a thread, *T1*, is working on variable ax and another thread, *T2*, is concurrently (on another CPU core) working on variable bx. So, think about it: when thread *T1*, running on CPU 0, accesses ax from main memory (RAM), its CPU caches will get populated with the current values of ax and bx (as they fall within the same cacheline!). Similarly, when thread *T2*, running on, say, CPU 1, accesses bx from RAM, its CPU caches will get populated with the current values of both variables as well. *Figure 7.4* conceptually depicts the situation:

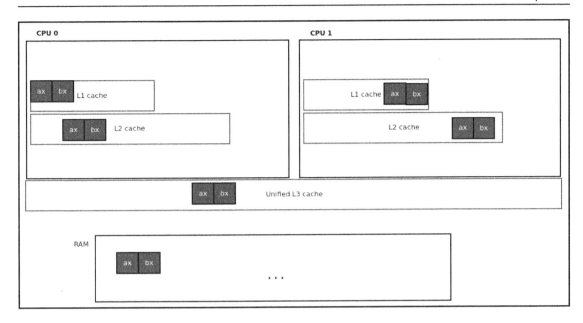

Figure 7.4 – Conceptual depiction of the CPU cache memory when threads T1 and T2 work in parallel on two adjacent variables, each on a distinct one

Fine so far; but what if *T1* performs an operation, say, `ax ++`, while concurrently, *T2* performs `bx ++`? Well, so what? (By the way, you might wonder: why aren't they using a lock? The interesting thing is, it's quite irrelevant to this discussion; there's no data race as each thread is accessing a different variable. The issue is with the fact that they're in the same CPU cacheline.)

Here's the issue: **cache coherency**. The processor and/or the OS in conjunction with the processor (this is all very arch-dependent stuff) will have to keep the caches and RAM synchronized or coherent with each other. Thus, the moment *T1* modifies `ax`, that particular cacheline of CPU 0 will have to be invalidated, that is, a CPU 0-cache-to-RAM flush of the CPU cacheline will occur to update RAM to the new value, and then immediately, a RAM-to-CPU 1-cache update must also occur to keep everything coherent!

But the cacheline contains `bx` as well, and, as we said, `bx` has also been modified on CPU 1 by *T2*. Thus, at about the same time, the CPU 1 cacheline will be flushed to RAM with the new value of `bx` and subsequently updated to CPU 0's caches (all the while, the unified L3 cache too will be read from/updated as well). As you can imagine, any updates on these variables will result in a whole lot of traffic over the caches and RAM; they will bounce. In fact, this is often referred to as **cache ping-pong**! This effect is very detrimental, significantly slowing down processing. This phenomenon is known as **false sharing**.

Recognizing false sharing is the hard part; we must look for variables living on a shared cacheline that are updated by different contexts (threads or whatever else) simultaneously.

 Interestingly, an earlier implementation of a key data structure in the memory management layer, `include/linux/mmzone.h:struct zone`, suffered from this very same false sharing issue: two spinlocks that were declared adjacent to each other! This has long been fixed (we briefly discussed *memory zones* in the companion guide *Linux Kernel Programming - Chapter 7, Memory Management Internals – Essentials*, in the *Physical RAM organization/zones* section).

How do you fix this false sharing? Easy: just ensure that the variables are spaced far enough apart to guarantee that they *do not share the same cacheline* (dummy padding bytes are often inserted between variables for this purpose). Do refer to the references to false sharing in the *Further reading* section as well.

Lock-free programming with per-CPU variables

As you have learned, when operating upon shared writable data, the critical section must be protected in some manner. Locking is perhaps the most common technology used to effect this protection. It's not all rosy, though, as performance can suffer. To realize why, consider a few analogies to a lock: one would be a funnel, with the stem of the funnel just wide enough to allow one thread at a time to flow through, no more. Another is a single toll booth on a busy highway or a traffic light at a busy intersection. These analogies help us visualize and understand why locking can cause bottlenecks, slowing performance down to a crawl in some drastic cases. Worse, these adverse effects can be multiplied on high-end multicore systems with a few hundred cores; in effect, locking doesn't scale well.

Another issue is that of *lock contention*; how often is a particular lock being acquired? Increasing the number of locks within a system has the benefit of lowering the contention for a particular lock between two or more processes (or threads). This is called **lock proficiency**. However, again, this is not scalable to an enormous extent: after a while, having thousands of locks on a system (the case with the Linux kernel, in fact) is not good news – the chances of subtle deadlock conditions arising is multiplied significantly.

So, many challenges exist – performance issues, deadlocks, priority inversion risks, convoying (due to lock ordering, fast code paths might need to wait for the first slower one that's taken a lock that the faster ones also require), and so on. Evolving the kernel in a scalable manner a whole level further has mandated the use of *lock-free algorithms* and their implementation within the kernel. These have led to several innovative techniques, among them being per-CPU (PCP) data, lock-free data structures (by design), and RCU.

In this book, though, we elect to cover only per-CPU as a lock-free programming technique in some detail. The details regarding RCU (and its associated lock-free data structure by design) are beyond this book's scope. Do refer to the *Further reading* section of this chapter for several useful resources on RCU, its meaning, and its usage within the Linux kernel.

Per-CPU variables

As the name suggests, **per-CPU variables** work by keeping *a copy* of the variable, the data item in question, assigned to each (live) CPU on the system. In effect, we get rid of the problem area for concurrency, the critical section, by avoiding the sharing of data between threads. With the per-CPU data technique, since every CPU refers to its very own copy of the data, a thread running on that processor can manipulate it without any worry of racing. (This is roughly analogous to local variables; as locals are on the private stack of each thread, they aren't shared between threads, thus there's no critical section and no need for locking.) Here, too, the need for locking is thus eliminated – making it a *lock-free* technology!

So, think of this: if you are running on a system with four live CPU cores, then a per-CPU variable on that system is essentially an array of four elements: element 0 represents the data value on the first CPU, element 1 the data value on the second CPU core, and so on. Understanding this, you'll realize that per-CPU variables are also roughly analogous to the user space Pthreads **Thread Local Storage** (**TLS**) implementation where each thread automatically obtains a copy of the (TLS) variable marked with the __thread keyword. There, and here with per-CPU variables, it should be obvious: use per-CPU variables for small data items only. This is because the data item is reproduced (copied) with one instance per CPU core (on a high-end system with a few hundred cores, the overheads do climb). We mention some examples of per-CPU usage in the kernel code base (in the *Per-CPU usage within the kernel* section).

Now, when working with per-CPU variables, you must use the helper methods (macros and APIs) provided by the kernel and not attempt to directly access them (much like we saw with the refcount and atomic operators).

Working with per-CPU

Let's approach the helper APIs and macros (methods) for per-CPU data by dividing the discussion into two portions. First, you will learn how to allocate, initialize, and subsequently free a per-CPU data item. Then, you will learn how to work with (read/write) it.

Allocating, initialization, and freeing per-CPU variables

There are broadly two types of per-CPU variables: statically and dynamically allocated ones. Statically allocated per-CPU variables are allocated at compile time itself, typically via one of these macros: DEFINE_PER_CPU or DECLARE_PER_CPU. Using the DEFINE one allows you to allocate and initialize the variable. Here's an example of allocating a single integer as a per-CPU variable:

```
#include <linux/percpu.h>
DEFINE_PER_CPU(int, pcpa);        // signature: DEFINE_PER_CPU(type, name)
```

Now, on a system with, say, four CPU cores, it would conceptually appear like this at initialization:

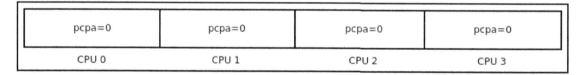

Figure 7.5 – Conceptual representation of a per-CPU data item on a system with four live CPUs

(The actual implementation is quite a bit more complex than this, of course; please refer to the *Further reading* section of this chapter to see more on the internal implementation.)

In a nutshell, using per-CPU variables is good for performance enhancement on time-sensitive code paths because of the following:

- We avoid using costly, performance-busting locks.
- The access and manipulation of a per-CPU variable is guaranteed to remain on one particular CPU core; this eliminates expensive cache effects such as cache ping-pong and false sharing (covered in the *Cache effects and false sharing* section).

Dynamically allocating per-CPU data can be achieved via the `alloc_percpu()` or `alloc_percpu_gfp()` wrapper macros, simply passing the data type of the object to allocate as per-CPU, and, for the latter, passing along the `gfp` allocation flag as well:

```
alloc_percpu[_gfp](type [,gfp]);
```

The underlying `__alloc_per_cpu[_gfp]()` routines are exported via `EXPORT_SYMBOL_GPL()` (and thus can be employed only when an LKM is released under a GPL-compatible license).

> As you've learned, the resource-managed `devm_*()` API variants allow you (typically when writing drivers) to conveniently use these routines to allocate memory; the kernel will take care of freeing it, helping prevent leakage scenarios. The `devm_alloc_percpu(dev, type)` macro allows you to use this as a resource-managed version of `__alloc_percpu()`.

The memory allocated via the preceding routine(s) must subsequently be freed using the `void free_percpu(void __percpu *__pdata)` API.

Performing I/O (reads and writes) on per-CPU variables

A key question, of course, is how exactly can you access (read) and update (write) to per-CPU variables? The kernel provides several helper routines to do so; let's take a simple example to understand how. We define a single integer per-CPU variable, and at a later point in time, we want to access and print its current value. You should realize that, being per-CPU, the value retrieved will be auto-calculated *based on the CPU core the code is currently running on*; in other words, if the following code is running on core 1, then in effect, the `pcpa[1]` value is fetched (it's not done exactly like this; this is just conceptual):

```
DEFINE_PER_CPU(int, pcpa);
int val;
[ ... ]
val = get_cpu_var(pcpa);
pr_info("cpu0: pcpa = %+d\n", val);
put_cpu_var(pcpa);
```

The pair of {get,put}_cpu_var() macros allows us to safely retrieve or modify the per-CPU value of the given per-CPU variable (its parameter). It's important to understand that the code between get_cpu_var() and put_cpu_var() (or equivalent) is, in effect, a critical section – an atomic context – *where kernel preemption is disabled and any kind of blocking (or sleeping) is disallowed. If you do anything here that blocks (sleeps) in any manner,* it's a kernel bug. For example, see what happens if you try to allocate memory via vmalloc() within the get_cpu_var()/put_cpu_var() pair of macros:

```
void *p;
val = get_cpu_var(pcpa);
p = vmalloc(20000);
pr_info("cpu1: pcpa = %+d\n", val);
put_cpu_var(pcpa);
vfree(p);
[ ... ]

$ sudo insmod <whatever>.ko
$ dmesg
[ ... ]
BUG: sleeping function called from invalid context at mm/slab.h:421
[67641.443225] in_atomic(): 1, irqs_disabled(): 0, pid: 12085, name:
thrd_1/1
[ ... ]
$
```

(By the way, calling the printk() (or pr_<foo>()) wrappers as we do within the critical section is fine as they're non-blocking.) The issue here is that the vmalloc() API is possibly a blocking one; it might sleep (we discussed it in detail in the companion guide *Linux Kernel Programming - Chapter 9, Kernel Memory Allocation for Module Authors – Part 2*, in the *Understanding and using the kernel vmalloc() API* section), and the code between the get_cpu_var()/put_cpu_var() pair must be atomic and non-blocking.

Internally, the get_cpu_var() macro invokes preempt_disable(), disabling kernel preemption, and put_cpu_var() undoes this by invoking preempt_enable(). As seen earlier (in the companion guide *Linux Kernel Programming* chapters on *CPU scheduling*), this can be nested and the kernel maintains a preempt_count variable to figure out whether kernel preemption is actually enabled or disabled.

The upshot of all this is that you must carefully match the {get,put}_cpu_var() macros when using them (for example, if we call the get macro twice, we must also call the corresponding put macro twice).

The get_cpu_var() is an *lvalue* and can thus be operated upon; for example, to increment the per-CPU pcpa variable, just do the following:

```
get_cpu_var(pcpa) ++;
put_cpu_var(pcpa);
```

You can also (safely) retrieve the current per-CPU value via the macro:

```
per_cpu(var, cpu);
```

So, to retrieve the per-CPU pcpa variable for every CPU core on the system, use the following:

```
for_each_online_cpu(i) {
    val = per_cpu(pcpa, i);
    pr_info(" cpu %2d: pcpa = %+d\n", i, val);
}
```

> FYI, you can always use the smp_processor_id() macro to figure out which CPU core you're currently running upon; in fact, this is precisely how our convenient.h:PRINT_CTX() macro does it.

In a similar manner, the kernel provides routines to work with pointers to variables that require to be per-CPU, the {get,put}_cpu_ptr() and per_cpu_ptr() macros. These macros are heavily employed when working with a per-CPU data structure (as opposed to just a simple integer); we safely retrieve the pointer to the structure of the CPU we're currently running upon, and use it (per_cpu_ptr()).

Per-CPU – an example kernel module

A hands-on session with our sample per-CPU demo kernel module will definitely help in using this powerful feature (code here: ch13/2_percpu). Here, we define and use two per-CPU variables:

- A statically allocated and initialized per-CPU integer
- A dynamically allocated per-CPU data structure

As an interesting way to help demo per-CPU variables, let's do this: we shall arrange for our demo kernel module to spawn off a couple of kernel threads. Let's call them `thrd_0` and `thrd_1`. Furthermore, once created, we shall make use of the CPU mask (and API) to *affine* our `thrd_0` kernel thread on CPU 0 and our `thrd_1` kernel thread on CPU 1 (hence, they will be scheduled to run on only these cores; of course, we must test this code on a VM with at least two CPU cores).

The following code snippets illustrate how we define and use the per-CPU variables (we leave out the code that creates the kernel threads and sets up their CPU affinity masks, as they are not relevant to the coverage of this chapter; nevertheless, it's key to browse through the full code and try it out!):

```c
// ch13/2_percpu/percpu_var.c
[ ... ]
/*--- The per-cpu variables, an integer 'pcpa' and a data structure --- */
/* This per-cpu integer 'pcpa' is statically allocated and initialized to 0
*/
DEFINE_PER_CPU(int, pcpa);

/* This per-cpu structure will be dynamically allocated via alloc_percpu()
*/
static struct drv_ctx {
    int tx, rx; /* here, as a demo, we just use these two members,
                   ignoring the rest */
    [ ... ]
} *pcp_ctx;
[ ... ]

static int __init init_percpu_var(void)
{
    [ ... ]
    /* Dynamically allocate the per-cpu structures */
    ret = -ENOMEM;
    pcp_ctx = (struct drv_ctx __percpu *) alloc_percpu(struct drv_ctx);
    if (!pcp_ctx) {
        [ ... ]
}
```

Why not use the resource-managed `devm_alloc_percpu()` instead? Yes, you should when appropriate; here, though, as we're not writing a proper driver, we don't have a `struct device *dev` pointer handy, which is the required first parameter to `devm_alloc_percpu()`.

By the way, I faced an issue when coding this kernel module; to set the CPU mask (to change the CPU affinity for each of our kernel threads), the kernel API is the `sched_setaffinity()` function, which, unfortunately for us, is *not exported*, thus preventing us from using it. So, we perform what is definitely considered a hack: obtain the address of the uncooperative function via `kallsyms_lookup_name()` (which works when `CONFIG_KALLSYMS` is defined) and then invoke it as a function pointer. It works, but is most certainly not the right way to code.

Our design idea is to create two kernel threads and have each of them differently manipulate the per-CPU data variables. If these were ordinary global variables, this would certainly constitute a critical section and we would of course require a lock; but here, precisely because they are *per-CPU* and because we guarantee that our threads run on separate cores, we can concurrently update them with differing data! Our kernel thread worker routine is as follows; the argument to it is the thread number (0 or 1). We accordingly branch off and manipulate the per-CPU data (we have our first kernel thread increment the integer three times, while our second kernel thread decrements it three times):

```
/* Our kernel thread worker routine */
static int thrd_work(void *arg)
{
    int i, val;
    long thrd = (long)arg;
    struct drv_ctx *ctx;
    [ ... ]

    /* Set CPU affinity mask to 'thrd', which is either 0 or 1 */
    if (set_cpuaffinity(thrd) < 0) {
        [ ... ]
    SHOW_CPU_CTX();

    if (thrd == 0) { /* our kthread #0 runs on CPU 0 */
        for (i=0; i<THRD0_ITERS; i++) {
            /* Operate on our perpcu integer */
            val = ++ get_cpu_var(pcpa);
            pr_info(" thrd_0/cpu0: pcpa = %+d\n", val);
            put_cpu_var(pcpa);

            /* Operate on our perpcu structure */
            ctx = get_cpu_ptr(pcp_ctx);
            ctx->tx += 100;
            pr_info(" thrd_0/cpu0: pcp ctx: tx = %5d, rx = %5d\n",
                ctx->tx, ctx->rx);
            put_cpu_ptr(pcp_ctx);
```

```
        }
    } else if (thrd == 1) { /* our kthread #1 runs on CPU 1 */
        for (i=0; i<THRD1_ITERS; i++) {
            /* Operate on our perpcu integer */
            val = -- get_cpu_var(pcpa);
            pr_info(" thrd_1/cpu1: pcpa = %+d\n", val);
            put_cpu_var(pcpa);
            /* Operate on our perpcu structure */
            ctx = get_cpu_ptr(pcp_ctx);
            ctx->rx += 200;
            pr_info(" thrd_1/cpu1: pcp ctx: tx = %5d, rx = %5d\n",
                ctx->tx, ctx->rx);
            put_cpu_ptr(pcp_ctx);
        }
    }
    disp_vars();
    pr_info("Our kernel thread #%ld exiting now...\n", thrd);
    return 0;
}
```

The effect at runtime is interesting; see the following kernel log:

```
[ 2052.643407] percpu_var:init percpu_var(): inserted
[ 2052.646162] percpu_var:thrd_work(): *** kthread PID 34971 on cpu 0 now ***
[ 2052.646648] percpu_var:thrd_work():    thrd_0/cpu0: pcpa = +1
[ 2052.647036] percpu_var:thrd_work():    thrd_0/cpu0: pcp ctx: tx =    100, rx =      0
[ 2052.647549] percpu_var:thrd_work():    thrd_0/cpu0: pcpa = +2
[ 2052.647942] percpu_var:thrd_work():    thrd_0/cpu0: pcp ctx: tx =    200, rx =      0
[ 2052.648506] percpu_var:thrd_work():    thrd_0/cpu0: pcpa = +3
[ 2052.648884] percpu_var:thrd_work():    thrd_0/cpu0: pcp ctx: tx =    300, rx =      0
[ 2052.649384] percpu_var:disp_vars(): 000) [thrd_0/0]:34971  | .N.0  /* disp_vars() */
[ 2052.649979] percpu_var:disp_vars():   cpu  0: pcpa = +3, rx =      0, tx =   300
[ 2052.650486] percpu_var:disp_vars():   cpu  1: pcpa = +0, rx =      0, tx =     0
[ 2052.650999] percpu_var:thrd_work(): Our kernel thread #0 exiting now...
[ 2052.655130] percpu_var:thrd_work(): *** kthread PID 34972 on cpu 1 now ***
[ 2052.655750] percpu_var:thrd_work():    thrd_1/cpu1: pcpa = -1
[ 2052.656255] percpu_var:thrd_work():    thrd_1/cpu1: pcp ctx: tx =      0, rx =   200
[ 2052.656932] percpu_var:thrd_work():    thrd_1/cpu1: pcpa = -2
[ 2052.657440] percpu_var:thrd_work():    thrd_1/cpu1: pcp ctx: tx =      0, rx =   400
[ 2052.658275] percpu_var:thrd_work():    thrd_1/cpu1: pcpa = -3
[ 2052.658746] percpu_var:thrd_work():    thrd_1/cpu1: pcp ctx: tx =      0, rx =   600
[ 2052.659370] percpu_var:disp_vars(): 001) [thrd_1/1]:34972  | .N.0  /* disp_vars() */
[ 2052.660051] percpu_var:disp_vars():   cpu  0: pcpa = +3, rx =      0, tx =   300
[ 2052.660684] percpu_var:disp_vars():   cpu  1: pcpa = -3, rx =    600, tx =     0
[ 2052.661280] percpu_var:thrd_work(): Our kernel thread #1 exiting now...
```

Figure 7.6 – Screenshot showing the kernel log when our ch13/2_percpu/percpu_var LKM runs

In the last three lines of output in *Figure 7.6,* you can see a summary of the values of our per-CPU data variables on CPU 0 and CPU 1 (we show it via our disp_vars() function). Clearly, for the per-CPU pcpa integer (as well as the pcp_ctx data structure), the values are *different* as expected, *without explicit locking.*

The kernel module just demonstrated uses
the `for_each_online_cpu(i)` macro to display the value of our per-CPU variables on each online CPU. Next, what if you have, say, six CPUs on your VM but want only two of them to be "live" at runtime? There are several ways to arrange this; one is to pass the `maxcpus=n` parameter to the VM's kernel at boot – you can see if it's there by looking up
`/proc/cmdline`:
`$ cat /proc/cmdline`
`BOOT_IMAGE=/boot/vmlinuz-5.4.0-llkd-dbg`
`root=UUID=1c4<...> ro console=ttyS0,115200n8`
`console=tty0  quiet splash 3 **maxcpus=2**`
Also notice that we're running on our custom `5.4.0-llkd-dbg` debug kernel.

Per-CPU usage within the kernel

Per-CPU variables are quite heavily used within the Linux kernel; one interesting case is in the implementation of the `current` macro on the x86 architecture (we covered using the `current` macro in the companion guide *Linux Kernel Programming - Chapter 6, Kernel Internals Essentials – Processes and Threads*, in the *Accessing the task structure with current* section). The fact is that `current` is looked up (and set) every so often; keeping it as a per-CPU ensures that we keep its access lock-free! Here's the code that implements it:

```
// arch/x86/include/asm/current.h
[ ... ]
DECLARE_PER_CPU(struct task_struct *, current_task);
static __always_inline struct task_struct *get_current(void)
{
    return this_cpu_read_stable(current_task);
}
#define current get_current()
```

The `DECLARE_PER_CPU()` macro declares the variable named `current_task` as a per-CPU variable of type `struct task_struct *`. The `get_current()` inline function invokes the `this_cpu_read_stable()` helper on this per-CPU variable, thus reading the value of `current` on the CPU core that it's currently running on (read the comment at `https://elixir.bootlin.com/linux/v5.4/source/arch/x86/include/asm/percpu.h#L383` to see what this routine's about). Okay, that's fine, but an FAQ: where does this `current_task` per-CPU variable get updated? Think about it: the kernel must change (update) `current` *whenever its context switches* to another task.

That's exactly the case; it is indeed updated within the context-switching code (`arch/x86/kernel/process_64.c:__switch_to()`; at `https://elixir.bootlin.com/linux/v5.4/source/arch/x86/kernel/process_64.c#L504`):

```
__visible __notrace_funcgraph struct task_struct *
__switch_to(struct task_struct *prev_p, struct task_struct *next_p)
{
    [ ... ]
    this_cpu_write(current_task, next_p);
    [ ... ]
}
```

Next, a quick experiment to show per-CPU usage within the kernel code base via `__alloc_percpu()`: run `cscope -d` in the root of the kernel source tree (this assumes you've already built the `cscope` index via `make cscope`). In the `cscope` menu, under the `Find functions calling this function:` prompt, type `__alloc_percpu`. The result is as follows:

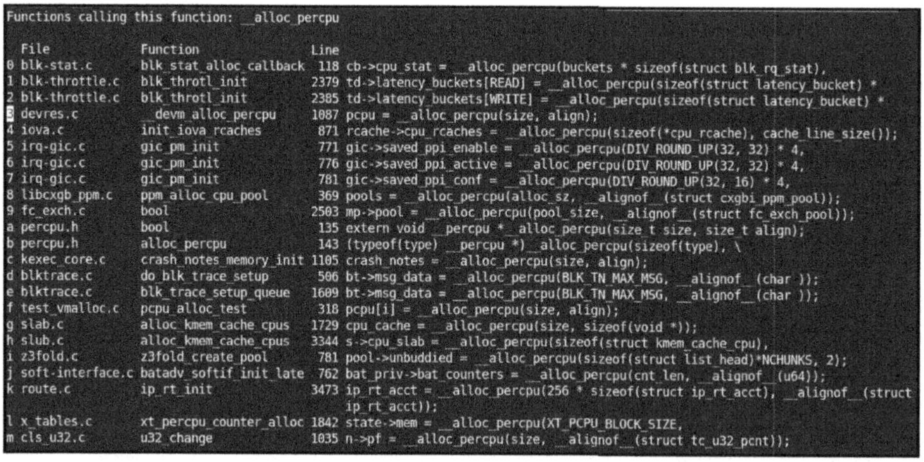

Figure 7.7 – (Partial) screenshot of the output of cscope -d showing kernel code that calls the __alloc_percpu() API

This, of course, is just a partial list of per-CPU usage within the kernel code base, tracking only use via the `__alloc_percpu()` underlying API. Searching for functions calling `alloc_percpu[_gfp]()` (wrappers over `__alloc_percpu[_gfp]()`) reveals many more hits.

With this, having completed our discussions on kernel synchronization techniques and APIs, let's finish this chapter by learning about a key area: tools and tips when debugging locking issues within kernel code!

Lock debugging within the kernel

The kernel has several means to help debug difficult situations with regard to kernel-level locking issues, *deadlock* being a primary one.

Just in case you haven't already, do ensure you've first read the basics on synchronization, locking, and deadlock guidelines from the previous chapter (Chapter 6, *Kernel Synchronization – Part 1*, especially the *Exclusive execution and atomicity* and *Concurrency concerns within the Linux kernel* sections).

With any debug scenario, there are different points at which debugging occurs, and thus perhaps differing tools and techniques that should/could be used. Very broadly speaking, a bug might be noticed at, and thus debugged at, a few different points in time (within the **Software Development Life Cycle** (**SDLC**), really):

- During development
- After development but before release (testing, **Quality Assurance** (**QA**), and so on)
- After internal release
- After release, in the field

A well-known and unfortunately true homily: the "further" a bug is exposed from development, the costlier it is to fix! So you really do want to try and find and fix them as early as possible!

As this book is focused squarely on kernel development, we shall focus here on a few tools and techniques for debugging locking issues at development time.

Important: We expect that by now, you're running on a debug kernel, that is, a kernel deliberately configured for development/debug purposes. Performance will take a hit, but that's okay – we're out bug hunting now! We covered the configuration of a typical debug kernel in the companion guide *Linux Kernel Programming* - Chapter 5, *Writing Your First Kernel Module – LKMs Part 2*, in the *Configuring a debug kernel* section, and have even provided a sample kernel configuration file for debugging here: https://github.com/PacktPublishing/Linux-Kernel-Programming/blob/master/ch5/kconfigs/sample_kconfig_llkd_dbg.config. Specifics on configuring the debug kernel for lock debugging are in fact covered next.

Configuring a debug kernel for lock debugging

Due to its relevance and importance to lock debugging, we will take a quick look at a key point from the *Linux Kernel patch submission checklist* document (`https://www.kernel.org/doc/html/v5.4/process/submit-checklist.html`) that's most relevant to our discussions here, on enabling a debug kernel (especially for lock debugging):

```
// https://www.kernel.org/doc/html/v5.4/process/submit-checklist.html
[...]
12. Has been tested with CONFIG_PREEMPT, CONFIG_DEBUG_PREEMPT,
CONFIG_DEBUG_SLAB, CONFIG_DEBUG_PAGEALLOC, CONFIG_DEBUG_MUTEXES,
CONFIG_DEBUG_SPINLOCK, CONFIG_DEBUG_ATOMIC_SLEEP, CONFIG_PROVE_RCU and
CONFIG_DEBUG_OBJECTS_RCU_HEAD all simultaneously enabled.
13. Has been build- and runtime tested with and without CONFIG_SMP and
CONFIG_PREEMPT.

16. All codepaths have been exercised with all lockdep features enabled.
[ ... ]
```

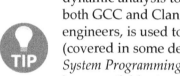 Though not covered in this book, I cannot fail to mention a very powerful dynamic memory error detector called **Kernel Address SANitizer (KASAN)**. In a nutshell, it uses compile-time instrumentation-based dynamic analysis to catch common memory-related bugs (it works with both GCC and Clang). **ASan (Address Sanitizer)**, contributed by Google engineers, is used to monitor and detect memory issues in user space apps (covered in some detail and compared with valgrind in the *Hands-On System Programming for Linux* book). The kernel equivalent, KASAN, has been available since the 4.0 kernel for both x86_64 and AArch64 (ARM64, from 4.4 Linux). Details (on enabling and using it) can be found within the kernel documentation (`https://www.kernel.org/doc/html/v5.4/dev-tools/kasan.html#the-kernel-address-sanitizer-kasan`); I highly recommend you enable it in your debug kernel.

As covered in the companion guide *Linux Kernel Programming* - Chapter 2, *Building the 5.x Linux Kernel from Source – Part 1*, we can configure our Linux kernel specifically for our requirements. Here (within the root of the 5.4.0 kernel source tree), we perform `make menuconfig` and navigate to the `Kernel hacking / Lock Debugging (spinlocks, mutexes, etc...)` menu (see *Figure 7.8*, taken on our x86_64 Ubuntu 20.04 LTS guest VM):

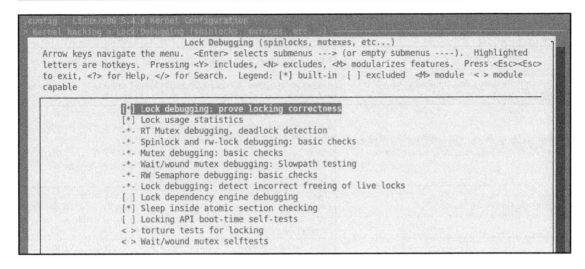

Figure 7.8 – (Truncated) screenshot of the kernel hacking / Lock Debugging (spinlocks, mutexes, etc...) menu with required items enabled for our debug kernel

Figure 7.8 is a (truncated) screenshot of the `<Kernel hacking > Lock Debugging (spinlocks, mutexes, etc...)` menu with required items enabled for our debug kernel.

Instead of interactively having to go through each menu item and selecting the `<Help>` button to see what it's about, a much simpler way to gain the same help information is to peek inside the relevant Kconfig file (that describes the menu). Here, it's `lib/Kconfig.debug`, as all debug-related menus are there. For our particular case, search for the `menu "Lock Debugging (spinlocks, mutexes, etc...)"` string, where the `Lock Debugging` section begins (see the following table).

The following table summarizes what each kernel lock debugging configuration option helps debug (we haven't shown all of them and, for some of them, have directly quoted from the `lib/Kconfig.debug` file):

Lock debugging menu title	What it does
Lock debugging: prove locking correctness (CONFIG_PROVE_LOCKING)	This is the `lockdep` kernel option – turn it on to get rolling proof of lock correctness at all times. Any possibility of locking-related deadlock *is reported even before it actually occurs*; very useful! (Explained shortly in more detail.)
Lock usage statistics (CONFIG_LOCK_STAT)	Tracks lock contention points (explained shortly in more detail).
RT mutex debugging, deadlock detection (CONFIG_DEBUG_RT_MUTEXES)	*"This allows rt mutex semantics violations and rt mutex related deadlocks (lockups) to be detected and reported automatically."*

Spinlock and `rw-lock` debugging: basic checks (`CONFIG_DEBUG_SPINLOCK`)	Turning this on (along with `CONFIG_SMP`) helps catch missing spinlock initialization and other common spinlock errors.
Mutex debugging: basic checks (`CONFIG_DEBUG_MUTEXES`)	*"This feature allows mutex semantics violations to be detected and reported."*
RW semaphore debugging: basic checks (`CONFIG_DEBUG_RWSEMS`)	Allows mismatched RW semaphore locks and unlocks to be detected and reported.
Lock debugging: detect incorrect freeing of live locks (`CONFIG_DEBUG_LOCK_ALLOC`)	*"This feature will check whether any held lock (spinlock, rwlock, mutex or rwsem) is incorrectly freed by the kernel, via any of the memory-freeing routines (`kfree()`, `kmem_cache_free()`, `free_pages()`, `vfree()`, etc.), whether a live lock is incorrectly reinitialized via `spin_lock_init()`/`mutex_init()`/etc., or whether there is any lock held during task exit."*
Sleep inside atomic section checking (`CONFIG_DEBUG_ATOMIC_SLEEP`)	*"If you say Y here, various routines which may sleep will become very noisy if they are called inside atomic sections: when a spinlock is held, inside an rcu read side critical section, inside preempt disabled sections, inside an interrupt, etc..."*
Locking API boot-time self-tests (`CONFIG_DEBUG_LOCKING_API_SELFTESTS`)	*"Say Y here if you want the kernel to run a short self-test during bootup. The self-test checks whether common types of locking bugs are detected by debugging mechanisms or not. (if you disable lock debugging then those bugs wont be detected of course.) The following locking APIs are covered: spinlocks, rwlocks, mutexes and rwsems."*
Torture tests for locking (`CONFIG_LOCK_TORTURE_TEST`)	*"This option provides a kernel module that runs torture tests on kernel locking primitives. The kernel module may be built after the fact on the running kernel to be tested, if desired." (Can be built either inline with 'Y' or externally as a module with 'M')."*

Table 17.4 – Typical kernel lock debugging configuration options and their meaning

As suggested previously, turning on all or most of these lock debug options within a debug kernel used during development and testing is a good idea. Of course, as expected, doing so might considerably slow down execution (and use more memory); as in life, this is a trade-off you have to decide on: you gain detection of common locking issues, errors, and deadlocks, at the cost of speed. It's a trade-off you should be more than willing to make, especially when developing (or refactoring) the code.

The lock validator lockdep – catching locking issues early

The Linux kernel has a tremendously useful feature begging to be taken advantage of by kernel developers: a runtime locking correctness or locking dependency validator; in short, **lockdep**. The basic idea is this: the `lockdep` runtime comes into play whenever any locking activity occurs within the kernel – the taking or the release of *any* kernel-level lock, or any locking sequence involving multiple locks.

This is tracked or mapped (see the following paragraph for more on the performance impact and how it's mitigated). By applying well-known rules for correct locking (you got a hint of this in the previous chapter in the *Locking guidelines and deadlock* section), `lockdep` then makes a conclusion regarding the validity of the correctness of what was done.

The beauty of it is that `lockdep` achieves 100% mathematical proof (or closure) that a lock sequence is correct or not. The following is a direct quote from the kernel documentation on the topic (`https://www.kernel.org/doc/html/v5.4/locking/lockdep-design.html`):

> *"The validator achieves perfect, mathematical 'closure' (proof of locking correctness) in the sense that for every simple, standalone single-task locking sequence that occurred at least once during the lifetime of the kernel, the validator proves it with a 100% certainty that no combination and timing of these locking sequences can cause any class of lock related deadlock."*

Furthermore, `lockdep` warns you (by issuing the `WARN*()` macros) of any violation of the following classes of locking bugs: deadlocks/lock inversion scenarios, circular lock dependencies, and hard IRQ/soft IRQ safe/unsafe locking bugs. This information is precious; validating your code with `lockdep` can save hundreds of wasted hours of productivity by catching locking issues early. (FYI, `lockdep` tracks all locks and their locking sequence or "lock chains"; these can be viewed through `/proc/lockdep_chains`).

A word on *performance mitigation*: you might well imagine that, with literally thousands or more lock instances floating around, it would be absurdly slow to validate every single lock sequence (yes, in fact, it turns out to be a task of order `O(N^2)` algorithmic time complexity!). This would just not work; so, `lockdep` works by verifying any locking scenario (say, on a certain code path, lock A is taken, then lock B is taken – this is referred to as a *lock sequence* or *lock chain*) **only once**, the very first time it occurs. (It knows this by maintaining a 64-bit hash for every lock chain it encounters.)

Primitive user space approaches: A very primitive – and certainly not guaranteed – way to try and detect deadlocks is via user space by simply using GNU ps(1); doing ps -LA -o state,pid,cmd | grep "^D" prints any threads in the D – *uninterruptible sleep* (TASK_UNINTERRUPTIBLE) – state. This could – but may not – be due to a deadlock; if it persists for a long while, chances are higher that it is a deadlock. Give it a try! Of course, lockdep is a far superior solution. (Note that this only works with GNU ps, not the lightweight ones such as busybox ps.)

Other useful user space tools are strace(1) and ltrace(1) – they provide a detailed trace of every system and library call, respectively, issued by a process (or thread); you might be able to catch a hung process/thread and see where it got stuck (using strace -p PID might be especially useful on a hung process).

The other point that you need to be clear about is this: lockdep *will* issue warnings regarding (mathematically) incorrect locking *even if no deadlock actually occurs at runtime!* lockdep offers proof that there is indeed an issue that could conceivably cause a bug (deadlock, unsafe locking, and so on) at some point in the future if no corrective action is taken; it's usually dead right; take it seriously and fix the issue. (Then again, typically, nothing in the software universe is 100% correct 100% of the time: what if a bug creeps into the lockdep code itself? There's even a CONFIG_DEBUG_LOCKDEP config option. The bottom line is that we, the human developers, must carefully assess the situation, checking for false positives.)

Next, lockdep works upon a *lock class*; this is simply a "logical" lock as opposed to "physical" instances of that lock. For example, the kernel's open file data structure, struct file, has two locks – a mutex and a spinlock – and each of them is considered a lock class by lockdep. Even if a few thousand instances of struct file exist in memory at runtime, lockdep will track it as a class only. For more detail on lockdep's internal design, we refer you to the official kernel documentation on it (https://www.kernel.org/doc/html/v5.4/locking/lockdep-design.html).

Examples – catching deadlock bugs with lockdep

Here, we shall assume that you've by now built and are running upon a debug kernel with `lockdep` enabled (as described in detail in the *Configuring a debug kernel for lock debugging* section). Verify that it is indeed enabled:

```
$ uname -r
5.4.0-llkd-dbg
$ grep PROVE_LOCKING /boot/config-5.4.0-llkd-dbg
CONFIG_PROVE_LOCKING=y
$
```

Okay, good! Now, let's get hands-on with some deadlocks, seeing how `lockdep` will help you catch them. Read on!

Example 1 – catching a self deadlock bug with lockdep

As a first example, let's travel back to one of our kernel modules from the companion guide *Linux Kernel Programming - Chapter 6, Kernel Internals Essentials – Processes and Threads*, in the *Iterating over the task list* section, here: `https://github.com/PacktPublishing/Linux-Kernel-Programming/blob/master/ch6/foreach/thrd_showall/thrd_showall.c`. Here, we looped over each thread, printing some details from within its task structure; with regard to this, here's a code snippet where we obtain the name of the thread (recall that it's in a member of the task structure called `comm`):

```
// ch6/foreach/thrd_showall/thrd_showall.c
static int showthrds(void)
{
    struct task_struct *g = NULL, *t = NULL; /* 'g' : process ptr; 't':
thread ptr */
    [ ... ]
    do_each_thread(g, t) { /* 'g' : process ptr; 't': thread ptr */
        task_lock(t);
        [ ... ]
        if (!g->mm) {     // kernel thread
            snprintf(tmp, TMPMAX-1, " [%16s]", t->comm);
        } else {
            snprintf(tmp, TMPMAX-1, " %16s ", t->comm);
        }
        snprintf(buf, BUFMAX-1, "%s%s", buf, tmp);
        [ ... ]
```

This works, but there appears to be a better way to do it: instead of directly looking up the thread's name with `t->comm` (as we do here), the kernel provides the `{get,set}_task_comm()` helper routines to both get and set the name of the task. So, we rewrite the code to use the `get_task_comm()` helper macro; the first parameter to it is the buffer to place the name into (it's expected that you've allocated memory to it), and the second parameter is the pointer to the task structure of the thread whose name you are querying (the following code snippet is from here: `ch13/3_lockdep/buggy_thrdshow_eg/thrd_showall_buggy.c`):

```
// ch13/3_lockdep/buggy_lockdep/thrd_showall_buggy.c
static int showthrds_buggy(void)
{
    struct task_struct *g, *t; /* 'g' : process ptr; 't': thread ptr */
    [ ... ]
    char buf[BUFMAX], tmp[TMPMAX], tasknm[TASK_COMM_LEN];
    [ ... ]
    do_each_thread(g, t) { /* 'g' : process ptr; 't': thread ptr */
        task_lock(t);
        [ ... ]
        get_task_comm(tasknm, t);
        if (!g->mm) // kernel thread
            snprintf(tmp, sizeof(tasknm)+3, " [%16s]", tasknm);
        else
            snprintf(tmp, sizeof(tasknm)+3, " %16s ", tasknm);
        [ ... ]
```

When compiled and inserted into the kernel on our test system (a VM, thank goodness), it can get weird, or even just simply hang! (When I did this, I was able to retrieve the kernel log via `dmesg(1)` before the system became completely unresponsive.).

What if your system just hangs upon insertion of this LKM? Well, that's a taste of the difficulty of kernel debugging! One thing you can try (which worked for me when trying this very example on a x86_64 Fedora 29 VM) is to reboot the hung VM and look up the kernel log by leveraging systemd's powerful `journalctl(1)` utility with the `journalctl --since="1 hour ago"` command; you should be able to see the printks from `lockdep` now. Again, unfortunately, it's not guaranteed that the key portion of the kernel log is saved to disk (at the time it hung) for `journalctl` to be able to retrieve. This is why using the kernel's **kdump** feature – and then performing postmortem analysis of the kernel dump image file with `crash(8)` – can be a lifesaver (see resources on using kdump and crash in the *Further reading* section for this chapter).

Glancing at the kernel log, it becomes clear: `lockdep` has caught a (self) deadlock (we show relevant parts of the output in the screenshot):

```
[ 1021.429110] thrd_showall_buggy: inserted
[ 1021.431264] ------------------------------------------------------------------
                  TGID   PID       current    stack-start    Thread Name   MT? # thrds
               ------------------------------------------------------------------

[ 1021.440804] ===========================================
[ 1021.442856] WARNING: possible recursive locking detected
[ 1021.445129] 5.4.0-llkd-dbg #2 Tainted: G           OE
[ 1021.447157] --------------------------------------------
[ 1021.449384] insmod/2367 is trying to acquire lock:
[ 1021.451361] ffff88805de73f08 (&(&p->alloc_lock)->rlock){+.+.}, at: __get_task_comm+0x28/0x50
[ 1021.453676]
               but task is already holding lock:
[ 1021.457365] ffff88805de73f08 (&(&p->alloc_lock)->rlock){+.+.}, at: showthrds_buggy+0x13e/0x6d1 [thrd_showall_buggy]
[ 1021.461623]
               other info that might help us debug this:
[ 1021.465332]  Possible unsafe locking scenario:

[ 1021.468871]        CPU0
[ 1021.470563]        ----
[ 1021.472349]   lock(&(&p->alloc_lock)->rlock);
[ 1021.474591]   lock(&(&p->alloc_lock)->rlock);
[ 1021.476870]
               *** DEADLOCK ***

[ 1021.482086]  May be due to missing lock nesting notation

[ 1021.485550] 1 lock held by insmod/2367:
[ 1021.487884]  #0: ffff88805de73f08 (&(&p->alloc_lock)->rlock){+.+.}, at: showthrds_buggy+0x13e/0x6d1 [thrd_showall_buggy]
```

Figure 7.9 – (Partial) screenshot showing the kernel log after our buggy module is loaded; lockdep catches the self deadlock!

Though a lot more detail follows (including the stack backtrace of the kernel stack of `insmod(8)` – as it was the process context, in this case, register values, and so on), what we see in the preceding figure is sufficient to deduce what happened. Clearly, `lockdep` tells us `insmod/2367 is trying to acquire lock:`, followed by `but task is already holding lock:`. Next (look carefully at *Figure 7.9*), the lock that `insmod` is holding is `(p->alloc_lock)` (for now, ignore what follows it; we will explain it shortly) and the routine that actually attempts to acquire it (shown after `at:`) is `__get_task_comm+0x28/0x50`. Now, we're getting somewhere: let's figure out what exactly occurred when we called `get_task_comm()`; we find that it's a macro, a wrapper around the actual worker routine, `__get_task_comm()`. Its code is as follows:

```
// fs/exec.c
char *__get_task_comm(char *buf, size_t buf_size, struct task_struct *tsk)
{
    task_lock(tsk);
    strncpy(buf, tsk->comm, buf_size);
    task_unlock(tsk);
    return buf;
}
```

```
EXPORT_SYMBOL_GPL(__get_task_comm);
```

Ah, there's the problem: the `__get_task_comm()` function *attempts to reacquire the very same lock that we're already holding, causing (self) deadlock!* Where did we acquire it? Recall that the very first line of code in our (buggy) kernel module after entering the loop is where we call `task_lock(t)`, and then just a few lines later, we invoke `get_task_comm()`, which internally attempts to reacquire the very same lock: the result is *self deadlock*:

```
do_each_thread(g, t) {    /* 'g' : process ptr; 't': thread ptr */
    task_lock(t);
    [ ... ]
    get_task_comm(tasknm, t);
```

Furthermore, finding which particular lock this is easy; look up the code of the `task_lock()` routine:

```
// include/linux/sched/task.h */
static inline void task_lock(struct task_struct *p)
{
    spin_lock(&p->alloc_lock);
}
```

So, it all makes sense now; it's a spinlock within the task structure named `alloc_lock`, just as `lockdep` informs us.

`lockdep`'s report has some amount of puzzling notations. Take the following lines:

```
[ 1021.449384] insmod/2367 is trying to acquire lock:
[ 1021.451361] ffff88805de73f08 (&(&p->alloc_lock)->rlock){+.+.}, at:
__get_task_comm+0x28/0x50
[ 1021.453676]
              but task is already holding lock:
[ 1021.457365] ffff88805de73f08 (&(&p->alloc_lock)->rlock){+.+.}, at:
showthrds_buggy+0x13e/0x6d1 [thrd_showall_buggy]
```

Ignoring the timestamp, the number in the leftmost column of the second line seen in the preceding code block is the 64-bit lightweight hash value used to identify this particular lock sequence. Notice it's precisely the same as the hash in the following line; so, we know it's the very same lock being acted upon! `{+.+.}` is lockdep's notation for what state this lock was acquired in (the meaning: + implies lock acquired with IRQs enabled, . implies lock acquired with IRQs disabled and not in the IRQ context, and so on). These are explained in the kernel documentation (https://www.kernel.org/doc/Documentation/locking/lockdep-design.txt); we'll leave it at that.

A detailed presentation on interpreting `lockdep` output was given by Steve Rostedt at a Linux Plumber's Conference (back in 2011); the relevant slides are informative, exploring both simple and complex deadlock scenarios and how `lockdep` can detect them:
Lockdep: How to read its cryptic output (`https://blog.linuxplumbersconf.org/2011/ocw/sessions/153`).

Fixing it

Now that we understand the issue here, how do we fix it? Seeing lockdep's report (*Figure 7.9*) and interpreting it, it's quite simple: (as mentioned) since the task structure spinlock named `alloc_lock` is already taken at the start of the `do-while` loop (via `task_lock(t)`), ensure that before calling the `get_task_comm()` routine (which internally takes and releases this same lock), you unlock it, then perform `get_task_comm()`, then lock it again.

The following screenshot (*Figure 7.10*) shows the difference (via the `diff(1)` utility) between the older buggy version (`ch13/3_lockdep/buggy_thrdshow_eg/thrd_showall_buggy.c`) and the newer fixed version of our code (`ch13/3_lockdep/fixed_lockdep/thrd_showall_fixed.c`):

```
-static int showthrds_buggy(void)
+static int showthrds_fixed(void)
 {
     struct task_struct *g, *t;   /* 'g' : process ptr; 't': thread ptr */
     int nr_thrds = 1, total = 0;
@@ -60,7 +58,7 @@
     read_lock(&tasklist_lock);
 #endif
     do_each_thread(g, t) {      /* 'g' : process ptr; 't': thread ptr */
-        task_lock(t);
+        task_lock(t);   /*** task lock taken here! ***/

         snprintf(buf, BUFMAX-1, "%6d %6d ", g->tgid, t->pid);

@@ -70,12 +68,21 @@
         snprintf(tmp, TMPMAX-1, "  0x%016lx", (unsigned long)t->stack);
         strncat(buf, tmp, TMPMAX);

+    /* In the 'buggy' ver of this code, LOCKDEP did catch a deadlock here !!
+     * (at the point that get_task_comm() was invoked).
+     * the reason: get_task_comm() attempts to take the very same lock
+     * that we just took above: task_lock(t);  !! This is obvious self-deadlock...
+     * So, we fix it here by first unlocking it, calling get_task_comm(), and
+     * then re-locking it.
+     */
+        task_unlock(t);
         get_task_comm(tasknm, t);
-/*--- LOCKDEP catches a deadlock here !! ---*/
+        task_lock(t);
```

Figure 7.10 – (Partial) screenshot showing the key part of the difference between the buggy and fixed versions of our demo thrdshow LKM

Great; another example follows – that of catching an AB-BA deadlock!

Example 2 – catching an AB-BA deadlock with lockdep

As one more example, let's check out a (demo) kernel module that quite deliberately creates a **circular dependency**, which will ultimately result in a deadlock. The code is here: `ch13/3_lockdep/deadlock_eg_AB-BA`. We've based this module on our earlier one (`ch13/2_percpu`); as you'll recall, we create two kernel threads and ensure (by using a hacked `sched_setaffinity()`) that each kernel thread runs on a unique CPU core (the first kernel thread on CPU core 0 and the second on core 1).

This way, we have concurrency. Now, within the threads, we have them work with two spinlocks, `lockA` and `lockB`. Understanding that we have a process context with two or more locks, we document and follow a lock ordering rule: *first take lockA, then lockB*. Great; so, one way it should *not* be done is like this:

```
kthread 0 on CPU #0              kthread 1 on CPU #1
   Take lockA                       Take lockB
      <perform work>                   <perform work>
                                       (Try and) take lockA
                                       < ... spins forever :
                                             DEADLOCK ... >

   (Try and) take lockB
   < ... spins forever :
         DEADLOCK ... >
```

This, of course, is the classic AB-BA deadlock! Because the program (*kernel thread 1,* *actually*) ignored the lock ordering rule (when the `lock_ooo` module parameter is set to 1), it deadlocks. Here's the relevant code (we haven't bothered showing the whole program here; please clone this book's GitHub repository at `https://github.com/PacktPublishing/Linux-Kernel-Programming` and try it out yourself):

```
// ch13/3_lockdep/deadlock_eg_AB-BA/deadlock_eg_AB-BA.c
[ ... ]
/* Our kernel thread worker routine */
static int thrd_work(void *arg)
{
    [ ... ]
    if (thrd == 0) { /* our kthread #0 runs on CPU 0 */
        pr_info(" Thread #%ld: locking: we do:"
            " lockA --> lockB\n", thrd);
        for (i = 0; i < THRD0_ITERS; i ++) {
            /* In this thread, perform the locking per the lock ordering
'rule';
```

```
       * first take lockA, then lockB */
      pr_info(" iteration #%d on cpu #%ld\n", i, thrd);
      spin_lock(&lockA);
      DELAY_LOOP('A', 3);
      spin_lock(&lockB);
      DELAY_LOOP('B', 2);
      spin_unlock(&lockB);
      spin_unlock(&lockA);
}
```

Our kernel thread 0 does it correctly, following the lock ordering rule; the code relevant to our kernel thread 1 (continued from the previous code) is as follows:

```
  [ ... ]
  } else if (thrd == 1) { /* our kthread #1 runs on CPU 1 */
        for (i = 0; i < THRD1_ITERS; i ++) {
            /* In this thread, if the parameter lock_ooo is 1, *violate*
the
             * lock ordering 'rule'; first (attempt to) take lockB, then
lockA */
            pr_info(" iteration #%d on cpu #%ld\n", i, thrd);
            if (lock_ooo == 1) {          // violate the rule, naughty boy!
                pr_info(" Thread #%ld: locking: we do: lockB -->
lockA\n",thrd);
                spin_lock(&lockB);
                DELAY_LOOP('B', 2);
                spin_lock(&lockA);
                DELAY_LOOP('A', 3);
                spin_unlock(&lockA);
                spin_unlock(&lockB);
            } else if (lock_ooo == 0) { // follow the rule, good boy!
                pr_info(" Thread #%ld: locking: we do: lockA -->
lockB\n",thrd);
                spin_lock(&lockA);
                DELAY_LOOP('B', 2);
                spin_lock(&lockB);
                DELAY_LOOP('A', 3);
                spin_unlock(&lockB);
                spin_unlock(&lockA);
            }
      [ ... ]
```

Build and run it with the lock_ooo kernel module parameter set to 0 (the default); we find that, obeying the lock ordering rule, all is well:

```
$ sudo insmod ./deadlock_eg_AB-BA.ko
$ dmesg
[10234.023746] deadlock_eg_AB-BA: inserted (param: lock_ooo=0)
```

```
[10234.026753] thrd_work():115: *** thread PID 6666 on cpu 0 now ***
[10234.028299] Thread #0: locking: we do: lockA --> lockB
[10234.029606] iteration #0 on cpu #0
[10234.030765] A
[10234.030766] A
[10234.030847] thrd_work():115: *** thread PID 6667 on cpu 1 now ***
[10234.031861] A
[10234.031916] B
[10234.032850] iteration #0 on cpu #1
[10234.032853] Thread #1: locking: we do: lockA --> lockB
[10234.038831] B
[10234.038836] Our kernel thread #0 exiting now...
[10234.038869] B
[10234.038870] B
[10234.042347] A
[10234.043363] A
[10234.044490] A
[10234.045551] Our kernel thread #1 exiting now...
$
```

Now, we run it with the `lock_ooo` kernel module parameter set to 1 and find that, as expected, the system locks up! We've disobeyed the lock ordering rule, and we pay the price as the system deadlocks! This time, rebooting the VM and doing `journalctl --since="10 min ago"` got me lockdep's report:

```
=========================================================
WARNING: possible circular locking dependency detected
5.4.0-llkd-dbg #2 Tainted: G OE
---------------------------------------------------------
thrd_0/0/6734 is trying to acquire lock:
ffffffffc0fb2518 (lockB){+.+.}, at: thrd_work.cold+0x188/0x24c
[deadlock_eg_AB_BA]

but task is already holding lock:
ffffffffc0fb2598 (lockA){+.+.}, at: thrd_work.cold+0x149/0x24c
[deadlock_eg_AB_BA]

which lock already depends on the new lock.
[ ... ]
other info that might help us debug this:

 Possible unsafe locking scenario:

       CPU0                    CPU1
       ----                    ----
  lock(lockA);
                          lock(lockB);
                          lock(lockA);
```

```
    lock(lockB);
```

*** DEADLOCK ***

```
    [ ... lots more output follows ... ]
```

The `lockdep` report is quite amazing. Check out the lines after the sentence `Possible unsafe locking scenario:`; it pretty much precisely shows what actually occurred at runtime – the **out-of-order (ooo)** locking sequence on `CPU1 : lock(lockB); --> lock(lockA);`! Since `lockA` is already taken by the kernel thread on CPU 0, the kernel thread on CPU 1 spins forever – the root cause of this AB-BA deadlock.

Furthermore, quite interestingly, soon after module insertion (with `lock_ooo` set to 1), the kernel also detected a soft lockup bug. The printk is directed to our console at log level `KERN_EMERG`, allowing us to see this even though the system appears to be hung. It even shows the relevant kernel threads where the issue originated (again, this output is on my x86_64 Ubuntu 20.04 LTS VM running the custom 5.4.0 debug kernel):

```
Message from syslogd@seawolf-VirtualBox at Dec 24 11:01:51 ...
kernel:[10939.279524] watchdog: BUG: soft lockup - CPU#0 stuck for 22s!
[thrd_0/0:6734]
Message from syslogd@seawolf-VirtualBox at Dec 24 11:01:51 ...
kernel:[10939.287525] watchdog: BUG: soft lockup - CPU#1 stuck for 23s!
[thrd_1/1:6735]
```

(FYI, the code that detected this and spewed out the preceding messages is here: `kernel/watchdog.c:watchdog_timer_fn()`).

One additional note: the `/proc/lockdep_chains` output also "proves" the incorrect locking sequence was taken (or exists):

```
$ sudo cat /proc/lockdep_chains
[ ... ]
irq_context: 0
[000000005c6094ba] lockA
[000000009746aa1e] lockB
[ ... ]
irq_context: 0
[000000009746aa1e] lockB
[000000005c6094ba] lockA
```

Also, recall that `lockdep` reports only once – the first time – that a lock rule on any kernel lock is violated.

lockdep – annotations and issues

Let's wrap up this coverage with a couple more points on the powerful `lockdep` infrastructure.

lockdep annotations

In user space, you will be familiar with using the very useful `assert()` macro. There, you assert a Boolean expression, a condition (for example, `assert(p == 5);`). If the assertion is true at runtime, nothing happens and execution continues; when the assertion is false, the process is aborted and a noisy `printf()` to `stderr` indicates which assertion and where it failed. This allows developers to check for runtime conditions that they expect. Thus, assertions can be very valuable – they help catch bugs!

In a similar manner, `lockdep` allows the kernel developer to assert that a lock is held at a particular point, via the `lockdep_assert_held()` macro. This is called a **lockdep annotation**. The macro definition is displayed here:

```
// include/linux/lockdep.h
#define lockdep_assert_held(l) do { \
        WARN_ON(debug_locks && !lockdep_is_held(l)); \
    } while (0)
```

The assertion failing results in a warning (via `WARN_ON()`). This is very valuable as it implies that though that lock `l` is supposed to be held now, it really isn't. Also notice that these assertions only come into play when lock debugging is enabled (this is the default when lock debugging is enabled within the kernel; it only gets turned off when an error occurs within `lockdep` or the other kernel locking infrastructure). The kernel code base, in fact, uses `lockdep` annotations all over the place, both in the core as well as the driver code. (There are a few variations on the `lockdep` assertion of the form `lockdep_assert_held*()` as well as the rarely used `lockdep_*pin_lock()` macros.)

lockdep issues

A couple of issues can arise when working with `lockdep`:

- Repeated module loading and unloading can cause `lockdep`'s internal lock class limit to be exceeded (the reason, as explained within the kernel documentation, is that loading a `x.ko` kernel module creates a new set of lock classes for all its locks, while unloading `x.ko` does not remove them; it's actually reused). In effect, either don't repeatedly load/unload modules or reset the system.
- Especially in those cases where a data structure has an enormous number of locks (such as an array of structures), failing to properly initialize every single lock can result in `lockdep` lock-class overflow.

The `debug_locks` integer is set to `0` whenever lock debugging is disabled (even on a debug kernel); this can result in this message showing up: `*WARNING*  lock debugging disabled!! - possibly due to a lockdep warning`. This could even happen due to `lockdep` issuing warnings earlier. Reboot your system and retry.

Though this book is based on the 5.4 LTS kernel, a powerful feature was (very recently as of the time of writing) merged into the 5.8 kernel: the **Kernel Concurrency Sanitizer (KCSAN)**. It's a data race detector for the Linux kernel that works via compile-time instrumentation. You can find more details in these LWN articles: *Finding race conditions with KCSAN*, LWN, October 2019 (`https://lwn.net/Articles/802128/`) and *Concurrency bugs should fear the big bad data-race detector (part 1)*, LWN, April 2020 (`https://lwn.net/Articles/816850/`).

Also, FYI, several tools do exist for catching locking bugs and deadlocks in *user space apps*. Among them are the well-known `helgrind` (from the Valgrind suite), **TSan (Thread Sanitizer)**, which provides compile-time instrumentation to check for data races in multithreaded applications, and lockdep itself; lockdep can be made to work in user space as well (as a library)! Moreover, the modern [e]BPF framework provides the `deadlock-bpfcc(8)` frontend. It's designed specifically to find potential deadlocks (lock order inversions) in a given running process (or thread).

Lock statistics

A lock can be *contended*, which is when, a context wants to acquire the lock but it has already been taken, so it must wait for the unlock to occur. Heavy contention can create severe performance bottlenecks; the kernel provides lock statistics with a view *to easily identifying heavily contended locks*. Enable lock statistics by turning on the `CONFIG_LOCK_STAT` kernel configuration option (without this, the `/proc/lock_stat` entry will not be present, the typical case on most distribution kernels).

The lock stats code takes advantage of the fact that `lockdep` inserts hooks into the locking code path (the `__contended`, `__acquired`, and `__released` hooks) to gather statistics at these crucial points. The neatly written kernel documentation on lock statistics (`https://www.kernel.org/doc/html/latest/locking/lockstat.html#lock-statistics`) conveys this information (and a lot more) with a useful state diagram; do look it up.

Viewing lock stats

A few quick tips and essential commands to view lock statistics are as follows (this assumes, of course, that `CONFIG_LOCK_STAT` is on):

Do what?	Command
Clear lock stats	`sudo sh -c "echo 0 > /proc/lock_stat"`
Enable lock stats	`sudo sh -c "echo 1 > /proc/sys/kernel/lock_stat"`
Disable lock stats	`sudo sh -c "echo 0 > /proc/sys/kernel/lock_stat"`

Next, a simple demo to see locking statistics: we write a very simple Bash script, `ch13/3_lockdep/lock_stats_demo.sh` (check out its code in this book's GitHub repo). It clears and enables locking statistics, then simply runs the `cat /proc/self/cmdline` command. This will actually trigger a chain of code to run deep within the kernel (within `fs/proc` mostly); several global – shared writable – data structures will need to be looked up. This will constitute a critical section and thus locks will be acquired. Our script will disable lock stats, and then grep the locking statistics to see a few locks, filtering out the rest:

```
egrep "alloc_lock|task|mm" /proc/lock_stat
```

On running it, the output we obtained is as follows (again, on our x86_64 Ubuntu 20.04 LTS VM running our custom 5.4.0 debug kernel):

```
$ sudo ./lock_stats_demo.sh
[+] Checking that locking statistics config is enabled    [OK]
[+] clearing lock stats ...
[+] enabling lock stats ...
cat/proc/self/cmdline[+] disabling lock stats ...
                        class name    con-bounces    contentions    waittime-min   waittime-max waittime-total   waittime-avg   acq-bo
unces   acquisitions    holdtime-min  holdtime-max holdtime-total   holdtime-avg
                        dup mmap_sem.rw sem-R:           0                         0           0.00          0.00          0.00          0.00
      0            1        627.78       627.78         627.78         627.78
                        &mm->mmap_sem/1:                 0                         0           0.00          0.00          0.00          0.00
      0            1        624.38       624.38         624.38         624.38
                &(&mm->page_table_lock)->rlock:          0                         0           0.00          0.00          0.00          0.00
      0           21          0.34         0.77           9.73           0.46
                        tasklist_lock-W:                 0                         0           0.00          0.00          0.00          0.00
      2            3          2.14        20.39          29.36           9.79
                        tasklist_lock-R:                 0                         0           0.00          0.00          0.00          0.00
      1            3          0.38         2.51           3.45           1.15
                &(&p->alloc_lock)->rlock:                0                         0           0.00          0.00          0.00          0.00
      2           15          0.32         1.63           8.67           0.58
                        &mapping->i_mmap_rwsem:          0                         0           0.00          0.00          0.00          0.00
      9          104          0.33         2.87          63.88           0.61
                        &mm->mmap_sem#2-W:               0                         0           0.00          0.00          0.00          0.00
      0           32          0.35       626.64         986.59          30.83
                        &mm->mmap_sem#2-R:               0                         0           0.00          0.00          0.00          0.00
      1          328          0.21        51.52        1803.33           5.50
       mmu_notifier_invalidate_range_start:             0                         0           0.00          0.00          0.00          0.00
      0           58          0.22         0.79          14.16           0.24
                        &mm->context.lock:               0                         0           0.00          0.00          0.00          0.00
      0            1          0.53         0.53           0.53           0.53
                &(&mm->arg_lock)->rlock:                 0                         0           0.00          0.00          0.00          0.00
      0            2          0.40         0.61           1.01           0.51
                        &ei->i_mmap_sem-R:               0                         0           0.00          0.00          0.00          0.00
      3            5          1.35         2.13           8.43           1.69
$
```

Figure 7.11 – Screenshot showing our lock_stats_demo.sh script running, displaying some of the lock statistics

(The output in *Figure 7.11* is pretty long horizontally and thus wraps.) The time displayed is in microseconds. The `class name` field is the lock class; we can see several locks associated with the task and memory structures (`task_struct` and `mm_struct`)! Instead of duplicating the material, we refer you to the kernel documentation on lock statistics, which explains each of the preceding fields (`con-bounces`, `waittime*`, and so on; hint: `con` is short for contended) and how to interpret the output. As expected, see, in *Figure 7.11*, in this simple case, the following:

- The first field, `class_name`, is the lock class; the (symbolic) name of the lock is seen here.
- There's really no contention for locks (fields 2 and 3).
- The wait times (`waittime*`, fields 3 to 6) are 0.
- The `acquisitions` field (#9) is the total number of times the lock was acquired (taken); it's positive (and even goes to over 300 for mm_struct semaphore `&mm->mmap_sem*`).

- The last four fields, 10 to 13, are the cumulative lock hold time statistics (`holdtime-{min|max|total|avg}`). Again, here, you can see that mm_struct mmap_sem* locks have the longest average hold time.
- (Notice the task structure's spinlock named `alloc_lock` is taken as well; we came across it in the *Example 1 – catching a self deadlock bug with lockdep* section).

> The most contended locks on the system can be looked up via `sudo grep ":" /proc/lock_stat | head`. Of course, you should realize that this is from when the locking statistics were last reset (cleared).

Note that lock statistics can get disabled due to lock debugging being disabled; for example, you might come across this:

```
$ sudo cat /proc/lock_stat
lock_stat version 0.4
*WARNING* lock debugging disabled!! - possibly due to a lockdep warning
```

This warning might necessitate you rebooting the system.

All right, you're almost there! Let's finish this chapter with some brief coverage of memory barriers.

Memory barriers – an introduction

Last but not least, let's briefly address another concern – that of the **memory barrier**. What does it mean? Sometimes, a program flow becomes unknown to the human programmer as the microprocessor, the memory controllers, and the compiler *can reorder* memory reads and writes. In the majority of cases, these "tricks" remain benign and optimized. But there are cases – typically across hardware boundaries, such as CPU cores on multicore systems, CPU to peripheral device, and vice versa on **UniProcessor** (**UP**) – where this reordering *should not occur*; the original and intended memory load and store sequences must be honored. The *memory barrier* (typically machine-level instructions embedded within the *mb*() macros) is a means to suppress such reordering; it's a way to force both the CPU/memory controllers and the compiler to order instruction/data in a desired sequence.

Memory barriers can be placed into the code path by using the following macros: `#include <asm/barrier.h>`:

- `rmb()`: Inserts a read (or load) memory barrier into the instruction stream
- `wmb()`: Inserts a write (or store) memory barrier into the instruction stream
- `mb()`: A general memory barrier; quoting directly from the kernel documentation on memory barriers (`https://www.kernel.org/doc/Documentation/memory-barriers.txt`), "*A general memory barrier gives a guarantee that all the LOAD and STORE operations specified before the barrier will appear to happen before all the LOAD and STORE operations specified after the barrier with respect to the other components of the system.*"

The memory barrier ensures that unless the preceding instruction or data access executes, the following ones will not, thus maintaining the ordering. On some (rare) occasions, DMA being the likely one, driver authors use memory barriers. When using DMA, it's important to read the kernel documentation (`https://www.kernel.org/doc/Documentation/DMA-API-HOWTO.txt`). It mentions where memory barriers are to be used and the perils of not using them; see the example that follows for more on this.

As the placement of memory barriers is typically a fairly perplexing thing to get right for many of us, we urge you to refer to the relevant technical reference manual for the processor or peripheral you're writing a driver for, for more details. For example, on the Raspberry Pi, the SoC is the Broadcom BCM2835 series; referring to its peripherals manual – the *BCM2835 ARM Peripherals* manual (`https://www.raspberrypi.org/app/uploads/2012/02/BCM2835-ARM-Peripherals.pdf`), section 1.3, *Peripheral access precautions for correct memory ordering* – is helpful to sort out when and when not to use memory barriers.

An example of using memory barriers in a device driver

As one example, take the Realtek 8139 "fast Ethernet" network driver. In order to transmit a network packet via DMA, it must first set up a DMA (transmit) descriptor object. For this particular hardware (NIC chip), the DMA descriptor object is defined as follows:

```
// drivers/net/ethernet/realtek/8139cp.c
struct cp_desc {
    __le32 opts1;
    __le32 opts2;
    __le64 addr;
};
```

The DMA descriptor object, christened `struct cp_desc`, has three "words." Each of them has to be initialized. Now, to ensure that the descriptor is correctly interpreted by the DMA controller, it's often critical that the writes to the DMA descriptor are seen in the same order as the driver author intends. To guarantee this, memory barriers are used. In fact, the relevant kernel documentation – the *Dynamic DMA mapping Guide* (`https://www.kernel.org/doc/Documentation/DMA-API-HOWTO.txt`) – tells us to ensure that this is indeed the case. So, for example, when setting up the DMA descriptor, you must code it as follows to get correct behavior on all platforms:

```
desc->word0 = address;
wmb();
desc->word1 = DESC_VALID;
```

Thus, check out how the DMA transmit descriptor is set up in practice (by the Realtek 8139 driver code, as follows):

```
// drivers/net/ethernet/realtek/8139cp.c
[ ... ]
static netdev_tx_t cp_start_xmit([...])
{
    [ ... ]
    len = skb->len;
    mapping = dma_map_single(&cp->pdev->dev, skb->data, len,
PCI_DMA_TODEVICE);
    [ ... ]
    struct cp_desc *txd;
    [ ... ]
    txd->opts2 = opts2;
    txd->addr = cpu_to_le64(mapping);
    wmb();
    opts1 |= eor | len | FirstFrag | LastFrag;
    txd->opts1 = cpu_to_le32(opts1);
    wmb();
    [...]
```

The driver, acting upon what the chip's datasheet requires, requires that the words `txd->opts2` and `txd->addr` are stored to memory, followed by the storage of the `txd->opts1` word. As *the order in which these writes go through is important*, the driver makes use of the `wmb()` write memory barrier. (Also, FYI, RCU is certainly a user of appropriate memory barriers to enforce memory ordering.)

Furthermore, using the `READ_ONCE()` and `WRITE_ONCE()` macros on individual variables *absolutely guarantees that the compiler and the CPU will do what you mean*. It will preclude compiler optimizations as required, use memory barriers as required, and guarantee cache coherency when multiple threads on different cores simultaneously access the variable in question.

For details, do refer to the kernel documentation on memory barriers (`https://www.kernel.org/doc/Documentation/DMA-API-HOWTO.txt`). It has a detailed section entitled *WHERE ARE MEMORY BARRIERS NEEDED?*. The good news is that it's mostly taken care of under the hood; for a driver author, it's only when performing operations such as setting up DMA descriptors or initiating and ending CPU-to-peripheral (and vice versa) communication that you might require a barrier.

One last thing – an (unfortunate) FAQ: will using the `volatile` keyword magically make concurrency concerns disappear? Of course not. The `volatile` keyword merely instructs the compiler to disable common optimizations around that variable (things outside this code path could also modify the variable marked as `volatile`), that's all. This is often required and useful when working with MMIO. With regard to memory barriers, interestingly, the compiler won't reorder reads or writes on a variable marked as `volatile` with respect to other volatile variables. Still, atomicity is a separate construct, *not* guaranteed by using the `volatile` keyword.

Summary

Well, what do you know!? Congratulations, you have done it, you have completed this book!

In this chapter, we continued from the previous chapter in our quest to learn more about kernel synchronization. Here, you learned how to more efficiently and safely perform locking on integers, via both `atomic_t` and the newer `refcount_t` interface. Within this, you learned how the typical RMW sequence can be atomically and safely employed in a common activity for driver authors – updating a device's registers. The reader-writer spinlock, interesting and useful, though with several caveats, was then covered. You saw how easy it is to mistakenly create adverse performance issues caused by unfortunate caching side effects, including looking at the false sharing problem and how to avoid it.

A boon to developers – lock-free algorithms and programming techniques – was then covered in some detail, with a focus on per-CPU variables within the Linux kernel. It's important to learn how to use these carefully (especially the more advanced forms such as RCU). Finally, you learned what memory barriers are and where they are typically used.

Your long journey in working within the Linux kernel (and related areas, such as device drivers) has begun in earnest now. Do realize, though, that without constant hands-on practice and actually working on these materials, the fruits quickly fade away... I urge you to stay in touch with these topics and others. As you grow in knowledge and experience, contributing to the Linux kernel (or any open source project for that matter) is a noble endeavor, one you would do well to undertake.

Questions

As we conclude, here is a list of questions for you to test your knowledge regarding this chapter's material: `https://github.com/PacktPublishing/Linux-Kernel-Programming/tree/master/questions`. You will find some of the questions answered in the book's GitHub repo: `https://github.com/PacktPublishing/Linux-Kernel-Programming/tree/master/solutions_to_assgn`.

Further reading

To help you delve deeper into the subject with useful materials, we provide a rather detailed list of online references and links (and at times, even books) in a Further reading document in this book's GitHub repository. The *Further reading* document is available here: `https://github.com/PacktPublishing/Linux-Kernel-Programming/blob/master/Further_Reading.md`.

Other Books You May Enjoy

If you enjoyed this book, you may be interested in these other books by Packt:

Mastering Linux Device Driver Development

John Madieu

ISBN: 978-1-78934-204-8

- Explore and adopt Linux kernel helpers for locking, work deferral, and interrupt management
- Understand the Regmap subsystem to manage memory accesses and work with the IRQ subsystem
- Get to grips with the PCI subsystem and write reliable drivers for PCI devices
- Write full multimedia device drivers using ALSA SoC and the V4L2 framework
- Build power-aware device drivers using the kernel power management framework
- Find out how to get the most out of miscellaneous kernel subsystems such as NVMEM and Watchdog

Linux Kernel Development

Kaiwan N Billimoria

ISBN: 978-1-78995-343-5

- Write high-quality modular kernel code (LKM framework) for 5.x kernels
- Configure and build a kernel from source
- Explore the Linux kernel architecture
- Get to grips with key internals regarding memory management within the kernel
- Understand and work with various dynamic kernel memory alloc/dealloc APIs
- Discover key internals aspects regarding CPU scheduling within the kernel
- Gain an understanding of kernel concurrency issues
- Find out how to work with key kernel synchronization primitives

Leave a review - let other readers know what you think

Please share your thoughts on this book with others by leaving a review on the site that you bought it from. If you purchased the book from Amazon, please leave us an honest review on this book's Amazon page. This is vital so that other potential readers can see and use your unbiased opinion to make purchasing decisions, we can understand what our customers think about our products, and our authors can see your feedback on the title that they have worked with Packt to create. It will only take a few minutes of your time, but is valuable to other potential customers, our authors, and Packt. Thank you!

Index

Y

Made in the USA
Las Vegas, NV
13 September 2021